KING KHAMA, EMPEROR JOE,
AND THE
GREAT WHITE QUEEN

Figure 1. Bathoen, Sebele (with flowers) and Khama.
Standing: Revs. W. C. Willoughby and Edwin Lloyd

KING KHAMA
EMPEROR JOE
AND THE
Great White Queen

*Victorian Britain
through African Eyes*

NEIL PARSONS

The University of Chicago Press
Chicago & London

Neil Parsons is a professor of history at the University of
Botswana. His books include *Seretse Khama, 1921–1980*
and *A New History of Southern Africa.*

The University of Chicago Press, Chicago 60637
The University of Chicago, Ltd., London
© 1998 by Neil Parsons
All rights reserved. Published 1998
Printed in the United States of America

07 06 05 04 03 02 01 00 99 98   5 4 3 2 1

ISBN (cloth): 0-226-64744-7
ISBN (paper): 0-226-64745-5

Library of Congress Cataloging-in-Publication Data

Parsons, Neil.
    King Khama, Emperor Joe, and the great white queen :
Victorian Britain through African eyes / Neil Parsons.
        p.   cm.
    Includes bibliographical references and index.
    ISBN 0-226-64744-7 — ISBN 0-226-64745-5 (pbk.)
    1. Africans—Travel—Great Britain—History—19th
century.   2. Public opinion—Great Britain—History—
19th century.   3. Chamberlain, Joseph, 1836–1914—
Views on Africa.   4. Africa—Foreign public opinion—
Great Britain.   5. Great Britain—History—Victoria,
1837–1901.   6. Botswana—Foreign relations—Great
Britain.   7. Great Britain—Foreign relations—Botswana.   8. Khama, African chief, 1830 (ca.)–1923.
I. Title.
DA125.N4P37   1998
327.4106883—dc21   97-37111
                                              CIP

⊚ The paper used in this publication meets the minimum
requirements of the American National Standard for Information Sciences—Permanence of Paper for Printed Library
Materials, ANSI Z39.48-1992.

For Professor Isaac Schapera on his ninetieth
birthday

To get it right always takes a little longer

Bojang ga bo bofane

(Grass does not bind itself)

CONTENTS

ILLUSTRATIONS

Maps

Figures

PREFACE AND
ACKNOWLEDGMENTS

This book can and should be read as a simple narrative, telling a tale that has not been told in such detail before. It can also be seen as a contribution to a number of areas of scholarly inquiry and debate.

First, it is a study in the historical anthropology of "Western" capitalist society, at the height of British imperial power and industrial might, as seen by intelligent outsiders. The reconstruction of the "discoveries" of imperial Europe and North America by observers from Africa, Asia, South America, and the Pacific is, as Apollon Davidson points out in his *Cecil Rhodes and His Times* (Moscow: Progress Publishers, 1988), a great challenge for "historians, psychologists and ethnographers." There is also a fascination in fiction about seeing "ourselves as others see us," to use Robert Burns's phrase—a fascination that goes back in English literature at least as far as Jonathan Swift's *Gulliver's Travels* (1726), and that continues through works such as *A Bayard from Bengal,* the adventures of "Baboo" in Britain (1902). If we may translate that fascination from fiction to nonfiction and put it in "postmodern" literary terms, this present book may be said to be an attempt to allow imperial "subalterns" to speak for themselves—portraying Western society as "other" rather than as "us."

Second, this book may be seen as a contribution to the social and political history of late Victorian Britain. It reveals a cross-section over a few months of provincial and metropolitan England, Scotland, and Wales, and the workings of so-called middle-class morality in public opinion and the press. It gauges the extent to which jingoism or imperialist fervor had overcome the body politic; and indicates how the Liberal "Nonconformist conscience" and Tory "romantic anticapitalism" can be understood in terms of then current ideas of evangelicalism and humanitarianism, temperance, and even pacifism.

Third, this book is a contribution in the recently revived field of imperial history. Khama, Sebele, and Bathoen immensely complicated and thereby undermined Cecil Rhodes's preparations for the so-called Jameson Raid. This book shows how Joseph Chamberlain, star politician of the new Conservative-Unionist government and colonial minister, was compromised by the three chiefs as specters from his radical past and by his prior knowledge of Rhodes's secret plans.

Fourth, and perhaps most importantly, this book is a contribution to the history of Africa. It demonstrates just how difficult it was to achieve the diplomatic alternative to armed resistance against colonialization—to preserve a measure of autonomy rather than inviting conquest and dispossession. It shows the "subimperialism" of African rulers exercising leverage within European imperialism and pursuing their own agenda of expansionism, and how colonial and missionary designs could be subverted and used for other purposes. Specifically for Botswana history, this book adds fuel to the debate as to whether it was the success of the three chiefs or the failure of the Jameson Raid that preserved the Bechuanaland Protectorate from incorporation into Rhodesia and South Africa.

Finally, on a personal note, this book is a study of the intersection of the antecedents of two societies with which I am familiar today—Britain and Botswana. It is the product of a long personal quest for the roots of an African civilization that startled me on first acquaintance as a late adolescent. It is also a form of apology for adolescent vandalism, inspired by parents born into an age of reaction against Victorian culture, in helping to destroy decorative plaster on the exterior of a late Victorian house in London.

✣ ✣ ✣

The idea of this book was suggested, as the centenary of 1895 approached, by Prof. Isaac Schapera, the doyen of scholars who have studied Botswana and its people. But my study of 1895 has been many more years in gestation.

The visit of the three kings or chiefs from Botswana to Britain first intrigued me when I was an eighteen-year-old at Moeng College in Botswana. I read about the visit in Anthony Sillery's *Bechuanaland Protectorate* (1952) and learned about its significance in Botswana's history from my headmaster, the late B. C. Thema. Later, as a postgraduate student in African Studies at the University of Edinburgh, I was encouraged to pursue my interest through research by Prof. "Sam" Shepperson.

Among others who have helped me with this book, and the previous work out of which it grew, I must single out Isaac Schapera in London, "Sam" Shepperson, now retired in Peterborough, and the late Anthony Sillery of Oxford; John Aldridge, David Jeffery, and Kevin Shillington in

London; Rev. Andrew Sellwood and David North (for the family of Alice Young) in Enderby, Leicestershire; Sekgoma Khama of Serowe, now in Stockholm; Tom Tlou, Jeff Ramsay, and Barry Morton in Gaborone; the late Jack Chirenje of Harare; and Apollon Davidson of Cape Town and Moscow.

Finally, I wish to acknowledge the assistance of library and office staff on two continents.

In Europe I have to thank the staff of the library of the University of Edinburgh and its former Centre of African Studies, and the National Library of Scotland in Edinburgh; Selly Oak Colleges Library in Birmingham; the former libraries of the London Missionary Society (Congregational Council for World Mission) and of the Royal Commonwealth Society in London (now at the School of Oriental and African Studies, University of London, and the University of Cambridge respectively); the Public Record Office formerly in Chancery Lane and now at Kew; the British Library's newspaper repository at Colindale; the archives of Madame Tussaud's waxworks in Marylebone; the office of the Lord Mayor of London (for a telephone inquiry); and the library of the University of London's Institute of Commonwealth Studies.

In Africa I have to thank the staff of the archive library of the Khama III Memorial Museum in Serowe; the libraries of the Botswana National Archives, of the University of Botswana, and of the National Museum and Art Gallery in Gaborone; the libraries of the University of Zambia in Lusaka and of the National Archives of Zimbabwe in Harare; the William Cullen Library at the University of the Witwatersrand; and the African Studies Library at the University of Cape Town. Finally a word of thanks to the staff and students of the Department of History, University of Cape Town, for helping me to muster ideas for the first chapter.

For permission to reproduce illustrations from originals I am grateful to Mr. David North of Enderby, Leicestershire, the grandnephew of the missionary teacher Alice Young (figs. 20–23), and to Ms. Fiona Barbour of the Duggin-Cronin Gallery at the McGregor Memorial Museum in Kimberley (fig. 30). I also acknowledge the courtesy of the School of Oriental and African Studies Library, University of London, for allowing me to use copies of other figures (map 3 and fig. 26). Special thanks go to John Aldridge of the Aldridge Press in Chiswick, London, for splendid print preparation of maps and illustrations, many of them from murky copies, and to Max Ellis for coloring the cover illustration. Finally my gratitude goes to David Brent and his editorial team at the University of Chicago Press, whose helpfulness has made them into friends.

A NOTE ON TERMINOLOGY

The term "Great White Queen" as applied to Queen Victoria (ruled 1837–1901) was put into the mouths of "native" supplicants by British settler records around the world and came to be accepted in metropolitan Britain as correct "Sambo" pidgin. Mary Queen of Scots was the original White Queen, as she wore widow's white. Perhaps Victoria, who wore widow's black, should have been the Black Queen. In the Setswana language she was known as *Mma-Mosadinyana*, that is, as Mrs. Little (Old) Lady. *Mma-Mosadinyana* continued to be used after Victoria's death by Tswana people to refer to the British government in London.

"Emperor Joe" was one of Joseph Chamberlain's many nicknames, referring to his tenure as colonial secretary (June 1895–October 1903). As a young republican he was "Radical Joe." He continued to be "Pushful Joe." After his betrayal of Charles Stewart Parnell and Irish home rule, Irish nationalists called him "Judas."

Khama (ruled 1875–1923) was usually referred to as "King Khama" (or as "Khama the Good") in Britain; and "the three kings" had a neat biblical ring that appealed to the British press in 1895. Sebele and Bathoen, on the other hand, were more commonly called "chiefs" in the press— though all three men were equal in traditional status. The words *chief* and *king* are used interchangeably in this book.

The Setswana word for chief is *kgosi* (plural *dikgosi*). But Khama, Sebele, and Bathoen were greater men than mere chiefs. Each one was a *Kgosi e kgolo* ("great chief" or paramount chief).

The term *Bechuanaland Protectorate* used in the text is synonymous with the boundaries of today's Republic of Botswana. Other "Bechuana" territories (including the colony called *British Bechuanaland* between 1885 and 1895) today constitute much of the North West and Northern Cape Provinces of the Republic of South Africa.

The word *Bechuana* (i.e. *Be-chuana*) is an archaic version of the modern word *Batswana* (i.e. *Ba-tswana*), referring to Tswana people in the plural. The word *Bechuana* continued in official use almost until the end of the colonial period in 1966. The singular word for a Tswana person was *Mochuana* (now *Motswana*), and Tswana language and culture were *Sechuana* (now *Setswana*).

Epiphany on Clifton Bridge

◆▸══◕ ◔══◂◆▸

CLIFTON SUSPENSION BRIDGE CROSSES A DIZZYING gorge near Bristol where the river Avon cuts through a hillside toward the Severn and the Bristol Channel. The bridge, completed in 1829, is a monument to the ingenuity of its architect, the twenty-three-year-old engineer Isambard Kingdom Brunel (1806–59). With iron frame, wooden planking, brick and masonry towers—and suspension chains taken from London's Hungerford footbridge, demolished to make way for Charing Cross railway bridge over the Thames in 1864—the narrow span stretches for 630 feet (190 meters).

It was across this bridge that four gentlemen could be seen cautiously making their way one morning in September 1895. Three Africans of obvious seniority and respectability, in sober gray woolen suits, were being cajoled to walk onward by a short, bespectacled white man with a pointed beard.

The pathfinder was William Charles Willoughby, an ordained minister of the London Missionary Society (LMS). He had been serving in the southern African mission field of Bechuanaland for four years. His reluctant followers—Khama, Sebele, and Bathoen—were all chiefs or kings of the "Bechuana" (Batswana) people of Britain's Bechuanaland Protectorate.

Reverend Willoughby had sprung the novel experience of the Clifton Bridge on the three dignitaries as a prank to catch them unawares "before they knew where they were." He had taken them for a ride in a horse carriage over the hills on the edge of the city of Bristol, along a road that suddenly jutted out into space across Clifton gorge.

They alighted next to the bridge and looked down into the ravine to see "people and carriages like little spots below them." They were "astonished . . . beyond measure," but "it was a matter of dignity with them to manifest surprise at nothing."

Willoughby took them to the beginning of the bridge, but the three chiefs refused to walk any further: "We are afraid. We'll go back."

Willoughby chided them, "I'll go on then."

"It's dangerous," they said.

"I've a wife at home," said Willoughby, "and am not a likely man to go into danger. I'm going across anyhow."

He strode out along the footpath on one side of the bridge. The chiefs hesitantly followed him: "At first they went holding fast by the uprights" on the footpath. They then found that it felt much safer to walk down the center of the carriageway. According to the *Bristol Mercury*, "They were much struck with the view from the middle of the gorge, and then they carefully retracted their steps."

As they regained their balance and good sense, no doubt the three men saw the humor of the situation, joshing at each other's "cowardice." Willoughby was certainly pleased by the experiment in breaking down the reserved manners of his three royal protégés. He later told a journalist from the *Westminster Gazette:* "There is nothing, in fact, more *infra dig.* for a South African chief than to show he is astonished." [1]

Nonconformist missionaries like Willoughby saw it as their duty to wear down the stoicism of their converts and to encourage them to express their emotions of pain and joy—to cry out and confess the Lord. Willoughby was the inheritor of a Puritan tradition that, as James Boswell's father had reminded Dr. Johnson, had taught kings they had a joint in their necks. It was a tradition that was antagonistic toward aristocrats and traditional rulers, and that had found a new form in the "moral purity" movement of late Victorian Britain. The movement was characterized by the "Nonconformist conscience" checking corruption in public life, by the temperance movement against drunkenness, and in more radical forms by "Little Englandism" opposed to imperial expansion and by the peace movement against wars in general.

Yet the success of Christian mission work in Bechuanaland was very dependent on the patronage of local royals and aristocrats, and upon the ultimate backing of British imperial control. Missionary societies in Bechuanaland operated through "tribal" state churches, based on royal prerogative and aristocratic privilege. Hence Willoughby and other LMS missionaries were more than a little ambiguous toward African royalty and toward European imperialism in general. Willoughby had a reputation in colonial circles of being an "*enragé* missionary," because of his exposure in the magazine *Truth* of the brutalities of the colonial conquest of Rhodesia. [2]

Willoughby had an immediate purpose in wanting to puncture the dignity and reserve of Khama, Sebele, and Bathoen in September 1895. It was now ten days since their arrival in Britain, and they were still proving to be rather too hesitant in front of the congregations that they were facing almost daily.

After their arrival, Khama, Sebele, and Bathoen had been mobbed by journalists, pampered by ministers of religion, and presented to hundreds of people in London. They had also achieved their first interview with the most powerful and glamorous politician of the age, Joseph Chamberlain, the secretary of state for the colonies (colonial minister) in the new Conservative and Unionist government, who held their fate in his hands.

Chamberlain had slipped away on a Mediterranean vacation, promising to attend to their matter on his return. It was decided that Khama, Sebele, and Bathoen would use the interim period to good effect by whipping up support in chapel and town meetings across the country. So that when Chamberlain returned he would find such a groundswell of support in "the provinces," that it would counteract the metropolitan and colonial interests that otherwise held colonial ministers in the palms of their hands. The provincial city of Bristol was chosen as the first stop on this most demanding phase of the Bechuana chiefs' mission to Britain. As their tour manager, Willoughby was determined that the three chiefs' tour of the provinces should be a barnstorming success from the start.

✤ ✤ ✤

Khama, Sebele, and Bathoen were suitably impressed with the Clifton Bridge's hanging seemingly unsupported over the abyss. Recalling the seasick sixteen-day voyage from Africa, they humorously suggested: "Well, if you can support a bridge in the air like this, why not build one from London to Cape Town?"[3]

A similar suggestion had been made ninety years before in an English version of the magical fake-memoirs of Baron Munchausen. The baron had found more gold dust and pearls in the Kalahari than he could carry, as well as a civilized empire in this part of the interior of southern Africa with "so polished and refined a people." He therefore proceeded to build a bridge—the eighth wonder of the world—between the Kalahari and Europe.

The Travels of Baron Munchausen was a work of many hands, a satire on contemporary mores, originally published in German in 1796. The civilization in the Kalahari first appeared in an English-language edition published in, or soon after, 1806. The book was a satire on accounts of current exploration by Europeans in Africa. It portrayed the Africans discovered in the Kalahari as more levelheaded and civilized than contemporary

Europeans. The notion of a Kalahari bridge mocked the British in particular, who had been crazed by contemplating the possibilities of mechanical and engineering progress during the Industrial Revolution.

Baron Munchausen's civilization in the Kalahari was not a complete figment of anyone's imagination. It was based on an account of "Booshuana," that is, Botswana, which was published in a book of 1806 eccentrically titled *A Voyage to Cochin China, in the years 1792 and 1793 . . . To which is appended an account of a journey to the residence of the chief of the Booshuana Nation*.[4]

Nor was the idea of a mechanical bridge through the air, from the Kalahari to Europe, to remain for ever fantasy. As the *African Critic* responded to the suggestion of the three Bechuana chiefs in 1895: "Well, even that may come to pass. The age of flying-machines will, however, surely precede it."[5]

A mere quarter of a century later, in 1919–20, three years before Khama died, landing fields for the Cape-to-Cairo air route were laid out in his country at Palapye and Serowe. Six or seven decades later there was to be an "air bridge" of jet airliners flying in little more than half a day between Europe and the capital city of the Republic of Botswana.

✤ ✤ ✤

By an act of singular foresight, the Bechuana chiefs in 1895 commissioned Durrant's Press Cuttings agency in London to clip the newspapers for references to themselves.

More than one copy of such press clippings survives. One copy covering the period up to October 15, originally belonging to Bathoen, is now held in the library of the National Museum of Botswana in Gaborone. Another copy, compiled for Sebele for a period two weeks longer, and by no means identical to Bathoen's for previous weeks, survives in microform in the library of Rhodes House at Oxford University—made on behalf of Dr. Anthony Sillery in the 1950s by the University of Witwatersrand, from an original that has since disappeared at Molepolole. A third copy of the press clippings, made for Khama and likely to be the most complete record, may or may not survive: it appears to have been taken on to Hartford, Connecticut, and then to Birmingham, England, by W. C. Willoughby—and has possibly been left to a descendant.

This collection of press clippings is an extraordinary resource for the study of British public opinion in the autumn of 1895. The clippings are taken from 135 different newspapers and periodicals—including thirteen London daily newspapers, thirty-one London weeklies or monthlies, seven London international periodicals, and twelve London or national Christian publications. The English provinces are represented by fifteen newspapers from the South, sixteen from the Midlands, and twenty-four from the North of England. There are also clippings from twelve Welsh, Scots, or Irish newspapers, and two from New York dailies.

The British press was fascinated by the "Three Kings" from the outer reaches of the ever expanding empire. Newspapers commented on the amount of news coming out of Africa, and on the increasing number of visits to Britain by "dusky potentates" from all over the world—be they Afghan, Swazi, or Ashanti. Press men and press women clamored to get interviews with Khama, Sebele, and Bathoen. The *Westminster Gazette* remarked on how much one would like to "read a Roman interview with some contemporary of Armenius who had come to Rome to get his wrongs righted."[6]

Bathoen's and Sebele's press clippings form the basis for this book. They also set the pattern on which the book is written—keeping the story as authentic as possible by using the original words of primary sources, and thus heeding the advice given to a journalist by Khama in 1895: "Be sure now, and only write as I have spoken to you, nothing more than my words."[7]

The chiefs had dubbed journalists the "hunters of words." At an important meeting in Birmingham's Council House, Khama remarked:

> I know that you live a long way off, and it is difficult for those who live a long way off to distinguish between words. Words are words, and it is hard to tell which are the right words and which are the wrong when they are spoken.

City dignitaries responded with cries of "Hear, hear."[8]

Khama, Sebele, and Bathoen appreciated the political value not only of spoken words but also of written words carried in official correspondence and newspaper reports. They were literate in their own language, Setswana ("Sechuana") and could read letters and newspapers as well as Scriptures in it. Sebele and Bathoen also spoke, and possibly read, Dutch in its Afrikaans variant. But they and Khama had a mere smattering of English and could only communicate effectively in English through interpreters.

As otherwise proficient linguists and litigious politicians, the three chiefs were acutely conscious of the importance of words and meanings. On landing in Britain, they told of the difficulty of relating the Setswana language to the new technology of steamships, steam trains, electric lighting, telegraphs, and telephones.

> It will be very difficult to make our people understand how iron and wood can move without being pulled by someone. Formerly we blamed the missionaries for not making these things plain, and we thought it was their imperfect knowledge of our language.

"Yes," Bathoen continued in philological vein, "we shall now have to tell our people that although we are masters of their language, we cannot explain these new ideas, because we have no words to correspond."[9]

The illustrious Rev. Dr. Parker of the City Temple, London's Congregationalist "cathedral," saw other virtues in the Setswana language in one of his sermons. Commenting on Khama's talk from his pulpit a week earlier, when the interpreter had had to use three or four sentences in English to expound on three or four syllables from Khama in Setswana, Parker remarked of the English language:

> We are foot-caught in our own dictionaries. Our words and modes of speech belong to the decaying aristocracies and fallen princedoms in language.[10]

ONE

Then Let Us All Be Philistines

⤜⇒ ⇐⤛

BRITAIN WAS NEVER GREATER AS A WORLD POWER THAN in 1895, when it was at the peak of its industrial strength and imperial self-confidence. The Royal Navy ruled the waves, the British army was garrisoned on six continents, and ancient Queen Victoria dominated the other monarchs of Europe—while at home "middle-class morality" ruled triumphant.

The 1890s saw the culmination of the second phase of the Industrial Revolution: the era beginning in the 1870s of electricity and steel, industrial chemicals and petroleum power, added to the earlier adoption of coal and iron and steam power. Britain had led the first phase of the Industrial Revolution a century earlier. But now, during the 1890s, it was being overtaken in industrial production and inventiveness by both the German Empire and the United States of America.[1]

There are two features, one economic and one political, that mark out the year 1895 as being crucial in the middle of a decade of critical change. In economic history, 1895 is the year in which the pound sterling is recorded as having reached its highest ever purchasing power.[2] In political history, 1895 marks the end of the Pax Britannia, when Britain and most of the world was at peace because its imperial might was virtually unchallengeable.

It was the so-called Jameson Raid, which set off on the last two days of December 1895, that in the words of Winston Churchill began the "violent times" of the twentieth century. The humiliating failure of the raid in South Africa opened the way for the exercise of German naval power against Britain and started the rush to arms that led to the Great War of 1914–18.[3]

✣ ✣ ✣

Britain had become "the first industrial society." It had ceased to be a mainly agricultural society. The countryside as we know it today was transformed into the hinterland of great cities by a dense network of canals and railways. Meanwhile the modern world was emerging through the crossing of the oceans by British steamships and penetration of the continents by British steam trains.

The measure of time itself, as we understand it today, was brought into being by the needs of the railway and the telegraph. Railway timetables for Britain were based on the standardized time of noon at the Greenwich observatory in London. The telegraph (and soon the telephone) necessitated and made possible the adoption of Greenwich time for the whole of Britain in 1880. By the 1890s the whole world was divided into standard time zones, all based on the meridian of Greenwich.

Modern urban life was created in the last quarter of the century by sanitation and transportation, after the cleaning (and sometimes clearing) of city-center slums and the incorporation of urban villages as city suburbs. By 1895 the power and light generated by coal was being augmented by the conversion of coal into electricity through steam turbines. But the use of electric lighting was not yet widespread. The gas-lit Colonial Office in London was not electrified until after Joseph Chamberlain took charge in 1895. London awaited the grid and power lines from its first major electric power station, which was being built on the side of the Thames at Deptford, dwarfing the church where the poet Christopher Marlowe lay buried.

London had had suburban railway lines for half a century, and there were also steam trains running along subway tunnels between the mainline terminal stations in London. Electricity now opened up the possibility of trains in tube tunnels deep underground and the possibility of an electrified tram system to replace horse-drawn trams and omnibuses in the crowded streets.

A prediction in 1894 of the "tram of a century hence" showed an elevated tram-car (with passengers seated on its open top) hanging from two overhead rails, traveling from Notting Hill to Bank along the sides of Oxford Street shops. From the United States came news of a projected railroad from New York to Washington, D.C., called the Brott Rapid Transit System, down which electric trains might travel at 125 miles an hour. More realistically, there was news of the construction of elevated steel viaducts for steam trains in New York City, and of the London-Aberdeen express breaking records with a 540-mile journey at an average speed in excess of sixty miles an hour. (Meanwhile in South Africa, the 600-mile trip by train between Kimberley and Cape Town averaged little more than sixteen miles an hour.)[4]

There were so many horse-drawn vehicles in London that there were traffic jams in major streets during rush hours. Street sweepers were employed at every corner to continually clear away horse manure. Ironically, the press hailed the new "four-wheeled petroleum gig" or "horseless carriage," still at a very experimental stage of development, as a future solution to urban pollution by horses.[5]

Already to be found in the homes of the rich and modern, with lines stretching from London as far as Plymouth by February 1896, was that revolutionary Scots-American invention, the telephone. Telephone lines were strung alongside the well-established national network of telegraph lines. Telegraphs had initially followed and only served the railway lines but began to stretch far and wide and even undersea as far as the Cape of Good Hope by the 1870s.

With up to six daily postal collections and deliveries a day, neither telegraph nor telephone were really necessary for communications within London. But the telephone and other pieces of new technology were changing the pattern of office work. Typewriters, onionskin carbon copies, and duplicators were beginning to become commonplace. They promoted the rise of bureaucracy and permitted the growth of administrative departments—helping to extend impersonal networks of communication and command even to the ends of the earth. Telephone exchanges and typewriters also opened up employment for armies of female clerical laborers.[6]

A similar revolution in organization was overtaking the newspaper trade in the 1890s. Cheap and rapidly degrading newsprint paper from acidic pine trees made possible the emergence of the "yellow press" serving the newly educated masses.

Photography began to move from professionals and studios to amateurs and households with the growing popularity of cheap, handheld Kodak box cameras. The most advanced households now possessed phonographs, or "gramophones," using wax cylinders—to supplement the piano and other musical instruments in family evening entertainments.

In warfare the Maxim-Nordenfeld (later Vickers) machine gun proved its worth as a horrendous people-reaper in the 1893 Anglo-Ndebele War conducted by Rhodes's company troops in Zimbabwe. The Sino-Japanese War of 1894–95 was the proving ground of naval battle between the big guns of iron-clad battleships made in Europe. Naval strategists predicted future warfare between (British and French) iron-clads with Maxims on their mastheads.[7]

Among technical innovations to first see the light in 1895 and to become commonplace within a decade were Röntgen's "photography by means of invisible radiations," or x rays; Diesel's compression engine;

Marconi's radio transmissions, or "wireless telegraphy"; and Gillette's disposable razor blade—invented by King C. Gillette after much brain racking for a patentable commodity that had to be regularly thrown away and replaced. Of these inventions two were German, one Italian, and one American—none British, though Guglielmo Marconi lived and worked in Britain as the best marketplace for his inventions.

There was also during 1895, in Paris, the first public showing of movie films by the cinema or "bioscope" projector by Auguste and Louis Lumière. Meanwhile, in New York City, the first pizzeria was opened. The world's first automobile road race ran from Chicago to Milwaukee, and Norwegian explorers made the first human landfall on the Antarctic continental mass—rather than merely on the surrounding pack ice.[8]

Not all projected technical developments were equally practical. Predictions, at least half a century old, of bullet trains running at breakneck speeds down pneumatic tubes from London to Scotland, resulted in little more than a few blowtubes for mail under central London by the 1890s. The 1894 prediction of underground tube trains "ventilated and worked by tidal force" has proved equally unattainable.[9]

✤ ✤ ✤

Britain's commitment to international "free trade" was wilting under the impact of an import flood of cheap and often shoddy German and American manufactured goods. (Hence the insistence on such imports to Britain being marked "Made in Germany," etc. to distinguish them from superior goods "Made in England.") But Britain managed to maintain international financial dominance through the banking and insurance services in the square mile demarcated by the old walls of the City of London.[10] The pound sterling was the world's main currency. It was seen as being "as safe as the Bank of England."

The international importance of the Bank of England was enhanced by its close association with the gold standard, which emerged as the benchmark of world currency values in the 1890s—with the U.S. dollar a late joiner in 1896. The key to the Bank of England's role was its virtual monopoly on the sale and distribution of gold from the Witwatersrand gold mines in the Transvaal republic—an arrangement developed in cooperation with the Rothschild banking house after the Baring banking crisis of 1894. By 1895 the Witwatersrand was producing a quarter of the world's gold supply, and its production was ever increasing.

The London Stock Exchange, in Throgmorton Street close by the Bank of England's Threadneedle Street premises, was the heart of the City's financial wheeling and dealing. During 1894–95 it saw a great flurry of buying and selling in South African gold shares. The best bet was shares in Witwatersrand (Rand) goldmining companies, such as "Johnnies"; the worst bet turned out to be "Chartereds" speculating in the attempt by Rhodes's company to find a "Second Rand" north of the Limpopo.[11]

South African gold shares were known in humorous stock Exchange parlance insensitive to South African usage as "Kaffirs" (a term roughly the South African equivalent of "niggers" and equally as derogatory and degrading).[12] Hence the ring of dealers in such shares was called the "Kaffir Circus," and the boom of 1895 in such shares was called the "Kaffir Boom."

An article in the journal called the *Nineteenth Century* explained the 1894–95 boom in South African gold shares as resulting from the creeping realization among stockbrokers of the significance of the fact that the Witwatersrand gold seam stretched fifty miles long and twelve hundred feet deep, with an incidence of gold content in its ore that, if low, was more regular than that of any other goldfield in the world. Stupendous possibilities were being opened up by new methods of gold extraction from its ore, notably the Forrest-MacArthur cyanide process patented in the United States, which would make even marginal gold-mines superprofitable.[13]

In the words of the London weekly magazine *South Africa*, whose fortunes were closely tied to the "Kaffir Circus," 1895 came in roaring like a lion and went out like the proverbial lamb. Shares in deep-level Rand mines, introduced early in 1894 at around five pounds each, were changing hands at twenty-three pounds on the London Stock Exchange by the beginning of 1895. This was despite the fact that there was only one deep-level mine yet in full production.[14]

At the end of 1894 Cecil Rhodes rushed to London to make his pickings from "Chartereds," attracting considerable publicity for a shareholders meeting of his British South Africa Company ("Chartered Company") at Cannon Street Station Hotel in January 1895.

The bantam fighter figure of Barney Barnato, cockney music-hall entertainer turned diamond-and-gold king, turned up in London twice during the year, and also astounded the Paris bourse. At Monte Carlo he failed to fulfill the words of the already well known song as "The man who broke the bank." But he went one better and founded his own bank. Its fortunes were, however, short lived:

> Barney, Barney, full of blarney,
>   Started a bank in town,
> And people laughed when the shares went up;
>   But not when the shares went down.[15]

In April 1895 there were scuffles with police outside the London Stock Exchange, as perspiring young "Kaffir Circus" brokers crowded on the sidewalk in shouting clusters that overflowed onto the street. Women cyclists had to dismount to pass along the crowded street, and policemen grew hoarse with the monotonous chant of "Keep the pavement clear, gentlemen, if you please."

The first dip in the gold share boom was in late May, when Scottish banks declined to accept gold shares as security for bank loans. But frenzied activity on the Paris, Brussels, and Berlin stock exchanges reflated the boom in June and July, and it was not until the end of August that the market finally peaked.

One of the investors who got out in time was former president Harrison of the United States, who put one hundred pounds into "Kaffirs" in early 1894 and sold them in August or September 1895 for twenty thousand pounds. He could not have done the same on Wall Street, because the New York Stock Exchange did not deal in gold shares, even American ones.

Sixty-four million pounds was wiped off the value of South African gold shares between their peak value in August 1895 and December of that year. This was referred to by stockbrokers as the "chill" or the "hump."

> After the rise, the fall
> After the boom the slump
> After the fizz and the big cigar
> The cigarette and the "hump." [16]

✣ ✣ ✣

London was a name familiar in even in the farthest reaches of Setswana-speaking country, because of "Lontone"—the London Missionary Society. (There was familiarity elsewhere in southern Africa with the names of Paris, Berlin, and Rome as the sources of other Christian missionaries.)

During 1895 the LMS was to celebrate the centenary of its foundation. It now occupied an office building in Blomfield Road, near Broad Street in the City, an area of recent slum clearance. The area between Broad Street in the east and Long Acre in the west was generally known as Seven Dials. It had been for centuries reckoned to be London's most notorious slum, or "rookery," crammed with humanity in close-set alleys and courtyards, and strewn with dung heaps and "dust" heaps.

A million chimney stacks poured out dark and greasy coal smoke, and London became ever more segregated between the rich living upwind to the west and the poor living downwind to the east. But much of the London that Dickens had known had changed almost beyond recognition in the years between his death in 1870 and 1895.

An American visitor of 1895, writing in *Harper's Monthly* on his return to London after a twenty-five-year absence, was pleasantly surprised by the care now given to West End parks and streets, with numerous trees growing and window boxes of flowers decorating the street side of private houses. London had for him become a hospitable town, fit to lead the world, with innumerable art galleries, theaters, and other public facilities. The new National Gallery (seeded by the private collection of a Russian trader), on the north side of Trafalgar Square, was still abuilding in 1895, being opened in April the following year.[17]

In and around the City there was a building boom in offices, which were replacing even the brick residences built after the Great Fire two centuries previously.

On the South Bank of the Thames, old medieval and Tudor sites had been covered over by small industries and ugly warehouses. One of the buildings due to be demolished in 1895 was the Queen's Head Inn in Southwark, a wooden structure around a courtyard built in 1587 on the site of an earlier 1452 inn. It had at one time been inherited and sold by a Cambridge University graduate called John Harvard, who took the money to America. So the inn was in a sense the acorn out of which grew the mighty oak of Harvard University. However, in the 1890s the inn was treated in the manner typical of property developers: first left to rot, and then demolished on the grounds of its structure being unsafe.[18]

North of the Thames, the main thoroughfare planned through Nine Dials was to run from the Strand to High Holborn—named Kingsway on its completion during the reign of Victoria's successor. This and related developments were set to destroy the maze of old streets. But David Garrick's Drury Lane Theatre received a merciful reprieve, as did a few tall Tudor buildings in High Holborn. New buildings sprouting in the area included the London School of Economics in the Aldwych, opened for business in September 1895, and the monstrous redbrick edifice of Prudential Assurance near Chancery Lane.[19]

✣ ✣ ✣

London's theater life was never more vigorous than in the 1890s. There were vaudeville music halls in every inner suburb, providing entertainment for the masses. The music halls had evolved from song-and-supper evenings in inns, such as the Eagle in the City Road, into custom-built theaters with liquor saloons attached. By the 1890s the saloons were screened from the performance—much to the indignation of young "toffs" like Winston Spenser Churchill, who had rioted in protest.

There were some "legitimate" theaters in western suburbs, such as the Hammersmith Lyric, which reopened with a flourish in 1895—the prologue to the play starring Lillie Langtry, the famous actress and model for

Pears' Soap advertisements, as well as mistress of the Prince of Wales. But "legitimate" theaters were mainly concentrated in London's West End.

West End drama in 1895 ranged from the long-running musical comedy *The Shop Girl* at the Gaiety Theatre, to recently knighted Sir Henry Irving's company at the Lyceum, and to soon-to-be-knighted Beerbohm Tree's company at the Theatre Royal, Haymarket.

The Gaiety Theatre (later buried under Aldwych redevelopments) was famous for its pretty Gaiety Girls in the chorus, and for its top-hatted stage-door Johnnies lined up outside after performances seeking to marry one of the girls. One of them married Woolf Joel, nephew and most trusted business partner of Barney Barnato.[20]

At the Lyceum Theatre, in a small street just north of the Strand at Waterloo Bridge, Henry Irving and his leading lady, Ellen Terry, played Arthur and Guinevere early in 1895. They then went off to boom and trill their Macbeth and Lady Macbeth in the Abbey Theatre on Broadway in New York, leaving Forbes Robinson and Mrs. Patrick Campbell to triumph as an overly mature but effective Romeo and Juliet at the Lyceum.[21]

At the Haymarket, Beerbohm Tree (brother of the witty cartoonist Max Beerbohm) had had a string of successes with the plays of Oscar Fingall O'Flahertie Wills Wilde. But Tree failed to secure Wilde's new play, *The Importance of Being Earnest,* which was fortunate for him, as it was closed soon after its premiere in February 1895 because of the sudden scandal surrounding the author. Tree turned to a play that was all the rage of the New York stage, *Trilby.* It was tried out in Manchester and Leeds and opened at the Haymarket in October and was to make Tree's fortune (a fortune big enough to build a new theater opposite his old one, and to found the Royal Academy of Dramatic Art).

Trilby was adapted from a new six-shilling novel by George du Maurier, in which a young, Irish, artist's model living in Paris is literally mesmerized by the evil Dr. Svengali to become Europe's sweetest singer. For purposes of the play, her Bohemian nature was sanitized and modishly recast as a "New Woman," dressed in a baggy military jacket, shoeless, and smoking a cigarette.[22]

The character of Svengali is said to have been based on that of William Hunt, also known as Gilarmi Farini, the Canadian-American show business impresario whose other achievements included the recruitment of Bushmen direct from the Kalahari in 1885 and the invention of the tip-up theater seat. Beerbohm Tree, however, played Svengali as a Fagin-type European Jew.

Another Jewish villain, Meikstein, based on the "Randlords" of the Transvaal (Marks, Beit, and Eckstein?) and on the Scottish trader who remained loyal to Lobengula in the Anglo-Ndebele War, featured in the great patriotic extravaganza musical *Cheer, Boys, Cheer* on the cavernous stage of Drury Lane, toward the end of 1895. The climax of the play was the reenactment of "Wilson's Last Stand," an incident in the Anglo-Ndebele War two years earlier that had fast gained mythological status.[23]

Novels published during 1895 included H. G. Wells's *The Time Machine* and Thomas Hardy's *Jude the Obscure*. Hardy's next novel, provisionally entitled "The Simpletons," was being serialized in *Harper's Bazaar:* it was published in book form as *Tess of the d'Urbervilles*. Messrs. Longman Green, the publishers, launched a new series of Penny Popular Novels, starting with an abridged version of Rider Haggard's *She*, based on the myth of the eternal rain-queen of the northern Transvaal. In children's literature the *Blue True Story Book* featured "Wilson's Last Fight" by Rider Haggard and "The Life and Death of Joan the Maid" by Andrew Lang.

In France the end of the year saw the death of the novelist Alexandre Dumas *fils*—one of the illustrious figures in European literature (together with his father, the author of *The Three Musketeers*, and Alexander Pushkin) who were of partial African ancestry.

Though 1895 was the year in which W. B. Yeats published his *Poems* in one volume, the vigorous verse of the British Indian colonial-expatriate Rudyard Kipling were far better known. The influential journalist Walter Besant, literary campaigner and founder of the Society of Authors, thought that Kipling ought to succeed Tennyson as Britain's poet laureate. But the job went instead at the end of October 1895 to a dull doggerel-monger called Alfred Austin.[24]

1895 also saw the death of the leading writer of children's hymns, Mrs. C. F. Alexander, whose hymns ("There Is a Green Hill," "Once in Royal David's City," etc.) were disciplinarian, teaching children to be "mild, obedient," as well as devotional.

Meanwhile, in Vienna, Sigmund Freud published his *Studies in Hysteria*, while in Russia Pyotr Ilich Tchaikovsky's ballet *Swan Lake* made its debut in St. Petersburg. In England the conductor Charles Hallé, doyen of Manchester music since 1850, died suddenly after a sea voyage from Cape Town. London's premier concert hall, the new Queen's Hall in Langham Place, just north of Oxford Circus, launched "promenade concerts," conducted by young Henry Wood, to bring in summer crowds on cheap stand-up tickets during the "dull season" when fashionable society deserted the metropolis for the Continent.[25]

✣ ✣ ✣

Our American visitor writing about Britain in *Harper's Monthly* magazine missed the feeling of social equality, as well as potential turmoil, that he found in France and already knew in the United States. The English might pride themselves in their traditional (i.e. seventeenth- and eighteenth-century) liberties, but they had been overtaken by the American and French Revolutions and by their own Industrial Revolution. There was too much truth still in the old adage:

> God Bless the Squire and his Relations,
> And Keep Us in Our Proper Stations.[26]

Middle-class culture had made inroads to grab the moral high ground of Victorian society—promoting Liberal political and Nonconformist religious values, with missionaries and humanitarians on its right wing and the democratic socialists of the "respectable working class" on its left wing.

The temperance movement, calling for checks and bans on public consumption of alcohol, gave a template for the local activities of Nonconformists and humanitarians. (Temperance interests in local politics were an important constituency for Gladstonian Liberals in national politics.) The very name *temperance* shows how the movement, meeting regularly through voluntary associations such as the Good Templars, attempted to give itself a moderate and middle-ground image. Its opponents, on the other hand, saw it as a movement of extremists determined to restrict the freedom of others. Temperance masked the hidden agenda of prohibition. There was indeed a patronizing tone of middle-class morality in sentiments such as that Drink was the curse of the working classes (neatly reversed by Oscar Wilde into Work being the curse of the drinking classes).

Both "gentlemen" and "roughs" were obliged to play by the new middle-class rules of sports and games. Enthusiasm for the strange English game of cricket was at its height in the 1890s. Big, dark-bearded Dr. W. G. Grace was the most popular man in England in 1895, after hitting his hundredth century. An all-white cricket team from England was touring Australia (by contrast the first Australian cricket team to tour England had been all black). Meanwhile the game was popular in such outlandish places as Bechuanaland (where the Palapye cricket club was founded in 1895) and even in the United States.[27]

Both the "low life" of the proletariat and the "high life" of the aristocracy were under attack from respectable middle-class values.

The entertainment of the urban masses centered on gin and gambling had been channeled into tea in the parlor and into the public house or "pub," licensed to sell beer within restricted hours. The few holidays were no longer marked so much as "holy days" but as bank holidays when financial institutions closed.

The Whit Monday bank holiday of 1895 saw half a million Londoners out-of-doors in an "amazing whirl of locomotion": 125,000 at the commercial fun-palaces of Earl's Court and Crystal Palace, 27,000 at the London

Zoo, and 100,000 enjoying themselves more traditionally on Hampstead Heath. The latter, on the Easter Monday bank holiday, were described as cockney "'Arries and 'Arriets" hurrying toward "'appy 'Ampstead." People were blowing into great paper snakes that inflated and elongated "with alarming suddenness and rapidity." Young women "mashers" (flirtatious dancers) from the East End were "dancing like so many marionettes" with deadpan faces, their ostrich-feather headpieces bobbing to the sound of the "latest music-hall song" played on a barrel organ.[28]

The manipulation of popular culture, the financial journalist J. A. Hobson remarked in his essay of 1900, *The Psychology of Jingoism*, was most insidious in the propagation of music hall songs and in the "yellow press" manipulated by big press barons.[29] Such forms of popular culture served the commercial aims of big business and supported imperialist aggression abroad in particular. If you look at periodicals published in 1895, you can see the emergence of what was even then called public relations, and of advertising that can be quite startling in conflating fact with fiction.

Probably the least ethical and acceptable adverts to modern eyes are the claims of patent medicine in 1895 periodicals. Thus the figure of Christ dispenses Clark's Embrocation to his disciples, and cigarettes are said to be healthful for women, children, and asthmatics. Soap advertisements reveal other current preconceptions:

> Soap is the pioneer of civilization.—Prior to soap there was barbarism; as soap extended its sphere, enlightenment followed; and from the time of the introduction of Pears' Soap to the present day civilization has advanced by leaps and bounds.

An advertisement for Eno's Fruit Salts describes it as an "imperative hygienic need" for those engaged in "The Antiseptics of Empire" and "Civilisation of the World."[30]

✤ ✤ ✤

For the upper stratum of London society the 1890s are remembered as the "Naughty Nineties." After the dark dress of early and mid-Victorian times, the Nineties were known for the fashionable display of supposedly dissolute colors: mauve, the base color of modern coal-tar aniline dye; yellow, the color of Aubrey Beardsley's softly pornographic *Yellow Book* magazine, as well as of the new popular yellow press; and green, the color of the carnations that Oscar Wilde and his friends wore, hinting at delicious decadence because of its very lack of meaning.

It was Oscar Wilde (of Tite Street, Chelsea) who provided the great scandal of London high society in 1895, though it was barely mentioned in the newspapers. He was imprisoned "on a certain charge" on May 25, after failing to disprove the libel of boxer Lord Queensbury's assertion that he was "posing as a Somdomite [*sic*]." Imprisonment seems to have enhanced Wilde's prestige in France: his *Portrait of Dorian Gray* became a bestseller and his new play *Salomé* was due to be put on by the Théâtre Libre in Paris.

Newspaper response to Wilde's conviction was necessarily guarded toward a crime simply not discussed in polite society. It was easier to comment on and condemn the aesthetic movement that Wilde represented: the belief in art for art's sake, that "art, being non-moral, has no ethical bearing whatever." The conviction of Wilde was seen as a victory over aristocratic decadence for the forces of moral vigilance, of straightforward "middle-class morality" and the Nonconformist conscience—which even the Conservatives were now ready to adopt after the infusion of Chamberlain's Unionists. As the *Daily Telegraph* remarked in an editorial of May 27, 1895, castigating Wilde's aesthetic ideas:

> And if such a reaction towards simpler ideas [of Art] be called Philistinism, then let us all be Philistines, for fear of national contamination and decay.

The Wilde affair revealed the criminal network of vicious exploitation of juveniles in homosexual as well as heterosexual prostitution in London's West End.[31] But one should be cautious with the guesstimates of later generations, reacting against the hypocrisies of their fathers, which turn a very significant proportion of working-class women in Victorian London retrospectively into prostitutes.

The press of 1895 was full of references to someone called the New Woman. She was educated and self-assertive. For many male observers that meant she was trying to be a man. Worse still, she was trying to be independent of men. A survey of British and American women university graduates showed that many were declining to get married. Cartoons characteristically represented the New Woman as an aging bluestocking wearing a tweed suit.

Press reports linked the emergence of the New Woman with the rise of the bicycle. The parks of London suddenly filled with respectable women cyclists in 1894–95. The duke of Cambridge, retiring commander in chief of the British army, attempted but failed to stop women cyclists from entering Hyde Park lest they scare the horses.

A preacher in Atlanta, Georgia, was reported as thundering against the "satanic contagion" of women on bicycles. Bicycles took women out of the house and necessitated new forms of dress, exposing previously hidden calves and ankles, icons of Victorian eroticism, to general view. The *Daily Telegraph* reported that Somali visitors to London were shocked beyond measure at seeing women in knickerbockers cycling on the Brixton Road. Even the great actress Sarah Bernhardt, visiting London, deplored outdoor life and the bicycle as exposing women to danger (presumably from men). The French were said to disparage English women for being so dominated by their servants that they fled their houses to shop, to see friends, or to exercise in the park.

W. T. Stead, former editor of the *Pall Mall Gazette* who now ran his own influential journal called the *Review of Reviews,* acclaimed the bicycle as a vehicle that would at last "humanise" mollycoddled middle-class women. It would make them fit and give them a taste of the meaning of exertion and exhaustion, hunger and thirst, and thus awaken a sense of adventure in them. The *North American Review,* on the other hand, argued against strenuous cycling by adolescents in case they overheated their bodies and distorted the growth of their brains.[32]

Among men, especially working men escaping their wives and the fumes of the city at weekends, the great new popular sport and vent for recreation made available by trains and bicycles was fishing on rivers and canals. A working-class man without fishing was like a middle-class woman without a bicycle.

✤ ✤ ✤

The 1890s saw continuance of the gradual democratization, socialization, and feminization of politics in Britain and elsewhere in North America and northwestern Europe.

The concept of democracy, propagated so assiduously in France and the United States, was regarded with suspicion in Britain, at least until the early twentieth century, perhaps because of its too close association with the twin concept of republicanism. But Britain experienced three great reform acts in the nineteenth century (1832, 1867, and 1884) that progressively extended the parliamentary franchise to nearly all male adults. There were also significant reforms in setting up and extending the franchise of local government.

The relative lack of success of local democracy in British history has blinded most historians to advances in the political enfranchisement of women householders in local elections, long before women got votes in national elections. Single (but not married) women rate-payers got to vote for town councils in 1882, and for the county councils created in 1888. From 1894 nearly all married as well as single women householders had the vote, and the right to stand as candidates, in such local elections.

The London County Council was the most significant forum of local democracy in Britain from 1888 until its abolition a century later. (As early as 1895 Prime Minister Rosebery was complaining that the LCC was meddling in "imperial" or national affairs rather than sticking to local issues.) In the LCC elections of March 1895 there was a tie between fifty-nine Progressive (Liberal) and fifty-nine Moderate (Conservative) seats. The working-class areas of inner London, which had been voting Progressive, had had their previous majority removed by newly incorporated suburbs that voted for the Moderates.[33]

With the extension of the franchise, the Conservatives had worked hard to wean working-class voters from working-class movements, socialism in general and trade unionism in particular. The secret weapon launched by Disraeli as Conservative leader in the late 1870s was the appeal of imperialism to working-class interests. In its crudest form it was "jingoism," the name derived from a music hall song that was the rallying cry of "patriots" in the anti-anti-imperialist Hyde Park riot of 1878. In its higher form the appeal to workers of imperialism was the extension of British markets abroad resulting in more jobs at home.

The first socialists to be elected members of Parliament sat on the Liberal benches in 1892—Ben Tillet for a Bradford seat, John Burns for Battersea in South London, and Keir Hardie for a seat in the East End of London. The foundation of the Independent Labour Party followed in 1893. The ILP conference at Newcastle-on-Tyne in April 1895 turned down a motion to rename itself the National Socialist Party and adopted a platform of "industrial commonwealth founded upon the socialisation of land and capital." But Hardie lost his seat in the 1895 election, and the operation of an effective Labour Party separate from the Liberals seemed far off in the future.

The year 1895 was a temporary low point for British working-class movements, as workers were enjoying relative prosperity. There were no strikes in vital industrial sectors: strikes were confined to industries such as boot making in the Midlands and waitressing in London. Yet only a few years earlier England had faced an almost revolutionary climate, fueled by international working-class solidarity. Even the Household Cavalry guarding the queen had mutinied under the influence of what she termed "horrid Socialists."

The high point of discontent had been "Bloody Sunday," on November 13, 1887, described by the historian Asa Briggs as "the most exciting day in London's nineteenth-century political history." Unemployed men seeking work, employed workers demanding an eight-hour working day, and Irish workers demanding home rule for their country, clashed at the Strand corner of Trafalgar Square with London police and Guards cavalry brought in from Whitehall. (South Africa House was later built at this corner.) A hundred workers were wounded; two died.

People's sudden fury against bourgeois law-and-order at this time, all over Europe and America, is partly explained by the arbitrary execution by hanging on November 11, 1887, of four men in the United States. The "Haymarket martyrs" were hanged simply because they had been the speakers at a workers' demonstration in a Chicago square when policemen were killed by a terrorist bomb.

Bloody Sunday had its connections with southern Africa, and Bechuanaland in particular, through the figure of Sir Charles Warren, London's commissioner of police. Warren, an impetuous "god-fearing and intelligent man," military engineer and southern African bush fighter, Arabist and pioneer archaeologist of Jerusalem, theoretician on planetary motion—and former enemy of Cecil Rhodes and failed Liberal parliamentary candidate—had basked in glory in 1884–85 as the leader of an expedition that expelled Boer filibusters from southern Bechuanaland simply by a show of superior force and modern technology. He tried the same tactics in Trafalgar Square, but the demonstrators, unlike the filibusters, did not flee; instead, they attacked the police lines.

Warren was obliged to resign his post and retreated to Singapore until 1895 as commander in chief of the British army in the Far East. His resignation has also been explained as part of a top-level conspiracy to cover up the supposed failure of his police to solve the "Jack the Ripper" murders in the East End.

One version has it that the Prince of Wales's perverted and soon dead oldest son, "Eddy," duke of Clarence, was the real Ripper. A more credible explanation is that Warren took the rap because the proven Ripper could not be tried in court—he had already been committed to a North London lunatic asylum. At a time of extreme social tension, it was believed that confirmation of the Ripper's oft-rumored Polish-Jewish identity might lead to a bloody pogrom by lynch mobs in London's East End. Given Warren's moral and religious background, and his close association with Palestine, this latter version of events is not implausible.[34]

✤ ✤ ✤

The downfall of Rosebery's Liberal ministry in June 1895 and the general election of July ushered in eight years of Conservative and Unionist rule. The leader of the Unionists, who for the first time formed a joint ministry with the Conservatives in June 1895, was Joseph Chamberlain.

Chamberlain was a Birmingham capitalist who had moved from screw manufacture into civic government, pioneering the city's "gas-and-water socialism" as its lord mayor, and entering the Westminster Parliament as a radical and republican member of the Liberal Party. Chamberlain rose to be a member of Gladstone's cabinet, as president of the Board of Trade. It was now, between 1882 and 1886, that he took the steps that set him on the path of his future career as an ardent imperialist and opponent of Irish home rule.

The first step was, by a twist of strange prescience, precipitated by events in Bechuanaland and the Transvaal. Chamberlain had been outraged over Gladstone's economy measure of withdrawing British rule over the Transvaal in 1881, after its Boers had defeated a relatively minor British force at Majuba. But the events of 1882 in Egypt, with the British victory over Arabi Pasha's nationalists at Tel-el-Kebir on September 3, aroused imperial self-confidence once again.

Ten days later Chamberlain was contacted by his close political ally Rev. Dr. R. W. Dale, keeper of Birmingham's Nonconformist conscience. Dale relayed the resolution of a meeting in the town hall addressed by Rev. John Mackenzie of the London Missionary Society. The resolution called for British support of southern "Bechuana" chiefs who were resisting Boer invaders or "filibusters" from the Transvaal.

During the spring of 1883 "Chamberlain told his colleagues that the bitter cry of the Bechuana must be heard . . . [but] failed to carry the Cabinet." Chamberlain brought the issue of Bechuanaland back before Cabinet in October 1884. The Transvaal republic, encouraged by German colonization across the Kalahari on the Namibia coast, had once more infiltrated filibusters to take over southern Bechuanaland.[35]

The result was vindication for Chamberlain: the dispatch of the four thousand men of the Warren Expedition, before whom the Boer filibusters simply melted away, sometimes reappearing to seek work as transport drivers.

Chamberlain now made a bid for the future leadership of the Liberal Party by, as W. T. Stead said, "putting ambition before principle." He finally broke with Gladstone in March 1886 over home rule for Ireland. Voting against the First Home Rule Bill in June that year, he was greeted by Irish Nationalist MPs with cries of "Traitor! Judas!" and was accused by Parnell of being the man who killed the bill.[36]

Chamberlain's rightward tilt toward Tory democracy was strengthened by his marriage to the daughter of a right-wing Democrat in the U.S. administration of President Grover Cleveland, who had been voted into power in 1884 over the protests of "Tammany Hall" Irish Catholics. Chamberlain led the Unionists on the Liberal benches at Westminster, dedicated to the continuing union of Great Britain and Ireland and to the promotion of British imperialism.

In 1892 Chamberlain became the leader of a separate Unionist Party, which allied with the Conservative Party against Gladstone's Second Home Rule Bill in 1893. Thus it was invited to join the new Conservative government of Lord Salisbury in June 1895. Chamberlain was undoubtedly the star figure on the new government's front bench in the House of Commons.[37]

To the surprise of many, Chamberlain chose to take the relatively junior position of secretary of state for the colonies in the new cabinet of 1895. He saw it as the platform for a program of popular imperialism that would shoot him to prominence as a national leader. By strange coincidence, Chamberlain's first problem in office was to be a reprise of the situation that had first engaged his interest in imperialism more than a decade earlier—only this time the "Bechuana" chiefs were northerners, and the filibusters were Britishers.

✤ ✤ ✤

Two events in 1893 helped to whip up jingoism, or popular imperialism and militarism, into a froth by 1895. The first event was the loss of the Royal Navy's flagship *Victoria* in a stupid collision of June 1893 that sent it to the bottom of the Mediterranean. Gladstone, economical as ever, refused to replace it with another bigger and better ironclad battleship. The popular response, no doubt encouraged by military-industrial interests, was hysteria about Britannia's duty of ruling the waves and calls to build up the Royal Navy in strength to face all other navies combined.[38]

The second event of 1893 was the declaration of war by the British South Africa Company on the Ndebele kingdom in western Zimbabwe. The BSA, or Chartered Company, had been formed in 1888–89 by a combination of commercial interests, headed by Cecil J. Rhodes, seeking to extend British colonialism through Bechuanaland to the Zambezi and beyond.

Rhodes was a Kimberley diamond magnate who had first come to political prominence in 1884–85, when he supported the land claims of Boer filibusters in Bechuanaland against General Warren and Reverend Mackenzie. By 1890 he was prime minister of the Cape Colony, Britain's largest and richest possession in Africa, as well as chairman of the BSA Company, of the Kimberley diamond monopoly, and of a Witwatersrand gold-mining group.[39]

As we will see in the next chapter, the Anglo-Ndebele War of October–December 1893 was a double victory for the BSA Company. It was a victory over the Ndebele kingdom that cleared the land and conquered the labor for the gold mines and settlers farms of the colony to be called Rhodesia; and it was a carefully nurtured triumph over what Rhodes called the "Imperial Factor"—colonial rule from imperial London rather than from within the colony.

When Rhodes appeared at the January 1895 shareholders' meeting of the BSA Company at Cannon Street Station Hotel in the City of London, he was at the height of his power and wealth—a "Colossus" of capitalism matched only by the likes of J. P. Morgan and the Rockefellers in America, and by the Rothschilds in Europe.

Rhodes and his partner Dr. Jameson had arrived in London, a place they visited but rarely, in November 1894 to negotiate with the Foreign Office for the extension of BSA territory beyond the Zambezi to Lake Malawi (Nyasaland). Rhodes was also rewarded by the queen with a seat on the Privy Council, Britain's supreme unelected council of state, while Jameson was admitted to the Order of the Bath.

They then went off to Ottoman Turkey with their bachelor friend Rochfort Maguire, an Irish MP. (Rhodes's association with Irish nationalists, because of his desire for home rule in the colonies, got him blackballed at this time from joining a prestigious gentlemen's club in London, the Traveller's.)

After consultations with the sultan's government at the Porte, apparently over such matters as the supply of teachers to the Cape Muslim population and the export of prize angora (Ankara) goats to the Cape, they "filled up leisure hours by making a closer acquaintance with both the people and places outside the Sultan's Palace." Was this when the Jameson Raid was planned? Or did the enjoyments of Rhodes and Jameson in Stamboul bathhouses match those of Oscar Wilde and Arthur Douglas, holidaying with André Gide elsewhere on the Mediterranean littoral (in the town of Blydah, thirty miles from Algiers)?[40]

The unexpected delay of Rhodes and Jameson in Turkey also delayed the annual general meeting of the BSA Company in the Cannon Street Station Hotel.

The meeting was a triumph of orchestrated publicity to raise capital for the BSA Company and boost its shares—after the "difficult and embarrassing position" at the previous year's annual stockholders' meeting, which had persisted until a few months before. Not a single mine in the supposed "Second Rand" of BSA Company territory had actually started gold production. But the past few months had seen an "Alice in Wonderland" tale of rags to riches, with the "unbounded enthusiasm" of money men rushing to subscribe half a million pounds or more in the company. In the words of the *East Anglian Daily Times:*

> Mr. Rhodes was greeted by the audience standing, cheering and waving hats and handkerchiefs and umbrellas; some of the women wept for joy.
> . . . at the close of the meeting he had the utmost difficulty in evading the embraces of his "oofish" sisters. That we are a nation of territory lovers was proved by the shouts of delighted "Ah!'s" which greeted Mr. Rhodes' announcement that the proprietors of the Company possess "a very large piece of the world."

The main point made by Rhodes was the extreme economy and efficiency of his company's elimination of the AmaNdebele (Matabele). Jameson, who had led the BSA Company troops, was greeted by the shareholders yet more enthusiastically than Rhodes himself. *Truth*, the mouthpiece of the acerbic radical MP Henry Labouchère, had another view:

> I fail to see why Mr. Rhodes should take credit to his Company for the low price at which they slaughtered the Matabele and seized their territory.
>
> They collected the scum that floats on the surface of civilisation, by a promise of the share in the cattle that they could loot, and in the land they could secure by the simple process of slaying its owners.

Likewise, the political commentator Wilfrid Scawen Blunt came to believe that the "gangrene of colonial rowdyism" that led to the Jameson Raid originated in the "slaughter for trade" of the Matabele war.[41]

⁘ ⁘ ⁘

Labouchère had begun his attack on the BSA Company early in 1894 after receiving intelligence of the Anglo-Ndebele War from Reverend Willoughby of the LMS at Khama's capital of Palapye in the Bechuanaland Protectorate. Willoughby had sent a letter that "inveighed" against a patrol sent out to hunt down the Ndebele king, Lobengula, in December 1893. Part of this "Shangani patrol," under Allan Wilson, had been besieged and wiped out by an Ndebele counterforce. Willoughby described the patrol as "a man-hunting, man-slaying expedition . . . indicating that its participants deserved their fate."[42]

Labouchère and Blunt were among those Englishmen, known by their detractors disparagingly as "Little Englanders," who had not been seduced by the lure of imperialism. What they saw as crude expropriation and racial arrogance, others justified by humanitarian or even socialist ends.

Chamberlain, the "People's Joe" who was not afraid of being called a socialist (though he was not), spoke in support of the candidacy of the explorer H. M. Stanley for the London working-class parliamentary seat of North Lambeth in July 1895. (Stanley had been being cuttingly contrasted with Dr. Livingstone in the liberal *Daily Chronicle:* "his African fantasias have been set to the crack of the rifle and the shriek of the dying native," while "Livingstone lived and died a friendly white man among friendly black men.") Speaking in the well-known Canterbury Music-Hall in Lambeth, Chamberlain said:

> I wish sometimes that the working classes would pay a little more attention to the history of the growth of this Empire; I wish they would think more of the questions concerned with its further expansion. I can show you in a minute that they are life and death to you.

He went on to praise Stanley for opening up new colonial markets that would enable the rapidly breeding working class to find employment in producing exports and to find sustenance from food imports.[43]

Such strange conjunction between the aims of imperialism and socialism was not unusual in 1895. When the great Friedrich Engels died, the oration at his cremation on August 12, 1895, was delivered by Judge Samuel Moore, the senior administrator of the Royal Niger Company in what was to become Nigeria. As a very good friend of Karl Marx, Moore had done the same at Marx's funeral. Moore's socialist credentials were impeccable. Not only did he translate *The Communist Manifesto* into English; he was also cotranslator of *Capital*.

Socialists of a different ilk included Sidney Webb (later Lord Passfield) and Sydney Olivier (later Lord Olivier, an uncle to the actor). Both were Fabian socialists, and both were officials in the Colonial Office in the 1890s. Sidney's journalist wife Beatrice married him only after she had given up on a long unconsummated relationship with Chamberlain.[44]

Critics of the practices if not of the purposes of imperialism extended Right as well as Left. American-born Sir Ellis Ashmead-Bartlett, the MP for Kingston in the House since 1880, was a Conservative. During the first half of 1895 he kept up a steady barrage of questions and assertions at Westminster and in his periodical publication *England and the Union* on behalf of the Swazi nation. His conscience had originally been aroused by Gladstone's "betrayals" in African policy in the early 1880s. (He also intervened in Gladstone's campaign over the Armenian question, in support of the Turks rather than the Armenians.)

Swazi delegates, who came to London in early 1895 to protest at Swaziland's being handed over to the Transvaal by the Liberal government, found Ashmead-Bartlett so energetic on their behalf that they gave him the praise name "Silomo"—meaning someone spoiling for a fight.

Silomo made mincemeat of Liberal government policy toward the Boers of the Transvaal, considered by the Conservatives ever since 1881 as much too indulgent. The issue at stake in early 1895 was the brutal nature of current military campaigns by the newly enriched Transvaal state to impose its rule on previously independent African peoples north of Pretoria. The Liberal government's spokesman in the Commons, Sydney Buxton, was forced to admit that the British consul general in the South African Republic (Transvaal) was dependent on its government for information "and that, except we obtain official information, we are not aware of what takes place.'

A Cape Town resident interviewed in the *Times* put the question of "native rights" in the Transvaal even more bluntly: "The question is not one of ethics; but of emphatically affirming the principal that the white man must be the unquestioned master in South Africa."[45]

✣ ✣ ✣

The idea that the human race consisted of a number of separate and superior or inferior "races" underpinned nineteenth-century nationalisms and imperialisms. The British philosopher Herbert Spencer (1820–1903) invented the phrase "the survival of the fittest," his interpretation of Darwin's evolutionary theory that he applied first to biology, then to sociology, psychology, and education. He featured, together with Chamberlain and Khama, in one of the biographical sketches of great men of the times in W. T. Stead's monthly *Review of Reviews* in 1895.

Spencer's "Social Darwinism" was probably more influential in the United States, in the aftermath of its Civil War, than in Britain, for which "other" races were a feature of empire overseas, not at home. Discussion of racial ideas in Britain was usually done vicariously through discussion of developments elsewhere.

Discrimination against Jews featured in stories from Vienna and Paris, where the infamous Dreyfus case was under way. Discrimination against blacks featured in stories about the United States, besides atrocity stories from foreign colonies in Africa—Boer, Portuguese, French, and Belgian.

Perhaps the most thoughtful piece on race and empire in the British press of 1895 was carried in the weekly *Spectator* on October 5, 1895, in a long article that began, "The white race is taking charge of the black race everywhere. . . . and it will have to make up its mind very soon as to the conditions of its guardianship":

> Twenty years hence no black will be able to live happily except by consent of some white people, and the responsibility assumed by the latter will be complete, and, we are compelled to add, most terrible.

The *Spectator* went on to condemn the outright trickery by which Southern whites had disenfranchised blacks in the United States and feared it would be "imitated in the Colonies of South Africa." The journal predicted:

> There will be perpetual discord, rising frequently to the dignity and horror of local civil war, and the end will be either white withdrawal, or more probably an angry and sullen submission on the part of the blacks, almost as fatal to true civilization as civil war itself.

Ironically, the solution of the *Spectator* was one that bears more than a passing resemblance to apartheid:

> black people should be declared to be foreign immigrants, guests of the State, entitled to the benefit of every law and every privilege, education,

for example, but debarred from political power. . . . they would be precisely in the position of the majority of Englishmen before 1832.

The *Spectator* concluded:

It will be said, of course, that the black man will resent his "legal inferiority"; but we do not find that the mass of white women in the States, or in South Africa, resent theirs.[46]

✤ ✤ ✤

Popular curiosity about the subjects of empire was fed by popular entertainment and education (particularly in the new subject called geography) as well as the press. But most people in Britain outside London and a few ports had probably never seen a person of color.

In London the impact of empire could be seen in entertainments such as the exhibition of Somali villagers from northeast Africa, put on at Crystal Palace in lieu of a South African exhibition that failed to materialize in 1895. (Perhaps the failure had something to do with the unsuccessful debut of South African fruit exports into Britain. The response of Covent Garden market porters to the first wizened and sour South African grapes in March 1895 was "Chuck 'em in the dustbin!")

The response to the Somali villagers when they walked about in working-class South London was terrifying, but not unlike the reception British workers might have received walking through some West African villages—they were hooted and whistled at, and even threatened with fisticuffs.[47] The response in upper-class areas of London would have been altogether more sophisticated, if we are to believe the *Morning Advertiser* commenting on the arrival of Khama, Sebele, and Bathoen in September 1895:

Black kings and princes are no longer the *rarae aves* that they were when his swarthy Majesty King Cetewayo first dawned upon an astounded London drawing room. Now an African of noble birth is to be met with at most fashionable receptions during the season, and black bishops talk theology with British deans at garden parties.

All roads, even that from Africa, lead to London. Any day you can hardly walk down Piccadilly without rubbing shoulders with an Afghan, a Zulu, a Hottentot, or a foreigner of some kind.[48]

As Khama, Sebele, and Bathoen were to discover, the manners and dress of class might take precedence over considerations of "race" in close encounters.

✤ ✤ ✤

Finally, the weather: 1895 was, as all years seem to be, unusual.

An unusually severe winter, of North American proportions, gripped northwest Europe. The river Thames was frozen and snow-covered from

Blackwall upstream in February; and nighttime skaters with candle lanterns could be seen gliding up and down the Serpentine (in Hyde Park) and across Hampstead Ponds as late as March 9.

Spring continued to be chilly, and then burst into warm weather at the end of April. Hot summer in late June and July contrasted with news of snow in South Africa, at Kimberley as well as on Table Mountain. The heat in London exceeded eighty degrees Fahrenheit (twenty-seven Celsius) in the shade in late July.[49]

After Khama, Sebele, and Bathoen arrived in England in early September 1895, they experienced the muggy heat of an Indian summer that they found much more oppressive than the dry summers of the African plateaus. That is, until the first week of October, when the weather plunged back into autumn chills.

TWO

A Trinity of
Dusky Kings

◀─◆─▷   ◁─◆─▶

THE "TRINITY OF DUSKY KINGS" WHO ARRIVED AT
Paddington railway station on the afternoon of September 6, 1895, were
the first Bechuana rulers to come to London. But news about Bechuanaland and the Bechuana had featured in British newspaper reports for
more than a decade, and British knowledge about land and people dated
from the beginning of the century. The chiefs themselves also had their
own preconceptions of Britain and about British people, drawn partly
from common historical experiences and partly from their biographies as
individuals from childhood upward.

✜ ✜ ✜

British knowledge of the Bechuana can be dated, as we have seen in
the introduction to this book, from the appendix on the "Booshuana
Nation" in the 1806 publication of *A Voyage to Cochin China*, satirized by
the authors of Munchausen's *Travels*. Early-nineteenth-century European
travelers lighted upon the Bechuana after a thousand-mile wagon trek
northward into the interior across scrub and semidesert. They found a
"nation" of town dwellers, with cultivated fields as well as flocks and herds,
practicing metallurgy and dressed in "decent" leather clothing—anxious
to trade with southerners bringing manufactured goods like firearms. By
contrast with the migrating herders and scattered hunter-gatherers seen
in the scrublands on the way, and "naked" warrior farmers seen in the
forests of the southeast coast, the Bechuana struck early Europeans as
being reassuringly familiar in lifestyle and positively "civilized" in their
demeanor.

Early-nineteenth-century European travel accounts thus praised the
civic and commercial virtues of the Bechuana. But these works, in German and French as well as English, were rarely reprinted and achieved

relatively small circulation, except in semiscientific libraries and among interested collectors in Western Europe and North America.

The Western image of the Bechuana was to be more fully built up in the nineteenth century by popular works of missionary travel and of big-game hunting, published in midcentury and frequently reprinted thereafter. The first of these was *Missionary Labours and Scenes in Southern Africa* by Robert Moffat, a Scots Congregationalist and former gardener turned missionary. It was published in 1842.

Moffat told a tale of evangelical, agricultural, and educational "labours" at the Kuruman mission station, on the southern edge of Bechuana territory. His main purpose was to raise sympathy and financial support for the London Missionary Society, and his portrayal of the Bechuana was often lurid and superficial—painting a picture of heathen darkness that only the light of Christianity could expunge. Though even he could not resist favorable physical comparison of the Bechuana with other Africans, contrasting their brown complexions with the yellowness of "Bushmen" and the blackness of "Negroes."

The two classic works of travel literature touching on the Bechuana, both published by John Murray and featuring among the best-selling books of the whole nineteenth century, were *A Hunter's Life in South Africa* by Roualeyn Gordon Cumming (1850) and *Missionary Travels and Researches in South Africa* by David Livingstone (1857). It was the latter especially that brought the Bechuana to the attention of English-speaking households around the world.

Over the next fifty years Cumming's *Hunter's Life* went through numerous editions, under a variety of titles such as *The Lion Hunter*. Dr. Livingstone's *Missionary Travels* was even more successful: the book was being given as a school prize to British pupils well into the next century.

Livingstone painted a generally sympathetic picture of the Bechuana, whom he saw as good friends who would help to extend commerce and Christianity into central Africa. It was *Missionary Travels* that brought to the world's attention the emigrant Dutch or "Boer" settlers of the Transvaal colony, or republic, whom he portrayed as slave-traders in conflict with the Bechuana—an image for which the Boers never forgave him.[1]

Meanwhile, after he abandoned his mission among the Bechuana, David Livingstone became famous in Victorian Britain and America as the great traveler—a missionary saint, and arguably the only working-class lad to become an unambiguous hero in Victorian Britain. Even the acerbic Lytton Strachey feared to criticize Livingstone when he debunked recent historical figures in his ironically titled *Eminent Victorians* (1918). The paring down to size was left to the editor of Livingstone's journals, Isaac Schapera, in the mid-twentieth century. Schapera pointed out that the supposedly great missionary had made only one full convert to Christianity—his close but somewhat wayward friend named Sechele.[2]

The death of David Livingstone in 1873, and the publicity whipped up by people like the journalist Henry Morton Stanley, who had linked his name with Livingstone's a few years earlier by a publicity stunt of "discovering" the doctor on Lake Tanganyika, helped to set off the imperialist fervor of the later 1870s.

It was another Scots missionary of the London Missionary Society, John Mackenzie, who most fully impressed the issue of Boers and Bechuana on British public opinion in the early 1880s. Mackenzie's agitation led to the Warren Expedition, which expelled the Boers of the Transvaal from Bechuana country *south* of the Molopo River in 1885. He pushed for the extension of British "protection" over the part of Bechuanaland and the Kalahari *north* of the Molopo River—the territories ruled by Livingstone's friend Sechele (father of Sebele), by Gaseitsiwe (father of Bathoen), and by Khama.

The result was the declaration of a British protectorate over Bechuanaland and the Kalahari in January 1885, which in September 1885 was divided into a Crown Colony called "British Bechuanaland" south of the Molopo, and a British protectorate called "the Bechuanaland Protectorate" north of the Molopo.

By the time Mackenzie produced his great polemical work entitled *Austral Africa: Losing It or Ruling It,* in 1887, the historian Daphne Trevor claims, "Bechuanaland was certainly not as important as Egypt . . . but Mackenzie's propaganda, Warren's expedition, and the controversy over his recall had impressed its existence on the newspaper reading public." [3]

But Mackenzie's humanitarian imperialism for Bechuanaland was rapidly overtaken by the capitalist imperialism associated with the name of Cecil Rhodes, the British South African diamond magnate and politician who was to become prime minister of the Cape Colony in July 1890. Rhodes had complex political affiliations. In Britain he was closer to Liberal imperialists than to Conservative imperialists, despite his antihumanitarianism, because of his espousal for colonial home rule—starting with Ireland. In South Africa he was allied with the Afrikaner Party at the Cape but was dead set against Afrikaner nationalism in the Boer republics.

The Cape Colony had made a brief bid to absorb Bechuanaland south of the Molopo in 1884. Rhodes revived the Cape Colony's claim to British Bechuanaland in 1888. He told the Cape Assembly in August 1888 that Britain would also be willing to hand over the Bechuanaland Protectorate to the Cape Colony at some future date. The message was passed on to the Tswana chiefs by Rhodes's old friend Sir Sidney Shippard (*Mo-*

rena Maaka, "Lord Lies"), who was both administrator of the colony and deputy (later resident) commissioner of the protectorate.[4]

The BaRolong people, based at Mafeking in British Bechuanaland and across the Molopo up to Pitsane in the Bechuanaland Protectorate, responded by holding protest meetings in October of that year. At Mafeking, leading Christian headman Israel Molema told the meeting that the Cape English were as bad as the Boers, and another headman proposed three cheers for the queen and three boos for the Cape. At Pitsane (later famous as the base for the Jameson Raid), the local BaRolong meeting in their *kgotla* (central court) resolved to fight rather than to accept Cape government.[5]

Rhodes soon changed his tune. In 1889 he and other mining capitalists based in South Africa combined with key financiers in the City of London (most notably the Rothschilds) and a royal duke or two to obtain a royal charter to colonize a vast area that a century later is covered by Botswana, Zimbabwe, Zambia, and Malawi. Mackenzie and Chamberlain protested, but the charter of the British South Africa Company was granted in October 1889. Knutsford, the colonial minister, said that the charter did not for the time being "supersede or affect" the administration of the Bechuanaland Protectorate by Shippard but regarded eventual transfer to BSA Company administration as inevitable.[6]

In 1892 Rhodes proposed what might a hundred years later be seen as a typical "privatization" ploy—speedy transfer of Bechuanaland Protectorate administration to his company in return for an annual subsidy from British government funds. The Colonial Office considered Rhodes's bid "stillborn," but arrangements were made to clear out rival mineral concessions from the Bechuanaland Protectorate in preparation for the full combination of administration and exploitation by the BSA Company. The Cape Colony was also building a railway from Kimberley to Vryburg in British Bechuanaland, from whence the line would be taken northward through Mafeking by the Bechuanaland Railway of the BSA Company. An editorial in the *Manchester Guardian* called the railway "the subject of one of the many friendly understandings between Mr. Rhodes the Cape Premier and Mr. Rhodes the representative of the British South Africa Company."[7]

The Colonial Office became instantly more sympathetic to Rhodes when Lord Rosebery, an out-and-out imperialist (married to a Rothschild), succeeded Gladstone as prime minister in March 1894. In May 1894 the BSA Company was formally given the right to administer on behalf of the Crown the land that soon came to be called (Southern) "Rhodesia," northeast of the Bechuanaland Protectorate.[8]

The BSA Company's need to incorporate the Bechuanaland Protectorate into Rhodesia became ever more pressing because of the impending extension of the Bechuanaland Railway across the Molopo from Mafeking—which would ultimately be financed by selling off the land along the line for white farmlands and townships. Hence while he was in London, in November 1894, Rhodes as chairman of the BSA Company put in a formal claim at the Colonial Office for "an assurance from Her Majesty's Government that their policy is unchanged, and that when, in their opinion, the time has arrived, they will transfer the administration of the Protectorate to the Chartered Company, thus carrying out the terms of the Charter and the former assurances of their predecessors." The reply of the colonial minister (Lord Ripon) to Rhodes was reassuring, though he added that the qualms of the "large and admiring classes in this country" who supported Khama in the Bechuanaland Protectorate, because of his opposition to alcohol, would have to be accommodated.[9]

Rhodes's reason for taking the Bechuanaland Protectorate became all the more urgent now that Rhodes and his co-conspirators had decided to use the protectorate as their springboard for a sudden attack on and coup d'état in the neighboring Boer republic of the Transvaal.

Meanwhile separate negotiations were being conducted by the Colonial Office with Rhodes as the Cape premier for the final incorporation of British Bechuanaland into the Cape Colony. When arrangements for this were being finalized in June 1895, Cape newspapers (all known to be more or less supporting Rhodes to the hilt) reported that the transfer of the Bechuanaland Protectorate to the Chartered Company would follow soon. It was this news that set the leading chiefs of the protectorate on their way overseas to appeal unto Caesar.

✤ ✤ ✤

In the early nineteenth century, Bechuana (BaTswana) views of the British and other traders, who came from the south to buy ivory and sell manufactured goods, were generally benign—just as were initial British views of the Bechuana.

It would be an exaggeration to claim that Westerners invented or "imagined" the Bechuana in the early nineteenth century. But Tswana or Bechuana identity developed in the nineteenth century under the cultural and linguistic impact of Western influence.

A general sense of Tswana identity undoubtedly predated the arrival of literate Europeans, before Messrs. Trüter and Somerville arrived in the southern Tswana kingdom of the BaTlhaping and referred to the "Booshuana Nation" in 1801–2. When asked about people to the north, BaTlhaping people referred to them as "Bechuana"—a word most likely derived from the verb *go tswa*, "to come from," meaning that people in the north came from the same origins. The ruling families of the Tswana states and statelets defined their identity by ultimate descent from common ancestor figures, who could be traced back five centuries or more. (*Be-tswana* rather than *Ba-tswana* seems to have been a southern dialectical variation among the BaTlhaping, indicating an overlap with Xhosa-speaking people of the southeast, who referred to Ba-tswana as *Abe-tswana*.)

During the course of the nineteenth century, the peoples all originally referred to as BaTswana or Bechuana became politically and linguistically differentiated under the impact of different Christian missions—Paris, Berlin, and London missionary societies respectively—as being "Sotho" and "Pedi" as well as Tswana. (A fourth possible political and dialectical variation, that of the Khalagari, who gave their name to the Kalahari "desert," had no powerful core state, never had its own missionary society, and never received such recognition of independence from Tswanadom.)

Western ideas of linguistic nation and nationality, and of the necessity for nation-states to politically represent them, were ill formed at the beginning of the nineteenth century but grew ever more certain thereafter. Such ideas were refracted back into the self-image of those Bechuana, who had access to literacy, rulers to whom newspapers were read, as well as preachers and teachers. A new sense of wider Tswana nationality grew among people in the dozen or more Tswana states and statelets.

Access to literacy was brought about by the linguistic studies and other activities, including printing and publishing, of the missionary societies. The key figure in the development of nineteenth-century Setswana literacy was Robert Moffat. He was the Martin Luther of the Setswana language, using the SeTlhaping dialect to produce the great *Bibela ee Boitshepo* (Holy Bible), which transformed spoken language into written form. With a team of BaTlhaping teachers and evangelists as his interpreters, Moffat produced complete translations of the New Testament (1840) and of the Old Testament (1857), which gave Setswana the distinction of being the first indigenous language south of Ethiopia with a complete Christian Bible.

The definition of the self goes hand in hand with definition of the other, and so it was with the self-definition of the Bechuana and their identification of the British—these were long processes with many lags and spurts.

Traders from the south like the British were all seen at first as *Makgoa*, a word that like its eastern and southeastern coastal equivalents (*Wazungu* and *Abelungu* respectively) seems to have originated as a generic term for alien traders from the ocean—but that in time became refined down to meaning Europeans ("whites" in twentieth-century parlance) in general and British, or English-speakers, in particular. The origin of *Makgoa* (singular, *Lekgoa*) is almost certainly originally associated with the long-haired traders who came from the east in the eighteenth century and earlier, up the Limpopo valley from the southern Mozambique coast. Derivations of the word *Makgoa* have been suggested from "Goa," the geographical origin of Portuguese-Indian traders, and from "Makua," the ethnic label of Portuguese-African traders from northern Mozambique—as well as from "go kgwa," to vomit, for those spewed forth by the ocean.

The first identifiable individual named "Lekgoa" in Tswana oral traditions is one Coenrad de Buys, a Boer who came north to exploit the Limpopo valley ivory trade soon after 1800. He and other southern traders came with horse and gun. Hence another possible derivation of the word *Lekgoa:* a red or white louse said to resemble a man seated on a horse.[10]

With the invasion of Boer and Griqua (people of mixed African and European ancestry) horsemen north of the Orange and Vaal Rivers in the 1830s and 1840s, they became distinguished from other Makgoa as *Maburu* (i.e. "Boers" or Afrikaners) and *Masetedi* (i.e. bandits, possibly "bright faces"), two terms used more or less interchangeably until the twentieth century. Among Makgowa, or Europeans proper, the distinctions of missionary and imperial nationalities became recognized by the distinguishing terms *Mafora* (French, inserting an "o" to get to grips with the guttural "r" in "Français"), *Majeremane* (German, from the English word "Germany"), and *Mayesemane* (English, from the word "Englishman"). Finally, in the decade before 1895, the Bechuana were of necessity learning to make a distinction that was seldom if ever completely sharp, between British people direct from Europe and English-speaking whites who had settled in Africa.

It is not clear, and is open to debate, when the political-racial language of color was adopted into Setswana from South African English and Afrikaans—referring to people as black *(bantsho)*, white *(basweu)*, and colored or brown *(bakgothu,* from *kgothu* meaning "copper"). White people were not seen as being white for much of the nineteenth century, but as "red" *(bahibidu)*, an understandable observation based on the complexion's response to climate—no doubt like the earliest Nordic and English references to black people being "blue." Hence a fifth, and last, possible derivation of the word *Makgowa*, from *go kgowa*, to peel, revealing the red underskin.

Indigenous southern African color symbolism was, as all such systems are, complex and sometimes contradictory. Red, black, white, and yellow in other contexts stood for young women, old women, young men, and old men respectively. Nor was color of complexion irrelevant in political-racial terms before "whites" appeared in southern African history. Oral

traditions record that people of darker complexion were generally accorded higher status and people of lighter complexion accorded lower
status—on the grounds of the latter's connection with servile Khoisan
("Hottentot" and "Bushman") communities.[11]

The history of British intervention among the Bechuana in the interior
of southern Africa, when read in retrospect, has an air of inevitability
about it. But for most of the nineteenth century it was by no means clear
that this was to be so. Before the 1870s the British were at the top of the
pile in the interior as well as on the coast, because they had the best access
to modern manufactured goods and weapons during the "imperialism of
Free Trade." But it was only the discovery of diamonds at Kimberley,
and the subsequent opening up of goldfields north and east of Bechuanaland, which brought British command, "protection," and overrule to the
interior.

To put the history of the nineteenth century into nineteenth-century
perspective, and to see the significance of British actions in African eyes,
we need to look at the life histories of the three chiefs or kings who went
to Britain in 1895.

Sebele

[Sebele] was the more kingly in the matter of head-gear; for he was wearing a new helmet of pith of a buff colour and draped with a pugaree. He is
a short thick set man, and quite unlike either of his companions. The cast
of his face is almost European, and if it were not for his dark copper hue
he might very well pose as the double of an eminent barrister whose features are well known to frequenters of the Temple and of the Courts.
. . . Had he been a white man he would have been a lawyer as surely as
Khama would have been a clergyman and [Bathoen] an inn-keeper."[12]

Sebele was born in about 1842. He was brought up in the shadow of a
remarkable father—the great *Kgosi* Sechele, who ruled the BaKwena of
Botswana for six decades up to 1892. In the latter years before he succeeded his father, Sebele was thus fond of comparing himself with the
successor to Queen Victoria:

I, Sebele, am the same age as the Prince of Wales. . . . I am the eldest son
of Sechele, the Chief of the Bakwena; Albert Edward, the Prince of Wales,
is the eldest son of the Queen of England. My father still rules and I do not
govern; it is the same with His Royal Highness—he does not rule in England. So I say I resemble the Prince of Wales.

The life of Sechele had been extraordinary, encapsulating nineteenth-
century Tswana history like the life of no other individual. He was born

in about 1810. One of the most notable events of that history, the assassination of his father, *Kgosi* Motswasele II, by his own people at the end of a battle he had lost, occurred when Sechele was about ten.

There are two very different popular traditions of this event. One tradition, written up with Shakespearean dimensions by the twentieth-century poet L. D. Raditladi in a play entitled *Motswasele II*, portrays the king as a tyrant who offended his barons by stealing their women and dogs. Another tradition has Motswasele as martyr to his people's treachery, the last monarch in times of relative peace, who left his people with a doom-filled prophecy of the future to come.

Motswasele is said to have prophesied the coming of armies of ants to revenge his death—first the Wars of the Black Ants; then the Wars of the Red Ants.[13]

The first black ants, in the form of Kololo marauders, arrived from the south within a year or two of Motswasele's death. The MaKololo, led by Sebetwane, dispersed the BaTswana of southeastern Botswana and robbed them of their cattle, before trekking north in 1826–27 to the Makgadikgadi pans, Lake Ngami, and the Chobe and Zambezi Rivers. In their place there came the AmaNdebele from the west, a well-organized military nation with a bloody reputation that took forcible tribute and stole women and children from the BaTswana.

The AmaNdebele themselves trekked north in 1836–37, to settle in the area around Bulawayo in western Zimbabwe. They had been expelled and replaced by the red ants, who settled around what became the towns of Potchefstroom and Zeerust in the western Transvaal (South Africa's North West Province today).

The first red ants had been Griqua horsemen and wagoners from the south, seeking elephant ivory and cattle, who raided the MaKololo and the AmaNdebele with firearms. The second group of red ants had similar arms and ambitions but had much greater resources—the Boers under Potgieter and others, trekking from the far south. They had left Cape Colony in search of free land obtainable by conquest, after the colony's new British rulers had cut them out of the land market in 1832 by insisting on auctions of open land to the highest bidder—rather than farmers obtaining tenure by squatting or seizure as before.

Together with Griqua and Tswana (BaRolong) allies, the Boers of Potgieter expelled Mzilikazi's AmaNdebele northward and established themselves as landlords and overlords of the BaTswana in the western Transvaal from about 1838 onward. The loose confederacy of Boer groups who had scattered north of the Vaal River eventually declared their statehood as the South African Republic, more plainly and simply known as "the

Transvaal," whose independence was recognized by the British by the Sand River Convention of 1852.

Sechele found himself declared *Kgosi* in about 1833 when, after twelve years exile more or less as an individual, he encountered a large group of BaKwena fugitives. Striding into their all-night dance dramatically at dawn, an uncle at his side, he was greeted by his brother Kgosidintsi with the tribute of a tortoise-shell filled with goat's milk.

Sechele built up his wealth and power as a close collaborator with the "English" (many being actually Scotsmen dressed in kilts) hunter-traders who came to his lands from Cape Colony in search of elephant ivory— supplying the ever expanding markets of Europe and North America with piano keys, billiard balls, and cutlery handles. Sechele hired out Kwena and Khalagari or Sarwa (Bushman) hunters to do the traders' work with muskets and became an excellent shot himself. He also opened up routes across the Kalahari "desert" to Lake Ngami, where greater concentrations of elephants roamed now that they were being exterminated in southern Botswana and the western Transvaal.[14]

It was Sechele's power and prestige, and his reputation for intellectual as well as commercial sharpness, that attracted the young Christian missionary David Livingstone to attach himself to Sechele's people in 1846. Together they settled at the village of Kolobeng, on the western side of the Ngotwane River in southeastern Botswana, in 1847.

In 1848 Livingstone baptized Sechele, who was qualified by remarkable progress in Setswana literacy and numeracy lessons as a full member of the London Missionary Society church, and able to take the full sacrament of Communion. In return Sechele put aside all his wives except one, Selemeng, the woman who had given birth to his heir Sebele about seven years earlier.

This multiple royal divorce alienated the patriarchs of the divorced wives' families and also caused mass female discontent. The women of Sechele's town staged a stay-at-home strike and downed their hoes, refusing to go the fields to plant and weed the crops. Normality returned when Sechele resumed sleeping with his favorite wife, Mokgokgong. But when Mokgokgong became pregnant, such evidence of "adultery" obliged Livingstone to bar Sechele from Communion. Both men seem to have accepted this philosophically, without rancor. (Sechele was not restored to LMS membership until 1890.)[15] Livingstone, unlike his father-in-law Robert Moffat, was tolerant of African traditions and beliefs.

Sechele attempted and managed to accommodate the traditional beliefs of his ancestors with the new doctrine of Christianity. Sechele has therefore been called "double-souled" by missionary commentators. Other writers have used Sechele, as the "only" convert who nevertheless "failed," as a stick to beat David Livingstone with.[16]

But the fact remains that Sechele was remarkably consistent in Christian belief and practice. He knew his Bible backward, finding texts to justify polygyny and circumcision and other Tswana practices, and did more to propagate Christianity in nineteenth-century southern Africa than virtually any single European missionary. Besides conducting services in the church of his home town, with the names of his ancestors painted on the wall behind the pulpit, Sechele personally took the Gospel to places as far away as Bulawayo—where the first European Christian missionaries were astonished to find that regular Sunday services conducted by Mzilikazi's headmen (after Sechele left) had preceded them by many years.

Sechele's conspicuous example legitimized Christianity and Western culture, including adoption of Western clothing, as well as coffee and cake, among Tswana and other African rulers. Among European Christians, through the writings of David Livingstone, he was one of the best-known African converts of the nineteenth century.

Sechele's Christianity and deep involvement in commerce involved him and his people in a long and complex three-way struggle with Boers and British. He successfully resisted the attempt of the Transvaal Boers to conquer his land, after the British gave them a free hand to do so by the Sand River Convention of 1852. Sechele even attempted to get to London, to negotiate an alliance with the British, in 1853, but failed to get further than Cape Town.

Sechele got on well with English gentlemen visitors, dining them in his metal-roofed house with china plates and silver cutlery under a chandelier, but he had much more everyday contact with Boer wagoners. He learned to speak good Dutch but barely spoke any English at all. Transvaal Boers were themselves by no means united in their approach to Sechele and other Tswana rulers. Boer farmers might look avariciously at Tswana labor, land, water, and wood supplies, but Boer hunter-traders saw the need for alliance and compromise to keep the ivory supply routes open.[17]

Despite periodic appeals for British assistance against the Boers, Sechele learned to live with his Transvaal neighbors. When General Sir Charles Warren came to Sechele's capital, Molepolole, in April 1885, to announce Queen Victoria's protectorate over "Bechuanaland and the Kalahari" north of the Molopo River, Sechele was noncommittal. His son Sebele actually told Warren, "We do not want any protection, we are strong enough to protect ourselves."

Sechele and Sebele were being somewhat ingenuous. Sechele actually received Warren on that Monday morning "gorgeously attired in a blue velvet coat, edged in white, with the Arms of England resplendent on his back." He was on recent record as preferring British imperial protection to any form of white-settler domination—British settlers in the form of Cape Colony, or Boer settlers in any form. He was obviously playing for a comparative advantage in the negotiations with Warren. As an Englishman who knew Sechele well had said in 1882, he was "an old fox, and I much fear the son and heir-apparent is worse than the parent." [18]

Sebele was even more educated and literate than his father, having been taught first by Livingstone and then at Moffat's Kuruman mission in the south. Sechele sent Sebele and two of his sisters to Kuruman after Livingstone left for the north. Some years later, Sebele rewarded his old teacher at Kuruman, William Ashton, with a royal eland skin as *malebogo a thupa,* "thanks for the rod." [19]

Described as "sullen and refractory" as a boy, Sebele was witty and convivial as an adult—and was pilloried as being a drunkard without morals by the missionaries—not unlike Albert Edward, the real Prince of Wales. Among his own people, Sebele had a somewhat mixed reputation. On the one hand, the Rev. Edwin Lloyd noted:

> There are few men who have a more complete mastery of the Sechwana language than Sebele, the son of Sechele. All customs, traditions, fairy tales, and folk-lore of his people, he has at ready command. When he begins to talk on these subjects, he generally goes on for hours together, retailing this kind of information . . . usually told on a pitch-dark night, around the blazing camp-fires, when travelling.

Among the favorite "fairy tales" were those about the canny hare who managed to trick both the lion and the hyena. [20]

On the other hand, Sebele had to contend with the idea that at heart he was a coward. In 1875 he had beaten an ignominious retreat from the failed Kwena assault on the Kgatla capital of Mochudi: "In battle, a Chief's place, when defeated," he was told, "is to be among the dead or wounded; he ought not to run away home."

The Kwena state that had flourished, with Sechele premier among all Tswana rulers, in the 1850s and 1860s, declined in the later 1870s when the center of commercial and political gravity in Botswana slipped north to the Ngwato kingdom of Khama III. Sebele found this intensely frustrating and chafed all the more at his subordination to an increasingly senile father. Once, during a heated *kgotla* debate at Molepolole, he ripped into his father, saying that if he did not die soon, he should be dispatched. This served to further alienate Sebele from many of his people. Though in fact an observant attender at church services, he was seen as the leader of the antichurch faction in Kwena politics. After succeeding as *Kgosi* of the BaKwena in 1892, on Sechele's death, he never really became a popular ruler.

Sebele was a thorn in the side of the colonial administrators of the Bechuanaland Protectorate. It was Sebele who took the initiative in calling a meeting between chiefs and administrators in 1888, but it was also Sebele who broke up the meeting in disarray. He opposed every extension of British power. In October 1890 he told the commissioner of the protectorate: "I wish to govern my country myself, and not have it governed by white people." He explained himself further in the next month:

> I do not want a magistrate. I want only independence. As to protection I say nothing. I liked it, but I do not like it any more. . . . We have received no assistance from you; all we have got from you is trouble.

When the new British magistrate at Gaborone tried to collect taxes from Boer and Indian traders at Molepolole, Sebele encouraged the traders to resist. When the British threatened him with military force, Sebele backed down—coughing up a ten-cow fine as a gesture of goodwill, but at the same time lecturing the magistrate: "Friendship does not mean giving laws to one another. Friendship is to advise each other." [21]

The high commissioner in Cape Town concluded that Sebele had to be taught the new meaning of British "protection," which had been greatly strengthened unilaterally in British law by the Foreign Jurisdiction Act passed by the Westminster Parliament in 1890.

Sebele was invited to Cape Town in June 1892, both to hear and see the extent of British power. At Vryburg, the capital of British Bechuanaland south of the Molopo River, Sebele caused outrage and dissent in the Boer or Afrikaans community, when he accepted an invitation to sit next to Pastor Wilcocks at a service in the local Dutch Reformed Church.

At Cape Town Sebele saw, like his father forty years earlier, ships and buildings and machinery. Unlike King Cetshwayo of the AmaZulu who had been pictured lounging on a cannon at Cape Town in 1882, he was not allowed to see the big guns in the forts of Cape Town in 1892 "on grounds of security." But he seems to have been sufficiently impressed by the trappings of British power: Sebele promised the high commissioner that in future he would behave himself.

Described as a "most pleasant, and a very kind and good-natured host," fond of his food as well as of his drink, the bald-pated Sebele was never the drunkard or the great sinner that some missionaries made him out to be.[22]

BATHOEN

[Bathoen] is an African of another stamp—taller by an inch or so than Khama, very stout and broad, with magnificent chest and shoulders, and a figure as erect as that of a drill-sergeant. He is a veritable Samson, and when he walks the earth seems to shake beneath him. He has a huge head—the flat spreading nose, the large open eyes, and the heavy lips of the true child of Ham. He was wearing a blue serge suit and a black bowler hat—with the front part of the crown knocked in.[23]

Bathoen was the son of Gaseitsiwe, *Kgosi* of the BaNgwaketse who lived immediately to the south of the BaKwena—abutting onto the Molopo River—and their friendly neighbors the BaRolong people of the Mafeking area.

The Ngwaketse kingdom, based on copper mining and hunting deep into the Kalahari, had been the biggest and most powerful Tswana state in the area of southeastern Botswana during the eighteenth and early nineteenth centuries. The Ngwaketse kingdom survived the Kololo invasion of 1824–26 but collapsed soon afterward when attacked by the AmaNdebele. BaNgwaketse remnants fled westward across the Kalahari, taking with them the nation's cattle.

Much like Sechele among the BaKwena—and others elsewhere on the South African plateau like Moshoeshoe of Lesotho—it was young Gaseitsiwe who reunited and led the BaNgwaketse back to prominence in the 1830s.

Known for his gentleness *(bokgewabo)*, Gaseitsiwe was described as "an unusually gentle, good-natured man [who] knew how to give the 'love that thinketh no evil.' . . . The very tones of his voice were most soft and mellifluous, as if pitched to disarm all hostility."[24]

Like Sechele, and his near neighbor to the south, *Kgosi* Montshiwa (Montsioa) of the BaRolong, Gaseitsiwe had to deal with the expansionism of Transvaal Boers from 1851–52 onward. The stone walls of the hilltop Ngwaketse capital of Kanye had to be reinforced once more, with musket loopholes. Gaseitsiwe himself was kidnapped by Boers when on a visit abroad. He was released after his son and heir, Bathoen, paid an enormous ransom of two thousand cattle.

It was to Gaseitsiwe at Kanye that Montshiwa fled in November 1884, escaping the predations of Boer filibusters at Mafeking. Gaseitsiwe was a much less powerful individual than Sechele, and unlike Sechele did not have a finger in many political pies abroad. But unlike the Kwena kingdom, the Ngwaketse kingdom weathered the storm of the later 1870s and early 1880s when hunting and hunting revenue dramatically declined—because of the rapid elimination of Kalahari wildlife due to widespread adoption of modern firearms. The Ngwaketse kingdom remained rich in cattle stocks, and it controlled the trade route from the Molopo across the Kalahari to central Namibia.

Guided by Montshiwa, Gaseitsiwe's reception of General Warren in April 1885 was scarcely enthusiastic. In the words of the *Diamond Fields Advertiser*, Gaseitsiwe like Sechele "no longer believe[d] in England's power to protect the black man." It was only Khama's example that persuaded Gaseitsiwe, like Sechele, to be more receptive to Warren when he passed through on his return southward in May.

Bathoen, son of Gaseitsiwe, was of a similar age and physique to Sebele, and like Sebele had proved himself to be no soldier—in a skirmish of 1882 at Ramotswa. But he found understudying his father as *Kgosi* much less stressful than Sebele did with his father.

From about 1885 Bathoen took on most of the governance of the Ngwaketse kingdom. He began to associate himself closely with his fellow *Kgosi* to the north, Khama, and also became Sebele's brother-in-law. Like Khama, Bathoen became a teetotaler, and he exceeded all other Tswana rulers as a Sabbatarian enforcing popular observance of the Lord's Day as a day of rest—such that in 1887 there was a short-lived revolt among the BaNgwaketse against his rule, which resulted in part of Kanye being burned down. Bathoen eventually succeeded Gaseitsiwe on the latter's death in 1889.

Bathoen had inherited Gaseitsiwe's easy relationship with the local London missionary, James Good, an undemanding fellow more interested in settling down to farming than in evangelism. The relationship was perpetuated by Good's son-in-law and successor, Edwin Lloyd. Good and Lloyd conveniently overlooked the fact that Bathoen's chosen wife, Gagoangwe, Sechele's remarkable one-eyed daughter, was already the wife of another man.[25]

A British antiquarian who passed through Kanye from the south in 1891 described first meeting a notice, at the bottom of Kanye hill, that banned wagons from entering or leaving town on Sundays. At the top of the hill lay the Dutch-gabled royal residence behind the *kgotla*, described as a "circular piazza for meetings planted with shady trees." BaNgwaketse men stood around, dressed in old military jackets and loincloths, ostrich feathers on their soft hats. North of Kanye the wagon road passed over broken wooded countryside, with red granite hills, before crossing a sandy plain of camel thorns that led to the hills of Molepolole.[26]

Like Sebele, seeing no further threat from Boers or Germans from east or west, Bathoen objected to the idea of colonial taxation in exchange for the protectorate. Like Sebele, therefore, he was invited to Cape Town by the high commissioner in 1892, to learn about colonial political economy.

In coming down the railway, the Chief stood on the front of the engine, [and experienced] in going through the valleys and gorges of the Hex River, surrounded by magnificent snow-capped hills, a sense of awe and grandeur in the extreme.[27]

Bathoen was the least remarkable in personality of the three chiefs or kings who visited Britain in 1895. His eyes stare out of photographs under perplexed brows. But this frown was the product of ingrowing eyelashes and short-sightedness, rather than any ill humor. He is otherwise described as kind and straightforward, with a good speaking voice, and given on occasion to joviality.

KHAMA

Khama . . . is a tall and very slender man. He stands slightly over six feet and is slim as a youth of twenty. He was the best dressed of the three; for a Cape tailor who knew how to use the shears had been at work upon his garb and had turned him out so that he should not disgrace the coloured population of Bloomsbury and Bayswater. He was clad in a jacket and vest of light check tweed and dark cloth trousers, and he wore a neat collar and light boots which will awake no noisy echoes in the corridors of the Colonial Office. His hat was of round white felt with a broad brim.

The face beneath the hat was of a singular though negroid type. It was a strikingly small face, and the head poised on a thin neck. . . . Khama looks about five-and-forty [sic]. His woolly hair is sparse and faintly tinted with grey.[28]

Khama III was the son of Sekgoma I, the *Kgosi* of the BaNgwato (otherwise BaMmaNgwato or "Bamangwato") people who lived to the north of the BaKwena people of Sechele and Sebele. The Ngwato kingdom claimed enormous marches in semidesert hunting areas of the north, said to stretch even as far as the Victoria Falls but very low in population density.

The Ngwato experience of the Wars of the Black Ants was quite as intense as that of Tswana states to the south. Khama was born on the southern edge of the great Makgadikgadi salt pans, in about 1835, after the Kololo invaders but before the Ndebele invaders passed—while his father was roaming as far as the Victoria Falls trying to collect the people together again. The MaKololo had taken most of their cattle; the Ama-Ndebele took the official heir to the Ngwato throne, a young boy called Macheng, half brother to Sekgoma.

Kgosi Sekgoma I, Khama's father, in much the same manner and at much the same time as Sechele and Gaseitsiwe to the south, brought his people back together into an expansionist state and ruled them for many decades. But his state, based at Shoshong, had a much greater potential for expansion and wealth in the long run, since it lay at a crossroads in the interior. It connected the so-called Missionaries' Road from Mafeking and Kuruman, and other southern wagon roads across the Limpopo from the Transvaal, with three roads to the north—to the Ndebele kingdom based at Bulawayo in western Zimbabwe; to the Zambezi, and to the Lozi kingdom that had overthrown the Kololo in the area of western Zambia; and to Ngamiland, the Okavango delta, and northern Namibia.

Sechele of the BaKwena attempted to keep Sekgoma of the BaNgwato under his thumb so as, in the words of John Mackenzie, "to obtain such influence in the town of the Bamangwato, as would enable him to secure some of the treasures of ivory and ostrich feathers which are brought from its extensive hunting grounds, extending northwards to the Zambese." The trade passing through Shoshong in the year 1877 was put at seventy-five tons of ivory from twelve thousand elephants, worth two hundred thousand pounds in then current values on the world market.

It was thus that Sechele, using his traditional seniority to the Ngwato *Kgosi*, in descent from a common ancestor, became the kingmaker of the BaNgwato. First, in 1857, he obtained the return of Macheng from the Ndebele kingdom and imposed him as *Kgosi* until the Ngwato aristocracy revolted: Sechele then reinstated Sekgoma, in 1858. Then, after civil war erupted between Sekgoma, the "grizzled old Tory," and his Christian sons, Khama and Kgamane, Sechele brought back Macheng as compromise candidate in 1866. Macheng remained *Kgosi* until 1872, when Khama overthrew him and, at Sechele's suggestion, was proclaimed *Kgosi* himself.

Khama was a militant convert to Christianity, baptized in 1860 at the age of about twenty-five. He had won his spurs in battle against the Ama-Ndebele in 1863, when tradition records that he wounded Lobengula of the AmaNdebele with a shot in the neck. In 1865–66, he had revolted against the "heathenism" of his father, leading the Christian youth literally as soldiers into battle. In 1866 he had left the kingdom in disgust at the restoration of his uncle Macheng, telling people that in future "My kingdom consists in my gun, my horses, and my waggon." Then in 1872 Khama had overthrown Macheng, with the help of a Kwena army led by Sechele's son Sebele.

Khama set about Christian kingship with a puritan vengeance on all things "heathen," including music and dancing and all forms of alcohol, and refused to lead traditional rainmaking, planting, and harvesting ceremonies. On New Year's Day of 1873 he summoned all the town's white traders and tore into them for holiday drunkenness. Khama sensed such hostility from people toward the new morality that he summoned his father home from exile in 1873 and withdrew to the Makgadikgadi salt pans to become independent once more. Sekgoma was now supported by his second son, Kgamane, but his rule had been fatally weakened by all the years of intrigue. When Shoshong was attacked by Macheng, with Boer and Ndebele supporters, from the south, Khama marched back in to seize power once more in February 1875—beginning a reign that was to last for forty-eight more years. Sekgoma and Kgamane fled abroad.

Khama was more conciliatory toward his people this time—particularly toward the overmighty aristocrats who wanted freedom to accumulate wealth (in cattle) from the spoils of hunting, at a time when the market for ivory, furs, and feathers was booming. But he showed he would take no nonsense from the increasing number of white hunter-traders passing through or resident in his country. First he banned all import and consumption of liquor, then he began to expel offenders. He also made it clear that no land or water-well in his country was ever for sale to anyone, and hunting by foreigners was strictly licensed and guided—though this could only moderate and not stop the drastic reduction in wildlife numbers that became evident by the end of the 1870s.

Khama soon came to the attention of the British authorities at Kimberley, far to the south, who were anxious for friends in the interior to send cheap "raw" labor to the new mines. A British official visitor of 1878 described Khama's country as "this native Utopia." The admiration was mutual. Khama had a weakness for supposedly Christian English gentlemen visitors and railed against the Boers who were seeking to invade his country from the Transvaal in support of Kgamane as their "puppet" candidate for *Kgosi*. But he only appealed for British "protection" once, in ·1876, at about the same time as Sechele, in all the years before the Warren Expedition arrived in 1885. (Old Sekgoma and Kgamane eventually returned home to live under Khama's rule, as broken men, Sekgoma dying in 1883.) [29]

Sir Charles Warren was more careful than he had been with Sechele and the Kwena, and he was better received, when he proclaimed the queen's protectorate to the Ngwato *kgotla* at Shoshong on May 12, 1885. The general found Khama to be a Christian soldier after his own heart, and "one of the big men of the nineteenth century." [30]

Warren had with him George Baden-Powell (elder brother of the later defender of Mafeking) and John Mackenzie, a missionary and mentor from Khama's youth. It was Mackenzie who managed to insert into Khama's message of acceptance to the queen the truly extraordinary offer of extensive Kalahari frontier lands, for the settlement of virtuous farmers direct from England, an offer that Khama was to rue: "He has never ceased to regret the arrangement in regard to his country which he says was Mr. Mackenzie's doing and not his" (1890).

With Khama's "magnificent offer" in hand, Warren and Mackenzie succeeded in extracting similar pledges from Sechele and Gaseitsiwe. However, all came to naught: the Colonial Office rejected the chiefs' gifts of land after protests from the Cape Colony at the implied insult to Afrikaners and colonial English.[31]

Growing numbers of white prospectors and speculators as well as hunter-traders now made the journey from the Cape through the Bechuanaland Protectorate to "Zambesia"—a journey immortalized in Rider Haggard's popular novel *King Solomon's Mines*, the "popular success of the decade."[32] Itinerants passing through Khama's capital gave him conflicting signals about the English. Two Ndebele *indunas* returning from England in 1889 gave him and his councillors "a wondrous account of England & its people & Queen," while hot-headed officers of the Bechuanaland Border Police, such as Frederick Carrington, gave Khama the impression that the English might attack and conquer him at any moment.

In 1889 Khama moved his capital from Shoshong to the new town of Palapye (in the hills east of the later railway station of that name). The *Cape Argus* called Palapye, which was laid out and constructed in two months, "wondrous" and not one whit less remarkable than the new cities of Kimberley and Johannesburg. It was linked to Cape Town by telegraph in 1890.

> Khama pervades everything in his town. He is always on horseback, visiting the fields, the stores, and the outlying kraals. He has a word for everyone; he calls every woman's "my daughter" and every man "my son"; he pats little children on the head.[33]

Like his fellow *Kgosi*, Bathoen of the Ngwaketse, Khama was out to profit financially from white penetration. He had a keen eye on market trends in oxen, horses, ostrich feathers, and the dying ivory trade. But, unlike Gaseitsiwe and Bathoen, Sechele and Sebele, he was extremely cautious in granting mineral and commercial concessions to foreign companies. Khama granted only one such concession—for mineral exploration—to a local trading company in 1887. This was sold through the Paris-based Caisse des Mines and the London-based Bechuanaland Exploration Company to be bought up by the British South Africa Company in 1892. The concession was then renegotiated directly by that company with Khama in July 1893.

Encouraged by the British government, and by Resident Commissioner Shippard in particular, Khama and the BaNgwato gave every assistance to Rhodes's BSA Company as the queen's representatives in colonizing what came to be called Rhodesia.

In 1890, when the BSA Company invaded Mashonaland, Khama

supplied scouts and labor for road building led by his half brother Raditladi. Not that Ngwato assistance was always appreciated: an American
"Rhodesian Pioneer" commented: "The Bamangwatos were the most an-
noying people it had ever been my misfortune to meet." They spent too
much time reading the Bible, singing, and praying. When white scouts
stopped for coffee, the Bangwato halted for prayer and complained about
the whites' frequent use of sacrilegious cursewords.[34]

In 1892 the BSA Company offered to take on the administration of the
Bechuanaland Protectorate in return for a large subsidy from the British
government. The offer was well publicized, and Khama protested about
it to Sir Henry Loch, Britain's high commissioner at the Cape. Loch denied that the press reports had any validity and then privately protested to
the Colonial Office at the speed of transfer contemplated. But the Colonial Office was unimpressed by Rhodes's offer and considered it "stillborn" from the start.[35]

In 1893 the BSA Company planned an invasion of the Ndebele kingdom
(Matabeleland) by an armed column, under the leadership of Dr. Leander
Starr Jameson, from its base in Mashonaland. But Loch insisted on an imperial column with Ngwato troops and colonial police also attacking from
the south.

Khama supplied seventeen hundred troops under the command of
himself and Raditladi, which joined the imperial column under Major
Goold-Adams—who like other local colonial policemen was a share-
holder in the BSA Company. This slow-moving wagon force from the
south bore the brunt of the fighting, against the AmaNdebele under the
command of their main general, Gambo, at the battle of Mangwe—while
the cavalry force under Jameson advanced rapidly on Bulawayo from
the east.

Ngwato scouts brought back intelligence that the AmaNdebele had
abandoned Bulawayo to Jameson's advance. As Khama put it later, "The
war was to all intents and purposes over and finished." There was also
smallpox in Matabeleland, and the BaNgwato wanted to return home to
catch the rains to plow after a previous season of famine. Goold-Adams refused to believe intelligence that no white man had gathered. "I cannot help
it if your men are slow," Khama told him, saying, "I know it is true. I believe
my men as you believe yours," as the two men parted in a huff.[36]

While newspapers in Britain were lauding Khama as "our loyal ally"—
the *Pall Mall Gazette* carried a character sketch of Khama, and the *Manchester Guardian* suggested that he should be made a Knight Commander
of the Order of St. Michael and St. George—Cecil Rhodes is said to have
"inquired how many men it would take to dispose of Khama and dispos-
sess him of his country." Rhodes strode into the great *kgotla* at Palapye

where Khama sat with his counselors and launched himself into a public diatribe against Khama as a deserter to the cause. Rhodes or his minions saw to it that a special Reuter's interview with Khama, giving his side of the controversy, never reached British newspapers.

What was now a personal matter of antagonism between Khama and Rhodes was not helped by the new London missionary at Khama's town, Rev. W. C. Willoughby, who supplied information highly critical of the Chartered Company to the Henry Labouchère's London news journal *Truth*.

When hostilities ceased, there was a white settler rush for Matabeleland and Mashonaland through Bechuanaland—in the words of the settler historian Hugh Marshall Hole, by "unsuccessful miners from California and Australia; fugitives from justice in England or other parts of Europe; men of decent birth who had come to grief, and men of low origin who were birds of prey by nature." The pastures around Palapye were grazed bare or denuded by travelers' careless fires. Cases of damage, rape, and other crimes by foreigners preoccupied Khama in *kgotla*.[37]

✤ ✤ ✤

Now it was established in Matabeleland, the Chartered Company began to claim as its own those parts of Khama's country that the Ndebele kingdom had claimed—the countryside between the Motloutse and Shashe Rivers (Bobirwa) in the northeast, and between the Nata and Shashe Rivers (Bokalanga) in the northwest. In August 1894 the company arrested Sarwa (Bushmen) hunters in Ngwato employment on the Nata.

In September 1894 the BSA Company attempted to take the northern part of Khama's country by sleight of hand, first placing it under the "Zambesian" rather than the South African customs union, and then proposing that the whole customs area should come under the company's administration. Khama objected furiously to the British government. Colonial Office officials in London, led by Edward Fairfield, supported Khama's view until December 1894, when Fairfield suddenly swung behind Rhodes. As Rhodes, who was in London at time, was fond of remarking, every man had his price.

In the last quarter of 1894 newspapers controlled by Rhodes began a concerted propaganda campaign against Khama and the "ant's nest of negrophilists" that supported him overseas ("Exeter Hall" in London) and in South Africa. John Smith Moffat, the assistant commissioner newly resident at Palapye, Robert Moffat's son, now beginning to regret his past in helping Rhodes to conquer the AmaNdebele, predicted that Khama was Rhodes's "next victim." Khama's only hope, wrote Moffat, was a direct appeal to the queen and people of England, a sentiment echoed by

Khama himself in a letter to Loch on July 4, 1894: "And if friendship with the Government does not help me at all in this matter [the Chartered Company claim to the Motloutse-Shashe 'disputed territory'], I ought to seek another way of approach by which I can speak to the Queen and the people of England."[38] (The British government, by contrast, was seen as compromised toward big capital. The replacement of Gladstone as Liberal prime minister by Rosebery, a Rothschild son-in-law, in March 1894, had given the government a plutocratic image.)

An anonymous article in the *South African Review* of January 1895, possibly by or inspired by J. S. Moffat, predicted that Rhodes would swallow Khama by the same means as he had swallowed Lobengula:

> Sooner or later some cause will be found to pick a quarrel with the chief: bogus parties of the enemy will be encountered by lonely patrols, Khama will be discovered to be massing his forces, and made responsible for some act of his subjects, and the dogs of war will be loosed upon him. . . . Rhodes's young men have tasted blood and wet their spurs.[39]

There were indeed to be a number of border incidents between Ngwato hunters and Rhodesian forces over the next few months and years, disputing land and cattle and labor. But Rhodes had bigger fish to fry than Khama alone. Together with Jameson he had arrived overseas in November 1894. They were plotting insurrection and armed intervention in Kruger's Transvaal republic a year hence, after swallowing not just Khama's country but the whole of the Bechuanaland Protectorate.

THREE

Another Sphere of Existence

-→⊨⊙ ⊙⊨←-

RHODES AND JAMESON ACHIEVED GREAT SATISFACTION during their visit overseas of November 1894–February 1895. As the journalist W. T. Stead was to remark:

> When Mr. Rhodes left England in February, 1895, he was at the zenith of his power. Alike in London and in South Africa, every obstacle seemed to bend before his determined will.

Rhodes left with the cheers of Chartered Company shareholders ringing in his ears, and with a seat on the queen's Privy Council. The boom in South African share prices on European stock markets had begun and was to soar upward as the months progressed. Lord Ripon, the colonial minister, had reassured Rhodes that the Chartered Company would be given the Bechuanaland Protectorate eventually. But Ripon had warned Rhodes about the "large and admiring classes in this country" who might be expected to support Khama.[1]

In the Bechuanaland Protectorate, Khama, like Sebele and Bathoen, had been greatly offended by the sudden appointment of a British magistrate (Assistant Commissioner J. S. Moffat) over him in 1892, "with power to levy taxes, issue licences, hold courts, and perform other acts of government." But High Commissioner Sir Henry Loch had not considered it necessary to summon Khama to Cape Town for an explanation. Khama was kept sweet toward the imperial factor by other means, such as the favorable treatment of Ngwato border claims against their Kwena and Kgatla neighbors in the south—which Resident Commissioner Sir Sidney Shippard, Rhodes's friend and collaborator, may have seen as a sop for Khama's losing out on his northern borders to the Chartered Company.

Loch (who was the governor of the Cape Colony as well as Britain's high commissioner for the rest of South Africa) kept his cards very close to his chest, but the evidence suggests that he had fallen out with Rhodes (who was prime minister of Cape Colony as well as chairman of the BSA Company) by the end of 1894 when Rhodes and Jameson went to London. Loch saw it as his job to assert the supremacy of imperial interests over colonial interests in South Africa, and he also saw Khama—representing some kind of native factor in the interior—as an ally in this endeavor. Hence it was on Loch's insistence that Khama's levies had been recruited to beef up imperial forces in the Anglo-Ndebele War.

At the end of 1894, Khama was invited for urgent discussions by Loch. He left Palapye on Christmas Day and went south by wagon to Mafeking, the new railhead, from whence he took the train to Cape Town without breaking the journey at any station on the way. Entering a railway carriage for the first time in his life, he was amazed at the smoothness and speed with which it moved. Khama arrived at Cape Town station at 12:55 in the middle of the day on Wednesday, January 2, 1895, in the company of J. S. Moffat and two attendants—his trusted adviser Ratshosa, and interpreter Simeon Seisa. They were accommodated in the imperial government's cottage at Newlands, the fifth stop between Rondebosch and Claremont on the suburban railway to Muizenburg and Simonstown. It appears that Loch had another visitor, Baron Ferdinand de Rothschild, MP, staying at his official residence.

Loch talked with some urgency of the Chartered Company's need for a railway extension from Mafeking to Palapye (from thence to be extended to Bulawayo), and of the proximate need for the imposition of direct taxation (the so-called hut tax) by the imperial authorities on the "tribes" of the Bechuanaland Protectorate. Khama was averse to neither proposal but said that they should be a matter of conditions—principally involving the restriction of liquor imports.[2] After several interviews with Loch, according to a local newspaper:

> The Chief afterwards announced that he had received a telegram from Queen Victoria, assuring him . . . upon her support in his righteous efforts to keep the curse of the liquor traffic from entering his country.

The reasons for Khama's visit to Cape Town were not well publicized. Some Cape and Transvaal newspapers suggested it was to "to implore the High Commissioner to save him from absorption by Mr. Rhodes." This was dismissed as "pure invention" by Flora Shaw (later Lady Lugard), the authoritative colonial correspondent of the *Times* of London, who was in close contact with officials in the Colonial Office and with Rhodes. Fears were even expressed in London, by Rev. Wardlaw Thompson, the energetic foreign secretary of the LMS, that Khama had made a volte-face and allied with Rhodes at last.[3]

Khama was a British ally more trusted than his brother chiefs who had previously visited Cape Town, and he was amiably received by the high commissioner. There was no "show of royal honours" by the authorities of Cape Colony, but Khama was entertained, on the afternoon of his first day or the morning of his second, by a spectacular parade of imperial soldiers at Wynberg. They were bidding farewell to their commander in chief, General Sir William Cameron, who shook Khama's hand—a handshake between white and black that was now rare.

Khama also inspected the flagship of the local imperial fleet, HMS *St. George,* probably down the peninsula at Simonstown. He was shown over a Union liner in the Cape Town docks. He inspected stacks of coinage in the vaults of the Standard Bank headquarters. He toured the great new five-storied shopping emporia of Garlick's and of Messrs. Thorne, Stuttaford and Co., on the morning of Monday, January 7. He was so entranced by the elevator lifts at the latter shop that his party was three-quarters of an hour late for the mayor and town clerk and other dignitaries of the Waterworks Committee of the Town Council, who stood patiently waiting outside the fire brigade headquarters in Berg Street. (See the ballad in the appendix of this book.) After a demonstration of the fire engine's capacity to arrive quickly and extend its telescopic ladders, the royal party was taken off to lunch by the mayor.

Cape Town had undergone a great transformation over the previous decade or so, with a largely new city center, new docks and new factories, and new middle-class suburbs along a railway line to the south. The aim had been to transform the city from "dirty white half-bred orientalism" into a typical Victorian metropolis. But the city did not entirely lose its character. It had a stunning physical setting in the bowl of Table Mountain, with green suburbs strung out around the mountain's further edge. Most of its one hundred thousand inhabitants were people of color living on the eastern side of the city center, among whom the Muslim Malay population was considered the most distinctive. As the London journal *South Africa* remarked, when editorializing at length on Loch's retirement:

> they help to give a picturesque air to the streets, and impart an air of Orientalism to what otherwise would be a prosaic city. . . . Malay women, dressed in gorgeous colours, and with stiffly starched and distended dresses . . . the priests [*sic*] in their robes and turbans and the Malay boys with their baskets of fruit and vegetables . . . at night, as they go to ball or party, they make the streets resound with the music of instruments played with no small amount of skill. Like the Australians, they believe in having plenty of holidays, and nothing will induce them to work continuously all the days of the week.[4]

Khama's lack of an official welcome from Rhodes's Cape Colony government "was more than compensated for by the expressions of sympathy and welcome emanating from the temperance societies and religious bodies of South Africa"—the local representatives of "respectable" Victorian English society, and from individuals such as the Cape parliamentarian and Rhodes critic Henry Beard. On Sunday, January 6, Khama attended the Congregational church at Claremont and afterward visited the "magnificent" gardens of a Mr. Arderne. On the afternoon of Wednesday, January 9, Khama, Moffat, and the other two men were photographed at Mrs. Elizabeth Hepburn's home in Wynberg by Mr. Barnard, an Adderley Street photographer. That evening Khama delivered a "touching little speech" in "sonorous Sechuana" at a social gathering in the Congregational church in Caledon Square:

> When I came to the Cape, I did not know that I had any friends. I felt like a lost man. I never expected to find such friendship here. I am a black man, and I have no personal friends among the white people, and I am astonished at the way you have received me.
>
> I thank you because I believe you will help me to fight the enemy that is called liquor. You must pray to God that he will help me in this matter, that the liquor may be spilt into the sea, the liquor which is the enemy of the world. If you can help me it will be a matter of great rejoicing to me, and God will be with you. God does not like destruction.

The next day Khama was fêted in the morning at the YMCA (Young Men's Christian Association) by a combined meeting of four local temperance bodies, and a local moral-vigilance association called the Law and Order League. After a formal address of welcome, Khama and J. S. Moffat made speeches. The meeting concluded with singing "God Save the Queen" and three hearty cheers for Khama. Then Khama was interviewed on the stoep (veranda) of the Newlands Cottage by the *Cape Times*, which after mutual handshakings and good-mornings in English found him a surprisingly reticent interviewee in Setswana interpreted by Moffat. Khama declined to comment generally on what he had seen at Cape Town beyond, "It is all so wonderful. It is something not to be talked about." When asked whether he saw any lessons from Cape Town municipal government that he could apply at Palapye, he replied:

> All the conditions of life up there are so different that I do not see how I can apply any of the great advantages that I see down here. It is another sphere of existence.

He was much more prepared to talk about his country. When taxed about the hostile newspaper reports on his country by a Cape Afrikaner parliamentarian, a wine grower and brandy distiller, one of Rhodes's closest political allies, "a broad incredulous smile spread over his wrinkled features": "How can Mr. De Waal know? He came in the night, and went away in the night without stopping."[5]

Khama and his party left Cape Town that night, Thursday, January 10, on the fast mail-train for the north. Khama like Sebele and Bathoen before him had now breached the symbolic barrier of long-distance travel to "another sphere of existence" and was psychologically more ready to travel onward over the seas.

1895 was the centenary year of the foundation of the London Missionary Society. Celebrations in London were planned to take place in September. Khama himself had long wished to greet the directors of the LMS at headquarters, and to see the homeground of his missionaries, including the English countryside about whose greenery he had heard so much from gentlemen visitors. There were also political considerations.

In February 1895 Wardlaw Thompson in London wrote to David Mudie, the LMS agent at Cape Town, about how pleased they would be to entertain Khama in England if only he made up his mind. "I hope," added Thompson, "that the necessity for such a visit ['the design of the Chartered Company and other interested persons'] has really passed away." In March Willoughby wrote to Thompson from Palapye that Khama's visit was "postponed for the present; but he is more anxious to go to England than ever he has been before." No one should be surprised if Khama turned up at the society's autumn celebrations.[6]

✢ ✢ ✢

On February 21, 1895, Rhodes and Jameson arrived back in Cape Town from their negotiations with the British government. On February 22 Sir Henry Loch announced his intention of retiring from his appointments at the Cape. His replacement would be Sir Hercules Robinson, who had been Loch's predecessor as high commissioner until 1889 and then became chairman of the London board of Rhodes's De Beers Company, and was now being reappointed as Rhodes's personal nominee for the job.

On February 27 Loch telegraphed the colonial minister, Lord Ripon:

> Chief Khama has ever been a faithful friend and ally of Her Majesty's Government, and to hand over that Chief, his people and his territory, to be administered by a commercial company, dependent for their prosperity upon what they may get out of the country, would be a breach of faith such as I am sure the Government would not for a moment entertain.[7]

Officially Loch denied that he was resigning, but he left the country suddenly, packing up a household that had been well established for a long stay at the Cape with his wife and two daughters. The appointment of

Robinson, an Irish Tory, was followed by widespread objections in press and Parliament—not least by Rhodes's critic Joseph Chamberlain—that he was merely Rhodes's pawn. As for Loch, he was honored with a peerage and a seat on the Privy Council. Lord Loch of Drylaw remained an open admirer of Khama but felt constrained from too publicly espousing Khama's cause.[8]

One of the points raised by Loch with Khama in January was the question of Ngamiland, the northwestern part of the Bechuanaland Protectorate, where an important concession for prospecting and development had been obtained (by deceit) for the Chartered Company from the Tawana kingdom of *Kgosi* Sekgoma Letsholathebe in 1893. Loch wanted Khama's cooperation in bringing the fractious Sekgoma Letsholathebe to heel. The latter came to see Khama at Palapye in April. Khama was mightily offended at the disrespect shown him by this "nephew," grabbing the most prominent place at Sunday church service, but learned probably with great alarm from Sekgoma Letsholathebe about Rhodes's moves to turn Ngamiland into "another Mashonaland with the difference that this time the pioneers would be Boers." The Boer settlement being set up by the Chartered Company at Ghanzi was particularly alarming. Sekgoma Letsholathebe could not accept Rhodes's argument that it was a frontier buffer against German South West Africa (Namibia), as the BaTawana had no quarrel with the Germans.[9]

Reports began to leak out, through the *Pretoria News,* of major military preparations by the BSA Company. The company was said to be trying to recruit and equip between five hundred and twelve hundred mounted men. Two to four Maxim-Nordenfeldt (later Vickers) machine guns, artillery, numerous rifles, and new uniforms, saddles, and camping equipment were being ordered from Britain. *South Africa,* the London weekly journal, tried to find out more at the beginning of April but found the Chartered Company "had adopted the tactics of the ostrich" and was imparting "an impenetrable air of secrecy surrounding the whole matter." The story died and revived only temporarily in June, when Sir John Willoughby was named by rumor as leader of the expeditionary force. *South Africa* concluded there were covert preparations being made to invade Barotseland—the Lozi kingdom north of the Zambezi—but expressed doubts about whether such measures were really necessary against a peaceful ally.[10]

On May 2 the Cape Colony parliament or Assembly opened with a Speech from the Throne by Governor Sir Hercules Robinson. He announced that Rhodes's government would soon submit resolutions to the House for the annexation of British Bechuanaland to Cape Colony. *Kgosi* Montshiwa of the Rolong reacted within a couple of days of the Cape newspapers being received at Mafeking. On behalf of his people he protested in a petition to the British government dated May 7. On May 8 the white citizens of Vryburg, the capital of the colony, reacted with a counterpetition in favor of annexation. On May 14 *Kgosi* Mankoroane of the Tlhaping south of Vryburg sent off his petition against annexation to the imperial authorities.

The future of the Bechuanaland Protectorate remained a matter of rumor and speculation. The Cape press assumed that its transfer to the Chartered Company would follow once the annexation of British Bechuanaland by Cape Colony had been achieved. This assumption grew stronger as the British Bechuanaland bill made its way through the Cape parliament. But no firm decision or timetable was ever announced. There were only hints in the air. One was the acknowledgment in the British Parliament, in the first week of June, that the expensive and underemployed Bechuanaland Border Police were soon to be drastically reduced in numbers. Another hint was an article later that month in *South Africa* titled "The Future of Bechuanaland." The article laid out Rhodes's ideas of pushing "the Cape system" of rule by "white men" in a federal or unitary state as far as Lake Tanganyika, to replace the "ease, slumber and vicious habits" among blacks tolerated by "Imperial control" even in Sir Sidney Shippard's Bechuanaland Protectorate.[11]

As for British Bechuanaland, the "Exeter Hall" element of missionary and humanitarian interests in London was evidently suffering from compassion fatigue. Wardlaw Thompson wrote to John Mackenzie on June 8:

> I am perfectly sick of going to Governments about such matters, and I am disposed to be content to let things work out their own way. If the majority of the people of this country [i.e. Britain] desire a certain course, and the minority cannot persuade them to change, it is quite hopeless for outsiders to exert any real influence to check the course of events.

What changed matters was the surprise defeat of Rosebery's Liberal government on June 23, and Rosebery's replacement as prime minister by Lord Salisbury, who formed a caretaker Conservative and Unionist administration on June 25—confirmed in power by a general election on July 12. Joseph Chamberlain, the Unionist leader, took the post of colonial minister, with Salisbury's son-in-law the earl of Selborne as his assistant minister. They were appointed on Friday, June 28, and started work on the Monday.

"Pushful Joe"—now "Emperor Joe" as well—had already been partly squared by Rhodes a couple of months earlier over his objections to Robinson's appointment as high commissioner, when Rhodes sent along their mutual friend Edward Grey—now the fourth earl Grey—to hint at Robinson's essential role in secret plans against the Transvaal that must not be upset. But Chamberlain regarded Rhodes as too cocky by half about the imperial factor, and on assuming office rapped Rhodes over the knuckles to show who was ultimate boss. Chamberlain knew, as did his successors and predecessors, that the protection of "native rights" was one of the most useful imperial sticks for beating colonial politicians. He refused to allow British Bechuanaland annexation to proceed without guarantees over "native" land and liquor laws.

These (ultimately unenforceable) guarantees were incorporated into colonial legislation considered on July 31 by the Cape Assembly. Over protests from all sides at the imperial interference in colonial prerogatives, Rhodes laconically told the assembled parliamentarians: "They must recognise that the Secretary of State was obliged to consider the views of the section who held the erroneous idea that the natives were badly treated." [12]

❖ ❖ ❖

Through press and telegraph Khama and Willoughby, Khama's new missionary who was at this time acting also as Khama's principal political secretary, kept a close watch on political development at the Cape and in Britain.

Khama was further alarmed by a report in June from his son and heir, Sekgoma, who had been hunting giraffes north of the Nata River. (A French missionary traveling north met Sekgoma Khama coming south on the eastern side of the Makgadikgadi salt pans, with six wagons, on June 2.). Sekgoma told Khama that he had met Chartered Company men who challenged his right to hunt there. When he told them, "This land is my father's, and we have hunted here and still we hunt," they told him: "If you speak in that way we will seize all your lands and property." Sekgoma Khama asked "by what right or custom" could they do so. They replied: "By reason of that custom by which we have taken the Matabele, and now it is our land." When Sekgoma further protested, the whites broke off the conversation and left. This followed on other reports of Khama's Bangwato being beaten up by Rhodesian police in May.

On June 28, 1895, Khama together with seven principal relatives and 128 others signed names or made their mark against a "PETITION to the Right Honourable JOSEPH CHAMBERLAIN, Her Majesty's Secretary of State for the Colonies." Khama was insistent that much of this and other documents had been drafted into English by Simeon Seisa, his well-educated private secretary, a former police court interpreter from Lesotho. But a rough copy in his personal papers shows that the petition had been redrafted by Willoughby. It began,

The petition of the undersigned Chief and Headmen of the Bamangwato tribe, resident at Palapye, in the British Protectorate, humbly showeth:—
That your petitioners have heard with alarm that their country is to be to placed under the Government of the Chartered Company, or under that of the Cape Colony. Your petitioners placed themselves under the British Government some years ago, believing that it was a wise and righteous government, which would not oppress them simply because their skins are black; and they still wish to remain under the Government of the Great Queen.

The petition was a well worked out mixture of what Khama felt and what Willoughby thought would appeal to the imperial government. It went on to dismiss the idea that the protectorate was too costly. Costs could be reduced by getting rid of the border police—"soldiers who have done harm and not good"—and by collecting the hut tax that had been only talked about so far. Then, with a Setswana idiom of being devoured that cannot be taken literally, the petition concluded with a rather pathetic passage that was subsequently to be much quoted:

your petitioners have heard much of the injustice and oppression which the Chartered Company inflict upon the tribes who live in the north; and your petitioners fear very much lest they should be killed and eaten by the Company. For the petitioners see that the Company does not love black people; it loves only to take the country of the black people and sell it to others that it may see gain.

Your petitioners have already given the Company the right to dig for minerals in their country, and they say: "Let the Company be satisfied with the minerals, and, as for us, let us continue to be the children of the Great Queen." [13]

Why did Khama and his people act just then? For a start—and this is an indication of how well-informed Palapye was about events in the outside world—the petition was addressed to Chamberlain by name, on his very first day in office. Khama was obviously trying to take advantage of Chamberlain's dozen years of association with John Mackenzie and Bechuanaland affairs, and his espousal of the imperial rather than colonial connection. Khama had also probably just received an anonymous circular, probably from the pro-imperial editor of the *Bechuanaland News* at Vryburg, begging the Bechuanaland Protectorate chiefs to speak up against "going under the Company." It is also possible that Willoughby got wind of the attempt on June 27, gagged by Rhodes as being *ultra vires*, by Beard and other opposition politicians in the Cape Assembly to protest at Chartered Company plans to take over the Bechuanaland Protectorate.[14] But the main incentive for Khama was undoubtedly the Shippard Award of the day before, June 27, which gave the Motloutse-Shashe "disputed territory" as an independent reserve to Khama's dissident brothers Raditladi and Mphoeng. As if he needed more proof, this showed that Shippard and other local imperial officials were blatant partisans of the Chartered Company, almost certainly under its pay and patronage.

Khama had been in dispute since 1892 with Raditladi, the half brother who had led the Ngwato scouts accompanying the "Rhodesian" Pioneer Column of 1890. Raditladi had taken issue with Khama over the enforced retirement by the Ngwato church of the aging Rev. James Hepburn, the missionary who was replaced by W. C. Willoughby. Together with Mphoeng, another half brother of Khama, Raditladi came to lead an opposition party of deacons within the church, who defied Khama's authority by conducting their own evangelism among low-status people in the Tswapong hills near Palapye. They also opposed Khama's liquor laws, particularly the prohibition of sorghum corn beer. Not unnaturally Khama emphasized that they were, in the later words of the *Cape Times*, "preaching beer"—rather than admitting that they were "preaching the Bible" and were thereby "making Khama's slaves 'cheeky.'"

The London Missionary Society took Khama's part. Wardlaw Thompson wrote to the Raditladi camp: "these days there is no more certain way of destroying your country and giving power to strangers than by becoming divided amongst yourselves." But the Chartered Company and local imperial officials took Raditladi's part. The company saw their friend Raditladi as the means for dividing and ruling Khama's country. As a party of dissident members within the body of the Ngwato church, Raditladi's followers also appealed to J. S. Moffat's latent evangelical spirit—their meetings on political strategy doubled as prayer meetings.[15]

At a time of increased tension over border incidents, the Chartered Company took advantage of the interregnum between the departure of Loch and the arrival of Robinson to begin demarcating its "customs line" border, which incorporated the Nata and Motloutse-Shashe areas into Rhodesia. The company admitted the line was for administrative purposes, and Khama reacted furiously: "as for administration was that not the same as *government?*" The Colonial Office told the company to hold off till Robinson could deal with the matter.

Khama's telegraphic greeting to Robinson, on the latter's arrival at the Cape, on June 7, complained of the company's "occupying my country without my permission" and added indignantly:

> I asked the Government of the Queen to enter into my country; I offered [in the "magnificent offer" of 1885], on behalf of my people, to give them a portion of my land, but they refused it. I also offered long ago to pay tax, but this also was refused.

. . . You mention Mr. Rhodes in your telegram. Is he not the man who insulted me in my own town after I had done all I could to help the Government in the Matabele War?

The final insult, and proof of complicity with Rhodes from the high commissioner himself downward, was the judicial commission under Resident Commissioner Shippard, to look into Raditladi's dispute with Khama. As an official in the Colonial Office later minuted, "Mr Moffat behaved as a violent partisan of Raditladi and practically dictated the award"— implying that Shippard had been almost as bad, and adding, "Thank goodness we are getting rid of him!"

Shippard's award of June 27 granted the whole Motloutse-Shashe area to Raditladi as a chief independent of Khama—sonorously concluding, "This is the Queen's decision and he who transgresses it will bring punishment upon himself."

Khama's response was twofold and immediate. First, he attempted and succeeded in undermining Raditladi by announcing that the brewing of corn beer would now be permitted—an act that drastically reduced the number of people prepared to follow Raditladi into independence. Second, he directed his people's petition toward Joseph Chamberlain the next day.[16]

✣ ✣ ✣

Khama's petition of June 28, 1895, was dispatched through the regular official channels—through Assistant Commissioner Moffat at Palapye to Resident Commissioner Shippard at Vryburg and then on to High Commissioner Robinson at Cape Town, before it could be enclosed in the official mail to London. Its contents do not appear to have been cabled, and Khama was too properly diplomatic to reveal it to the world until Chamberlain responded. Moffat forwarded it on July 2; Shippard waited until July 25; and Robinson passed it on on July 30. It is difficult to conclude otherwise than that it had been deliberately "sat upon" until Rhodes had had a chance to get the British Bechuanaland annexation bill through the Cape parliament.[17] Hence as late as July 20 the likeliest man in London outside the Colonial Office to know about Khama's petition, Wardlaw Thompson of the LMS, was writing to John Mackenzie in South Africa:

> You refer to Khama's country and the action of friends at home [i.e. in Britain]. We are powerless in these matters, and at the present time any attempt to get up feeling about Khama would be like flogging a dead horse. . . .
> If Khama and the Chiefs were to protest . . . we should at least have a text to appeal upon, but not a whisper has reached this country that I know

of, in the way of remonstrance against the proposed arrangements from the parties most interested in it.[18]

Meanwhile, the Chartered Company moved to head off any threat to its carefully laid scenario for the invasion of the Transvaal—the so-called Jameson Plan. Rhodes hurriedly shipped off his personal envoy, Dr. Rutherfoord Harris, another "slick doctor," from Cape Town on July 11—the day before the British general election. He arrived in England on July 27, to cultivate the press and government to Rhodes's orders, overtly to make arrangements for the immediate extension of the railway from Mafeking to Bulawayo. "Railway works" were to be the "cover" for the Jameson Plan. An extraordinary annual general meeting of the BSA Company was held in London on election day to raise £2,500,000 from the shareholders. A letter from Rhodes was read out saying that he would rather like another half a million in reserve. The railway was talked of as proceeding in stages—from Mafeking to the police camp at Gaborone, from Gaborone to Khama's capital at Palapye, and from thence to Bulawayo.[19]

With Chamberlain now become caesar in London, Khama determined to go there on appeal, in concert with fellow paramount chiefs of the Bechuanaland Protectorate. After his "killed and eaten" petition, Khama contacted Chiefs Sebele of the BaKwena and Bathoen of the BaNgwaketse, using Willoughby and the horse and the telegraph and the LMS missionary at Molepolole, Howard Williams, as channels of communication. (The LMS missionary at Kanye, Edwin Lloyd, had gone on furlough to Britain.) It is not clear if Khama contacted chiefs attached to other mission societies at this stage—Linchwe of the BaKgatla with a Dutch Reformed mission, Ikaneng of the BaLete with a Lutheran mission, and Montshiwa of the BaRolong with a Wesleyan Methodist mission. (LMS-connected Sekgoma Letsholathebe of the BaTawana had no telegraph and was a few weeks away in travel.)

Each chief was to pay for himself and a personal clerk-interpreter. Khama was to pay for Willoughby's travel and expenses. On July 29 Howard Williams telegrammed to Willoughby that Sebele and Bathoen were ready to go to England with Khama, and that the imperial authorities in Cape Town had been wired to this effect. The BSA Company was alerted: it owned the telegraph line and had access to any information transmitted. Rhodes alerted Jameson at Bulawayo, who arrived in haste at Palapye within the week, to conciliate Khama.

Bathoen's and Sebele's petitions were drawn up at about this time: they were transmitted to London by Robinson in August. The petition of Linchwe and the Raad (Dutch for parliament or *kgotla*) of the BaKgatla was signed on July 27. It protested against annexation by the Chartered

Company, who would enslave them, like the Boers had done to the
BaKgatla in the Transvaal.[20]

✢ ✢ ✢

Robinson ordered Khama to await Dr. Jameson's arrival at Palapye. His
wagons, with Willoughby, and Willoughby's small son who was also going
to England, left for the south on July 31. They expected to reach the railhead at Mafeking by August 15. Willoughby proceeded slowly, as the
oxen were weak. Khama would catch them up on horseback. Meanwhile,
Khama received a memorandum of sympathy and support from the white
residents of Palapye, praising him for the honesty, sobriety, and lack of
cattle rustling among his people.[21]

On Saturday, August 3, according to J. B. Shaw, a Palapye white trader
who sent this account on to Willoughby,

> [Jameson] arrived very early in the morning and repaired to the B.S.A.
> mess house. About ten Sekgomi [Sekgoma, Khama's eldest son] came in
> and asks Mr Walter and Self to go down with the Chief, also told us that
> Charles Ceask and Steve Hoare were going—went down to mess hut and
> saw Sadler; who said Humph! seems to be a public meeting!—the Dr. only
> wants to speak to Khama.
>
> However K. went in with Charles Ceask to greet J., and upon getting
> the greeting over sent out for Walter Hoare and Self, Walker went past
> Sadler and into the room but Sadler stopped me saying "No! I shall not
> alow [sic] any more to go in." I said to him Thank you? Well, Khama asked
> me here and he has called me here and now and I guess I am going!

As Khama did not trust the company, he insisted on other white witnesses
being present in his dealings with it.

Jameson made a point of relaying Rhodes's apology for his "unkindly"
words of 1893 over the retreat from the Matabele War. Jameson blamed
it all on young Howard Moffat at Bulawayo, who had misinformed Jameson, who had then misinformed Rhodes. Jameson added that "Mr Rhodes
often lost his temper, so would K. try to put it all out of his mind, and
think no more of it."

Next Jameson explained that the Chartered Company had been promised "this country" by Lord Ripon, in writing, to relieve the imperial government of a hundred thousand pounds a year in administrative costs.
The company must now take it over before it laid out a million-pound
railway through it. Jameson himself would be the protectorate's new administrator. So if Khama had any complaints, he should raise them now
with him. Jameson then unwisely went on to imply that Khama's griev-

ances were cooked up by Willoughby, the white man who had run away to avoid meeting the new administrator.

Khama had so far listened in silence. However,

> This put K.'s back up and he said if you wanted Mr W. why did you not wire or write him—Mr W. went away at my request.
>
> Asked by J. if he had anything to complain of or any messages to send to the High Commissioner—K. said No! I have heard all your words and they are *big!* ones, but I will say nothing, at any rate until after I return from England.[22]

Khama was more forthcoming to Jameson in a second interview, that afternoon. He opened up bitterly on J. S. Moffat's role in the Raditladi settlement. Jameson was equally rude about Moffat. He then offered to give Raditladi land in Rhodesia instead of the Motloutse-Shashe area designated by Shippard. This pleased Khama but did not stop his resolution to journey southward. He would still go to Cape Town to meet the new high commissioner, Robinson. And though political questions might possibly be settled there, he still wished to go on to England to see the English people.

Jameson then cabled Rhodes that a visit to England might even be a good idea in reconciling Khama to the company's rule.

Khama wanted to leave that evening on his horse, to meet up with Willoughby and his wagons at Palla camp on the Limpopo. But he agreed to await further negotiations with Jameson. Robinson telegrammed Khama on the Sunday not to leave till the Raditladi question had been settled finally with Jameson. As far as Robinson and Jameson knew, this was the only political issue that was driving Khama toward England.

Rhodes and Jameson conversed for an hour, speaking through telegraphists who tapped out their words, on Sunday morning. The stratagem they devised was to get Khama to retract all objections to company administration, and get him to commit himself to that end in a telegram to the high commissioner. Jameson said he no longer found Khama an "oyster" in negotiations, and he could see clearly Khama's point about Moffat's bias.

Rhodes and Khama conversed telegraphically that Sunday afternoon. Khama insisted that the Raditladi question should be settled once and for all now. Rhodes tried all he could to get Khama to send a recanting telegram to Robinson, so that Robinson could cable it to the Colonial Office to overtake the June 28 ("killed and eaten") petition, from Khama to Chamberlain, now dispatched on the high seas. Much to Rhodes's frustration, Khama sent a telegram to Robinson about Raditladi that afternoon but studiously made no comment on the Chartered Company. But Jameson reassured Rhodes:

> I see Khama has not mentioned the Protectorate question but Tom Fry
> my interpreter tells me that in walking up with Khama just now the latter
> stated that his only grievance was the veldt question [i.e. the land awarded
> to Raditladi] & he had no objection to the Chartered Coy. taking over
> Gov't.

Jameson was sure that he had converted Khama to the virtues of Chartered rule. Later he was to claim he had been cruelly deluded, and put the blame on Tom Fry's bluster and imperfect knowledge of Setswana. It was probably Tom Fry whom Khama later recalled, during a speech in Birmingham, as having told him before he left that he would meet only missionaries in England, and missionaries were "nobody."

The next day, Monday, Khama was "itching to be off," saying that he preferred to speak to Robinson in person rather than write to him on the question of company rule. Khama finally left on horseback on the morning of Tuesday, August 6.[23]

The Jameson Plan was reaching a critical phase. At about this time Rhodes wrote to his colleague Alfred Beit that "we must have the right of administration [over Bechuanaland Protectorate], to collect our forces at Gaberoones [*sic*]," as soon as possible, because "Johannesburg is ready"— for its *uitlander* revolution against Boer rule. What stood in the way was Chamberlain, and Khama:

> I may tell you that Khama is all right . . . but he is coming down with the
> missionary Rev. Willoughby, and the rascal, who detests me, may change
> Khama again on the road. Is it not awful to think that the whole future of
> the British Empire out here may turn on a wretched Kaffer [*sic*] and a
> Secretary of State who listens to some fanatic in the House of Commons?[24]

Major Frank Johnson, the originator of the first Jameson Raid from a "jumping-off ground" in Mashonaland to grab Matabeleland, was addressing electoral meetings in Mafeking for the new Bechuanaland division of Cape Colony. Cryptically he referred to "the Charter [of the BSA Company] as laying the foundation for the unification of South Africa."

An obviously Chartered-inspired report from Cape Town, the first indication of any dissent in the Bechuanaland Protectorate to reach the British public, appeared in the London *Times* on August 13. Khama, it reported, was grateful and well disposed toward the company and would visit the high commissioner in Cape Town—but it was now doubtful whether he would visit England since the Raditladi dispute has been settled by the good offices of Dr. Jameson.[25]

Beneath this clipping from the *Times*, a Colonial Office official scribbled a rough draft of the sovereign's consent to the Chartered Company taking over the administration of the Bechuanaland Protectorate. Such was the effectiveness of the Rhodesian propaganda machine that controlled the press cables from South Africa. Cecil Rhodes also wrote to Lord Rosebery, the former prime minister, at this time, to use his personal influence with Joseph Chamberlain to get a prompt and speedy transfer of the protectorate to the company.[26]

Khama eventually caught up with his wagons at Mochudi, capital of Linchwe's BaKgatla people. From Mochudi the party traveled southward past Gaborone through Ramotswa, the town of Ikaneng's BaLete people, and on toward Mafeking. Kgatla and Lete traditions record that they gave Khama their moral support, and Khama urged their chiefs to accompany him to England—but the chiefs declined. Why? Possibly because of lack of ready finance, possibly because of old tensions between Linchwe and Sebele, Ikaneng and Bathoen. Their refusal to go was to be greatly to their detriment. Both chiefs were on the intended line of rail and—while Khama, Sebele, and Bathoen were away—lost their lands to the Chartered Company. They also gave the company the excuse to assemble troops for supposedly punitive purposes and railway works protection at Gaborone and Pitsane, as part of the "cover" for the Jameson Plan.[27]

Meanwhile Sebele had left Molepolole on Tuesday, August 6, after a great farewell *kgotla* meeting the previous Thursday. Rev. Howard Williams declined to go to England with Sebele, whom he disliked. His wife had also just given birth to a baby. Accompanied by a young and somewhat gauche clerk-interpreter called Kehutile Gohiwamang, Sebele trekked south through Kanye, where he was to join up with Bathoen and proceed direct to Mafeking.[28]

Bathoen joined Sebele with two attendants. One was a middle-aged churchman, David Sebonego, who acted as clerk-interpreter. The other was a headman called Kwenaetsile (*Kwena-e-tsile:* "the crocodile has come"), variously described as Bathoen's half brother or as the husband of Bathoen's daughter, a self-important character who was imposed on Bathoen by a *kgotla* meeting that did not trust him to negotiate on his own. Sebele and Bathoen were also joined by Rev. James Good, Lloyd's father-in-law, who wanted to go as far as Cape Town to collect Miss Partridge, a new schoolmistress from England, to take her back to Molepolole.[29]

Khama, Sebele, and Bathoen met at Mafeking. Here they greeted and consulted with ancient *Kgosi* Montshiwa, a shrewd old "pagan" statesman with a great reputation as a rainmaker. Most of his land was in the Crown Colony, but a little was in the protectorate. Khama and the others suggested that Montshiwa send a delegate with them, but the Rolong *kgotla* had not decided by the time the three chiefs left. Khama, Sebele, and

Bathoen left Mafeking by train for the south probably on the morning of August 15.[30]

The Rolong decided to send delegates with the three chiefs on Thursday, August 15, just after the chiefs had left. Wesleyan missionary Appelbe and local white trader Gerrans proposed sending Stephen Lefenya, an effective evangelist and English teacher, to arouse the Christian conscience of Britain. Montshiwa insisted that his son and heir, Besele (or "Wessels") go too and gave Wessels and Lefenya one hundred pounds each for the journey.

On that same day a telegram from Cape Town printed in the London *Times* announced to the world that Chiefs Montshiwa and Mankoroane of British Bechuanaland had withdrawn their objections to Cape Colony rule. Rhodes and Robinson, who had no doubt instigated the news agency report, were therefore most disconcerted to hear about Besele coming south. A new Rolong petition to the queen against both colony and company was presented to the Mafeking magistrate on Friday, August 16.[31]

✤ ✤ ✤

The first leg of the chiefs' train journey was from Mafeking to Vryburg. They spent the first night in the Central Hotel at Vryburg as official guests of Resident Commissioner Shippard: their expenses record ten shillings in hotel tips, plus cabs and station cloakroom tickets. Shippard and his wife entertained them and gave them letters of introduction to friends in England, and they were photographed sitting with him on the wooden balcony of his residency. Reverend Good, who was accompanying the chiefs, seems to have been a good friend of the Shippards: he had attended the wedding of Shippard's daughter to Captain Gosling at Vryburg a month before.

They then resumed their journey southward on the Friday morning train. The small wood-burning locomotive of the Bechuanaland Railway stopped periodically at stations to load fuel and water. They stopped for meals at station hotels. Lunch (£1 3s. 6d. for the whole party) on August 16 was at Warrenton, on the Vaal north of Kimberley. From Kimberley, which they left on the evening of the sixteenth, the chiefs and their party were provided with their own saloon all the way to Cape Town. It is not known if meals were taken at station hotels or in a dining car attached to the train. The price of the last evening's dinner (£1 9s. 6d.), after previous cheaper meals, suggests that it might have been taken at the high-price Matjiesfontein station hotel.[32]

The train arrived in Cape Town before breakfast on the eighteenth. It seems that some or all of the party went to stay at Wynberg with the

Hepburns. They now learned that Besele and Lefenya were following them and would arrive the next day. Confused messages flew between Cape Town, Vryburg, and Mafeking, as to whether Besele should be allowed to proceed to England, or whether indeed he and Lefenya were really coming at all. Just in case, Willoughby booked two extra passages on the *Tantallon Castle*, which was due to sail on the afternoon of Wednesday, August 21.[33]

On the twentieth, High Commissioner Sir Hercules Robinson made a last-ditch attempt to persuade Khama, Sebele, and Bathoen to turn back. Robinson demanded to be told their exact purpose in going to England, so that he could telegraph the Colonial Office. He warned them that all matters of politics had to be dealt with first by him in Cape Town. The chiefs declined to answer Robinson directly. Khama said he would not speak until he was face-to-face with Mr. Chamberlain. If Chamberlain was going abroad on vacation, as he was now told, then he would wait in England until Chamberlain returned in November. It was a private visit and the chiefs were paying all their expenses: there was no question of waiting to be invited on a paid official visit.

On the morning of August 21, the chiefs traveled by train to Rondebosch, where they saw Cecil Rhodes on his grand Cape Town estate, Groote Schuur. The meeting had been arranged by David Mudie, businessman and Cape Town treasurer for the LMS (Mudie was an admirer of Rhodes, with whom he had had dealings on August 15, when Rhodes handed over checks for £847 and £500 for the LMS in a matter unrelated to the chiefs). The interview between the chiefs and Rhodes was interpreted by "young Hepburn," with Reverends Good and Willoughby assisting.

Rhodes, who was recovering from a heavy bout of influenza, addressed Khama plainly and directly. He made him three promises that he would keep when the protectorate became his. First, he did not want Khama's land. Second, he would respect his prohibition on liquor—as Rhodes had said on another occasion, he believed in no liquor and no vote for the natives. Third, the chiefs would retain their judicial powers in cases not involving white men.

Rhodes then claimed that the queen had already given the protectorate to him, and only the timing of the transfer was not yet fixed. There was thus no point in the chiefs going to England on a political mission. He finished by reminding Khama of his triple promise and added that "those who knew him, knew that he did not break his word." Khama and the other two were unresponsive, determined to take the ship the next day and holding their counsel.[34]

After seeing High Commissioner Robinson once more, Khama was interviewed by Mr. Cowen of the *Cape Times*, using Seisa as interpreter. Cowen claimed their conversation ran like this:

"Have you met Mr. Rhodes since you came down this time?"
At this question the old chief straightened himself, his face assumed a new expression, his eyes brightened, his intelligence seemed alight. . . . he replied:
"Yes. . . . And he told me a thing with respect to my country. He said the Colonial Secretary (Mr. Chamberlain) had informed him that later on the Protectorate over it would be passed over to the Chartered Company."
"He told you that all was decided?"
"Yes, all decided."
"Not immediately?"
"No; but later on. When, he did not state."

Cowen was astounded to hear this, an obvious "scoop," and sought confirmation with Seisa as interpreter and then turned back to Khama:

"Mr. Rhodes told you that?"
"Yes."
"And what did he say?"
"Nothing."
"Did you mention to the High Commissioner what Mr. Rhodes had said?"
"Yes."
"And what did His Excellency say to it?"
"He said nothing; not a word."
"Are you quite sure he made no remark?"
"Yes. He said nothing."

The interview was "spiked" by the editor of the *Cape Times* and was not published until September 21, when it was picked up by the *African Critic* in London.[35]

The journey of the three chiefs had been fully budgeted up to a return in early November, when it was reckoned that the weather would turn too cold in England—and full accounts of the expenses of the three chiefs and their attendants were kept by Willoughby until their return to each of the home towns. Khama's account begins with a "wire" sent from Palla (3s. 3d.) and food bought at Mochudi and Gaborone. The cost in one-way fares to Cape Town for himself, Willoughby, and Seisa was £28 11s. The chiefs' joint account began with four shillings expenditure at Vryburg station cloakroom.

Sebele and Bathoen paid for their own return ship passages. Like Khama they traveled first class, at £73 14s. each—Willoughby's fare was discounted at £66 6s. 6d., as Khama's partner and possibly together with his son (for whom he paid) in the same cabin. The four attendants traveled second class at £47 5s.

Willoughby arrived in Cape Town with the further sum of £560 collected from the three chiefs—of which £160 belonged to Sebele. Of this amount £110 was left behind in Mudie's safekeeping, to be used on their return to Cape Town. The remainder was transmitted to a London bank account by Mudie on their behalf.

On the afternoon of Wednesday, August 21, the delegation spent three shillings on cabs to the docks and boarded the liner *Tantallon Castle* in Cape Town's new Victoria basin docks. (Vessels that had recently been in port included the U.S. warship *Gaul*.) Khama drafted a last-minute telegram to his people and his son, Sekgoma Khama, who was acting as his regent at Palapye:

> Bo-Raditladi must leave at once. See that our people make no trouble. Take those who claim cattle and their witnesses to Lieutenant Williams who will decide. Sail today Tantallon Castle. Letter follows. *Dumela dumedisa Bamangwato*. Give Mission [for] trek oxen eight pounds ten.[36]

✤ ✤ ✤

Henry Beard, Cape opposition politician and LMS supporter, was less than optimistic about Khama's chances in a letter to Wardlaw Thompson. If Khama returned from London empty-handed, then Rhodes would have no compunction in welching on his promises to Khama. Beard feared that control of the newspapers by great monied combinations, or more Armenian atrocities, would drown out Khama's voice in England.

Mudie, on the other hand, wrote to Thompson warning him, "Our friend Mr. Willoughby has strong feelings. . . . I therefore trust that if public meetings are held you will be able to keep him moderate." In this he concurred with the opinion of Fairfield in the Colonial Office, who, on similar cursory inspection, also saw Willoughby as the demon of the plot—the "*enragé* missionary." Another Colonial Office minute-writer, on August 20, welcomed the chiefs' visit as a chance to clear the air and counteract Willoughby's poisoning of Khama's mind against Rhodes.

News of the chiefs' journey reached the British press in the dispatch of a "well-informed" correspondent from Cape Town, published in the *Times* on August 21. It reported that Khama was leaving for England, to acquaint himself with the country, its people, and its queen, and to hear the views of the Colonial Office on the future of his country. The correspondent added: "It is understood that for the present he wishes to remain directly under the Queen," but negotiations in England might change his mind. The *Times* commented that "time and his own words will show us" what is on Khama's mind, and "so shrewd a man will carry back with him a better account of England *and its power* [emphasis added] than he could gather from a whole library of books." [37]

Meanwhile, as the chiefs sailed to England, there were straws that pointed to a change in the winds of Rhodes's fortune. The Cape press made great play of a lecture, "The Political Situation," published by the semi-radical writer Olive Schreiner and her politician husband Cronwright, attacking Rhodes's obsession with northward expansion of the Cape Colony as a drain on its resources, and adding that Boer rule was preferable to Cape rule for the whole of South Africa. Schreiner had been a great admirer of Rhodes as a seemingly boundless visionary—indeed she had thought herself in love with him. But her moment of disillusion had come at Matjiesfontein station in the Little Karoo, northeast of Cape Town, in November 1890, when Rhodes had tried to rope Cronwright into a corrupt land deal. On August 13, 1895, she wrote to a friend:

> I sometimes think Rhodes is coming near the end of his course. . . . We would have loved him so, honoured him, followed him!—but he has chosen . . . narrow self-interest. . . . He is to me an almighty has-been. [38]

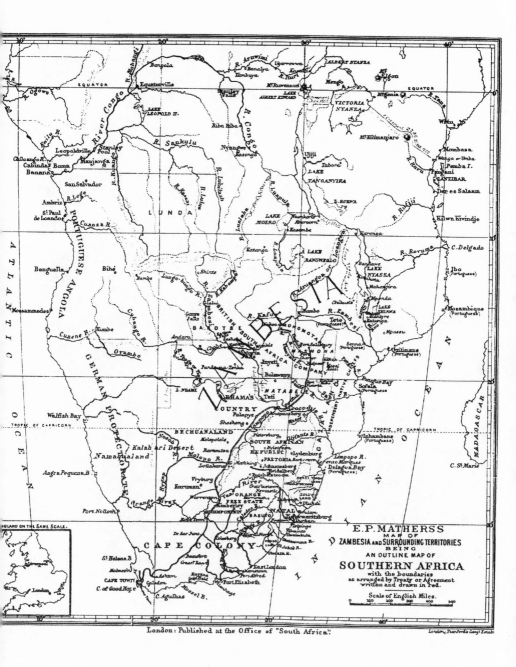

Map 1. Southern Africa in the 1890s. Most of the borders were still
fantasies only to be found on European maps of Africa. "Zambesia" began to
be called "Rhodesia" from 1895. (Reprinted from E. P. Mathers,
Zambesia, or England's El Dorado in Africa, fold-out map at end.)

THE TRAM OF A CENTURY HENCE.

Figure 2. 1894 Vision of a Century Hence: aerial tramway running along
the sides of department stores in Oxford Street, London. Note the rain and smog.
(Reprinted from *Review of Reviews* 9 [1894]: 399.)

Figure 3. The "New Woman" (1): Woman as Athlete. Advertisements
for rubbing embrocation showing middle- or upper-class women in activities as
diverse as bicycling, cricket, and tennis. (Reprinted from
Illustrated London News 106 [1895]: 785.)

THE NEW WOMAN AT THE SEASIDE.

BATHING WOMAN TO NEW DITTO: "You can't come 'ere, Sir. The gen'lemen bathes t'other side of the Pier."

Figure 4. The "New Woman" (2): Woman as Aesthete. "Blue-stocking" intellectual mistaken for a man by woman bathing attendant. (Reprinted from *Home Budget of the Cape Times Weekly Edition*, 14 Sept. 1895.)

From the *Westminster Budget.*]   [November 17, 1893.

MR. RHODES: THE NAPOLEON OF SOUTH AFRICA.

Figure 5. Expanding Empires (1): Anti-Rhodes. Rhodes as the Napoleon
of South Africa, against a background of slaughter after the conquest of
Matabeleland, 1893. Cartoon from the *Westminster Budget* newspaper.
(Reprinted from *Review of Reviews* 8 [1893]: 595.)

m *Moonshine*.] [November 25, 1893.

IN MATABELELAND.—THE MAN IN POSSESSION.

GLADSTONE (to Rhodes): "You've done the fighting, but—if you have no objection—the plunder belongs to us."

Figure 6. Expanding Empires (2): Pro-Rhodes. Rhodes as "the man in possession" of Matabeleland, faces penny-pinching "Little Englanders" Gladstone and Labouchere. Cartoon from humorous magazine *Moonshine*. (Reprinted from *Review of Reviews* 9 [1894]: 17.)

Gloire

From *Kladderadatsch*.]   [Sept. 29th, 1895.

GLORY IN MADAGASCAR.
A German View.

Figure 7. Expanding Empires (2): French colonialism, 1895. Cartoon
from German satirical magazine *Kladderadatsch* commenting on the French
invasion of Madagascar. Death in a French helmet weighs a pile of dead
Malagasy against a few French casualties. (Reprinted from
Review of Reviews 12 [1895]: 292.)

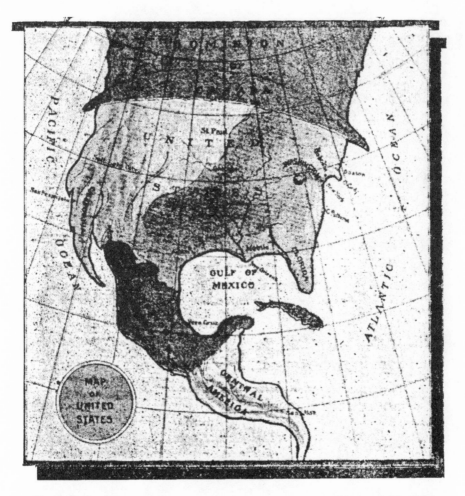

From *Judge*.]   [August 10, 1895.

THE TROUBLE IN CUBA.

UNCLE SAM : "I've had my eye on that morsel for a long time ; guess I'll have to take it in ! "

Figure 8. Expanding Empires (3): Jingoism in America, 1895. Cartoon from the American journal *Judge*, 10 August 1895, commenting on Uncle Sam's attitude to Cuba. (Reprinted from *Review of Reviews* 12 [1895]: 195.)

Figure 9. Khama at Cape Town, January 9, 1895. From left: Khama's Setswana secretary Ratshosa *(standing)*, John Smith Moffat and Khama *(seated)*, Khama's English secretary Simeon Seisa *(standing)*. A contrast in headgear, photographed by Barnard (of Adderley Street) in the garden of Mrs Elizabeth Hepburn's house at Wynberg. (Reprinted from G. W. H. Knight-Bruce, *Memories of Mashonaland*, frontispiece.)

Figure 10. The British General Election, July 1895: election night in Fleet
Street. Results being posted outside a newspaper office. Such displays of public
fervour were later called "mafficking." Enthusiasm for the new Conservative and
Unionist government was fed by the coming to power of its star politician
Joseph Chamberlain, who chose to become Colonial Minister.
(Reprinted from *Illustrated London News* 107 [1895]: cover.)

MR. CHAMBERLAIN'S CHAMBER OF HORRORS.

Figure 11. "Mr Chamberlain's Chamber of Horrors." Haunted by his previous political incarnations as Irish home ruler, Church disestablishmentarian, anti-Lords democrat, fashionable republican, Jacobin revolutionary, and rural populist. Cartoon from *Westminster Budget*. (Reprinted from *Review of Reviews* 12 [1895]: 114–34.)

THE CHAMBERLAIN HEN AND THE BECHUANA DUCKLING.

The Hen (on dry land, with fussy solicitude, to the Cape duck): Now
take care of the new duckling, and mind *you don't go too far!*
The Cape Duck (striking out): Oh yes—of course, of course—anything
you like—ta-ta!
The Hen (with a louder cluck): And mind *you "mention in debate that you
have given me this assurance"!*

Figure 12. "The Chamberlain Hen and the Bechuana Duckling."
Cartoon from the Cape press on Chamberlain's vain attempt to put some
checks on "native policy" when Cape Colony annexed British Bechuanaland
in 1895. (Reprinted from *Cape Times Weekly Edition*, 7 August 1895, 35.)

THE RULERS OF BECHUANALAND.

Figure 13. En route to Cape Town, Friday, August 16, 1895: the Chiefs
with Sir Sidney and Lady Shippard at Vryburg. Seated in front *(from left):* Bathoen,
Khama, Sebele, with Kwenaetsile standing. Shippard (with mutton-chop
whiskers) seated behind them on the *stoep* (verandah). (Reprinted
from *Review of Reviews* 12 [1895]: 311.)

THE C.R.M.S. "TANTALLON CASTLE," 5700 TONS REGISTER.

Figure 14. The *Tantallon Castle* and Capt. Robinson. It was the Castle
Line's fastest and most comfortable ship. (A few years later the ship was wrecked
on Robben Island near Cape Town.) (Reprinted from *South Africa* 26
[15 June 1895]: 549 and 551.)

Figure 15. Passengers on board the *Tantallon Castle*. (Reprinted from *South Africa* 26 [15 June 1895]: 553.)

SEBELE, CHIEF OF THE BAKWENA.

BATHOEN, CHIEF OF THE BANGWAKETSE.

KHAMA.

REV. W. C. WILLOUGHBY.

THE BECHUANA CHIEFS.

(From a photograph taken by Russell and Sons, for the " Illustrated London News.")

Figure 16. "The Three Kings of Africa": Sebele, Bathoen, Khama, and Willoughby as they appeared in the *Illustrated London News* on September 21: a studio portrait. (Reprinted from *Review of Reviews* 12 [1895]: 302–17.)

BUNG IN AFRICA.

Right Hon. J. Ch-mb-rl-n (*to* King Khama). "'*Local Veto*' for Bechuanaland?
H'm!—A rather ticklish business! Upset a government *here* the other day!"

Figure 17. "'Bung' in Africa": Khama and Chamberlain as they appeared
in *Punch*, on September 21, 1895. The word "Bung" (derived from a retort from Doll
Tearsheet to Pistol in Shakespeare's *Henry IV, Part II*, act ii, 4) was applied to brewers
and the anti-Temperance liquor interest in British politics, who had supported the
Conservatives and helped turn out the Liberals in June of the same year.

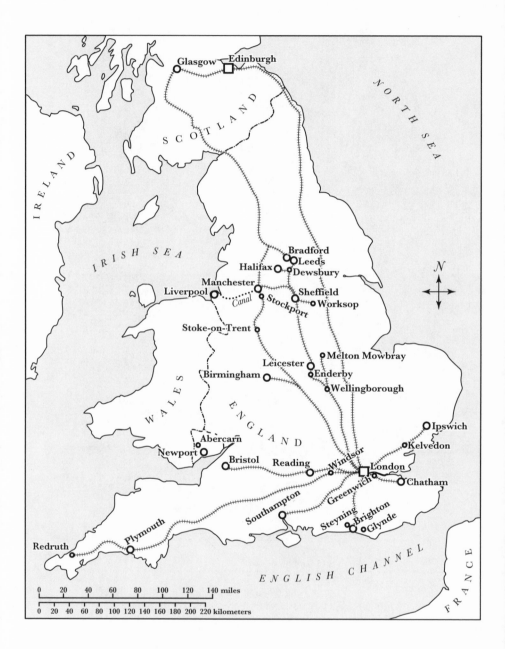

Map 2. Great Britain, 1895: where the Bechuana Chiefs went (by train).
(Map by author.)

FOUR

We See You with Our Eyes

-✦-==◉ ◉==-✦-

THE *TANTALLON CASTLE,* 5,636 TONS, WAS THE CASTLE Line's fastest ship. It had been used by Gladstone for a cruise to the opening of the Kiel Canal that June, when the guests had included Khama's friend from 1885, the Liberal MP Sir George Baden-Powell. The ship carried 150 first-class, 100 second-class, and 80 third-class passengers.[1]

Captain Robinson of the *Tantallon Castle* (who kept in touch with Khama until the latter's death in 1923) later told how Khama's face "grew longer and longer as Table Mountain melted away and nothing appeared to rise up and take its place." Khama stayed in his cabin some days with seasickness. An even later writer, L. D. Raditladi, a grandson of Khama's dissident brother, waxed more poetic.

> At last, when that prodigy of the human mind, that great big house which floats upon the bosom of the sea, left Cape Town, and plunged majestically through the waves of the ocean, Khama's dream was to become a reality. . . .
>
> Slowly and confidently the huge floating house steamed into the Atlantic. The Continent of Africa quietly receded and disappeared below the swelling waves of the ocean. What now linked Khama to his fatherland was but a thin memory, a sudden longing for his beloved tribe he had left behind. Day after day the sun arose from the eastern horizon of the blue deep and sunk to its rest in the west beneath the crimson lining of the liquid foam which spread itself around that lonely steamer for miles and miles like a huge translucent carpet.

Captain Robinson's more prosaic account continues:

> On regaining his liberty Khama took in the sea from all points, and grew more silent day by day, until we neared the Equator, when he confided to Willoughby his fears that the "White Chief" (myself) had lost his way, and that there was neither mountain, hill, trail, nor tree in all that vast wilderness of water, water, water.

One of the chiefs explained: "They showed us some irons; they called it a compass, which they said showed us the roads by which we went. . . . Captain Robinson showed us all these things, and was very kind to us. We have not seen any man so kind."

Two days after crossing the equator Robinson invited Khama up to the bridge at 5 A.M. As dawn broke, they saw "The Paps" of the Cape Verde Islands emerge on the horizon. Robinson watched Khama carefully. Khama said nothing till he moved away and caught the captain's eye; then he asked Willoughby to thank him and to apologize for his previous doubts in Robinson.

Another incident on the journey was the theft of Sebele's trousers. A fireman stole them from the sailor who laundered them, and then exchanged them for a parrot in Madeira. This was not discovered until after the voyage by Robinson, who was horrified by what he thought was the robbery of a black Christian by a white heathen.[2]

On Monday, September 2, the *Tantallon Castle* anchored off the Spanish-owned Atlantic island of Madeira. Bathoen and Sebele bought chairs here—all three chiefs had previously bought chairs in Cape Town as well—and spent a shilling each on fresh fruit. There were also telegrams awaiting the delegation at Madeira. Willoughby was invited to preach in his old church at Brighton on the fifteenth; Khama and the rest were greeted with "Welcome to Europe" and invited to stay at the house of a Mr. Mosely, "half hour railway from London away from noise and bustle."

The chiefs also made friends on board. One of them was Mr. A. de Sales Turland, a manufacturer from England who had abandoned his former radical principles and had become an ardent imperialist. He had been traveling in South Africa, residing for a time with a brother in Johannesburg. He invited the chiefs to be his guests in Northamptonshire. Other passengers on board included a European nobleman, Count Carnace, and families with children and maids.

On the morning of Friday, September 6, at 6 A.M., after a four-hour delay by heavy mists, the liner docked in the Sound off Plymouth. The passage, excluding stoppage time, had taken fifteen days, nine hours, and twenty minutes, with what was described as "average weather." Freight on board included mail from East Africa, Natal, Cape Town, and Madeira, and forty-two boxes of raw gold worth £127,821.

Wardlaw Thompson of the London Mission and Rev. A. Sharp, a Setswana-speaking Wesleyan missionary home "on furlough," and one Reverend Professor Chapman of Plymouth came on board the *Tantallon Castle* in Plymouth Sound to greet the Bechuana. Sharp had come to take charge of Besele and Stephen Lefenya.

Press representatives who boarded the ship in the Sound inquired after the health and welfare of the chiefs. They politely confirmed their good health and pleasure at their reception. Willoughby, as their press manager, declined to issue a statement until they had seen the secretary of state. But the Liberal *Daily Chronicle* and the local *Western Mercury* asked Khama whether he was satisfied with Rhodes's and others' promises that he would retain his rights under any change of government. Khama replied:

> No; the words would be worth nothing if they are not placed on record, to speak for themselves when these men will not be alive or in office, so that we may turn to them.[3]

Willoughby paid out £11 6s. 6d. on the chiefs' behalf in tips to eleven stewards on the boat. The first action of the chiefs on dry land, after going through customs (tipping the customs porters a half-crown), was to have breakfast: at three shillings per person for eight people. They all then caught the 8:10 express train of the Great Western Railway to London.[4]

✣ ✣ ✣

On August 23 the question of the Bechuanalands at last came up for debate in the House of Commons. Speakers against the transfer of the territories from imperial rule were Khama's old friend Baden-Powell and Captain Bethell—a relative of Christopher Bethell, whose death near Mafeking had helped to precipitate the Warren Expedition in 1884–85. Ashmead-Bartlett tried to divert the debate into condemnation of the Transvaal republic and its treatment of the Swazi people in particular.

Chamberlain explained that the Cape Colony could now take over British Bechuanaland because it was providing guarantees on "native policy" that it had refused to provide a decade earlier. He looked forward to a greater South African state at some time in the future but said that its constituent parts should first be built up. The Bechuanaland Protectorate would remain as it was under imperial rule for the time being.

The Commons met on the morning of Thursday, September 5, for the last time of that parliamentary session before the summer and autumn recess. Three questions were asked in the half-hour sitting, all on African affairs: on the Stokes affair of a missionary-trader murdered by a Belgian officer in the Congo Free State, on the French invasion of Madagascar, and on Boer "atrocities" in Swaziland.[5]

There was a dearth of home news for the press. As W. T. Stead's monthly survey of the British press, as well as of North American and continental European journals, called the *Review of Reviews*, commented at the end of the month:

> In Home politics there has been an extraordinary lull . . . in the perfect weather we have had in September. The Liberals have been perfectly dumb. . . . After the General Election everyone rests.

But, Stead added, you did not have to dig far beneath the surface in the ranks of the ruling Conservative Party "to find how rancorous and bitter is the feeling on the part of the Tory rank-and-file against Mr. Chamberlain" and "the Birmingham gang [the Unionist allies of the Conservatives]."

The press was hungry for entertainment. The pomp of the state visit of the Shahzada of Afghanistan, who had left England three days before the Bechuana chiefs arrived, had done something to provide this. "High society" had ebbed away in the "dull season" from the capital into the countryside or to the Continent. Home news was mostly holiday news about the seaside and the weather. The press called it the "silly season" even in 1895, as the *Bristol Mercury* of September 10 observed:

> It is more than probable that their Majesties Sebele, Khama, and Batwen know nothing at all about the Silly Season, but if their desire is to be talked and written about, interviewed, and photographed, they could not have chosen a better time than the present in which to visit this country. But if, as they must be, [they are] seriously anxious to succeed in their mission, it is questionable whether the moment of their arrival is equally well chosen.

There was a vacuum in the press to be filled, but there was also a dearth of enthusiasm that could have proved fatal to the chiefs' cause. Wardlaw Thompson went along to see the lively Liberal MP Arnold-Foster, one of John Mackenzie's collaborators and the main butt of Rhodes's hatred at Westminster, about whipping up interest in the visit and received little encouragement.[6]

✢ ✢ ✢

The chiefs' train crossed the countryside of southwestern England and arrived unpunctually in London, at Paddington Station, at 4:30 that afternoon. The *St James's Gazette* reporter thought that the Bechuana were pretty docile for kings, staring, as they were, up at the great sooty glass roof, in the cacophony of steam inside the canopy of the station. He noted down the smart appearance of the three men, with details that have been quoted in a previous chapter of this book. He was most intrigued by Khama:

> The features carried one's mind at a flash to the Egyptian friezes and sculpture in the British Museum, where many types of negro are represented, but where there is one distinct type remarkable for the narrowness of the face from cheek to cheek and from the profile to the back of the head. There are any number of Khamas in the sculpture of ancient Egypt. The face is but slightly prognathous, the eyes small and elongated in form, and the lips lacking in the excessive fullness of the ordinary African. The expression was benignant and the smile delightful.

The *Gazette* reporter wanted to interview Khama while he waited for the baggage to be collected from the guard's van. The reporter first tried to use Willoughby as interpreter but was rebuffed. He then recruited a Setswana-speaking army officer, Hamilton Goold-Adams, who had come to the station to greet the chiefs.

In answer to the ritual inquiry about his well-being, Khama told the *St James's Gazette* that he was well enough, though he had been sick for the first few days at sea. What were his first impressions of England?

> Everything is looking so marvellously fresh and green—such fine pastures and trees so rich in foliage! I have never seen so beautiful a country as that we passed through today.

After a brief comment on his liquor laws, Khama said he could not comment on the political situation until he had seen Chamberlain. At this point the reporter was spotted by Willoughby:

> the little missionary relaxed his vigilance in the matter of luggage, swooped down upon us, and with a peremptoriness born by association with subject races, forbade the King to hold any conversation.

The *St James's Gazette* concluded that the missionaries had the Bechuana chiefs in their pocket and meant to keep them there.[7]

While the Wesleyans went their own way from the station, the LMS party were taken straight by cab and bus to the LMS headquarters at No. 23 Blomfield Street, near Liverpool Street and Broad Street Stations. London Mission House—otherwise known as Livingstone House, King's Court—was an imposing but by then soot-grimed office building, with the Livingstone Book Shop at its base, built less than twenty years earlier (architect: E. C. Robins). All in all it was a shrine to the London Missionary Society's most famous son, David Livingstone, whose posthumous image was assiduously cultivated by the society. Here the chiefs offered thanks to the Almighty for their safe delivery from the deep, and partook of afternoon tea.

Their chiefs' hotel was round the corner from London Mission House in South Place, just off Finsbury Pavement—the main road connecting Moorgate with the City Road. Armfield's South Place Hotel was a temperance hotel. It described itself as a first-class hotel for two hundred guests "entirely re-built in the very best style," with perfect sanitation, bathrooms and lavatories, on every floor, lit throughout by electricity, and with an American (Otis?) passenger elevator to all floors. The *Manchester Courier* dismissed it as a cheap hotel; another newspaper called it "unpretentious." The LMS picked up the bill eventually, but it is not clear if its offer to do so was made at the start.

That Friday night Willoughby wrote from Armfield's to Chamberlain advertising the chiefs' presence and requesting an interview.[8]

SATURDAY, SEPTEMBER 7

The next day, Saturday, the chiefs were taken out to buy further clothing. They took a 2s. 9d. cab to the stores and bought hats, overcoats, boots, umbrellas, haberdashery, and other clothing to the tune of £10 12s. 5d. (Bathoen), £9 5s. 9d. (Sebele), and £11 1s. 1d. (Khama). Khama soon afterward bought another £5 4s. 6d. worth of shirts and collars, dress ties and handkerchiefs, and the like. The three chiefs and Kwenaetsile, who was always to assert his status as more than a mere attendant, were now wearing top hats, though as the *Cape Argus* remarked, not all of them "appear comfortable in this particular item of metropolitan attire."

Sebele also spent £3 10s. on a gold watch-chain on Saturday morning, and 2s. 6d. on a pocketbook and pen. He also got £6 cash for his own spending money.[9] Unlike the others, he seems to have made a habit of venturing out on public transport and into the shops, with Gohiwamang in tow as his interpreter. Given the warm weather, he may have dearly wanted to take a drink in a bar or "pub" but is said to have remained teetotal for the whole trip.

That Saturday afternoon and evening the chiefs were the subjects of the "new" investigative journalism when they were interviewed through Willoughby by representatives of the two main Liberal daily newspapers, the *Daily News* and the *Daily Chronicle*. The first interview was at London Mission House, with a representative of the children's magazine of the LMS, *News from Afar*, also in attendance. The second interview, after the evening meal, seems to have been at the hotel.

For the *Daily News* Khama and Sebele began by explaining the relationship between the chiefs. "From his land," Khama is reported to have said, gracefully gesturing toward Sebele, "our race sprang. Although I am from Bechuana, we are all Bantus, and we look upon Sebele's people as our fountain tribe." (The English terminology was Willoughby's, who had adopted the term *Bantu* from scholarly linguistic studies.) Yes, Sebele added, referring to Khama and Bathoen, "My younger brothers, but we are all of one race."

The *Daily News* tried to steer Khama toward the question of his "desertion" from the Matabele War, but Khama interjected:

> I am reluctant to talk about war. I hate it. It is a thing of the past. I have never waged war, but have only defended. I prefer not to talk about it, it brings back such sad thoughts. Peace reigns in my country, and I hope ever will—as a Christian I am opposed to war.

In an apparent reference to the Chartered Company, he went on: "I will not allow my people to follow up fugitives and take prisoners. If we are attacked, we must fight; but it must be short, sharp, and then done with."

What did Khama fear most? His exact reply was prolix; his words were rendered more succinctly and romantically in *News from Afar:*

> Two things I fear most, Drink and the Devil. You send us your Bible, and you send your fire-water as well.

Khama told the *Daily News* that the British authorities were undermining his laws by allowing liquor imports. Here Bathoen chipped in—"the short, burly-looking chief who up till now had kept silent":

> I am an abstainer from drink, just like Khama. I have prohibited it in my land, and with my own hand destroyed five waterpots which I found had been filled with beer.

Reiterating Khama's criticism of liquor imports, Bathoen continued in characteristically naive strain:

> England is a country where all are Christians, and so you send your bad men away and they come to us. They drink and they go out shooting on Sundays, and when we see their evil ways we remind them that they would not dare to do that in England.

At this the journalist muttered an aside to Willoughby, "They are not disillusioned yet." Willoughby replied:

> No. There has fortunately not yet been an opportunity, for so far our time has chiefly been spent with the tailors and the bootmakers. All the chiefs, and especially Bathoen, are very particular about their dress, and even Khama's small feet must be shod to the best advantage before he meets the authorities over here.

The next question from the journalist was about slavery. "A puzzled look came in to their faces," and they set about a dialogue between themselves "as to whether their interviewer meant *slave, serf,* or *servant.*" Finally came their defensive response:

> As a rule each man works for himself, but if bushmen work for us we give them cows, and then they buy waggons, and in time become independent. If to hire a man is to make a slave, then we have them; but if it is not slavery to work for another for pay, then we have no slaves. To work without pay we do not ask; it is the Boers who do that.

This disingenuous reply was complicated further by Willoughby's choice of the word "bushmen" for the word *batlhanka,* when the chiefs were evidently referring to vassals in general, who could even be lords in their own right with sway over other vassals.

Then in a significant addendum, after explaining that his own brother had been enslaved by the Boers until he had redeemed him, Bathoen added: "We no longer act thus ourselves."

What did they most want to achieve in England? "Next to success in the object of our visit," said one of the chiefs, "we wish to see the Queen— or, as our people call her, 'the one who listens,' or 'the little woman of many days *[MmaMosadinyana].*'" Khama went on to explain that many Bechuana doubted her existence:

> They think to say she is alive is a lie, and many of my people have mixed notions; they think the Queen is like God, and the Prince of Wales like Jesus Christ. Of course we do not speak of ourselves, but of the very ignorant people.

Ever the canny statesman, he used this to underscore a point to be made with the powers-that-be.

> If we return and say we have not seen her they will say: "See, it is as we said, all lies." We believe it would be of great use from a diplomatic point of view for us to have audience of her Majesty.

What had struck them most on their journey and in England? Not surprisingly, the chiefs remarked: "We marvel most at the ships, the trains, the telegraphs, and the telephones." (Telephones were still uncommon, and they had probably not used one before they arrived in London.) The interview with the *Daily News* ended with a discussion of the difficulty of interpreting such new concepts through Setswana.

The children's magazine representative sitting in on the interview, Florence Balgarne, remarked of the Setswana language: "It is musical, and reminds me a little of Welsh." [10]

The next interview, with the *Daily Chronicle,* was on that Saturday night, after the evening meal. The first question was as to why they had come to England. Khama, acting as spokesman, gave a carefully modulated reply:

> We hear of annexation; we hear of things we do not understand. We are afraid changes of this kind may mean much. We want to understand them. When we have understood them, when we know what they mean, we shall be able to put our thoughts before the Queen's Secretary of State for the Colonies.
>
> Our first work is to ask questions. Then it will be for us when we have received information to consult together and see what we are called upon to do. . . . according to our custom we think it would be wrong to speak to others about our business until we have spoken to the high officers of the Queen, whom we hope to see as soon as they can make it convenient.

Further pursuit of this line of questioning was futile. The *Daily Chronicle* turned to the delicate question of Khama's "desertion" in the Matabele War. Khama replied that his men were threatened by the smallpox in

Matabeleland, and some were wounded and had to be taken home. The rains had begun to fall, after a long dry season and near famine, and it was essential to plow (while the hard-baked ground was still wet):

> Moreover, the Matabele had quickly been conquered by *our column* [emphasis added], and they had been conquered also by the forces advancing from the other side [Mashonaland]. They had fled north, and the war was, to all intents and purposes, finished.

The journalist moved on to the more sensitive point of Rhodes's scolding of Khama in his own *kgotla*. Khama responded:

> No, I don't not want to speak about that, because since then Mr. Rhodes has asked me to forgive him for words which he said when he was misinformed, and I cannot go back on what I have already forgotten.

The interview ended with Khama's general comments on the "progress" of his people, from "old customs that are bad" such as male polygamy to "better ways." His particular obsession, of course, was his liquor laws. He had (very recently) "found it necessary to modify these laws as to the people making their own beer. [But] I punish drunkenness."

Would his people always grow better and better?

> I do not know what will come; the future only can show. But I hope they will still progress if there are no hindrances in the land to prevent them. . . . You can never, though, speak of a people as if they were one man, and say "He is good," or "he is bad." People are different the one from the other, and they always must be different.

It was as the *Daily Chronicle* interviewer was leaving that Khama gently wigged him with humorous but earnest words of warning: "Be sure now, and only write as I have spoken, nothing more than my words." [11]

SUNDAY, SEPTEMBER 8 – MONDAY, SEPTEMBER 9

On Sunday morning the Bechuana went down to the City Temple for divine service. They probably walked the mile or so, through the streets to the Holborn Viaduct. The City was quiet on a Sunday because there was relatively little traffic on the roads; financial and commercial houses were closed for the day, and few people actually resided within the square mile demarcated by the remains of the old city walls. As they walked, the Bechuana would have had good views of St. Paul's Cathedral, dominating the metropolis from the top of Ludgate Hill.

The City Temple was London's premier Congregational church, presided over by the great preacher Rev. Dr. Parker, keeper of London's Nonconformist conscience. The church stood next to Holborn Viaduct.

The viaduct was an elevated roadway, thirty feet high and a quarter of a mile long, stretching from Newgate to Hatton Garden. It crossed over the valley of the Fleet River or ditch (now a covered sewer) that separated the City from the West End of London. It had cost two million pounds to build in 1863.[12]

On the Monday morning there was a trip to Madame Tussaud's Wax-Works. The Bechuana party of eight adults took four-penny tickets on the Metropolitan subway railway, popularly known as "the Drain," from Moorgate to Baker Street Stations. The entry fee to Madame Tussaud's was 8s. 6d.: one wonders if the 6d. constituted an extra admission fee to the "Chamber of Horrors," or if the chiefs were giving young Master Willoughby a treat.

Madame Tussaud herself had been dead for forty-five years, and her exhibition of 190 wax-headed and limbed figures, sculpted from measurements of dead bodies and live people, had been expanded to 350 figures by 1895. One wonders how many of the figures would have meant anything to the chiefs, or to the majority of other tourists passing them. But the chiefs were undoubtedly impressed by the verisimilitude of the life-sized figures in appropriate dress, with glass eyes staring at them. When Sebele later met ceremonially dressed soldiers standing rigidly to attention in the corridors of Windsor Castle, he thrust a finger at one's face to check if he was real.

Then, as now, the tableaux of figures at Madame Tussaud's consisted of some strange juxtapositions amid general order. The first hall consisted of a pantheon of royal ancestors from William the Conqueror to Queen Anne, but Queen Elizabeth stood in the next hall or Grand Salon—with Victorian royalty and politicians, famous actors and writers. Here, the chiefs would have encountered Joseph Chamberlain for the first time, vicariously, as figure no. 148. There were also General "Chinese" Gordon, an eccentric military engineer not unlike Sir Charles Warren—whom the chiefs may have known about from his Basutoland adventures—and his archfoe the so-called Mahdi of the Sudan; the archbishop of Canterbury, John Knox, Martin Luther, George Washington, Abraham Lincoln, the emperor of Germany; Rosebery and Gladstone, Salisbury, and a late visitor to Bechuanaland, Lord Randolph Churchill. There was also Sir Wilfrid Lawson, the Liberal humanitarian MP who was to ally with the chiefs' cause. In the next hall there were the late khedive of Egypt and the sultan of Turkey, John Wesley standing next to the vaudeville exhibit "General Tom Thumb," a tableau of Her Majesty the queen next to Victor Hugo, and Joan of Arc standing in armor almost next to David Livingstone in his characteristic consul's hat. No doubt

Queen Victoria (no. 193) and Livingstone (no. 208) produced the loudest cries of recognition and wonder.

After that, no. 222, "A Royal Tiger Hunt," and no. 228, "Death of Nelson," and endless pieces of Napoleona, such as Napoleon's coach from Waterloo, which had been among Madame Tussaud's prize acquisitions, might have been an anticlimax for the Bechuana. Next in line was the Chamber of Horrors, ordinary-looking murderers transformed into model Victorian villains by dim lighting, grimy clothes, and malicious looks on their faces, with a scatter of blood-drenched memorabilia from the French Revolution. Maybe some or all of the Bechuana avoided this hall in the basement and merely saw the last hall on the ground floor—consisting of various (East) Indian princes and William Booth of the Salvation Army (recently sailed for the Cape of Good Hope) and his late wife next to scenes from "Cinderella" and *Robinson Crusoe.*

Finally, after scenes including the poignant execution of Mary Queen of Scots, a university boat race, a meet of the hounds, and a "football scrimmage," there were figures that—if well sculpted—must have seemed the most familiar of all to the Bechuana. Standing at the exit to receive the greeting and farewell of the party, were figures 348–49: Cetshwayo, king of the Zulu, defeated by the British sixteen years previously, and his favorite wives (how many wives is unspecified in the catalog). Six years earlier the two Ndebele envoys sent by Lobengula were shown the same wax figure in Madame Tussaud's museum and were told that it "was Cetshwayo in person, punished thus for his unruliness." [13]

At this point, emerging into the light of day, the chiefs may have returned back to Moorgate at once. Alternatively, if they had sandwich lunches packed at Armfield's, they might have made a whole day of their outing by crossing Regent's Park to the London Zoological Gardens and back to "the Drain" at Great Portland Street Station.

That evening the chiefs were interviewed in the hotel's upstairs drawing room (accessible by elevator) by a "lady journalist" from the *Christian World.* Lloyd as well as Willoughby was on hand to interpret. She described her uneasiness at entering the room from the elevator. She revealed her preconceptions by describing Setswana as a "primitive language," the chiefs as "negroids rather than negroes," Khama as being "of a remarkably fine type," and by referring to them as "primitive man" with "very patriarchal simplicity . . . much after the manner of the Book of Job." Such awkwardness proved to be mutual:

> During the preliminary hand shakings KHAMA's face lighted up with an amused smile. Presently, the contagion spreading to the other chiefs, Mr. LLOYD turned to me and said, "You must excuse the slight embarrass-

ment which the chiefs seem to feel: the fact is, they are not accustomed to be interviewed, and least of all by a woman. You will readily guess," he added with a merry twinkle "that the ladies of Bechuanaland have not yet taken to journalism."

The woman's response was fairly forthright: "That leads up to the very point I want to learn: What has Christianity done for the women, why have the chiefs not brought their wives for a European trip?" None of the chiefs answered the latter part of the question. Khama, twice a widower, had lost his second wife only a year before. But he, despite being described as "the most reticent of the three," seems to have monopolized the talking, referring to women of the upper class at home:

> KHAMA: One thing I can reply is that since the missionaries have taught us that our wives are our equals, we no longer expect them to dig. Formerly they did all the work. It is a sure sign of advance when you see the men use the ploughs which have come to us from Sweden and America; the men are proud to drive two oxen in a plough.
>
> A little Bechuana boy is said to have described his home as a place where women work and men dress their hair and fight and talk; but this is no longer true. This generation of women can many of them cut dresses and sew for themselves, and sew for their husbands as well.
>
> CHRISTIAN WORLD: Have they, then, made as much progress as the men?
>
> KHAMA: No; I fear not, they have not as much zeal as the men. I can't tell you why, but they look to see what the men do, and then follow them. I wish they did learn more to spin and weave, but they mostly string beads.
>
> CHRISTIAN WORLD: But do you give them the same chance as yourselves?
>
> KHAMA: Perhaps not, but I have heard even missionaries say that it were better the women still worked in the field than be idle at home. There is much to be done yet for them.

Next all three chiefs had their say on the liquor question. Khama referred to alcohol as "the destruction of my people; they lose their good standing, and their food and speech because of it." Bathoen, "the least interesting looking of the three chiefs, but he is an earnest man," complained that drink "teaches unkindness and causes man to love sleep. . . . all kinds of evil come out of the beer-pot."

This sparked off Sebele, the temporary rather than total abstainer, into the strongest denunciation of all—"much in the style of some Hebrew prophet, he proceeded in a low, musical voice emphasized by frequent gestures" (and displaying on the way considerably less gender sensitivity than Khama):

> SEBELE: I can say more about the habit of liquor than my younger brothers, for, alas! I know it in my own personal experience as the great

destroyer. If a man should drink the fire-water of the traders, although he be a king, although he be a Christian, he will grow drowsy. Although he be a judge, he will no longer know how to speak amongst the people.

Liquor is the cause of quarrelling; liquor makes men to be of a feminine heart—it is no true gift. The work of liquor is rascality. There is no pleasing man who drinks.

CHRISTIAN WORLD: Then you had no strong drink before the Europeans came?

SEBELE: Yes, we had it, there was no good in it; but the English [liquor] is worse, it is so strong, it is like fire. . . . In the olden days we did not give liquor to the young men; now all have it.

The white man's brandy is stronger than our *khadi* (honey beer). I do not profess to observe very closely, but so it seems to me. My father forbade it in our country. I tell you I have seen its evil workings in myself, and I, too leave it alone. I would that the English would help to keep it out instead of sending it into our lands.[14]

TUESDAY, SEPTEMBER 10

The first two official engagements now fixed for the chiefs were an introduction to the directors of the London Missionary Society on the afternoon of Tuesday the tenth, and a preliminary interview with Secretary of State Joseph Chamberlain on the afternoon of Wednesday the eleventh.

Before a packed centenary meeting of the board of directors of the London Missionary Society, at London Mission House, Wardlaw Thompson introduced the three chiefs—Sebele first, as the senior. Khama then spoke, interpreted by Lloyd:

> We rejoice to meet with the London Missionary Society. We have long heard of you with our ears while we were still in our own countries, and we give thanks to God today that we see you with our eyes, just as we see you now, and our hearts rejoice very much on account of the way, the handsome way, in which you have received us.
>
> When I was in Mangwato, my country, I thought I would like to come to England. It is to see the wonderful things in England that I have come, and also to have the pleasure of meeting with the Directors of the Society; but on account of the many duties I had in my country I lacked time to come. But when I did see time, I said to my missionary: "Now I want to go to England to see the Directors of the Society." So we came through the country of Africa.
>
> I am glad to be able to beg help from you today, and say to you: "Will you help us?" We do not know the customs of you white people even as you do not know our customs, who are black people. We are in difficulties. Will you help us, please? We ask you to pray to God for us, and to help us in our need. We are people who try to learn while we are in our country,

because the things of our own country are things which keep us back and cause us to go back. And the Word of God does not go forward as we should desire in our own country.

Various destructive things come amongst us and destroy the Word of God amongst us. And it is on account of these destructions and difficulties that we come to you today, and plead with you to help us in our time of need, because, with regard to our country, we know that it is passing away hence from us; but still, if we put our trust in Christ, we know that we can live best by means of Him, because it is he who comforts our hearts. These are my greetings to you.[15]

The London Missionary Society had emphasized that it had no official connection with the political mission of the Bechuana chiefs. But after Khama's speech, the directors adopted a motion that they would be willing to support the chiefs in a delegation to the secretary of state. However, Chamberlain turned this down.

The LMS thus had no direct role in organizing the political campaign tour of Britain now being set up by Willoughby, in response to numerous requests for the chiefs to speak (unlike its direct role in John Mackenzie's campaign tour of the early 1880s, and John Philip's campaign in an earlier age). But its centenary celebrations provided a network of meetings in churches and halls across the land, at which Khama, Sebele, and Bathoen could press their cause. Khama was now, after all, the society's most famous convert—even if his actual baptism had been Lutheran!

Khama's reputation was enhanced by the publication by Hodder and Stoughton, in time for the LMS centenary, of the collected letters of Rev. James Hepburn, Khama's late missionary, under the title *Twenty Years in Khama's Country*. The fortuitous publication of this book, in September, was extremely important in cultivating the favor of the British press toward the Bechuana chiefs, whose cause, according to Wardlaw Thompson, "when they arrived . . . seemed very low."[16]

Extracts from *Twenty Years in Khama's Country* appeared in the British press as early as September 7, in the *Daily Graphic*. The book was actually published about ten days later. The review of the book in the *Bradford Observer* on September 17 remarked, "Even apart from all the miraculous circumstance with which the piety of the good missionary has surrounded it, the story is still a remarkable one." The *Spectator* of September 21 trusted that no reader of the book would fail to hope that the British government would support the rule of "our loyal friend and ally Khama the Good."[17]

There was also another book being hurriedly written, for publication as soon as possible, by the LMS missionary Edwin Lloyd, who was on "home leave" alternately accompanying the Bechuana chiefs and attending his pregnant wife at Clapham. The book was to be called *Three Great African Chiefs*.

WEDNESDAY, SEPTEMBER 11

"Joe" Chamberlain (motto: *Je tiens ferme,* translated satirically as "I own this firm") was in Birmingham. On the eleventh he returned to London specifically to meet the three chiefs from the Bechuanaland Protectorate, before proceeding on his continental vacation arranged by the travel agents Thomas Cook and Co. The interview had been arranged between Albert Spicer, MP, and Chamberlain's deputy minister, Lord Selborne. Given his radical imperialist and Nonconformist background, and the need to assuage the temperance lobby, which had been roughly dealt with by the Conservatives in the recent election campaign, Chamberlain needed little persuading. The Khama deputation was the first public test, as a Conservative and Unionist minister in his chosen ministry, of a man who for ten years or more had made public his intention of becoming prime minister.

The promotion of temperance in Africa was a sop to the temperance movement that left the question of temperance in Britain begging. Chamberlain thereby espoused the interests of "legitimate" imperial big business without offending "Bung"—the contemporary slang for beer and liquor interests represented in the Conservative Party. The cheap spirits imported into the West Coast of Africa were mostly not British but German or Portuguese. As for South Africa, Chamberlain had remarked: "Cape smoke [i.e. cheap brandy from the Cape] eats the life out of honest business. Therefore, if only that our workingmen may get employment at home, let us cease from poisoning our dark-skinned brethren abroad." His bluestocking friend Flora Shaw made similar points in the columns of the *Times*.[18]

The interview between Chamberlain and the chiefs, however, was intended to be brief and purely social, leaving aside all political issues till November, when Chamberlain returned from his Spanish-Mediterranean holiday. Had not the general election occurred, Chamberlain would have taken his annual vacation in the Cape Colony as a guest of the opposition there.

Given wariness about Willoughby, it is not surprising that the Colonial Office arranged for Lloyd rather than Willoughby to be the interpreter at the meeting. The Colonial Office view of the white man as the real power behind the supplicant chiefs is reflected in the *Daily Telegraph*'s account of the day, which puts Willoughby before Khama:

Shortly before three o'clock, the Rev. W. C. Willoughby arrived at the
Colonial Office, accompanied by Khama, who wore a tall silk hat and
black clothes, the coat being a fashionably cut "frock," and except for the
decidedly African cast of his features, and his woolly hair, might well have
been taken for an English gentleman. The chiefs Sebele and Bathoen, the
former a well-proportioned man with slight grey beard, arrived shortly
afterwards, accompanied by Mr. Edward [sic] Lloyd, one of the London
Missionary Society's missionaries, lately returned from abroad, and the
party was conducted to one of the waiting rooms.

The Secretary of State did not arrive at Euston [Station, from Birming-
ham] till shortly after three o'clock, and his visitors had been waiting some
time before he reached his office. The visitors were at once shown to his
private room. The interview proved far longer than had been anticipated,
and at a quarter to five the right hon. gentleman, whose carriage had been
awaiting him in Downing Street, sent a message to his coachman directing him not to remain longer. It was not until about ten minutes past five
that the interview came to an end, and the visitors were then escorted by
Mr. H. F. Wilson, Mr. Chamberlain's private secretary, with whom they
all shook hands at parting.

A correspondent of the *East Anglian Daily Times,* who saw the chiefs waiting
in the antechamber of the Colonial Office, remarked on how he "was
much struck with their intelligence and pleasing appearance. They are
tall and of really fine physique. Attired, as they are, in well-fitting morning dress, they might easily pass for European gentlemen if not for their
swarthy hue."

Chamberlain had listened for two hours to the chiefs, consenting to
hear their case despite the original attention not to; and "the chiefs felt
satisfied, from the Secretary of State's demeanour, that they might hope
for the favourable consideration of their desire for the Government's protection." Sebele began, with Bathoen and then Khama following,

> over the whole question, of which the chief item was their objection to the
> possibility of being taken over by the Chartered Company, while there
> were minor points dealing with reforms or alterations which they desired
> in the present condition of things in the Protectorate.

The narrative of the interview was taken up by a Colonial Office press
release through the Press Association:

> Mr. Chamberlain listened with great patience and interest while they were
> unfolding their case in "their own picturesque but at the same time intel-
> ligent and forcible manner," occasionally asking questions which seemed
> to afford them the opportunity of making clear their precise meaning on
> any doubtful or obscure points. As to the main issue, Mr. Chamberlain
> naturally deferred until after the further hearing. . . . with respect to the
> minor matters . . . he invited his visitors to re-submit their views in writing.

Willoughby told the press afterward that "there was very little in connexion with the interview which he felt himself at liberty to communicate." But Khama's petition had not been mentioned, and "great misunderstanding evidently prevailed about that document"—as it had "been prepared and forwarded in June last, when there seemed little possibility that the chiefs would have an opportunity of personally laying their case before the Government."

Khama, Sebele, and Bathoen, according to the *Methodist Recorder* of September 12, were impressed by Chamberlain's dignity and knowledge, but thought him a little too young to govern such a large empire.[19]

❖ ❖ ❖

Willoughby's financial accounts reveal that at some time on the Monday or Tuesday there was a cab fare to pick up tailoring ordered and fitted on the previous Saturday.

Sebele was still missing a pair of trousers. When Captain Robinson discovered their fate, he came round to Armfield's with money in recompense and gave it to Sebele. A day later he was summoned before Khama, who asked him to take the money back, apparently because Robinson had given it to Sebele without Khama's knowledge. When Khama became insistent, the captain told him a parable. Once a chief sold a trader a horse. The price was high because the horse was "salted" (inoculated), and the chief gave a year's guarantee against the horse getting horse-sickness. Three weeks later the horse died of colic. The chief gave the trader his money back. The trader declined to accept because the horse had not died of horse sickness. But the chief insisted that the trader accept his money back or leave his country for ever. "And the trader had to take it because he loved the Chief."

Of course Captain Robinson was telling Khama a true story about himself, as told to Robinson by Willoughby. While Robinson told the story, "Khama's face was a study. He never raised his eyes, but sat with folded hands and without moving." At the story's conclusion, Khama stood up; he raised his eyebrows and smiled broadly and then bowed with silent dignity, thanking Robinson for his visit. There was no question of Robinson taking the money back.

When Robinson told the story in later years, he wrote: "Many a lesser man has found a resting place in Westminster Abbey." But we may justly ask, from Sebele's viewpoint, just what was Khama trying to prove? His business acumen, or just that he wanted to have and keep the whip hand over his fellow chiefs?

Two other men also came up from the seaside, both from Eastbourne, to see Khama during the week. One was H. A. Bryden, the author of

With Gun and Camera in Southern Africa, who had visited Bechuanaland in 1890 and whose letter awaited Khama on arrival. The other was Sir George Baden-Powell, who exchanged cables with Khama and Willoughby, before coming up to entertain the chiefs in London on Thursday the twelfth. He promised Khama telegraphically: "I will ask leading public men meet you as some return for your kindness to me when visiting you with Sir Charles Warren 1885 Shoshong." [20]

FIVE

Besieged by a Curious Crowd

◂┅═◉ ◉═┅▸

EDITORIAL RESPONSE IN THE BRITISH PRESS TO THE
arrival of the three chiefs on September 6 was generally positive, particularly toward Khama as an individual.

On Saturday, September 7, many newspapers cited Khama's "killed
and eaten" petition against the Chartered Company, quoted in full in the
St James's Gazette and described as "rather pathetic" by the *Daily Telegraph*.
Biographical sketches of Khama promoted his image as a remarkably
sagacious Christian leader of his people—in daily newspapers and in spe-
cialist weekly journals, such as H. Rider Haggard's *African Review* and E. P.
Mathers's *South Africa* published that Saturday. An ironic popular review
called *Modern Society* said "Khama is almost too good to live—so Cecil
Rhodes is beginning to think."

Contemporary racialism was evident in some newspaper comments
that day. The *Yorkshire Evening Post*, for example, credited Khama with "remarkable wisdom for a member of the coloured race" and said that his
rule had improved his people mentally and physically, whereas other "native races" had deteriorated. But this newspaper obviously had a taste for
hyperbole, as it described Khama as "one of the most remarkable native
rulers the world has even seen."

Saturday's *Nottingham Guardian* concluded:

> There is room in South Africa for several native protected States, just as
> there is room for feudatory states in India, and there is much to be said,
> from many points of view, for encouraging, if it be possible, the growth of
> semi-independent native civilizations.

The *Western Morning News* of the seventh argued that unless Khama's rights
were preserved, even under the company, "Khama will have on his side
every Christian man and woman in England." But the groundswell of

support for the chiefs was not reflected in the more Conservative and establishment London newspapers, which were altogether cooler. The *Times* of September 7 carried only a cursory report of the chiefs' arrival.[1]

By Monday, September 9, the press was beginning to comment more on issues rather than personalities. The London *St James's Gazette* saw the chiefs' mission to Britain as denoting "that the incessant conflict of racial and material interests between the white man and the black in Southern Africa has entered upon a further and acute stage. The fundamental issue is whether *Kraal rule* or *Rhodes rule* shall prevail—whether, in fact, the black man or the white is to be the actual lord of the soil and master of the destinies of its inhabitants." The *Lincolnshire Echo* of the ninth reported not inaccurately that the chiefs were constitutional rulers at home who had been compelled to come to Britain by force of public opinion among villagers.

The Conservative *Morning Post* of September 9 could not see why Khama was complaining when he got his protection free of charge. But the Liberal *Daily News* on Monday, September 9, argued that Chamberlain "must delay his travels until he has given audience to the three most important native rulers to be found in all our colonies."[2]

The latter point was taken up the next day, Tuesday the tenth, by the *Dundee Advertiser:* "Mr. Chamberlain has a splendid chance to see what he can do as a diplomat." The *Bristol Times* pointed out how the Bechuana were much more important than the Swazi delegates who had been privileged to see Queen Victoria in 1894.

The *Newcastle Leader* of that Tuesday was quite blunt on the main political issue—the threatened takeover of the Bechuanaland Protectorate by the BSA Company. The company was in the hands of "mere speculators or rough settlers." Its rule would be a "cramping monopoly, supported by the harshest tyranny" over the native population:

> The settler as a rule has not a very high opinion of the black races among whom he lives. He finds them treacherous and not very honest. He believes that the only way to make them useful is to keep them strictly in subjection. In all cases in which the interests of the two colours come into conflict black must yield to white. And as the chief interest of the white man is to make as much money as he can in the shortest possible time, it often happens that the "nigger" experiences treatment which is sadly at variance with the high principles which the teachers sent out by the white men seek to inculcate.
>
> Wherever the Imperial Government has had direct control, its representatives have been looked on as the defenders of native rights, and as far as the impediments of officialdom permitted they have justified the reliance put on them.

It was an "African correspondent" of the (radical-imperialist) *Pall Mall Gazette*, Stead's old newspaper, who contributed the most stinging criticism of Khama, on September 10—whereas the newspaper itself was much more sympathetic. Khama's self-conceit, wrote the correspondent, was only equaled by his narrow-mindedness. His demands on the British government smacked a little too much of "Native Home Rule," in which regard to he was plainly an incompetent ruler. Palapye was "the most awful bed of pestilence" and prostitution in Africa. Let Khama be entertained at Exeter Hall and otherwise ignored, argued the correspondent. Chamberlain should listen only to Rhodes. As for Khama, he should meditate on La Fontaine's fable of the frog and the bull.[3]

The *Aberdeen Free Press* of September 11, on the other hand, was stern rather than hostile: Khama should be protected from the British South Africa Company so long as he and his people "fulfil their obligations."

The *Times* was now ready with an editorial "first leader," which appeared on the eleventh. It reflected the Colonial Office point of view, combining the caution of the establishment with the company's need to downplay the chiefs' grievances. Rhodes had assiduously cultivated its editor, Moberley Bell, and had recruited its colonial correspondent, Flora Shaw, as some kind of secret agent for the Chartered Company in November 1894. The *Times* faithfully printed Rhodes's press releases, including a report attempting to preempt Khama's meeting with Chamberlain by saying that he had accepted company rule when Jameson went to meet him at Palapye.

The *Times* now acknowledged that Khama "has earned for himself the admiration and confidence of an influential section of opinion in this country" and trusted that he would be well received in the British towns he would tour. Khama had come to London to be informed about his country's future. The Bechuanaland Protectorate must eventually pass from imperial control to "some form of local government" (i.e. white colonial government), but it was unlikely that this would be that soon. Meanwhile Rhodes must have guarantees for the extension of the railway from Vryburg to Palapye.

The *Times* repeated Rhodes's libel on Khama's "withdrawal" from the Matabele War, without any mention of Khama's viewpoint and Rhodes's apology to him as carried in the *Daily Chronicle* interview two days before. (Next day the *Realm*, a popular right-wing London newspaper, described Khama's version of events as "specious.")[4]

Chamberlain's cordial reception of the chiefs on Wednesday, September 11, put the Unionist and Nonconformist seals of approval on the Bechuana chiefs, who had been already approved by the Liberal opposition. But the old Whig and Tory Anglican establishment of landed interests would take longer to win over. The *Times* and the *Morning Post* of September 12 reported that "a large number of persons of position" had promised the chiefs assistance, and invitations to them from all the large provincial towns were pouring in—so that "during the next few weeks they will spend their time in visiting the chief centres of British industry."

The press had fun at the expense of Chamberlain's disquiet on the liquor question. The *Manchester Guardian* of September 12 published a long satirical poem in which Chamberlain remarks to Khama that he might grant protection from "Bung" (the liquor lobby) in Bechuanaland, but Bung was his ally in Britain (see the appendix of this book). *Punch* on September 21 portrayed Chamberlain telling Khama that the issue of local government liquor prohibition ("Local Veto") had helped to unseat the Liberals in the recent elections.

A number of newspapers picked up on the idea of "Rhodes rule versus Kraal rule"—home rule for African rather than Irish natives. (The Dutch word *kraal*, properly referring to corrals or livestock pens, had become equated with small African villages in colonial parlance.) The *Realm* of Thursday, September 12, modified its espousal of inevitable "Rhodes rule" with the acknowledgment that "we are bound by ties of honour and friendship to treat the Bechuana chieftains with delicacy." If Khama was really wise, he would spend "the remainder of his days in leading his people to an acceptance of direct rule by the whites."

The *Globe* newspaper of September 12, and a letter in the *Yorkshire Post* of the next day, hailed Khama as "exemplifying, as he does, in an eminent degree, Carlyle's definition of a king as 'a man who can.' He is a man of stern religious principle, of the Puritan type, who holds that it is the duty of a ruler not only to practise the cardinal virtues himself, but to enforce them on his subjects." [5]

Khama's Nonconformist appeal was confirmed in the pages of the evangelical Christian and temperance press. "King Khama interviewed by a lady" appeared in the *Christian World* on September 12. That week the *Christian*, the *Christian Commonwealth*, the *Christian Globe*, and the *Rock* all pledged their support for Khama against speculators, land-grabbers, and liquor merchants. The *Woman's Signal*, an organ of the "white ribbon" WCTU (Women's Christian Temperance Union), the most powerful women's organization in the English-speaking world, portrayed Khama as "the friend of women":

> Women, children, subjected races, all have been defended and guarded from the evil and barbarous customs which had prevailed. Their status has been raised, their lives secured, their rights as citizens recognised.

Women, accustomed to till the fields, have by the tact and perception of their ruler been imperceptibly relieved of at least a portion of their hardest tasks, while the men have been induced in some degree to share in agricultural pursuits. The daughters of Christian converts have been ceaselessly watched over by him and Mabisi [Mma-Besi, Khama's wife, who died in 1889].[6]

England and the Union (price 2d.), recently bought by the Massachusetts-born Tory humanitarian MP Sir Ellis Ashmead-Bartlett, said it would be "simply infamous if Khama is now betrayed. . . . It is a splendid opportunity for honour and fair play, and we trust it will not be lost." The edition on Saturday, September 14, also went to town on the systematic deception of public opinion by news reports from Cape Town, which were "Like almost all the news that comes from South Africa . . . sent by order of one of the two great influences that control all the South African Press, with one or two exceptions . . . the Chartered Company and the Kruger gang."

The *African Critic* of the same date began with personal remarks on the "perpetual youth" of bright-eyed Khama, who looked forty-five but must be sixty-five: "Tall, slight and wiry, he looks as tough as steel." The writer, probably H. A. Bryden, who had first met Khama five years before, was gratified to find that Khama recognized and greeted people whom he had met at Palapye. The *African Critic* reported that Khama, Sebele, and Bathoen had been impressed not only by green fields and sheep and cattle seen from trains, but also by "the endless miles of houses and innumerable thousands of souls that go to make up London."

The writer credited these "intelligent farmers" with an understanding of the English class system that would benefit them: "They appear to have formed more adequate and precise notions of what is meant by our nobility—our headmen they term them—than any previous native visitors from South African shores."

The *African Critic* of September 14 commented on the interview with the chiefs in the *Daily Chronicle* a week earlier. The *Chronicle* had called Khama's refusal to rehearse his quarrel with Cecil Rhodes—because "Mr. Rhodes has asked me to forgive him"—the answer of a true king. The *African Critic,* quoting Tennyson, thought the answer more that of a kind heart than of a coronet.

The *African Critic* and the Cape newspapers picked up on comments in the German press. *Berliner Zeitung* suggested that Rhodes might bear in mind that Khama could ally with the Boers or the Germans instead. *Vossiche Zeitung* made a similar point: "The power of England on the Limpopo and the Zambesi is not so firmly established that British statesmen can afford to despise the friendship of native rulers."[7]

THURSDAY, SEPTEMBER 12

Armfield's Hotel was by now, as the *Home Budget of the Cape Times* noted, "besieged by a curious crowd, which eagerly awaits the comings in and goings out of our dusky visitors." The reporter of *South Africa*, probably its editor, E. P. Mathers (1850–1924), who arrived at the hotel for a 9:30 A.M. appointment on Thursday, discovered that "the hall porter finds he has rather more to do than he likes in the way of answering inquiries." *South Africa* was made to wait in the hotel lobby until a previous visitor had finished with Khama upstairs:

> Still I possessed my soul in patience, watching the burly forms of Sebele and Bathoen flitting in and out of the smoking room, followed by their black attendants. Many and inquisitive were the looks cast in their direction by the fair maidens and their attendant swains.

South Africa was to return on more than one subsequent occasion to observations on the sexual frisson that the swarthy visitors excited for some British women. Sebele and Khama's secretary Seisa were probably regarded as the most attractive, while Kwenaetsile was the most directly flirtatious.

> It was great fun, too, watching the Bechuanas walking downstairs; they seemed so painfully nervous, a feeling born, doubtless, of sad experiences [in rolling ship's corridors] on board the *Tantallon Castle*. But, at last, Mr. Willoughby appeared upon the scene, looking quite worn out with all the wear and tear of the last few days.

The reporter was taken upstairs to "a comfortable room on the first floor" with a mantelpiece "decked with sundry Bibles." Khama sat there "in company with a portly, sleek-faced native"—probably Seisa, though Besele or Stephen Lefenya from the Wesleyan delegation may also have been visiting to pick up intelligence on the previous day's meeting with Chamberlain.

> The Chief rose and greeted me courteously, English-wise, with a hearty hand-shake and "How do you do?" Taking a chair, and producing the inevitable note book and pencil, I took stock of the much-talked-of Khama. He is tall and remarkably slender, with a look of determination and energy on his face, though at times when asked a question he half closes his eyes in a sleepy fashion.

Had Khama seen Mr. Chamberlain yesterday? Yes, he had: "I spoke about some matters with him, but he was not able to go fully into them [until] he returns." Why had Khama come to England—to see the sights and "wonders of civilisation," to see the queen, or for some political reason? *South Africa* added: "Would you mind telling us your real object?"

Khama gave an evasive answer: "There is nothing more to hear. Everybody knows. I really can say nothing."

Willoughby intervened with the explanation that Khama was tired of being asked the same questions and having to give the same answers over and over again in interviews. After a somewhat frosty exchange with Willoughby, the reporter managed to get the point about journalistic rivalries across to Khama through Willoughby:

> I rejoined, [saying] well, let him know that there are the same jealousies among interviewers as there are between his indunas, and that instead of helping one another we try to conceal news. At this the Chief laughed heartily, and my drooping spirits revived.

Khama explained "in mellifluous Sechuana" that he had come to England because he and his people had heard news of [Rhodes announcing] his country's impending annexation, and "They had naturally enough followed the course of events in Rhodesia, and disapproved of the way in which the Chartered Company had dealt with the land in Matabeleland." He saw hundreds of wagons full of liquor going to Matabeleland and feared that the company would curtail his "rights and privileges." So he had come to the imperial government to get "full possession of the facts of the case . . . and to defend the interests of his people."

The interview went on to explore the issues raised by Khama. The land issue was one of "water rights" as well as "garden rights." Khama tackled the "mistaken impression" given by some white travelers that his country was underused by his people and their cattle. They saw only the water points ("permanent waters" including wells and riverbeds) on the "main transport roads," which his people avoided with their cattle for fear of infection by bovine lung-sickness among transport oxen. As for the rest of his country,

> There are indeed very few of the pastures near the permanent waters that are not stocked with as many cattle as they can carry, though it may be that some few could carry a little more.

As for the apparently excess land around a "reserve" for his own people that Khama had offered to the British ten years before in 1885—the so-called magnificent offer—that offer had had to be withdrawn "owing to the great increase both of population and the number of cattle." There was also no question of surrendering hunting land, as Khama "insists . . . that all game in the country belongs to the Chief."

Khama's next point was the need for maintenance of the traditional system of justice for his people. The *South Africa* report continues:

> The circumlocution and terminology of English law were quite beyond their comprehension, and our pleadings and counter-pleadings are in their

eyes a sheer waste of time. They have a simple way of administering justice of their own, and of trying cases and sifting evidence by which they contrive to get to the bottom of the matter and find out of the truth, by which it is utterly impossible to get a man off on a technical quibble.

. . . what a native does not understand he mistrusts. Our judges would never find out the truth, hence injustice would be done sheerly from ignorance both of the language and customs of the people. Every man would tell his chief the truth, or . . . twenty others would be prepared to speak against him. But it is constitutional in the native to keep back part of the truth at least from the white man, if not to speak falsely altogether. . . . As regards cases between white men and black, Khama is willing that they should, as at present, be remitted to a white judge; but even white men prefer these cases coming before the Chief, as they are settled more expeditiously, at no cost, and equal justice is done.

Of course, one must also ask how much this indirect version of Khama's views was not also colored by the white-settler viewpoint of *South Africa*.

Khama and the *South Africa* representative then discussed the claims of the British South Africa Company in and to his country. Khama emphasized that the existing company concession in his country was confined to mineral rights under the ground and was held simply because "They have taken over the rights originally held by Messrs. Heany and Johnson, which have, however, been re-stated and made out in the name of the Company." As for the railway proposed by the company, "I shall not oppose the construction of the railway; but the conditions must be clearly stated."

This prompted *South Africa* to ask whether it was a sudden influx of whites (for the impending construction of the railway) into his country that had caused Khama to come to England? No, replied Khama: whites were "welcome, and can be controlled as at present."

What then was it that brought on this crisis so suddenly and acutely?

—It was Mr. Rhodes' statement in the Cape House of Assembly, during the debate on the Bechuanaland Annexation Bill, that the whole matter had been settled. There had been the idea of a visit to England at the end of last year, but it was this speech [that] brought it to a head, and caused me to visit England at this season.

At this point, *South Africa* started to ask Khama further questions on the dispute with his brother Raditladi, but the interview was interrupted by the arrival of Sir George Baden-Powell, MP, at the hotel. He had come to take the Bechuana chiefs on a tour of the Houses of Parliament in Westminster. (One later report suggests that the chiefs first went to see the Tower of London, which was in the opposite direction to Westminster; but this appears to be a confusion with the itinerary of the next day, Friday.) The *South Africa* representative asked to come back later in the day to finish the interview, and Khama agreed to continue in the afternoon.[8]

Khama and his secretary, Seisa—for Khama has a very bright secretary—drove to Westminster in Sir George's carriage. The others, with their missionary friends . . . followed in cabs.

The chiefs were shown through the House of Commons, the House of Lords, the committee rooms, and, indeed through the whole building. They readily grasped the purposes of the Houses of Parliament as the meeting place of the representatives of the English people. They also followed an explanation of the difference in the methods under which the members of the two Houses have the right to sit in them.

Their guide for the two-hour tour, interpreted by Edwin Lloyd, was a policeman, Inspector Kendrick (who was tipped 2s. 6d. for his pains). He showed them the House of Commons library, "and they all marvelled at the number of books." It was the general impression given by paintings and statuary of past politicians, and "the architecture and the extent of the buildings," rather than "minor details" such as the bench on which Gladstone sat and the dispatch box on which he leaned, that really excited their admiration.

South Africa reported that the Bechuana chiefs were "most of all struck with the handsome ceiling of the Robing Chamber." The *African Review* said that "the surroundings—the splendour and the brilliance—left perhaps an impression of astonished admiration." Asked what he thought of the Houses of Parliament, Sebele was caught off guard and replied, "It is wonderful, and I cannot tell what I thought." One of the attendants, possibly young Gohiwamang, said something like, "The English are gods." This remark prompted the *Globe* newspaper to speculate on the amount of irony in Setswana humor.[9]

That night Sir George Baden-Powell entertained them to dinner at his Eaton Square house in Belgravia. Lord Selborne and General Sir Charles Warren were also present, as was George's yet unknown younger brother Robert "Stephe" Baden-Powell. George Baden-Powell had been one of Liverpool's MPs since 1885, when he stood as a Liberal after his return from the Warren Expedition in Bechuanaland. He had first come to prominence in 1879 when he published a book advocating a commercial remedy of the so-called great depression through free trade—firstly with Britain's white-settler colonies, and secondly with the interiors of Africa and Southeast Asia.[10]

Sir Charles Warren had also stood as a Liberal candidate in the 1885 elections but had been unsuccessful, after indulging in a bitter *Times* correspondence with Cecil Rhodes over the activities of Sir Hercules Robinson as Britain's high commissioner in South Africa. Warren was now one of the most senior generals in the British army, as commander in chief of the Southern Command based at Chatham on the Thames estuary. He had just returned from directing military maneuvers in the New Forest.

Many years later Robert "Stephe" Baden-Powell, by then famous as Boy Scout movement founder and leader, recalled that evening at his brother's Eaton Square house. Khama had played with his hosts' children (who must have been mere babes, as George had married only in 1893) and then sat down to dinner "as if he had been used to it all his life." By contrast, Khama's own recollection soon after the event suggests some initial unease:

> Seated at the grand table of Sir G. Baden-Powell, what made me feel at home was not the beautiful glitter of diamonds worn by the ladies, but the simple little flowers and the asparagus leaf decorations. In my country the asparagus grows wild, and here in England I saw it festooned at the first dinner party I went to.

Khama added that he "felt at home sitting next to Lady Powell, for she, too, is an abstainer, and by us, at any rate, there was no wine." [11]

FRIDAY, SEPTEMBER 13

On the next morning the chiefs toured the Tower of London and Tower Bridge next to it on the Thames at the eastern end of the City. Admission for the whole party to the Tower cost 9s. 6d. (while the horse bus and train return cost 2s. 6d. in total). This castle, which confusingly had four towers rather than one, had been built by William the Conqueror on the remains of a Roman tower and stood guard on the river approach to the City of London from the sea. Red-liveried "yeomen of the guard" acted as guides. After being shown the towers and dungeons the chiefs were taken to see the crown jewels stored in its treasure house.

Bathoen was particularly impressed by the treasures of the Tower and the elaborate precautions taken to preserve them from theft. He uttered intriguing words that the *Christian World* thought "meant more, no doubt, than they seemed," and that continued to be quoted weeks and even years afterward: "England takes good care of all her things, but throws away her people." [12] (Was he by any chance referring to emigration?)

Next to the Tower of London stood the enormous iron superstructure of Tower Bridge (not to be confused with the stone London Bridge to the west), the engineering wonder of the late Victorian world. It was still gleaming new, as it had been opened to traffic only the year before, after nine years of construction. There was a large rigid walkway strung across between the tops of its high bridge-towers, which housed the steam equipment that raised and lowered the two halves of the roadway to accommodate the masts of ships passing in and out of the Pool of London.

The chiefs were shown over the bridge and its machinery rooms and possibly witnessed the raising of the roadway to allow a ship to pass. The number of such ships had been drastically reduced by the construction of many docks further downriver, but the Pool of London stretch of the river between Tower Bridge and London Bridge was still a busy port area.

It was probably on the way to or from the Tower, in a horse cab crawling through the crowded streets of the City of London, that Sebele demonstrated "the intensity of the impression made on [his] mind by the number of people in the streets." Willoughby recalled:

> We were riding in a cab through Cheapside, when the Chief asked:—
> "Are there any locusts in England?"
> "No," said I.
> "It wouldn't matter," said he.
> "Why?" I asked.
> "Because," said Sebele, "the Queen would simply issue an order that every one of her people should catch one, and then there would be none of them left."

On this or another occasion one of the chiefs asked Willoughby why Londoners never did any work. He had been watching them for some time: "They spend all their time just walking about the streets." Many years later Willoughby pointed out parallels here with the formation of the European myth of the "lazy black" in Africa.

Sebele was the most worldly-wise of all the Bechuana, but even he had been sheltered from the life in the London streets. As Willoughby told one journalist at about this time:

> And, strange as it may seem to you, the chiefs have not yet realised the drunkenness and vice of our country. We are rarely out, except in daylight, and driving from place to place, unable to decipher a single sign-board; they are yet literally in ignorance of the drink system which assails people on all hands.[13]

The touristic round on that Friday the thirteenth continued with visits to the two main London churches of the established Church of England, St. Paul's Cathedral in the City and Westminster Abbey a couple of miles upstream.

The chiefs were already familiar from a distance with St. Paul's, the enormous late-seventeenth century domed temple on Ludgate Hill, designed by Christopher Wren to rival and outstrip St. Peter's in Rome. They now entered the building and "were amazed at its vastness."

In Westminster Abbey, overlooked by the Victorian-Gothic towers of the Houses of Parliament, their taste for statuary would have been sated by numerous monuments to the sometimes great and rarely good plastered on the lower walls of the medieval minster—which had become a shrine for national heroes not entirely unlike Madame Tussaud's. The main attraction in the abbey for the chiefs was the memorial stone set in the floor above the mummified body of David Livingstone (his heart and entrails having been buried where he died in Africa). Here the chiefs "bowed reverently." The central position of the grave in the lower nave would have brought home to the chiefs, especially to Sebele, who had known the man personally, the significance of Dr. Livingstone within contemporary British culture as a great national hero now buried in the national shrine.

Both of that Friday's visits to churches appear to have been private ones, not conducted by a senior Anglican cleric such as a dean or canon but probably by lay vergers. The chiefs were still very much associated with Nonconformism rather than Anglicanism. Quite possibly their main guides that day were from the headquarters staff of the LMS, which could also have covered their cab fares.[14]

The *South Africa* representative returned to Armfield's Hotel late that afternoon to finish the interview with Khama and Willoughby. Khama denounced his half brother Raditladi as "cunning, ambitious, extremely clever, but, above all, unscrupulous in his methods . . . to gain entire independence" and related the story of the Moffat inquiry and the arrival at Palapye of Jameson—who told Khama that his country's annexation had "already been settled between Mr. Rhodes and the great officers of the Queen."

It was probably on Friday evening that a representative of the *Illustrated London News* came round to talk to the chiefs, in preparation for a feature article signed by "J.M." to be published eight days later. Guided through linguistic pitfalls by Willoughby and Lloyd and Willoughby's little son, "J.M." probably got the most accurate estimates of the ages of the chiefs— Khama sixty-one, Sebele and Bathoen fifty-seven—given in any publication. The journalist gleaned guarded remarks on their political mission from Khama and had a much longer "chat" with Sebele—"who in some ways is the most remarkable personality of the whole group." Sebele told "J.M." enthusiastically how as a child he had been one of the first scholars in Livingstone's school:

> It was at this time that our nation began to read, and I still know the hymns we learned in the school. Also it was about this time the troubles of my father began with the Boers, and Livingstone said it would be better for him if he were living at another place in the land. I liked Livingstone very much as a boy, and all the people liked him.

"Why did you like him—didn't he whip you in the school?" added Willoughby jocularly. "Oh no, he didn't whip me." Sebele's reply caused all the chiefs and attendants to laugh too. "J.M." of the *Illustrated London News* then ventured a very large question indeed: what did Africans think of "the advance and increase of the white man in Africa?" Sebele replied:

> We distinguish between white men and white men, for there are those who remain and those who just seek gain that they may return home again. At first we saw the white people pass, and we said, "They are going to hunt for elephant-tusks and ostrich-feathers, and they will return where they came from." We saw first Oswald, then Gordon-Cumming, but now when we see the white men we say "Jah! Jah!" ("Oh dear! Oh dear!"). And now we think of the white people like rain, for they come down as a flood, and we [can] do nothing to stop the flood. When it rains too much, it puts a stop to us all.
>
> We never thought they would find gold and diamonds in the country, but now they have come to stop. It is not good for the black people that there should be a multitude of white men.

Here, no doubt with an eye on his missionary interpreter, Sebele quickly added that

> the natives simply rejoice to see the missionaries. They are our friends, and without them and the Gospel we should have no life at all, and we should not be in England now, for we should have had no friends.
>
> What we shall see in time to come I do not know, but I know we have seen trouble.[15]

SIX

A Kind of Middle-Class Royalty

-→⋗⧟⊃ ⊂⧟⋖←-

NOW THAT CHAMBERLAIN HAD BEEN CONTACTED, AND the long waiting period for his return began, Willoughby set about planning the itinerary of the Bechuana chiefs' great journey and speaking tour around Britain. Contacts were made with Nonconformist chapels anxious for the chiefs to visit, more often than not as part of local celebrations of the London Missionary Society centenary. The chiefs were also due to help start the centenary celebrations at LMS headquarters in London. But first they would test the waters in the provinces beyond London, by venturing to Brighton and Bristol.

Saturday, September 14 – Sunday, September 15

On Saturday, September 14, the chiefs and their attendants accompanied Willoughby by second-class train from London Bridge station (cabs 4s. 6d.) to Brighton (return railway fare £1 18s. 6d.) on the south coast. (Above the entry for these fares in Willoughby's accounts is three shillings for another "Baker St. Return" fare. Did the Bechuana chiefs go to Madame Tussaud's for a second look, this time free of charge, that Saturday morning?)

In Brighton they were to stay for two nights in the Ditchling Road residence of Mr. George E. Singleton, secretary of the Union Street Congregational Church. Willoughby himself stayed with other friends, while his young son stayed on with the chiefs, with whom by all accounts (as a native Setswana-speaker himself) he got on very well

Singleton took them all to the seafront on Saturday afternoon to see the fish swimming behind the glass walls of tanks in the Brighton Aquarium. The chiefs with young Willoughby as interpreter strolled along the seafront embankment and down the West Pier, causing quite a stir in their frock coats and silk hats, and listened to a promenade concert at the Brighton Pavilion.

The chiefs attended the Union Street chapel on Sunday, twice, both morning and evening. Willoughby was its former pastor and gave "addresses on mission labours." On the Sunday morning even the famous secularist and socialist G. J. Holyoake came to church that day. Holyoake, radical old author of *Sixty Years of an Agitator's Life* (1892), had devoted his career to weaning the labor movement from Nonconformism and religion in general. But the chiefs were not paraded before the congregation, on the contrary being relegated to a back pew.

Willoughby's sermon said how a century ago the map of Africa was a catalog of "blanks and blunders," as were the maps of India, China, Asia Minor—and South America, at least for Protestants. But now the world was tied up into one by the missionaries, aided by the progress of the (British) nation. There were now Scriptures in four hundred languages, and seven thousand Protestant missionaries with three million converts. Best of all, there were thirty thousand native evangelists, of whom three thousand were educated, responsible pastors—"for the world will never be Christianized by white lips alone." What more eloquent answer to the critics of missionaries could there be? It was true that social iniquities and anti-Christian sentiment persisted at home—had Willoughby spotted Holyoake in the congregation?—but this must not stop the work abroad.

The *Brighton Herald* recorded that at the end of the service "a large number of the congregation availed themselves of the opportunity of shaking the Chiefs by the hand." Khama beamed and bowed. Sebele received greetings with "gravity and stateliness." Bathoen was said to be "almost deferential" to those he met.

On the Sunday afternoon the chiefs visited a local magistrate, Mr. D. Hack, and had tea with Edna (Mrs C. H.) Lyall, née Bayly, the editor of James Hepburn's *Twenty Years in Khama's Country*. She was visiting England from Cape Town and had come to stay with a friend in Montpelier Road, Brighton, "with the express purpose of meeting the chiefs."

At the end of the evening service, after Willoughby's account of mission life in Khama's country, with the building crowded to the doors, the pastor of the church, Rev. R. J. Campbell, "asked those of the congregation who sympathised with Khama to rise, and immediately everyone rose. Mr Willoughby interpreted this to the chief, and then expressed Khama's thanks for the kind feelings which had been shown towards him." [1]

MONDAY, SEPTEMBER 16

The next morning the chiefs visited higher (primary) grade York Place School. Before returning to London on the train, Khama left three ostrich feathers (on which he had spent four shillings in packing material) for Mrs. Lyall, "the little lady whose eyes point out a kind heart." Khama said later that same day:

> I and my brother chiefs all agree that we like Brighton far better than London. There is beauty there, and air, and sun-shine, and sea. We met with kindness in London, but the friendliness of the people in Brighton made us feel really at home.

In London Khama, Sebele, and Bathoen stopped at their hotel in Finsbury before going on to the West Country that afternoon. Soon after they arrived at Armfield's, a journalist called Mrs. Fenwick Miller, who wrote under the name "Flora," came to interview Khama. The interview was published in the *Echo* two days later.

> Calling at his hotel, I found that he and the other chiefs, Sebele and Bathoen, had just returned from Brighton. They had already something of the fatigued look borne of too-pressing publicity.

Willoughby—"guide, philosopher and friend for the whole party"— explained:

> Only an hour ago we were back from Brighton; this evening we start for Bristol; then, by the wish of the Colonial Office, Khama is to visit Aldershot, and what with the (L.M.S.) Founders' Missionary Week in view, the Congregational Union meetings, with trips up the Thames and to the Crystal Palace thrown in, we have not an idle moment on our hands.

"Flora" lavished her attention on Khama, whom she described as having "one of the most delightful and fascinating smiles which ever irradiated a human presence [and which] flashes only now and again upon a thoughtful and somewhat stern expression." Khama had been described to her by "an enterprising phrenologist" as "A nineteenth century Oliver Cromwell, to whom the destinies of England might well be entrusted for a space."

She asked Khama what he thought of London. He replied:

> KHAMA: It is big, but not beautiful. St. Paul's is immense, your Parliament House and Westminster Abbey are grand. But your city is so big; it does not appeal to me. . . .
> FLORA: Then what do you admire most in England?
> KHAMA: Of all we have seen, there is one thing we marvel at more than at anything else, and that is the greenness of everything and the softness of the turf. I walked for the first time the other day over real turf, cut short, and soft as moss. We cannot comprehend how it is made to grow like that.

The next thing that strikes us is that you always have water enough and to spare. How I wish your turf and your water could be introduced into my country; but that is impossible. I admire these two things more than all your fine buildings and streets.

FLORA: You are a lover of Nature, then?

KHAMA: Yes, indeed, of all God's works—the flowers and the trees.

FLORA: What, then, may I ask, do you find to criticise over here?

KHAMA: There is one thing startles me more than any other. I am a great lover of animals, especially of horses and dogs. They are my constant friends and companions. I am quite proud of my stud. Now, over here, in your London streets, I notice so many, indeed, quite an extraordinary number, of your cab and omnibus horses go lame. If you watch you will see. I am trying to discover the cause. If the cause can be found, a humane people like the English will surely find a remedy.

You have splendid horses, and your St. Bernard dogs I admire more than any I have ever seen. I should take some home, but I fear the heat of our climate might not suit them.

But your cab horses are a puzzle to me. You have beautifully smooth pavements, and I can see many of these poor creatures have sore feet. But, then, we are here not to find fault, but to learn. We shall visit your cities, and especially your great manufacturing ones, for that purpose.

"Flora" thought it wise to retreat when Bathoen turned the tables on her. "He is puzzled," said the interpreter, "to find so many unmarried ladies over here, for with them marriage is almost absolutely universal—it puzzles him very much."

"Yes," added Bathoen," I want to know if you are married, and if not, why not? Has no man ever asked you?"

This led the *African Critic* to muse on how Bathoen could possibly have found out that there were so many unmarried ladies "over here": "Has he had a few offers from eligible spinsters who imagine him unable to distinguish between leap and non-leap years?"[2]

The chiefs then left for Bristol, traveling once more on the Great Western Railway, from Paddington Station (fare £5 10s.).

TUESDAY, SEPTEMBER 17

The chiefs had gone to Bristol with Willoughby and Lloyd to attend the local celebrations of the London Missionary Society centenary at a breakfast meeting in the Victoria Rooms, Clifton. (Three months earlier the same hall had been the scene of celebrations of a different kind—for the hundredth century scored by the great cricketer Dr. W. G. Grace). Lloyd had once lived in Bristol, attending Redland Park Chapel. Now in 1895 Bristol Congregationalists had raised £2,643 for foreign missions and had just sent a medical missionary, Dr. Ethel Tribe, to China.

The large hall of the Victoria Rooms was crowded out, with tickets oversubscribed, according to the *Western Daily Press* partly because of the advertised presence of the chiefs. The meeting was chaired by the tobacco baron S. D. Wills, who recalled that his father, the second H. O. Wills, had presided over a similar enthusiastic meeting to greet Robert Moffat twenty-four years earlier. His main point was to call for an increase in the number of women missionaries.

A Baptist speaker read the roll of honor of Free Church mission societies, beginning with William Carey's Baptist mission society in 1792 and the London mission in 1795, followed in the years up to 1815 by Scottish Presbyterians, Evangelical Anglicans, American Congregationalists, Wesleyans, and Lutherans—in that order. (He conveniently overlooked the Society for the Propagation of the Gospel of 1701, as well as bodies founded abroad, such as the Jesuits and the Moravians.)

At this point the three chiefs entered and took seats on the platform, bowing to the deafening applause. Khama was given a somewhat compromising introduction by the pacifistic Mr. F. N. Tribe, father of Dr. Tribe and secretary of the Bristol Missionary Society. He was introduced as one who had helped the British "in one of those wars they so much deplored in South Africa, but although they deplored the war they none the less appreciated [his] loyalty to England." Sebele was singled out by Tribe as "not a Christian . . . but taught to read by Livingstone himself, his father being an intimate friend and companion of Livingstone. (Applause.)"

Khama, Sebele, and Bathoen now faced a large crowded audience of the English public for the first time. (They had sat in "a back pew at the far end under a gallery, out of sight of many of the congregation" at Brighton.) Khama, with "well-lined features, his face looking careworn," delivered, with Lloyd interpreting, what was to be one of his shortest speeches during the odyssey of the chiefs:

> We rejoice to see you to-day and to greet the Christian churches in this city. We, the people of Bechuanaland—chiefs—have come to this country to see these lands, to greet the ministers and the Christian people in this land, and we rejoice very much on account of the way in which you have received and welcomed us. Although we are black people, we are only one people in Jesus Christ. (Applause.) Again, we are people who have very strong objections to strong drink. (Loud applause.) We rejoice that you receive such words so kindly, and we entreat you to help us with all your power in this battle against strong drink. Liquor—we fear it very much. It is a great destruction in all the country. It also destroys the churches. (Hear, hear.) Liquor is like armies that destroy all people. (Hear, hear.) These are all my words.

Bathoen spoke much the same: "Though a person has become a Christian, if he loves liquor he is in danger of being destroyed by it. (Applause.)"

The *Bristol Mercury* remarked on the contrast between the three chiefs in speech and looks: how light-complexioned Bathoen was by comparison with Khama, while "Sebele is very dark, with iron grey whiskers, and he speaks with much ease and fluency his native Sechuana tongue . . . full of figure and metaphor." Sebele's speech played on the name of David Livingstone, which he had discovered to be the magic mantra that cued applause from virtually any British audience:

> I began to see missionaries by seeing the first of them, namely, Livingstone. (Loud applause.) He came proclaiming the word of God. Before that lots of black people had come, and they said they were proclaiming the word of God, but we did not, and could not, understand properly, or what they were after. But when David Livingstone came it was then we really began to understand the meaning of the word of God.

After the meeting closed, the chiefs were taken on a tour of "the principal industrial centres of the city":

> As Mr. Charles Wills had placed his carriage at their disposal they first visited Messrs. Charles Wills and Sons' wholesale clothing manufactory in Rupert-street. They were received by Mr. Charles Wills, who assured Khama that he had followed his career with interest, and especially that period of it in which he did splendid service to the Mother Country. He also fully appreciated the views to which the Chiefs had given utterance with respect to the use of stimulants amongst their tribes.
>
> The Chiefs then went over the factory and examined the various processes of clothes making from the cutting of the cloth to the finished article and the making of button holes. This latter work seemed to interest them most of all, but they were not a little astonished when they learned in the button department that 144 buttons could be bought for eightpence. They thought it perfectly marvellous.

The *Western Press* added that besides the amazing buttonhole machines, which cut and sewed a new buttonhole every twelve seconds, they "saw the most modern machinery . . . cutting cloth and other material about twenty thicknesses at a time." The two-hour visit ended in the stockroom, where the chiefs asked more "pertinent questions" about made-up (ready-to-wear) clothing being piled up for export to South Africa and elsewhere.

At the end of the tour Bathoen remarked that England truly was "the fountain of clothes."

The chiefs, accompanied by their two missionaries, plus Rev. U. R. Thomas of the Methodists and Dr. Tribe's father, ventured onward on their industrial mission through the city of Bristol in their carriages—

Khama specially negotiating for a box seat, because he "was delighted to see the fine horses fast going at the mere wish of the coachman."

It was intended to show the Chiefs several other industries, but they had difficulty in getting further than the extensive tobacco factory of Messrs. W. D. & H. O. Wills in Bedminster, where they spent between two and three hours, nearly every moment of which was devoted to the minute examination of the various stages of manufacturing tobacco from the leaf into the smokable article.

Mr. George Wills and Mr. Melville Wills conducted the Chiefs round the large factory, where they were astounded to find nearly 1500 work-people employed in the various departments. The visitors were not a little astonished at the difference between the manufactured tobacco here and that which they smoke in Bechuanaland. The Rev. W. C. Willoughby, who interpreted . . . almost looked askance at the prospect before him of an-swering innumerable questions on all these matters when the visitors got him in a quiet corner in the evening. Before leaving the factory the Chiefs were invited to tea with the members of the firm.

It was at Clifton that Willoughby managed to get the chiefs unawares to walk onto Brunel's narrow iron road bridge above the deep gorge of the river Avon (see introduction of this book).

Bristol had, of course, once thrived on the proceeds of the West African slave trade. Such was the reason for the *Westminster Gazette*'s sarcasm, much resented by the *Bristol Mercury:* "Bristol was most impressed with the visi-tors—whom not very long ago she would have been anxious to secure as slaves." [3]

WEDNESDAY, SEPTEMBER 18

Early the next morning the chiefs traveled back toward London, stopping off for the day at Reading. Here at the station they "were received by the Hon. Eustace Fiennes (by whom the visit was arranged), Mr Martin J. Sutton, and other gentlemen." Even the *Times* the next day had a short note on this visit:

The party were entertained at breakfast by Messrs. Sutton, and afterwards went over the warehouses of that firm, inspecting the bulb rooms, the export department, and afterwards the seed grounds. Mr. Fiennes then entertained the visitors, as well as the borough and county members, at lunch at his residence near Reading. In the afternoon a visit was made to Messrs. Huntley and Palmer's biscuit factory.

The chiefs were reportedly "much pleased with all they saw."

Shortly after five o'clock they drove to the Great Western Railway Station, where Mr. Gibbs, the [railway?] divisional superintendent, with Mrs. and

Misses Gibbs, were introduced and shook hands. In reply to Mr. Gibbs, who through the interpreter conveyed his hope that the party had enjoyed their visit to Reading, Khama said he had been very much pleased with his reception and the large business establishments he had inspected.

A well-known representative of one of the Berkshire county papers, who was also introduced, expressed his hope that Khama's mission would be attended with satisfactory results, and that he and his companions would have a safe return to their native land. Khama warmly thanked the journalist for his good wishes.

The party left by the half-past five express for Paddington, their departure being witnessed by a considerable number of spectators.[4]

THURSDAY, SEPTEMBER 19 – FRIDAY, SEPTEMBER 20

That Thursday evening the Bechuana visited the Crystal Palace, the industrial exhibition hall made of iron and glass, bigger than a cathedral, that had been built for the 1851 Great Exhibition in Hyde Park and had then been reconstructed on the hills of Sydenham south of London.

They attended the 6:30 show of Carl Hagenbeck's Somali Display, East African Village, and ostrich farm (admissions 2s., 1s., or 6d.) at Crystal Palace. The ostriches would have been familiar to them, the sixty-five Somali villagers (from an African country as close to the Balkans as to Bechuanaland) much less so. There was also an exhibition of loan material from collectors of African arts and crafts, the sole remnant of the exhibition's originally planned southern African theme. The chiefs were treated to displays of the Somali racing horses, dromedary camels, and ostriches, and they were "greatly pleased by their entertainment."[5]

Their next appointment was on Friday afternoon with the Oceana Company, holders of a mineral concession in Bathoen's country and rivals of the BSA Company. Let the *South Africa* journal take up the story:

> On Friday afternoon, from four o'clock onwards, those who were strolling on the Thames Embankment, near Westminster, might have seen the steamer *Bismarck,* of the Victoria Steamboat Association, lying alongside Westminster Pier. She had two bright blue flags flying, each bearing in its centre a large white O, which, of course, represented the monogram of the Oceana Company. For they were to entertain the three Bechuana chiefs, and had chartered this steamer to carry their guests to Greenwich.
>
> From a few minutes after Big Ben had boomed out the hour of four, one by one smartly-dressed men came dropping down to the pier, looked at the boat, and stood chatting around. The deck of the steamer was covered with a bright crimson carpet, and on the seats were crimson red cushions. The minutes passed quickly by, but the chiefs did not put in an appearance, and anxious eyes wandered between the clock of the Houses of Parliament and the steps down which Khama and his fellows were ex-

pected to come; but still they lingered, and messengers were sent in all directions, and the telegraph called into use; all sorts of rumours flying round the while. Till finally, at a quarter-past five, the guests arrived, to the great relief of those who had been shivering on the pier.

First came the burly Bathoen (really the hero of the day), limping slightly, as though suffering from gout; then the slim, tall figure of Khama, who was perfectly well dressed, while, in his wake, the tall and stately Sebele sailed along, closely followed by Seisa, Khama's English-speaking Secretary, who was trained at Lovedale. It turned out eventually that the chiefs had been detained by the incursion of a deputation of ladies just as they were starting; and no wonder! Anyone might have been detained by so fair a cause, especially if they were sympathetic.

As soon as the party was on board, the *Bismarck* started, blowing off steam the while as a parting salute. As the boat went down the river, all the objects of interest, historical and otherwise, were pointed out to the illustrious visitors; though the trip did not last very long, Greenwich being reached in 35 minutes. . . .

When Greenwich was reached, the party straightaway left the boat and went up to the "Ship Hotel," the grounds of which were prepared for lighting up later on. Among those assembled in the ante-room before dinner were the three chiefs and their suite, Sir Frederick Young, Mr. T. Fowler, Rev. Brooke Lambert, Messrs. C. A. V. Conybeare, F. A. Bullock, H. F. J. Weber, Dicey, Foss, Schuster, Doctor J. Oppenheim, C. G. Kekewich, C. H. Pasteur, J. Ochs, Morton Lambert, A. L. Secretan, Murray, H. P. Hill, E. Hannan, G. H. Kearton, Toulmin, J. Smith, and Revs. C. J. [*sic*] Willoughby and E. Lloyd.

The dinner was most *recherché*, and reflected the greatest credit on the "Ship Hotel," and was well worthy the hospitality of the important company who were hosts on the occasion. The table was most elegantly decorated with flowers, to the great delight of the guests. The chair was taken by Mr. C. A. V. Conybeare, Managing Director of the Oceana Company, owing to the absence of the Chairman. It transpired that the Oceana Company acted as hosts on this occasion because of the very large interests they hold in the Bangwaketse Company, which has extensive concessions in Bathoen's territory. Hence he was the principal guest of the evening and sat on the Chairman's right hand, while Sebele was on the Chairman's left. The following was the

MENU
Tortue Claire   Tortue Liée
Gras Verts au Jus

—+ ≡+≡ +—

Carrelets Souché
Saumon Souché
Whitebait
Rissoles de Crevisres   Petites Soles Frites
Boudins de Merlans à la Danoise
Anguilles Etuvée à la Bordelaise

Omelette de Crabe au Cordon Bleu
Côtelettes de Saumon à l'Indienne
Rouge et Noir
Kari de Crevettes à l'Hindoostanie au Riz
Salade de Homard Mayonaisse

Ris de Veau à la Financière

Quartier d'Agneau Rôtis et Haricôts Verts

Coq de Bruyere et Perdreaux Rôtis
Pomme de Terre Frits

Asperges en Branches Glacé

Jambon Grillié et Salade de Tamate

DESSERT

Gelés au Vin   Dames d'Honneur
Meringues à la Crême
Nougat à la Chantilly

Pouding à la Neselrode

Glaces
Crême d'Ananas   Eau de Raisins

VINS

Pouché Frappé
E. I. Madeira
Macrobrunner Cabinet vint. 1862
Moet Imperial vint. 1884, Cuvée 1714
Irroy Carte d'Or vint. 1878
Liqueurs.
Chateau Lafite vint. 1874
Cockburn's Port vint. 1868
Brown Sherry vint. 1865

Café

When grace had been said by the vicar of Greenwich, the CHAIRMAN said it was proposed to have one or two toasts. It was his pleasure and his duty to propose "The Queen" . . . and he would therefore ask Mr. Lloyd to explain that Englishmen always honour their sovereign in this fashion at all gatherings of this kind. The toast was, of course, honoured by all; the chiefs drinking it in some teetotal beverage.

The CHAIRMAN then said that they would not indulge in a long toast list, but there were a few appropriate toasts; the first, the principal one of the evening, was that of the chiefs, Khama, Bathoen, and Sebele. He would propose it himself, and would ask Sir Frederick Young and Sir Douglas

Straight to second it, and Rev. Brooke Lambert to support it. The Oceana Company wished to show the chiefs whatever civility they could, not principally because they happened to be connected with their territories, but because it was the duty of all Englishmen to do what they could to make pleasant the first visit of these gentlemen to this country. . . . They who represented the Oceana Company took great interest in recognising in the chief Bathoen a nearer link, as they were his tenants.

Another report had the chairman "offering support to them in their attempt to keep out what was bad in Western civilization from their country." In this atmosphere of flowing wine and conviviality, Reverend Lambert struck a more sober note, maintaining "that we have something to learn as well as to teach, and that we must, in dealing with other races, drop our insular pride."

Sebele, in reply to the toast, remarked how pleased they were with the hospitality of England, picking up Bathoen's phrase used in Bristol about England being the great manufactory and source of all "things."

The Ship was the main inn on the Greenwich waterfront, on the site of the pre-Roman settlement on the western side of Greenwich Palace (taken over by University of Greenwich in 1997), where the riverboats landed their passengers. (The inn closed in 1908 and later made way for the *Cutty Sark*'s dry dock.) Like the Trafalgar on the eastern side of Greenwich Palace, The Ship was famous for its whitebait (sprat) fish dinners eaten by businessmen and politicians on annual trips by steamboat down the Thames.

A press dispatch—carried in such newspapers as the *Devon Gazette* and the *Nottingham Guardian*—reported that the Bechuana chiefs' evening in Greenwich was really a junket for sixty or seventy members and supporters of the Oceana Company, including "kindred spirits" from the London Stock Exchange "Kaffir market," one or two Colonial Office officials, and a City alderman. The menu was a "triumph of culinary science [with] every imaginable thing in season and out of season," and the wines "would make a world-wide reputation for the table of any private host." This fare ensured that everyone had "what schoolboys would call 'a right royal time' . . . [though] the conversation was decidedly 'shoppy.'"

> The dinner . . . which must have cost at least five guineas a head, was a thing to be remembered by all who were present.
> Poor old Khama, however, seemed rather bored with it all. Some of the delicate items in the programme did not seem to tickle his palate very much, but he ate tremendously of the dessert which, like everything else, had been provided regardless of the expense.

The *Court Journal* mused "There . . . seemed to be something lying very heavy on the King's mind—could it have been Mr. Chamberlain!" and added that the dinner ended with "a supplementary banquet of fruits of all kinds in the highest state of perfection." (The frequent additional expenditure on "fruit" recorded in Willoughby's financial accounts confirms such taste on the part of the Bechuana.) Though reported as so in some newspapers, it scarcely seems as if the chiefs would have had time that evening to have visited the sights such as the chapel and banqueting hall in the Palace between the Ship and Trafalgar Hotels, before returning on the steamboat to Westminster.

The raucous evening was not without deeper significance to be exploited. The cause of the Bechuana chiefs had now moved beyond preacher and pulpit into the realms of finance and big business, and of commercial interests jealous or suspicious of the monopolistic power of the Chartered Company. The ordinary general meeting of the Oceana Company's subsidiary Kanya [Kanye] Exploration Company, held in the first month of January 1895, had protested at the British government's obvious complicity with the Chartered Company in trying to wipe out rival concessions in Bechuanaland. The Kanya Company insisted on the "sovereign rights and powers" of *Kgosi* Bathoen, as its concession giver, as the bedrock of its rights over and against the Chartered Company.[6]

SATURDAY, SEPTEMBER 21 – SUNDAY, SEPTEMBER 22

After breakfast on the Saturday, the chiefs were interviewed once again by a press representative. They did not consider it surprising that they were such objects of interest. In a letter to Willoughby this particular journalist, from the *Westminster Gazette*, explained his motivation as being to collect

> the first impressions, made by a visit to the seat of a great empire, on men of intelligence but still in the tribal state of development. One would like very much to-day to read a Roman interview with some contemporary of Arminius who had come to Rome to get his wrongs righted. . . . his impressions of the Italian scene, and of the stir and movement of the Imperial city, would to-day be fascinating reading.

As a result he was granted an early morning appointment at the chiefs' hotel in Finsbury.

> When I arrived, the Chiefs, having finished breakfast, were at prayers, and consequently I had to wait a while. The minutes, however, passed pleasantly enough in conversation with Mr. Stead, who has chosen Khama as the subject of his next character sketch in the *Review of Reviews*. At last I was able to accompany Mr. Willoughby upstairs. . . .
>
>   In the breakfast-room, from the long central table of which the snowy damask cloth had not been removed, sat Khama, Bathoen, and Sebele. Their personal appearance has sufficiently been described already by oth-

ers, but it occurred to me that, save for the colour of their skins, they resembled a group of somewhat stolid but thoughtful English farmers. They made no sign of greeting which surprised me.

The journalist considered himself an old hand at interviewing African potentates:

> for I have been the object of the majestic courtesy of Prince Ademuyiwa, of Jebu Remo, and of the *camaraderie* which accompanied *insouciance* of Nonguana, that Prince of the Swazis at whose hands Sir Ellis Ashmead-Bartlett received the title and dignity of Silomo. I remember how Nonguanga, seated on the side of his bed, at my request sang a song of love, and then one of war.
>
> A glimpse of Khama, Bathoen and Sebele was enough to convince me that to ask for a solo, duet, or trio would be of the wildest tactlessness. Indeed, I was so filled by their reticent quiet, with a sense of their personal dignity, that, to recover my *aplomb* and ordinary ease of mind, I began the interview by putting a question to Mr. Willoughby.

The journalist contented himself with talking to Willoughby until Simeon Seisa, as another interpreter, "had taken his seat at the head of the table, and very alert and shrewd he looked with his bright, pleasant, genial smile." One suspects that there had been some disagreement between the chiefs and Willoughby, and between the chiefs themselves, which had been solved by calling in Seisa to interpret. This would not be the last time when there was tension between the chiefs and with Willoughby in their long and testing period of cohabitation.

The *Westminster Gazette* began with a prosaic question. Willoughby interrupted the journalist and asked him to rephrase it. The question was then put thus: "You have no sea in your country. What do you say of the great waters you crossed?" The answer was prosaic enough:

> "We think it is a wonderful thing to go upon the sea, where there is no road, and yet to go, day and night, straight to the point at which we wish to arrive. . . ."
>
> "Do the Chiefs know how the English sailors accomplished this marvel?"
>
> "Yes, they showed us some irons; they called it a compass."

Questions and answers on the chiefs' progress through England, interpreted probably through Seisa, carried on in like manner, except when Willoughby interjected with his own reminiscences and his views of their views.

> "Well," I began again, "was England what you expected to find it?"
>
> "We were very pleased to see England," replied the Chiefs, "and to see fine houses, fine gardens, and the green grass."

"The grass," interposed Mr. Willoughby, "struck them more than anything else. They were making remarks in the train all the way up on the beauty of the grass and the trees. Greenness like that is unknown in Bechuanaland."

"And some more impressions, please."

"We have seen people," said the Chiefs, "very many people indeed, who know well how to prepare tobacco. We have also seen a crowd of people who know how to prepare bread, biscuits, and cake"—they employed here a Bechuana word, which denoted anything baked—"we have seen again a very large number of persons sewing men's clothes, and, as for seeds, and how to sow, and prepare them."

"What did you think of the Underground Railway?"

"We were very much surprised to see the train go under the ground, like the conies burrowing under the rocks."

"I suppose you get the idea of conies from Scripture?"

"Oh no," said Mr Willoughby, "there are plenty about Palapye."

After Willoughby had told the tale of the chiefs' adventure on Clifton Bridge, the *Westminster Gazette* asked Willoughby:

> "And what do they think of all this interviewing, and the interviewers?"
> "They call the interviewers 'hunters of words,'" said Mr. Willoughby: "The interviewers have all been gentlemen, except such as were ladies."
> "And they understand the reason for it all?
> "Oh, yes, they understand that, being strangers, they are likely to be objects of interest."

The *Westminster Gazette* concluded that the Bechuana chiefs were "quiet, shrewd, self-possessed men" with "no trace of affectation, such as a cynic might have suspected in his Majesty Jebu Remo; of the rollicking Bohemian gaiety of the Swazi Prince; nor of the arrogant smartness of the Ashanti Envoys, when these latter had their tweed suits and their shoes on."[7]

Other journalists were more than a little disappointed by this unbefitting lack of glamour on the part of the three kings from Bechuanaland. They took aim at Khama as "an economical monarch," who according to the *Liverpool Mercury* "puzzles the splendour-loving cockney by acting like an ordinary mortal instead of like a king, though only an African king." Thus the *African Critic* of the twenty-first remarked:

> It seems to be quite a grievance with the scribe tribe that Khama is not living in quite such style as the last coloured visitor of note to this country [the Shahzada]. His hotel is by no means an expensive one, and he is not above the use of the homely but convenient penny 'bus. . . . But when one of the chiefs drove in a hansom [cab] along Threadneedle Street the other day, I suppose he partially expiated the omnibus offence.

The *Lichfield Mercury* on the other hand praised Khama as "a kind of middle-class royalty" with "no 'side' or swagger," saving his money for "a whole series of inspections of various industries and manufactures" and scorning social entertainments:

> Every day, it is said, he refuses a whole shoal of invitations, principally from middle-class and Dissenting quarters. He also declines steadfastly to exhibit himself at Exeter Hall, though he is much pressed to take part in some forthcoming missionary meetings.

From Scotland the *Dundee Courier* on the twenty-third was vigorous in its condemnation of those "stupid and ungracious reflections" on Khama's parsimony: Khama "is not housed at the public expense as was the Shahzada. Neither is he a rich man. . . . he is obeying maxims of prudence which are morally binding even on monarchs. He is living according to his means."

From the North of England the *Bradford Observer* of the nineteenth reflected on broader issues of European imperialism in Africa and Asia:

> Mr Herbert Spencer describes the present condition of public feeling as favouring an aggressive policy all over the world—giving State authorizations to filibustering companies, and permitting political burglaries everywhere.
>
> This diagnosis is too accurate not to give rise to some prickings of conscience in those of us who have any conscience left in the matter; and it is emphasised by the fact that the moment has been chosen for a series of appeals to us. . . . Malagasies, Swazis, Ashantis, Chitralis, to say nothing of chieftains like Gungunhama and Samory . . . and now the Bechuana chief and his comrades take their place and ask a decision of us.

The weekend of September 21 saw a cartoon of Chamberlain with Khama and "The Ballad of Bechuana" (see appendix of this book) in *Punch,* and the publication of the "J.M." interview and article in the *Illustrated London News.* Further comment, generally friendly to the chiefs' cause, appeared in publications as varied as the *West Australian Review,* the *Belfast Witness,* the *Naval and Military Review,* and the *Levant Herald.* The *New York Tribune* took another week to feature "King Khama, an African gentleman and monarch worthy of the name" on September 29.[8]

✠ ✠ ✠

That Saturday afternoon there was the first big event of the LMS Founders' Week, with a children's festival at the City Temple. Saturday, September 21, was the exact anniversary of the Monday in 1795 when Congregationalists, Presbyterians, and some Anglicans had met in the Castle and Falcon Inn, Aldersgate Street, to found the society "on a broad and

catholic basis for the spread of evangelical Christianity in heathen lands,"
following up an initiative started in a Change Alley coffeehouse during the
previous November.

The City Temple was packed with "young people," whose enthusiasm
was aroused to "tumultuous" cheers and clapping when the chairman,
Alderman Belsey of Rochester, grasped Khama's hand after first greeting
Bathoen and then Sebele. The chairman called on "the immense assemblage" to give the chiefs the so-called Chautauqua salute—adopted from
the New England movement for moral and religious education, named
for its summer school in upper New York state. Thereupon "the audience
rose and waved handkerchiefs, the City Temple being thus suddenly filled
with a mass of waving white."

Khama, obviously touched, delivered a speech "in a very low tone, but
with apparently no hesitancy," interpreted by Willoughby, exhorting
youth to do good works in God's name:

> I rejoice very much to be present here with you in this house of God,
> though I am filled with pain because I am unable to speak to you in your
> own language. I rejoice much to see so many young children, and I pray
> God that as we have been joined together in one body, so He will help us
> to join in one Spirit, the spirit to help people. . . . The work which we find
> on the earth is a work which tries men, and again it is a work that passes
> away, but the work of God has no ending. . . . I have not long words to
> speak. I am not a man practised in speech. I know how to do things better
> than to say them. But I give you joy with my words—the joy that I see in
> your faces.

Soon after "the great South African chief took a dignified departure"
from the rostrum, all the Bechuana left the hall. The children were then
treated to "popular, chatty" addresses—one of which quoted a missionary
bishop who had said "with Johnsonian emphasis, 'Yes, sir, and every missionary must be an adventurer—an adventurer for the cause of Christ.'"

Khama was to be the principal attraction in the next week of crowded
missionary gatherings, which was to take him as far as the English Midlands. Supporters of the Christian missionary movement saw Khama as
the tangible answer to the slights on their efforts overseas delivered at a
recent meeting of the British Association.

The coming week was to be the hottest of the year, rising to eighty-six
degrees Fahrenheit (thirty degrees Celsius) on Tuesday the twenty-fourth.
Khama was to complain that the weather was more oppressive than in
the Kalahari. The overcoats he had brought with him were superfluous.[9]

Sunday, September 22, seems to have passed without recorded incident. This may have been the day when Khama took a trip to Croydon
in Surrey, a visit possibly to some church or chapel congregation that cost

him personally 6s. 2d. in train fares for himself and whatever companions he chose.

That Monday evening in London the City Temple was again filled for LMS Founders' Week, for a thanksgiving meeting to round off the first full day of proceedings by delegates from many mission societies in conference. Against a gigantic missionary map of the world that covered the organ, the chiefs were greeted with cheers as "fruits of the labours of the missionaries." The chairman, Rev. J. P. Gladstone, who presided over the LMS board of directors, spoke of the history of the society. Wardlaw Thompson also spoke briefly, followed by Khama—interpreted by Lloyd; —who spoke about the war on strong drink and the need for schools in his land.

A feeling of exhaustion had evidently set in after the long previous proceedings. Many of the audience had evidently come only to hear Khama and left when the chiefs left.[10]

SEVEN

The Day a King Came to Enderby

◆╼═⊃ ⊂═╾◆

WITH EVANGELICAL CREDENTIALS NOW WELL ESTAB-
lished at the LMS centennial celebrations, it was time to brave the lion's
den of regional politics. On Tuesday, September 24, the chiefs left London
and headed for the heartland of Chamberlain's political support—the industrial Midlands.

The *St James's Gazette* in London was to remark on the "smartness that
would win the admiration of a showman" that had sent the "distinguished
negro converts" out of the capital to exhibit them "for the stimulation of
missionary enthusiasm in the provinces." Birmingham, in particular, was
not only the stronghold of "missionary non-conformity"; but also "the
name of the town is, to them, in a political sense, synonymous with that of
Mr. CHAMBERLAIN, in whose hands their future lies." [1]

Willoughby, as the chiefs' tour manager and main political adviser, set
out to court the Nonconformist and evangelical conscience of industrial
manufacturing areas. This ethic, associated with the skilled working class
up to the 1840s, had since slipped up the class scale to become "middle-
class morality," informing the radical wing of the Liberal Party, and now
being subverted to support Chamberlain. As the leading historian of Congregationalism has noted, the Nonconformist movement was broken and
began to fade by the end of the 1890s, precisely because of the splits en-
gendered by Irish unionism and imperialism. But for the moment the new
puritanism seemed to be triumphant.

Willoughby was still cautious about broaching too directly the actual
political issue that had brought them to England. Their main platforms
for speaking were being provided by provincial celebrations of the LMS
centenary, where they were to be paraded as visible tokens of the efficacy
of foreign Christian missions. Their mode of attack on the Chartered
Company was to concentrate on the issue of liquor. But it is evident that

Khama and the others wanted to tackle Cecil Rhodes and his Chartered Company more directly than Willoughby advised.

✤ ✤ ✤

One matter of business remained outstanding—the letter that Chamberlain had asked the chiefs to send laying out to the Colonial Office the details of their grievances.

The letter from the chiefs to Sir Robert Meade, permanent undersecretary for the colonies, was drafted by Willoughby from ongoing consultations with the chiefs, and was dispatched on September 24. Willoughby's hand is obvious in such emendations as "Do not let them take away the land which is the life of your people" becoming the altogether more pathetic " . . . which is the life of your children"—the appropriate "quaint expressions and picturesque arguments" for appealing to the master race. One also suspects that Willoughby had a hand in qualifying the chiefs' joint thoughts more diplomatically, such as in the second half of the sentence, "We know that the Officers of the Great Queen sometimes make mistakes; because they are not of our race and cannot think our thoughts or understand our customs." (They knew that such "mistakes" were often as not deliberate actions dictated by bias toward the interests of Cecil Rhodes.)

The chiefs' letter to Chamberlain began:

> You were good enough to ask us to put our words on paper and send them to you. We each have little words that we should like to speak to the Government. But the words that brought us to England are one, and we speak them as one mouth. . . .
>
> We came to England to ask the Government of the Great Queen to continue her protection over us. . . . there is no Government that we can trust as we trust that of the Great Queen. We pray you therefore not to throw us away as if we were troublesome children who would not listen to their mother's words. . . . we are anxious that you should tell us plainly that you will not give us away against our wishes.

They stated their objections to Chartered Company rule on a number of counts. First, because "we think they will take our land and sell it to others." Second, because "they will fill our country with liquor shops, as they have Bulawayo." Third, because "they are people without gratitude," as seen in their dealings with Khama. Fourth, "because we hear the words of the Makalaka and the Matabele who live under the Company, and we see that these people do not like their rulers."

If the British were really, as Rhodes had told them, irrevocably committed to handing over the protectorate to the company at some time yet undetermined, then let that transference be postponed for ten years. The chiefs also made reference to their anxiety over "our younger brothers" being encouraged by white men to challenge their rule; to their willingness "to pay a poll-tax" best collected by the chiefs (through "sub-chiefs and headmen, and from the little chiefs of the smaller tribes which live in our country") on behalf of the government; and to the need for "one of your own people, a good man who knows our speech and customs and is not bad-tempered and impatient" to live among them as the queen's officer "to become your eyes and ears, and to become also our mouth, which shall speak our words to you."[2]

The Colonial Office's response, described by the historian Anthony Sillery as "far from affable,' was to come on October 8 (see chap. 12).

TUESDAY, SEPTEMBER 24

The chiefs arrived at Wellingborough, a market and manufacturing town near Northampton, on Tuesday, September 24, at 12:13 midday off the London train. Here the chiefs' host was Mr. A. de Sales Turland, a local manufacturer whom the chiefs had met on board the *Tantallon Castle*.

Turland took the chiefs to lunch at the Hind Hotel. After lunch the party drove in coaches to visit one of the boot factories in nearby Kettering, arriving at about four in the afternoon. Seeing the vast quantity of output, Khama's first observation was on the enormous number of beasts that had been killed to make so many leather boots and shoes.

The chiefs stood in front of each machine in the factory watching the operators intently. The machine that punched eyelets for bootlaces in the leather was a main attraction, because it was operated by a mere boy. The chiefs eagerly pointed out to each other how another machine not only inserted but also twisted screws into position. They remarked on "the nicety and quickness" of the manufacturing processes and periodically "held up their hands in amazement."

They were themselves objects of great interest to bystanders in the factory. The workers strained to hear the strange language being spoken by the interpreter, Willoughby. But a local newspaper, the *Wellingborough Post*, thought there was "nothing formidable in the visitors. They looked like shrewd men . . . attired in English costume . . . big and well-built" but with characteristic "Ethiopian features."

After less than an hour and a half in the factory "they appeared so interested in the visit that it was only with difficulty Mr. Turland could induce them to leave in time to catch the 5.40 train." First there was a little ceremony in the office of the factory owner, Mr. Hanger, in which the chiefs expressed their thanks and Hanger offered them their choice of "a pair of boots of any design as a memento of the visit." Then they were driven in two landaus to the railway station, "raising their top hats to those assembled outside the factory, who cheered as they left." [3]

At supper they were once again guests of Turland at Wellingborough, from which they moved to a so-called *conversazione* in Salem Lane School. There Turland had assembled a crowd of about five hundred who had first supped at his expense. Among the "banners, greenery and mottoes" in the hall was a message in large letters proclaiming DOMELAUN BORRA (i.e. *Dumelang Borra*, "Welcome Sirs"), a phrase that Turland had no doubt picked up on his travels.

The chiefs arrived in the hall while Turland's other guests were still eating, "and were accorded a hearty reception." All five hundred went to the Congregational church next door, where even greater numbers sat waiting for a meeting arranged by Turland.

Hymns were sung and prayers said, and Khama was called upon to speak. He did so, interpreted sentence by sentence into English by his attendant Seisa. Inspired no doubt by the services of his own personal interpreter rather than Willoughby, and by the relatively secular nature of the gathering, Khama's made his first frontal move on the political issue that had brought him to England. The other chiefs did likewise for the first time in their short speeches that followed his.

Khama began with the words, "I have very few words to speak to you to-night," a preface in any language that invariably indicates the speaker's intention to expatiate at length on a subject:

> I want to tell you why I came to this country. While we were in Africa, we heard that the Imperial Government were going to hand us over to the Chartered Company, and we three chiefs came here to England to hear why the Imperial Government were going to hand us over. . . .
>   We don't want a new government; we want the old Government. Why should the great Queen throw us from being under her own government?

He concluded:

> We have been under the home Government for some time, and we don't want a new man to govern us.
>   These are all the words I want to speak to you to-night, and I hope God will help you . . . in this matter to speak for me. I thank you all.

There was, as yet, no public identification of the wrongs of the Chartered Company.

Sebele stood up and delivered a similar but more polished speech, picking up on the sorts of words and phrases that would appeal to the audience's sense of pathos:

> I greet you all with great joy, and I thank God because we have met here to-night. We did not think when we came here that we should have such a

welcome from you white people. We only see a very few white people in our country. . . . We came here with very sore hearts. . . . We want to be under the great Queen who has been our mother for long time.

He ended by underlining his main point once again: "We don't like a new government; we want to be under the great Queen."

The same points were repeated by Bathoen in his speech. All three "pathetic, and evidently earnest speeches, evoked loud applause." Speeches by Willoughby and Turland were followed by the adoption of "a proposition embodying the views of the speakers" to be sent to Mr. Chamberlain.[4]

The chiefs would have gone to bed that night, in the Hind Hotel, well satisfied with the beginning of their Midlands tour.

WEDNESDAY, SEPTEMBER 25

Meanwhile preparations were going ahead in the major manufacturing town of Leicester, and in the nearby village of Enderby, for the reception of "Khama the Good" and "his two brother chiefs."

Khama was going to Enderby to fulfill his parting promise made to one of his Palapye "lady missionaries," Alice Young, "a native of Enderby," that he would visit her parents in England. Miss Young had now been away from home for two years and was evidently concerned about her family. She was a much-admired young schoolteacher at Palapye who had been active in Leicester church and temperance circles. She had undergone teacher training prior to sailing for Africa by six months of observations in Leicester board schools.

So large was the expected turnout to hear the chiefs that the local organizers of the LMS centenary had booked two different Nonconformist chapels for meetings in succession on the evening of September 25, neither the Temperance Hall nor the Floral Hall having been available, due to prior bookings. The two meetings were to be open to ticket holders only, and applications for tickets had reached overflow level already on the day before. This produced the response in a dissatisfied letter to the *Leicester Daily Post* that there should be a town meeting for "the community at large" to meet the chiefs, organized by temperance bodies or by the local Leicester chamber of commerce. Leicester should also show off the best of its "clothing, hosiery and boots and shoes" to the representatives of the "millions of Africa."[5]

Late in the morning of Wednesday, September 25, "the three princes," as the *Post* called them, arrived at number 1 platform on Leicester's Midland Station at 11:30 on the dot. A large number of official welcomers surged around the chiefs' carriage to greet them. Alice Young's father and brother were given pride of place.

After introductions on the platform and in the street outside, the chiefs and their attendants and the Youngs proceeded in two vehicles—a carriage and a two-horse brake wagonette—to Enderby, where "the occasion was made apparently a general holiday."

As the party turned into the road leading into the village, the vehicles were mobbed by cheering schoolchildren who ran alongside. A large crowd of villagers had gathered to welcome them at the lych-gate outside the village church at the entrance to the village, including the vicar, Reverend Aylward, the squire, Captain Drummond, and the bishop of Trinidad, who happened to be visiting.

Amid "hearty cheers" the "illustrious visitors" were approached by Reverend Dickenson, the village's Congregational minister, who stepped up onto Khama's wagonette to deliver a little speech:

> In the name of the people of Enderby I beg to give you a very hearty welcome. Your fame and good works have preceded you, and we call to mind, as we look upon you this morning, something of the noble life you have lived, and we congratulate you from the depths of our hearts, and bid you a very hearty welcome.

The vicar seconded the welcome, and the bishop added that (though himself white) he was the bishop of "many thousands of your race in the West Indies." He told them, "I shall rejoice, when I go back, to be able to tell them I have met one of your eminent standing among their race." What Khama thought of this is not recorded. His response to all the greetings, through Willoughby, was simple and courteous enough: "Thank you all very much for the cordial welcome you have given us here."

The next part of the ceremony was the presentation to Khama of an illuminated and framed address resplendent in purple and gold from the local Charles Brook Lodge of the International Order of Good Templars, the main temperance group. The address expressed

> sympathy with you in your appeal to the British Government to prevent the sale of intoxicating drinks being imposed upon your country. . . . We know and greatly deplore the terrible evils arising from the drink traffic in our own country, and most earnestly pray that by the blessing of the Almighty Father you may for ever secure the entire and absolute prohibition of the traffic from your own native land.

Khama replied that he would take the "beautiful address" back home: "I will keep it in . . . the house in which I sleep, and there I shall hang it." (He was as good as his word: nine decades later the framed parchment still decorated the dining room of his son Tshekedi's widow's house at Pilikwe in Botswana.)

Accompanied by cheers, the chiefs walked to Dickenson's house for a rest, and then to the schoolhouse attached to the Congregational chapel for lunch with the Youngs and their friends.

During the meal Khama was much attracted by one of the children of the family with whom he was soon on terms of the greatest friendliness, nursing the child and exhibiting a most kind and affectionate disposition. He was also much interested in a sketch of himself made by Miss Sloane, and readily attached his autograph to it.

In the Young household there was a newly arrived letter awaiting Khama from Alice Young back in Palapye. It was read out to Khama. Among other items of recent news the letter reported the death, from smallpox, of one of the Bangwato student teachers at Palapye. Khama "was greatly moved, and for some time could not repress his sobs."

On leaving the Young household, the family presented Khama with a riding whip that much pleased him. The whole party was then photographed outside the house, before making its way along the crowded village street to the local national school. People pressed in to shake their hands, "and many of them were thus gratified." The children at the school performed with songs and musical exercises under the direction of the headmaster.

Next the chiefs were put in the charge of the Anglican vicar. They paid a call upon the hall, or feudal manor house, where they were entertained by Captain and Mrs. Drummond. They were shown over the house and gardens and "appeared to be particularly attracted by the trees laden with fruit, while Khama was delighted with the springy turf on which he walked." After tea and fruit, and the presentation of a bouquet to Khama by Drummond's daughter, the squire led his guests to his "well-kept stables and saddle and coach-houses." The chiefs showed great interest in the horses and ponies, and in the strange type of riding saddle used in England. They were also "evidently much pleased with a visit to the laundry," perhaps because it was equipped with hissing steam presses.

There was no time left to tour Rawson's granite works, the main source of local employment, where special arrangements had been made for blasting with dynamite to scare and delight the chiefs. So "the firm and its employees were greatly disappointed."

The chiefs were now handed back by the Establishment to the care of the Nonconformists. Yet more tea was dispensed at the Congregational chapel. An ancient minister, Rev. J. N. Robjohns, was produced in a Bath chair, in which he had been wheeled from the neighboring small village of Narborough. The chiefs enthusiastically plied the lively old man with questions interpreted by Willoughby. After tea there was an organ recital, and a large congregation came into the chapel to see, and hopefully to hear, the chiefs.

Khama obliged with a short speech, which was largely in praise of Miss Young, "who teaches my children beautifully." He greeted "my young people" of Enderby, as he had promised her, in her name. He had also been pained, he said, to hear today that "one she has taught has died. But he was a righteous fellow. This is the work God has done, and when God gives the order, where is the man to object to the order! Again, I rejoice to see you, and greet you. (Cheers.)"

> The party soon afterwards drove down the village street on their way to Leicester, and were loudly cheered by the crowds of people who lined the route, not a few waving hats and handkerchiefs from the upper windows of their houses. Thus ended a red-letter day in the history of Enderby, the inhabitants of which will not soon forget the enjoyable visit of Khama and his friends.

This extraordinary day in the life of an English village was later commemorated by a plaque, placed on the chapel lectern, recording the visit of King Khama. The lectern with its plaque still has pride of place in Enderby's United Reformed church, which replaced the chapel. Descendants of the Young family treasure photographs of the chiefs' visit. In 1980 there was at least one old lady living in Enderby who had been a small child there on that day in 1895. She could not recall any details but just remembered the excitement of "the day a King came to Enderby." [6]

⁜ ⁜ ⁜

That night Khama spoke twice in Leicester, after first being taken to tea— presumably a high tea with cooked food this time—at a private house. Khama's first speech was at Belvoir Street's Baptist chapel, a round classical building in the city center "packed in every part."

Khama followed a hard-hitting introduction by the chairman, Alderman Leonard, which while rejoicing in the mutual benefits of trade also deprecated injustice in the extension of empire. The visitors, said Leonard, "wanted to remain loyal partners . . . under the protection of this kingdom, and they objected to being handed over to the tender mercies of a company that, to say the least, existed in the main for aggrandisement and paying dividends. The mere fact that the two million sterling capital of that company was now valued on the stock exchange at 18 millions sterling showed what they motives had been and would be."

Alderman Leonard warned that whatever party was in power in Britain "it could not long remain and have real support unless it had the support of the *public opinion* of this country, and they were there that evening to voice the feelings of the town of Leicester, to support Khama's mission,

and to let the Government know"—as well as, he quickly added, to celebrate the London Missionary Society's centenary.

At this point a reverend gentleman stepped forward to appeal for missionary funds, and to boost the audience's expectations of Khama's impending speech:

> they were exceedingly fortunate in having upon their platform one of the
> greatest triumphs of the Gospel of Jesus Christ in heathen lands. (Cheers.)
> He referred to the apostle of social purity, that great temperance reformer,
> that perfect Christian gentlemen, that noble, enlightened ruler and gener-
> ous friend of missions, who was known among his own people as Khama
> the Good. (Cheers.)

The congregation still had to wait, however, while Reverend Willoughby "spoke at some length of the essential qualifications of a missionary." Willoughby then began to warm to the topic in hand—remarking
that the Ten Commandants applied to all, white or black, and people in
pursuit of riches had no more right to take native land in South Africa
than in the North of Scotland. Willoughby then took his seat back on the
platform, while Khama stepped forward with his personal interpreter,
Simeon Seisa, at his side.

Khama's Belvoir Street speech, interpreted by Seisa, for the first time
clearly identified the Chartered Company as the antagonist and hinted at
the possibility of war if the British government went ahead and abandoned the Bechuanaland Protectorate to Rhodes's Chartered Company.
The speech, freed from the restraints of Willoughby's interpretation, was
one of the most explicit and uninhibited of all the speeches made during
the chiefs' visit to Britain. Khama seems to have poured his heart and soul
into it, even to the extent of feeling unwell afterward. The speech is worth
quoting in full from the record in the *Leicester Daily Post*.

> Khama, who was very heartily cheered on rising to speak, then addressed
> the meeting, his speech being lucidly interpreted by one of his attendants.
> He said:
>
> Mr Chairman and all friends—I greet you tonight, and desire to say
> how very pleased I am to see you. You have honoured me very much,
> although I am a black man. (Applause.) Indeed, I can see you look on me
> as you look on a white man.
>
> I want to tell you, in very few words, why I came here. I heard while I
> was in my country in Bechuanaland that the Imperial Government was
> going to hand us over to the Chartered Company or the Colony, and we
> were very much afraid, for we did not know this, and only heard through
> the newspapers. So that we are come here to pray the Imperial Govern-
> ment that it should not hand us over to the new Government.
>
> You do not know the ways of the Chartered Company, because you are
> very far away and we are very near to them. We think that the Chartered

Company will take our lands. We have very much enjoyed being under the Imperial Government, and we say why should the Imperial Government throw us away to the new Government? We have come here, therefore, to ask your help, in order that we should not be handed over to the new Government. (Applause.)

We do not know much about the new Government. We black people live on the land; we live on the farms. We get our food from the lands, and we are afraid if the new Government begins in our country we will not get these things, and it will be a great loss to us to be given the Chartered Company. (Applause.)

We think that the Imperial government is throwing us away. The Chartered Company, when it came, found that we were under the Imperial government, and we say why should the Imperial government want to had us over to the Chartered Company? (Hear, Hear.)

I have been helping the Chartered Company a long time, but I do not think they ever thanked me for that. Besides that, the Chartered Company asked me for permission to let them inspect the minerals in my country. Of course I said, "You had better have the minerals if you like, because we don't look after them." But I don't think even then the Company thanked me for that. Now I am very much surprised; I do not know what they want, though I think what they want is the land, and not anything else. (Hear, Hear.)

Besides, we are afraid they are not very careful about the liquor in the country—(Applause)—and this makes us very pained. That is why we come here in England, to let the people know what it is we ask. We say why should the home Government hand us over to the other people without asking us? (Hear, Hear.)

They hand us over like an ox, but even the owner of the ox looks to where the ox will get grass, and water, land, that sort of thing. (Applause.)

I think they ought to have asked us, and found out first what we think about it. Although we are black people we have tribes that we rule over, but if a Chief wants to make a new law or anything he must speak with his people. (Applause.)

We were progressing very much under the Imperial Government, but now you are teaching us the word of war, and I think these things ought to cease. I think under the Imperial Government we should learn many things which are good, and the Imperial Government also protects us from war. (Applause)

Some of the Company are not very good people. We come to England to speak and let you hear what it is we ask, and these are the words I wish to speak tonight. I am very pleased indeed to see you here, and I hope God will help you to be a good people to everybody. (Applause.)

As prearranged by Willoughby for all the chiefs' public meetings, the Belvoir Street congregation then adopted a loyal petition to be sent to Mr. Chamberlain, begging that Bechuanaland be kept under imperial administration and not be given over to the British South Africa Company.

Meanwhile round the corner in the large redbrick Wesleyan chapel in Bishop Street, with unadmitted crowds still gathered outside in the central square, Bathoen was struggling manfully with a speech. The interpreter was Rev. E. Howard, another LMS missionary on leave from Bechuanaland.

They had come over from their own country, where they were kings and were free. They were brought to this country by means of words which brought them pain. They had been living under the shadow of Queen Victoria, and they rejoiced to be under the shadow of her Majesty. (Cheers.) They heard that the Queen was handing them over to the company. They did not love the company, and had come to speak to the Queen on the matter.

After more speeches by other speakers, "King Khama arrived, and had a splendid reception." Willoughby spoke first on his own account, with cautious words:

He was not there to pick holes in the Chartered Company or criticise their actions in Matabeleland or Mashonaland, but why should this Government throw them away just when the hardest of the difficulties had been overcome and when the people were loyal to their rule?

Khama then spoke but briefly. The exhaustion of the day in Enderby and the enervation resulting from his long speech in Belvoir Street had had their toll on the health of a sixty-year-old man, even a fit one. He was feeling distinctly unwell and spoke somewhat testily:

The company existed for the sake of wealth, and not for the sake of government or assisting mankind. Was he to be given away as a dog to a master he does not know?

A resolution of support by the meeting for the chiefs' cause was carried unanimously.[7]

Thursday, September 26

Next morning Khama had difficulty in getting out of bed and delayed the chiefs' tight schedule by an hour to recover from his fatigue by extra sleep.

Before he left for Birmingham, Khama was presented by the local temperance society at Leicester with a resolution praying for the success of the "Chief of Bechuanaland" with the British government. The *Leicester Daily Post* that day came out with an editorial arguing "The Case for Khama"—praying that "Mr. CHAMBERLAIN may be induced to make the desired concession, and so enable KHAMA THE GOOD and his brother chiefs to enter upon a fresh career of usefulness in Bechuanaland."[8] Khama's "plain unvarnished tale" had clearly swayed the Leicester public.

EIGHT

They Are Strong and We Are Weak

⤙⟹ ⟸⤚

THE CITIZENS OF BIRMINGHAM LIKED TO THINK THAT their metropolis was the "best governed city" in Britain. The "municipal socialism" of Mayor Joseph Chamberlain had given them modern gas and water supplies and grand streets with municipal buildings in Chamberlain's favorite architectural style of Italianate Victorian Gothic.

Birmingham was the capital of the prosperous Midlands and was beginning to rival Manchester in the older industrial North as England's second city. The city had a new self-confidence that belied the years when it used to self-consciously borrow the names of London locations and streets for its own. Metropolitan and provincial newspapers, which could almost ignore what happened in little Leicester, had to sit up and take note of what happened in big Birmingham.

The *Birmingham Mail* began reporting on arrangements for the "Visit of King Khama" on the Friday previous to the chiefs' visit. Clearly primed by interests close to the Chartered Company, the paper disarmingly reported that the chiefs' purpose in coming to Britain was to secure the prohibition of liquor traffic, and "it is said that Mr. Cecil Rhodes is willing to give the guarantee they seek."

Arrangements for the visit were being taken in hand by philanthropic, temperance, and missionary bodies, led by Rev. J. J. Rutherford—who had been bombarding Willoughby with telegrams for weeks. In the absence of the mayor of Birmingham on holiday in the Baltic, his deputy, Alderman Johnson, declined to offer a civic reception without authorization from the Colonial Office in London. But he agreed to unofficially entertain the chiefs to breakfast in the Council House library.

The *Birmingham Post* and the *Birmingham Gazette* reported in more detail on arrangements in their editions on the day after the *Mail*. Apart from a social reception in the town hall, all public meetings would be held under the aegis of the LMS centenary. Rev. Arthur O'Neill of the Peace Society was reportedly unwilling to be too deeply involved because of Khama's participation in the Anglo-Ndebele War. Otherwise, the Birmingham newspapers contented themselves with glowing portraits of Khama as an Alfred the Great and as a social reformer, and passed on good reports of the chiefs from the London press. Khama's missionary W. C. Willoughby, they added, had been partly trained at Spring Hill College, and his wife was a former Birmingham Sunday school teacher.[1]

THURSDAY, SEPTEMBER 26

Birmingham was in holiday mood for the Onion Fair in the extremely warm and humid weather of late summer.

A crowd of curious "excursionists from the country" and "city folk" milled in and around the New Street Station, where the chiefs were expected to arrive from Leicester via Rugby on the London and North-Western express train at 10:35 in the morning. Onlookers, some of whom had been waiting since 9:30, were said to be anticipating "a full-blown savage in his native regimentals." If so, they were to be sorely disappointed.

Khama's morning indisposition delayed the chiefs' arrival till 11:25, when their train drew up on platform 6. The chiefs were in their own first-class saloon attached to a slow, crowded "market special" train of the Midland Railway. After the platform was announced, a cordon was set up by railway staff to hold back the large crowd, and the stationmaster "by the exercise of considerable tact" ensured that the carriage halted on exactly the right spot.

The chiefs "emerged from the carriage faultlessly, but not picturesquely, attired in top hats, black suits, and modern ties, collars and—alas for lovers of the romantic and unconventional—umbrellas." A member of the reception committee was so enthusiastic in waving his hat that nosegays he meant to present to the chiefs fell out and had to be retrieved from the crowd's feet. He then stepped forward with a nosegay of tiny roses, which was accepted somewhat clumsily by Khama—"evidently suffering from a cold" and not sure what to do with it. Bathoen also received a nosegay and demonstrated to Khama how to attach it to the buttonhole of his fawn-colored light overcoat.

The *Birmingham Mail* observed that Khama was "a fine looking fellow. He is tall and but for a slight stoop would be soldierly" but was "slightly built" by comparison with his fellows. Sebele was "well-made, firmly knit." The *Birmingham Gazette* referred to his "all-round muscular figure." The *Post* said Bathoen looked "for all the world like a jolly old country farmer; he is stout, hale and hearty; and seems to have an overwhelming affection for his umbrella." The *Birmingham Post* thought Sebele and Bathoen "both men of a grand physique, and of a merry countenance withal," who would have "cut a very fine figure in the native garb." The press mistook Bathoen's sturdy brother-in-law in a soft felt hat for Chief Besele Montshiwa, who was no longer accompanying the party. The three comparatively lightweight attendants in billycock hats were also noted.

> Strange as it may seem, the heat occasioned them an immense amount of inconvenience, the Chief Bathoen being bathed in perspiration, and expressing to those around the discomfort he felt.

The chiefs acknowledged polite applause and any cheers from the otherwise curiously silent crowd by tipping their tall stovepipe hats, while they shook hands for several minutes with civic and religious dignitaries waiting with their wives on the station platform. There was also the familiar face of Turland, their host from Wellingborough. The party then proceeded in a single file led by Khama, acknowledging a burst of cheering from the crowd, to two landau carriages drawn by bay horses that were waiting to take them from the station.

The landaus went direct to the Shorthorn Show at Bingley Hall, where prime beef cattle were being paraded by the Birmingham Agricultural Exhibition Society. Khama was feeling "very ill" but showed himself to be "a shrewd judge of stock" as he thoroughly examined and asked questions about the cattle, expressing surprise that cows could grow so large in fifteen months. Khama assured his hosts of the superiority of English over Dutch (i.e. Afrikaner) beef and dairy livestock. "He is enjoying this far more than you think," Willoughby assured the exhibitors, who were worried by the expressionless look on Khama's face and feared he was bored.

Willoughby refused to allow Khama to be interviewed but told the Birmingham press in detail about Khama's inoculation of cattle against lung sickness. He assured the reporters of Khama's admiration for Birmingham's favorite son, Joseph Chamberlain, about whom Khama had said: "This man . . . will do righteousness." The press asked about Khama's leisure interests. Willoughby somewhat tetchily replied: "He has no amusement: life is too serious to him. When he is not fully engaged he is ready for a sleep, but he has no amusement."

After a quarter of an hour sitting together in reserved seats watching a cattle auction in the sales ring, the chiefs declined the stewards' offer of lunch and were whisked away to their next appointment at 12:25. They were shown around Messrs. Elkingtons' silversmithing works in Newhall Street. After inspecting design and modeling, stamping, turning, soldering, and casting, they reached the plating department. Here Sebele had the privilege of gilding three threepenny coins by immersing them in a vat of hot liquid gold "and triumphally withdrawing them with their auriferous coating." After cooling, each chief was presented with one of the coins to take away as a souvenir.

No chief or attendant had "so far forgot his dignity as to express astonishment or betray any vulgar affection," however much he might have marveled inwardly. No such inhibition, however, restrained Bathoen's brother-in-law Kwenaetsile, who "in the show-rooms burst into a perfect ecstacy over the figure of an angel designed to support a casket which is in making. He imitated the motion of wings with his arms and said he almost expected the figure to fly away: it looked so real."

Finally "the three chiefs signed their names in the visitors' book, in very fair and legible English calligraphy." Then it was time for lunch in Hagley Road with Mr. J. Hargreave, a Birmingham solicitor whose sister was another spinster "lady missionary" at Khama's town of Palapye.

After lunch, the rest of the party went on a tour of the Birmingham Small Arms factory at 4:30 while Khama and Willoughby stayed to rest at Hargreave's. Khama then transferred to the Cobden Temperance Hotel, where the party was to stay for two nights. He remained indoors for the rest of the evening, "fearing lest the night air might further indispose him."

Freed from the constraints of Khama and Willoughby, their taskmasters, the rest of the party did not maintain their "customary impassability" in their tour around the small-arms factory at Small Heath. Sebele became "the life and soul of the party":

> he chatted gaily about what he had seen, and added, jokingly "I know all about it now, and when I get home I shall be able to make as many guns as I want." [2]

✛ ✛ ✛

While Khama remained in the hotel, Willoughby joined the rest of the party at an early evening festival of Sunday school children in the Birmingham Town Hall. They were treated to two exciting dramatic sketches by the children, titled "The Lifeboat" and "The Fire Brigade," backed by organ, choir, lantern slide projector, and the sudden appearance of real city firemen rushing to the rescue with a hose and extendable ladder. An address was read by the chairman, and the chiefs were presented with a letter of tribute to "His Majesty King Khama."

Sebele, interpreted by Willoughby, leaped up to speak in reply. He greeted the children on behalf of the children of his country and said how glad he was to see so many children doing Bible studies. He added that he hoped soon to receive a lady teacher from England in his town. "The applause that greeted the dusky chief was enthusiastic, and at the end of Sebele's neat little speech he was loudly cheered."

The party left the Town Hall just before 8 P.M. and were driven to a combined LMS centenary and temperance meeting in Carr's Lane Congregational Chapel. Carr's Lane chapel was the former benefice of Chamberlain's old ally in municipal politics the late Rev. Dr. R. W. Dale, where the name "Bechuanaland" had often been heard in protest meetings over British policy in southern Africa a decade earlier.

The chairman, one Joseph Warden, began the meeting by recalling how Daniel O'Connell and other radical orators had "made these walls resound again and again with denunciations against the iniquity of slavery." Birmingham was the right city and the chapel was the right spot for Khama's crusade.

The next speaker, Reverend Morgan, introduced a mild pre-prepared motion expressing "great pleasure at the visit of King Khama to this city." The motion entirely missed out on the main matter that brought the "Bechuana" chiefs to Birmingham, though Morgan referred in his explanatory remarks to the need to distinguish Christian mission work from "anything in the nature of commercial booms" and from "our eminently aggressive commercialism—(hear, hear)."

A minister of religion and temperance advocate by the name of J. N. Knight rose to propose first a rider and then an amendment specifically mentioning support for Khama's temperance work. But he was overruled by the chairman on the grounds that the motion had already been seconded. (This led Knight to fire off several letters of self-justification to the press subsequently.)

Willoughby spoke of his Palapye mission work, emphasizing that the aim of mission work was to produce "Christianised" Africans and not "Europeanised" Africans, who he said were "a blot upon civilisation." He then interpreted the speech of Bathoen, who according to a press report expressed "a deep earnestness and fervency, marking his utterances as he detailed them sentence by sentence":

> I rejoice very much to see you, and see you just as you are gathered to-gether in the House of God, just as you yourselves wish it to be done.
>
> We rejoice that the English people have sent teachers into our land. . . . I ask that you will pray for us that the teaching may go forward, and that we may progress in the work of God. This is my greeting, and these are the words I speak to the gathering here to-night. I pray that God will help you, and help us, that we may all go forward along the better way— (applause).

In reading this speech and other speeches by Bathoen one can hear the cadences that were to mark him out as an effective speaker subsequently in Welsh chapels. If Bathoen were the Welshman, then the dour Khama was surely the Scot, while Sebele seemed to Englishmen almost the epitome of John Bull.

In LMS circles during the odyssey of the three chiefs round Britain, Sebele became known as "the sinner," since he was not a church member but "made the most pious speeches of the lot." Wardlaw Thompson, the foreign secretary of the LMS, was to say that Sebele "was certainly the best public speaker of the three, and had the knack of saying things which greatly pleased his auditors."

Hear then Sebele's speech at Carr's Lane, Birmingham—"a few sentences delivered with even more expressiveness than his companion":

> I rejoice to see you and to give you my best greeting.
>
> A very long time ago we began to see the teachers that came from your country, and the first teacher that I ever saw was David Livingstone— (cheers).
>
> It was he who taught me when a boy to read and write, and he taught us also of the Gospel, that God wanted men to love one another, because he loved them. And I see that these words must have some truth in them, because we who are men with the black skin are evidently loved by those who are here, though you have white skins and are different from us— (applause).
>
> And I rejoice to see that you are trying to act according to the words that are written in the Epistle to the Hebrews—"Brethren, love one another,"—(hear, hear).
>
> . . . And I hope that God will give us permission to go forward as you have gone forward in this land, that our children may learn, as I see your children learn in your schools, and that I and my people may become something like yourselves.
>
> Now 50 years have passed since Livingstone began to teach us, and we have seen some progress—(applause)—and we ask that you will give us your best wishes and the help of your teachers that we may be able to realise such great things. Again I say be greeted—(applause).

The "intelligent-looking young" Seisa, Khama's interpreter, spoke last, in place of his employer. His "fairly good English" demonstrated "an almost scholarly selection of words" despite "occasional hesitations."

Seisa began and ended his speech by assuring his audience that Khama "meets the prayer of the English people who pray for him"—whatever that may have meant. But the rest of the speech was somewhat of a putdown for Khama. Seisa said he almost felt sorry for him because Khama "speaks alone for himself" against old customs and had not—contrary to press reports Seisa had read in this country—succeeded in suppressing such customs among his people.

No doubt Willoughby and Khama frowned on this subversive streak in Seisa. He did not speak in his own right or interpret another major speech in public again.

At the close of the meeting the "Bechuana" returned to the Cobden Hotel in a closed carriage. The press was then told that Khama was recovering well and was in a sound sleep.[3]

Willoughby gave a long interview to the *Daily Post* that evening. He took the opportunity to present himself as amenable to negotiation with Rhodes and Chamberlain. He set out to debunk his image as a radical "Little Englander," declaring himself an ardent imperialist and an admirer of Cecil Rhodes. He appreciated what the Chartered Company had done in taking new lands for the empire, but could see no reason for its taking over an already loyal and peaceful territory like the Bechuanaland Protectorate—no reason, that was, except for pushing up its shares a pound or two. As for relieving the imperial government of excessive administrative costs, why would a commercial company take on a loss-making operation except to make a profit by taking and selling off the chiefs' lands? The costs of the Bechuanaland Protectorate's colonial administration could anyway be easily cut to twenty thousand pounds a year by running it along the lines of Basutoland (Lesotho). The reduced costs could be covered by poll tax, licenses, fines, and income from the territory's share of the South(ern) African customs union.[4]

FRIDAY, SEPTEMBER 27

The next morning Khama had quite recovered after a good night's rest. The chiefs prepared to attend the Birmingham Town Council breakfast, now to be held in the banqueting hall rather than the library of the Council House.

Khama seems to have been well aware that this would be his most crucial piece of oratory yet. Hence, as he was shortly to confess, one reason for his nervous indisposition the day before. Birmingham was the city of Mr. Chamberlain, upon whom the success of the mission ultimately depended. Within Birmingham, there was no more important body than the Town Council, whose aldermen and councillors were at the core of political support for their local magnate and former long-term mayor.

This was to be the event that would, through press notices and editorial responses in the weekend press as much as in the provincial and metropolitan dailies, make or break the success of the chiefs' political mission to Britain.

The Town Council breakfast was attended by the chairmen of the various committees of the council, including Chamberlain's brother-in-law Alderman William Kenrick, MP, and other aldermen and town councillors. Special guests included the chocolate manufacturer Richard Cadbury, Hargreaves the solicitor, and the bishop of Coventry. Kenrick sat close by the chiefs at table, with Seisa at hand to interpret for him.

Khama spoke after a few very cordial words from the deputy mayor. Interpreted by Willoughby, Khama told them how pleased he was to meet "the heads of this town." He added: "I have just now a very great joy in my heart, because I see that a man with a white face is not above taking in his arms one whose skin is black, as you have done me this very day—(applause)."

This was by contrast with their treatment at home. Khama explained that he and his colleagues had been obliged to come to Britain as the result of a great deal of debate among their people, after "it was said that the English Government had given away their country" to a company "who want to make wealth—(hear, hear)." He added:

> Concerning you, I know that you live a long way off, and it is difficult for those who live a long way off to distinguish between words. Words are words, and it is hard to tell which are the right words and which are the wrong when they are spoken—(hear, hear). And so the thing that brought us to England is to ask the great Government to treat us mercifully—(cheers).
>
> The Company has already a very large number of black people in its dominions, indeed several nations. In the name of those people I tell you that they [the Company] have not taken them in their arms nicely. . . .
>
> . . . But these words of course are but words to you, and whether I am speaking correctly, or the Company have spoken correctly, when they told you of their doings, you cannot judge. We live near, and we know.

He reiterated his faith in "the British people" and his desire "to give our children that learning which your children get," and his fears that the Chartered Company would flood his country with liquor. To illustrate the methods of the Chartered Company, Khama related the story of how his son, Sekgoma, had recently been confronted by whites while out hunting in the north of his father's country. They told him "we will seize all your lands and your property. . . . By reason of that custom by which we have taken the Matabele." Hence Khama and his people feared the loss of their lands and property under Chartered Company rule.

> We say that the English Government has helped us, and we can trust it, and we say, Let it govern us still, and still we shall find help. I give you thanks for the way in which you have taken me up in this town, and I say, may God give you all that safety and that progress which leads men for-

ward along the right road. I am a man of black skin, but my heart is just the heart which God moulded—(loud applause).

After the breakfast, at a stand-up reception, Khama was introduced to the mayor, Alderman Fallows. He had been unable to attend the breakfast, he said, due to his arrival just the day before from a Baltic cruise. Fallows "had a brief chat" with Seisa and with "those members of the African retinue who could converse in English."[5]

At this point Khama was drawn aside by a representative of the *Birmingham Mail*, who reported him as looking "delighted with the beaming and steaming countenance of half a dozen portly Aldermen." However,

> The transformation from good humour to grave concern that took possession of the kingly countenance on the mention of the word "weather" was something wonderful.

As he mopped his own "steaming" brow, "the mellow influence of a good breakfast" persuaded Khama to talk further, using Willoughby as interpreter:

> He stated that the weather here was much more inconveniently warm than in his own native country. In [his part of] Africa the air was pure and dry and by means so oppressive as that which he had experienced in England. The days were hot but the nights were cold, and that enabled them to get a good night's rest.
>
> When he was making arrangements to come to England he was advised to provide himself with plenty of thick overcoats, but he had since found that he might with advantage have left them at home. In this country he found that the air was laden with moisture and smoke, and the excessive heat not only affected him but his whole party.

Khama said that he had "never felt the heat so much as yesterday" traveling in that slow train from Leicester to Birmingham. But he was candid enough to add that his "indisposition" the previous day might not have been "entirely due to the heat but was contributed to by the keen anxiety he felt concerning his mission to England." He had also just received the shocking news of the death from smallpox of "a favourite teacher, to whom he had looked with great expectations."

The *Mail* reporter observed that though "King Khama and his party" were now sweltering, English weather was so perverse that they might "wake up to-morrow morning and find small icebergs floating down Corporation Street."

The interview was interrupted by colleagues seeking Khama's casting vote on whether next to visit the art gallery or Messrs. Cadburys' cocoa works. The Birmingham Art Gallery was one of the triumphs of Chamberlain's period of civic office, which had dispensed high culture for the people as well as gas and water.

His Majesty had to choose between cocoa and curios, and cocoa triumphed. The party accordingly made a move along the corridor to the main stair case.

The *Birmingham Mail* went on to describe an episode that one can conjecture most likely involved Bathoen's gauche brother-in-law:

Amongst the people watching the procession was a liveried attendant bedecked with such broad gold braid and brass buttons as only a corporation official can display with proper ceremony and state. The effect that this glitter had on one of the members of the royal retinue was extraordinary. He evidently conceived that such a gorgeous uniform could not be disported by anyone under the rank of commander-in-chief of the British Army, and with a deferential bow he raised his hat and passed on with the air of a man who had done the right thing.[6]

Shortly after eleven o'clock the party left in carriages for Bournville, Khama sitting on the box seat of one of the carriages to get a better view. The chiefs inspected the cocoa and chocolate works in the southern suburban village of Bournville, where the Quaker philanthropists Messrs. Cadbury had set up "a Worcestershire Eden" of model workers' houses as well as a manufacturing plant. Cocoa was still being imported from South America, but the crop was also now being taken up among coastal farmers on the Gold Coast of West Africa.

The chiefs "watched the various processes of manufacture with the deepest interest, and expressed astonishment at the number of people employed there." The *Birmingham Post* remarked on the continuing hesitation that the elderly Bechuana men, unused to multi-storey living until a couple of months before, still had in using stairs:

The distinguished visitors were a trifle sceptical in regard to some of the suggestions made to them.

Sebele, perhaps, was the most cautious member of the company. In leaving the underground dressing-room the party had to pass up a short flight of stairs, the entrance to which looked at the first glance a little dark. One of the guides motioned to Sebele to make the ascent, but the wary African hung back, and, when pressed, he pushed forward an attendant, who quickly made a trial trip, and called from the top of the stairs to his chief. Sebele then essayed the climb, not, however, without visible misgiving.

The objection to staircases is apparently shared also by Khama himself, for on being asked to descend from the cutting-room to another department he hesitated, pointing with an index finger down the stairs. Being reassured by Mr. Willoughby, he ventured on the journey.

Strangely enough, it was the shipping department of the factory that seemed to hold the most fascination for Khama. He "bestowed the keenest attention on a parcel which was being prepared," after being told that it was being packed so that its contents should remain intact wherever it was sent in the world, "even to his own country." The "Bechuana" party passed on to the next department and had to send back for Khama, who was "still intent upon an export packet." He had been waiting to see the finished article, perhaps as the *Post* remarked facetiously, in case "he would renew acquaintance with it in Africa."

After expressing their gratitude for the courtesy and kindness of the factory tour, the chiefs were presented with mementos in the form of "handsome boxes of fancy chocolates." They acknowledged the gifts "by profound bows and a ceremonious raising of hats, following which the King [Khama] took a pen and laboriously wrote his name on his parcel, an example which was immediately imitated by the other chiefs."

No doubt the chiefs and their attendants had some taste of the products of Messrs. Cadbury at Bournville. But they were now ready for lunch and an afternoon rest at the residence of Mr. Richard Cadbury—Uffculme, at Moor Green.[7]

Later in the afternoon, no doubt in time for afternoon or low tea, they made a visit to the home of Joseph Chamberlain, named Highbury after his London birthplace, and set in eighteen acres of its own land some five miles south of the city center.

The house was a grand orange brick and brownstone pile, designed in the Italianate Gothic style of the major public buildings built as a result of Chamberlain's tenure as mayor of Birmingham. The Highbury estate had long lines of greenhouses, where Chamberlain grew orchids and other exotic plants. The extensive gardens were landscaped with banks of roses and rhododendrons, and "delightful surprises" consisting of "dells, rocks and bogs, water scenes and rustic bridges."

The main drawing room at Highbury was typically late-Victorian, with satin-covered furniture, heavy drapes, excessive wall decoration, and dark natural lighting through color-tinted windows. Attached to the drawing room was a large conservatory, with flowers in bloom in every season and palm trees set around a fountain.[8]

No doubt rested by such cool surroundings, the chiefs were prepared for their final public meeting in Birmingham, when they would address a reception in the town hall "provided by the joint-committee of the Missionary, Temperance and Peace Societies of the city."

That evening the town hall at Birmingham was packed with men and women. The meeting began as a social gathering, at which tea was served between five and six o'clock. The chiefs then arrived to take their places on the platform, at the right hand of Richard Cadbury, who was to act as chairman for the evening. Their appearance "was the signal for the most enthusiastic cheering, which greatly pleased the visitors." Thirty-five other men, including aldermen and councillors as well as ministers of religion and society officials, joined them on the platform to face the audience.

Cadbury began by presenting the chiefs with an address on a sheet of vellum, signed by the organizing committee, on behalf of Christian and philanthropic groups including the Aborigines Protection Society. The address expressed sympathy with the chiefs as Christians associated with the names of Moffat and Livingstone, as workers for temperance or prohibition of liquor, and as promoters of the principles of peace between the tribes in Africa.

This was followed by three short speeches. One deplored drunkenness in Birmingham, which might lower Khama's opinion of them. A speech by Rev. Arthur O'Neill of the Peace Society went straight to the heart of the political matter. O'Neill "said he did not like the Chartered Companies in Africa, and he hoped the people of Birmingham would speak out and strengthen the hands of Mr. Chamberlain—(hear, hear, and applause)."

The chairman then announced, no doubt at Willoughby's instigation for fear of a repeat of Khama's previous "indisposition," that Khama would not after all be a main speaker that evening. Sebele rose to give a polished speech, further refining phrases from previous speeches by Khama and himself and beginning with these words:

> I rejoice very much to be amongst a nation of Englishmen who are very numerous, and to see so many of your great number present in one gathering tonight. My first acquaintance with Englishmen was when Dr. Livingstone came to our town to live and to teach us. (Applause.) He began to speak to us about the love that God has, and now I see that it is even as Dr. Livingstone said.

Sebele's father had known the Setswana Bible better than any missionary except Robert Moffat, and Sebele continued to speak in like vein—which, on being translated, sounded much like the English Bible:

> We were first prompted to come to England by certain words which we read in a newspaper, and which said that we were to be placed in the hands of a new Government.
>
> Then we three chiefs spoke one to another, and we said: "Can it be that we shall be given away in ignorance, the Government not knowing the things that they do, because we are not like a man's oxen, who can be given without consultation—(applause)—and it must be our work to go to England and speak to the great Queen, that she may know the things that we do [say] here today. (Hear, hear.)

Politics closer to home were also brought to the audience's mind:

> We know ourselves that we, standing alone, are without power to keep the company coming into our land. They are strong and we are weak, but we

have come seeking for mercy and for helpfulness, and asking that we may
not be given altogether away. (Applause.)

In matters of a purely native nature, in things between our own people,
we desire that we may be left as now to administer justice between those
who have a dispute.

What we wish is this, that concerning our own people we shall still have
the power to govern them and that they shall not be compelled to go to
the courts of the company in order that they may find there what they can
find easier at home.

At this point a voice in the audience shouted: "Home Rule!" Sebele
began to wind up his speech, ending once more with a note that touched
on the audience's sense of guilt over racial imperialism:

I rejoice very much because you have listened to me so nicely; because
your faces show that you are not tired when a black man speaks.

It was now Bathoen's turn to repeat much the same speech, encouraged
by the cheers of the audience and by his ability to make people laugh:

We don't like to be governed by men whose one object is to take out metals
from the earth—(laughter and applause)—and whose business in life is to
hunt for precious stones, for they might take it into their heads to dig us in
the same manner. (Laughter.)

He went on to make a serious bargaining point that had not been put in
public before:

And if it be said that we must be given to the company, then we said to
one another we will ask the Great Queen to keep us for ten years.

He then returned to the assault on the Chartered Company, pointing
out that after the missionary Moffat visited the Matabele there had been
"peace for many years; but when they were handed over to the company
they very soon found war, and a war that had one ending. (Shame.)"

These things make us to question and to wonder . . . and so before the
company began to deal with us, as they did with the Matabele, we have
come to England that we may see the Queen and ask her help.

The meeting ended with a resolution wishing every success to "the
mission of Khama and his companions" to the government and Mr.
Chamberlain.

Khama had not spoken, but he was to do so briefly at a second meeting that evening, held to mark Birmingham's celebrations of the LMS
centenary. His "eloquent address" is sparsely recorded, except for one
anecdote:

When it was known that I was coming to England, a certain white man
resident in my town said, it is useless coming to England with a missionary
because you will only see missionaries, and nobody of importance, for the

missionaries are nobody in our country. (Laughter.) And I gave answer that if I did see only missionaries I should still rejoice, for theirs is a work in which I can take pleasure. (Hear, hear.) And he who spake this is one whose chief employment is drunkenness, and outside this he has no work that is great.

Khama concluded by "expressing his great desire to see schools established in his country for the children."[9]

SATURDAY, SEPTEMBER 28

On Saturday morning Khama was up before breakfast to take an invigorating walk down the boulevard called Corporation Street. This street outside the hotel, otherwise known as "Rue Chamberlain," had been driven through the heart of the old city slums and was now flanked by trees and tall new buildings designed by Chamberlain's favorite architect.

Khama was seen to be "returning the salute of a friendly constable, and ready to reply to the greeting of any passer-by who felt disposed to recognise him." The *Birmingham Gazette* thought Khama's form of salute to be "well-meaning but awkward."

Sebele and Bathoen soon joined Khama on his morning exercise up and down Corporation Street. The chiefs breakfasted and, at their insistence, made a thorough inspection of the backstage facilities of the Cobden Temperance Hotel in which they had been staying—laundry, kitchens, and elevator lifts. Then the chiefs set out on their last two visits to the sights of modern Birmingham.

They proceeded in open carriages to the Central Fire Station in the Upper Priory—being "cheered by a small crowd of people who were awaiting their arrival." They were welcomed by municipal dignitaries and officials, who explained the functions of the fire brigade while the party looked over the horse stables and the appliances in the engine sheds. According to the *Birmingham Post,*

> The horses were very much admired by Khama and his companions, and the intelligence the animals manifested in answering to their names, as well as in almost putting on their own harness when an alarm was raised, drew from them marked signs of pleasure.

The *Gazette* continues:

> At the close of the inspection a [reviewing] stand was made at the end of the yard, and a display was given by the brigade. An alarm was raised, and in 18 seconds, the men and engines were in readiness for the most furious conflagration. A hose was run out, and a stream of water was shot into the air ["over the buildings" said the *Post*]. Simultaneously a fire-escape was placed against the building, six men quickly ascended, and carried from the room six others whose lives were supposed to be in danger.

The chiefs watched the display with feelings something akin to amazement. They expressed their delight at what they had seen, and on their behalf Mr. Willoughby expressed to Superintendent Tozer the pleasure they had derived from their visit.

Next they rode in their carriages to visit a button factory in Great Hampton Street. Khama "insisted on riding upon the box-seat, beside the driver, so that he might the better observe the action of the horses."

The button factory was owned by Messrs. Green and Cadbury, presumably Joel Cadbury and Councillor Green, who had been active in entertaining the chiefs over the previous two days. They were shown the manufacturing processes of pearl and linen buttons and "readily accepted several samples [of 'unfinished buttons'] as souvenirs of their visit."

> The large number of girls engaged at the works caused Khama to remark, "I am astonished at many things here, but the greatest is at what girls in England can do. They can do whatever they try."

There was no time left to visit the nail-and-pin works of Alderman Cook and Sons in Porchester Street, nor the edge-tool works of Messrs. Yates at Aston. The chiefs had a train to catch at 11:50 from New Street Station, where two first-class compartments had been reserved for them in the London express. They arrived at the station to find a big crowd come to see them off.

> A large number of people followed them on to the platform, and they sought refuge from the public gaze in the first-class refreshment room, where they partook of iced drinks.
>
> Before leaving Khama expressed through Mr. Willoughby the great pleasure his visit to the city had given him and his companions. He thanked everyone who had contributed to that end, and he especially thanked the police for their assistance.

In thanking the Birmingham city police force for their crowd control, Khama implicitly criticized the Bechuanaland Border Police, the corrupt colonial force that in theory enforced law and order in Bechuanaland: "We are glad to see how the police make peace and order, instead of trouble." [10]

✢ ✢ ✢

The chiefs had come clean with the British public, by identifying the Chartered Company rather than simply liquor as the enemy. They had gained sympathy for their cause, but there was still a long way to go in convincing people of its practicality.

No doubt as they traveled to London, and through London on to smokeless Brighton, on that hot Saturday at the end of September 1895,

Willoughby would have read and read out aloud some of the press comments that were appearing. The *Birmingham Gazette*, for example, expressed its admiration for Khama's speech at the Birmingham Council House breakfast as "the most remarkable which he has yet delivered in this country." But it described the "contest between King KHAMA and the Chartered Company" as "highly debateable." The *Birmingham Argus* was more persuaded by Khama's speech:

> His explanation excited the warmest sympathy and, so far as the representative opinion of Birmingham may influence the reception which Mr Chamberlain will give the representation of the chiefs, it will favourably dispose him towards the satisfaction of their legitimate claims.

This was an excellent omen for other cities, indicating the favorable impact that the Bechuana chiefs would have on the municipal elites on which Chamberlain banked for his basic support. The weekly journal *South Africa*, on the other hand, carried an omen altogether more sinister, in the form of a large fold-out supplement in its edition of September 28. The supplement was an extremely detailed (thirteen miles to the inch) map of the northern half of the Bechuanaland Protectorate from Palapye upward. The northwestern corner (Ngamiland) was demarcated as "British West Charterland" and the rest of the territory down to the Limpopo was marked as British South Africa Company territory. Palapye (Palachwe, 3,150 feet above sea level) was marked as the terminus of "Railway from Cape Town."

The *Illustrated London News* on September 28 refrained from political comment but observed of Khama's speechifying in the Midlands:

> The Bechuana chief, Khama, as a speaker, is improving since his arrival in this country. His utterance gets quite impassioned in its fluency, and the moment the interpreter has told the audience what the dark-skinned chief is saying, Khama hastens on sentence after sentence in impetuous eloquence.
>
> It is really an impressive sight to see this fine, tall, distinguished man addressing a great English audience in his native tongue. There is a mastery about his brow and an intelligence in the light of his eyes which account for the wide influence he has exerted, and the courage with which he has grappled with difficult questions of policy in his own country.

There was quite another type of comment that appeared the day before in a journal of the liquor trade, *Licensing World:*

> There has been quite a little Khama "boom" this week. To adapt Rudyard Kipling to the situation, it has been "Khama this, and Khama that, and Khama all over the shop." . . . in these dull times he must have been a boon and a blessing to hard-up editors.

The *Licensing World* continued on a sour note, accusing Khama of political interference in internal British affairs because of his opinions on temperance and prohibition:

> Khama on African topics may be worth listening to; but I really do not think it dignified on the part of the English people and the English Press to rave about a black man ["teaching white people the rudiments of political economy"], however distinguished a negro chief he may be.

Almost the same words were plagiarized in the magazine *Fun* on October 1, which added: "By the time the next interesting black man arrives we may have learned to be a little Khama—I mean calmer." [11]

✥ ✥ ✥

That *Kgosi* Khama's reception in England had been extraordinary was confirmed by the fate of the two BaRolong delegates, representing *Kgosi* Montshiwa of Mafeking. They had arrived on the *Tantallon Castle*, and together with their guide, Rev. A. S. Sharp, accompanied the other Bechuana on some early excursions. But Chamberlain and the Colonial Office had refused to see them at all, despite the fact that one fifth of their land fell within the Bechuanaland Protectorate rather than in "British Bechuanaland" now becoming part of Cape Colony. (This was yet another indication of Colonial Office complicity with the Chartered Company, as the "Barolong Farms" were the first target for company "railway works" expropriation within the protectorate.)

It became expedient to separate this "Wesleyan" delegation from their "LMS" brethren. Besele (Wessels) Montshiwa and Stephen Lefenya went their own way with Sharp. On September 24 they were reported to be touring Windsor Castle, being shown the state apartments, the chapels, and the royal mews. Soon afterward they took a mail ship, the *Drummond Castle*, which sailed from London for Cape Town on the twenty-seventh and from Southampton on the twenty-eighth. [12]

NINE

The Fountain whence Came the Missionaries

-◆→⟾◉ ◉⟾←◆-

THE CHIEFS TRAVELED STRAIGHT THROUGH LONDON that Saturday to Brighton for further rest and recreation, staying once again at the house of George Singleton. The journal *South Africa* claimed that they "fled to Brighton to escape the heat." At their request, Singleton had set up a number of trips to places of interest for them. Their stay was to extend to their appearance at the annual convention of the Congregational Union of ministers and lay leaders being held in Brighton during the following week.

This time they paid for themselves to revisit the aquarium (total admission 5s.), while separate lodgings were found for the attendants at the price of four pounds. As the chiefs strolled along the elevated stone and concrete promenade on the Brighton seafront, smartly dressed, "They seemed to care little for the curious glances of the crowd, but marched along with an air of stolid indifference." A Manchester newspaper speculated whether it was ennui rather than restrained interest that Khama and the rest were expressing in all that they saw.[1]

SUNDAY, SEPTEMBER 29

The next day the chiefs attended divine service in Union Street chapel in the morning once again. That evening Singleton arranged a musical evening for them at his house.

Five women singers, two men singers, and a pianist from the Lewes Road chapel entertained the chiefs and their attendants with Moody and Sankey hymns, lively revivalist church music with African-American resonances, which had taken nineteenth-century British Nonconformism by storm. The chiefs already knew many of the older songs on offer (albeit in Setswana rather than English) and first made a selection of which ones they wanted to hear. Their choice included "Will You Meet Me at the Fountain?" and other favorites such as "Hold the Fort," "Knocking, Knocking, Who Is There?" "Gospel Bells," and "Tell Me the Old, Old Story." Willoughby's small son was on hand as their interpreter.

Miss K. Holman opened the recital with a "very tasteful" solo rendition of "Will You Meet Me at the Fountain?" The audience in the Singleton drawing room settled back to listen with obvious pleasure:

> Khama, his friends, and the native attendants listened with undivided attention, Khama, in particular, beating time with his hand upon his knee and being keenly interested in the performance.

After an interval in midperformance, for the partaking of "zoedone and cake," the recital ended by special request with "God Be with You Till We Meet Again," during which "Khama and His Friends" stood up and remained standing. The chiefs then shook hands with all the singers and said, through their small interpreter, "Good night; thank you"—"apparently highly gratified at the musical treat."[2]

MONDAY, SEPTEMBER 30

On the Monday morning Singleton took the Bechuana to see the local board school in Elm Road, of which he had been chairman of the board of management in the previous year.

About twenty people descended on Elm Road School, including other friends of Singleton and Master Willoughby to act as interpreter. They found "one of the latest and finest" buildings erected by the Brighton School Board; "and the chiefs expressed themselves as greatly pleased at the brightness of the place, while they were evidently interested in the working of the school, and asked many questions through the interpreter." They used and repeated the English word *good* many times in their spoken observations.

The headmaster had arranged a tour that would "appeal to the eye and ear." First they entered the infants' department, where they inspected kindergarten work and were treated to a show of English traditional dancing. The children were circling around a maypole, boys in one direction and girls in the other each with a ribbon attached to the top of the pole. The chiefs were impressed by the precision and accuracy with which the small dancers weaved under and over each other and plaited their ribbons tightly round the pole. No doubt the implications of this supposedly ancient English fertility dance were not spelled out to the chiefs any more than to the children themselves.

The party then proceeded to the boys' school. On inspecting one of the smaller boys' workbook, one of the chiefs inquired as to whether the profusion of blue marks by the teacher indicated good or bad work by the pupil. The chiefs "seemed pleased" to see boys drawing maps of southern Africa, and electrical experiments in another classroom "amused the visitors greatly." In the girls' school they closely examined drawings on display and "listened with attention" to the singing.

Finally, after the Bechuana were photographed together in the girls' playground, "the three chiefs inscribed their names in English characters in the visitors' book."[3]

Meanwhile more than a thousand delegates were assembling for the annual assembly of the Congregational Union to be held over the next few days in Brighton. Such conventions were to become commonplace in seaside towns during the twentieth century, but the Congregational Union convention was sufficiently novel toward the end of the nineteenth century for the arrangements to draw detailed comment in the Brighton and national press.

A major effort was made by the other religious denominations in Brighton, including Anglican "Churchmen" and Jews, to make the Congregational delegates feel at home. The promise of an appearance or two by the three "Bechuana" chiefs at the meetings in the seaside town seems to have been the main reason for a record thirteen hundred delegates turning up. The delegates reported on arrival in the latter part of Monday to the Corn Exchange building, where the convention organizers gave them colored maps of Brighton and allocated them to stay in homes as well as hotels all over the town. The actual proceedings were to be held in the central complex of the Corn Exchange, the Dome, and the Royal Pavilion—the latter being a long, low building of domed and tented "oriental" shapes built during Regency days earlier that century. The London *Daily News*, which together with the London *Daily Chronicle* constituted the Nonconformist national press, remarked that delegates were afforded "ample accommodation for writing, conversation, and light refreshments on the spot," as well as spaces for committees and the gathering as a whole.

That evening, of Monday the thirtieth, the Dome was filled with more than three thousand people attending the welcoming service and sermon. A Congregational minister from Sydenham (Crystal Palace), south of London, conducted the devotional service. A young theologian of pronouncedly Modernist views from the Free Church College in Glasgow, preached the hour-long sermon—an exposition of the higher criticism based on the Second Epistle of St. Peter, chapter 3, verses 13 to 14. His refusal to accept everything in the Bible as literal rather than symbolic truth would have appealed to Willoughby, but not to much of his audience. His appeal for practical action to carry out Christian social ideals beyond "the elect" could have been just as controversial.

The temperance meeting that followed the sermon retained much of the audience. Its chairman, also the chairman of the Congregational Union, Rev. Urijah Thomas, urged upon his audience the need to support Khama's mission to Britain. But the chiefs themselves had not yet made an appearance.[4]

TUESDAY, OCTOBER 1

On the Tuesday the chiefs busied themselves during the morning with a visit to a dairy factory, producing butter and cheese, at Glynde—a village east of Lewes on the inland railway between Brighton and Eastbourne. (Today the area is best known for the Glyndebourne opera theater.)[5]

That afternoon the three chiefs and two of their attendants walked into the assembly of the Congregational Union in the Dome at Brighton, chaired once again by that Welshman with the (in the estimation of the *Pall Mall Gazette*) "magnificent" name of Rev. Urijah Thomas. The meeting was bedeviled by the acoustics of the hall, which baffled the more rapid speakers with bewildering echoes. The Bechuana entered the Dome during a debate on finances that was immediately wound up because of the "manifestation of delight" among the delegates, who "rose in enthusiastic welcome."

Wardlaw Thompson, the foreign secretary of the LMS, introduced the chiefs with the proud boast "that he had been entertained by each of them in their own capitals." Rev. Edwin Lloyd, taking time off from the book he was writing about them, acted as their interpreter on this occasion. Lloyd conveyed to the chiefs on behalf of the chairman "warm approval of the objects of their mission."

The *Christian World* reported, "The arrangement had been that only Khama should speak, but the Assembly insisted on a few words from each. Each began with a greeting."

Khama delivered a typically sincere little speech, rejoicing to see missionaries in their own country and thanking God that he had been able to see "the great churches of England." He went on to profess his recognition of Christ as Savior and his faith that Christ "could also destroy all the evil things in this world." He ended with the words, "May Christ join us together with joy" (to which the profane and irreverent *Pall Mall Gazette* added: "whatever he understands by that").

SEBELE "brought down the house" by saying that he saw long ago a teacher called Mr. Livingstone, and they had found that what he said was true, that the love of God is a genuine thing, and they found it was still so to-day. They rejoiced to see the fountain whence came the missionaries. It was manifest that the English Christians had the love of God in their hearts, because they made no difference between black men and white men.

After Bathoen had spoken similar words, and Willoughby had declined to speak on the grounds that time was pressing, the assembly considered and adopted with cheers a "spirited resolution" sympathizing with "Prince Khama and his fellow chieftains" and begging Her Majesty's Government to "find it possible in some way [for them] to remain under the direct protectorate of the British Crown."

When the chiefs arose to quit the platform there was a rush of delegates to shake hands with them. The chiefs smilingly held out their hands.

The *Christian World* adds that Rev. G. J. Woods, one of the platform speakers who had previously delivered an address on "Congregationalism in the Rural Districts," "at length found it necessary to interpose physically" so that the chiefs and their attendants might leave the Dome.

The proceedings continued without the Bechuana for another hour or two with the introduction of ministers from Australia and Tasmania, "rather wearisome discussion on the report of the committee appointed to consider the revision of the constitution," and "long, sharp and divided discussion" over ministers' conditions of service. It is scarcely surprising that the chiefs' visit to the Congregational Union was by contrast described by the Rev. Dr. Brown of Bedford as "both affecting and historic."[6]

WEDNESDAY, OCTOBER 2

The late or Indian summer lasted until the second day of October 1895, when the chiefs had the last of the warm weather to make a prearranged visit to a farm in the Sussex countryside. Singleton took the three chiefs and two interpreters by a local train to Steyning, a small country town eight or nine miles northwest of Brighton, where the climate and soil are propitious enough even to grow grapes.

They arrived at Steyning station at 12:15 after midday and were driven in a brake to "Newham," the house of Mr. W. Powell Breach, where they ate lunch. Breach was a local businessman and magistrate, and a friend of Singleton—presumably representing "new money" with Congregational connections, rather than the old squirearchy that normally supplied rural justices of the peace.

The first stop after lunch was Messrs. Breach and Sons' wool and leather factory. Here the chiefs were shown over the works by the Breach sons and "appeared to be deeply interested in the various processes [that] sheep's skins undergo in their transformation into parchment."

The next stop was the Steyning auction market, where calves were being auctioned by Messrs. Pearson and Farncombe. Here they listened to the barking and hectoring style of the auctioneer, Mr. Farncombe, and "the conventionality of the English mode of sale appeared to immensely tickle the visitors' fancy."

After "strolling through the market and inspecting the stock," the party was ready to drive to the Breach farm at Bramber. There was one more stop on the way, when the chiefs alighted to visit Mr. W. Potter's ornithological museum. The stuffed birds were "inspected with considerable interest," but it was the exhibition of a mantrap that most excited the chiefs. The trap was a potent symbol of the enclosure and privatization of former communal hunting land by the avaricious chiefs of England, an instrument of torture with heavy iron jaws that snapped onto the ankle of the would-be poacher.

The chiefs arrived at last at Horton Farm, which had been leased by the Breach family to raise sheep for their wool and leather factory. Here once again the chiefs "seemed delighted with everything that engaged their attention, and were not slow to solicit explanations as to the use of the farm implements." They strolled around the meadows, inspecting grazing livestock at close quarters, and expressing their customary "astonishment at the verdure of the trees and meadows." Either Sebele or Bathoen insisted on actively searching out the sources of water, such as streams and wells, on the farm.

After afternoon tea in the farmhouse, with the farm manager and his wife, Mr. and Mrs. Lambert, the Bechuana returned to Steyning. On their drive back through the villages of Bramber and Upper Beeding to Steyning, they "excited much interest among the townspeople and villagers" who flocked into the streets to see them.

At Steyning Khama, Sebele, and Bathoen were each presented with "a rug made of wool stripped from skins at the Steyning factory" as a memento of their day's visit. The whole party was then given "a hearty send-off" on the six o'clock train from Steyning station by "a large gathering of children."

The weather had at last turned. As the *Sussex Daily News* remarked, "They appeared to keenly feel the sudden change from the tropical heat to English autumnal weather."[7]

THURSDAY, OCTOBER 3 – SUNDAY, OCTOBER 6

Securely wrapped against the damp "sudden extreme cold," and at last able to wear their heavy greatcoats, the three chiefs took an "up" train for London at 11:00 on the morning of Thursday, October 3.

They were to stay in London for six nights, once again boarding at Armfield's South Place (Temperance) Hotel in Finsbury, in preparation for another sally northward. A correspondent writing to the *Brighton Gazette,* signing himself or herself "Colonial," said that the chiefs were going north "in answer to the direct invitation of the most influential people to Manchester, Liverpool, Leeds, and Sheffield, and, lastly, to Glasgow, where they hope to obtain a personal interview with the Queen [at Balmoral]."[8]

Friday, October 4, was spent at the "Empire of India" exhibition in Earl's Court, one of the great exhibition halls erected in West London. The chiefs were reportedly "delighted" with the dramatic pageant titled "India," staged at the exhibition during the afternoon or evening by the Hungarian theatrical entrepreneur Imry Kiralfy. No doubt the pageant presented India as a land of elephants and bejeweled maharajas. It would be interesting to know how the Africans reacted to this presentation of colonial life on another continent, but their comments are not recorded. They also went for "rides" in the funfair within the exhibition and particularly "enjoyed the sensation of a journey on the Big [Ferris] Wheel."[9]

It was possibly on Saturday, October 5, that the chiefs traveled down by train to Surbiton in Surrey (rail fare 18s. 6d. and then cabs 8s. 6d.). Surbiton was the nearest main-line railway station for civic-proud Kingston-upon-Thames, which had originally refused to accommodate a railway station. It was also the station for Chessington, where Chessington Hall had been a famous pleasure resort since the eighteenth century. Possibly the attraction at Chessington was a predecessor of the zoological park eventually set up there in 1931. Khama and other chiefs rounded up live animals for such collections—with the exception of ostriches, prized for their feathers in current hat fashions, whose live bodies and fertilized eggs were jealously guarded.[10]

MONDAY, OCTOBER 7 – TUESDAY, OCTOBER 8

On Monday the chiefs paid a long visit to the London Hospital, one of the London medical schools, in Whitechapel—the heart of the East End, where "Jack the Ripper" had operated a decade previously. Through Willoughby as interpreter, according to the *British Medical Journal,* Khama

> made numerous inquiries during his inspection of the wards, examining the beds and spring mattresses, ice safe, surgical appliances, etc., remarking frequently on the prevailing cleanliness.
>
> Khama is a tall, well-built man, with a quick and courteous manner. He asked many intelligent questions as to the management of the institution, and whether the patients paid; also as to the position of sisters and nurses. In speaking his face presents a pleasing and intelligent expression.

In the children's ward he made many friends among the little patients, with whom he shook hands, to their great delight; and he remarked of the nurse that the children "loved their new mother."

A week later the *Liverpool Courier* added a further tale about the visit of the chiefs to this London teaching hospital, indicating that Willoughby was once again complicit in springing a surprise on them:

> They were conducted into the dissecting room. It happened to be what is known as "a good day," there being about eight bodies in the room "for the knife."
>
> Immediately they saw what was going on—students slicing away at dead bodies—the three chiefs of a warlike race decamped at an undignified pace from the room, being apparently horror-stricken. The Rev. Mr. Willoughby followed them out and appealed to them thus—"Chiefs, surely you are not such cowards as to be afraid of dead men?"
>
> Upon their bravery being challenged they immediately consented to return to the ghastly spectacle. Their conductor then explained that "the bodies were being cut up so as to enable the doctors to save other lives."
>
> Their temporarily shocked belief in our Christianity was revived, and King Khama said he would not mind his body being cut up if it were to save other people's lives.[11]

The next day, Tuesday the eighth, Bathoen collected and paid for sets of reading glasses from George Spiller and Co., of No. 3 Wigmore Street—just north of Oxford Street, which was fast becoming London's main shopping street. There was one pair of gold spectacles price £2 10s., and a pair of gilt spectacles price 15s. 6d. Presumably the spectacles had been prescribed after an eye test a day or two earlier.

Meanwhile it was Sebele who spent significant sums on medicines, including ointment and ipecacuanha (emetic/purgative) cachets, and doctor's fees—the latter totalling £8 16s. 6d.

It was also about this time that the chiefs signed themselves up with Durrant's Press Cuttings, Ltd. of 103 Whitecross Street, E.C. (still going a century later). Sebele and Bathoen were charged £5 5s. each for collections of newspaper clippings from the beginning of September to the middle of October (with Sebele's a week or so longer). Whereas Khama is recorded as having paid £3 3s. for "Durrant's Press Fee." The discount may be explained by the agency donating the September clippings to Khama as an incentive for further orders.[12]

✠ ✠ ✠

The success of the Bechuana chiefs' mission to the provinces of Great Britain was by now indisputable. Provincial towns and cities clamored for the honor of a visit—though the assumption seems always to have been that the chiefs would pay their own way. The *Dundee Advertiser* of October 5, for example, revealed that the citizens of Dundee had written to Wardlaw Thompson of the London Missionary Society, but the society had proved to have nothing to do with arrangements for the chiefs. Their request was passed on to Willoughby as the chiefs' tour manager, but he had had to choose from literally "hundreds" of towns. The chiefs would only be able to visit forty-four.

The London press now began to respond to provincial press comments following the chiefs' tour of the English Midlands.

South Africa of October 5 commented that the connection with religious bodies that Khama exploited might be death to his cause: "his psalm-singing little ways" would make him appear ludicrous in the eyes of the British public. The London *Sunday Times* of October 6 cautioned that while pro-missionary sentiment in England was strong and growing during the chiefs' visit, it was associated with anti–South African Dutch feeling:

> The Khama visit therefore, by playing into the hands of the anti-Boer party, and skilfully availing [himself] of Jingo feeling and the Temperance movement, has created an extremely difficult position for Mr Chamberlain. If he conciliates Khama and the missionaries, he must antagonize Mr Rhodes.

The *Court Journal* of October 12 echoed fears of Khama's antagonizing Chamberlain: on missionary platforms "The black and white effects produced are singular, but not argument, or artistic."

But the Bechuana chiefs were beginning to receive support, and Cecil Rhodes to receive opprobrium, from two of the three most illustrious editors in the land—W. T. Stead in his *Review of Reviews* at the beginning of October, and Frank Harris in his *Saturday Review* at the end of the month (the third illustrious editor being W. E. Henly of the *Fortnightly Review*).[13]

Stead's "Character Sketch" of Khama was published on October 1, after Stead had fobbed off preemptive inducements by Rhodes's envoys to recruit him to the Chartered cause. This in itself was significant since Rhodes had some years before placed great store on winning Stead over from being an erstwhile supporter of Mackenzie and Chamberlain's South Africa Committee. In 1891 Stead had been named as second executor after Lord Rothschild of Rhodes's will, one of the guardians of Rhodes's eccentric plans to fund a secret society to rule the world after his death. The "Character Sketch" of Khama in 1895 appears to have been the exact point at which Stead broke with Rhodes, leading to his being dropped as an executor. As Stead himself put it later: "It was what seemed to me the inexplicable desire of Mr. Rhodes to obtain Bechuanaland as a jumping-off place which led to the first divergence of view between him and myself." The "Character Sketch" itself shows that Stead was influenced by the recent "trumpet blast" of "Olive Schreiner's manifesto" against Rhodes and his "gang of gambling speculators."

Stead's fifteen-page study of the life of "Khama, Chief of the Bamangwato" was based largely on reading of the works of John Mackenzie and James Hepburn. Stead indulged himself in abundant simile. Khama was like Clovis, the medieval Frankish king who built Rheims cathedral after his conversion. He actually looked like Abraham Lincoln; the Tswana were like the tribes of Israel; Rhodes—"the Dictator of South Africa"— was like Mammon in Milton's *Paradise Lost* ("his looks and thoughts were always downward bent [on] trodden gold"), and his vision of South Africa was like Milton's Pandemonium: "never since the world began has there been [such] a successful edifice of dominion which bore from its turret to its foundation stone [such an] impress of Mammon."

As for Khama,

> Perhaps the most notable feature of Khama is the extent in which he succeeds in impressing those who visit him with his superiority. One who knows him well states that "the odd thing about Khama is that all who meet him seem to find that he excels in whatever department they are interested in . . . The hunter . . . The missionary . . . The politician. . . ."
>
> In reality Khama is none of these. He is a thoroughly good man, honest and painstaking, self-possessed and resolute.

Stead told Rhodes "he had better let Khama alone for a season":

> Khama is the one man in the whole of Africa whose case commands the sympathy of a large section of the British public; his claim is moderate, founded in justice and right. And if there be a God who rules among the affairs of men, it does not seem probable that He wishes Mr. Rhodes to sacrifice Khama to the exigencies of political or financial adventure.

The "Character Sketch" ended on a note of warning: Khama was like a corn on John Bull's little toe. England's message to Cecil Rhodes must be: "Dodge the corn if you want to get the shekels." [14]

Apart from Stead and Olive Schreiner before him, there were now other signs that the tide was on the turn against Rhodes. The *Penny Illustrated Paper* of September 28 had praised Rhodes as another George Washington. But by October 6 the *Sunday Times* was mocking him as "the Poo Bah of Africa."

The *Westminster Gazette* carried an interview with a "negro agitator" in the shape of a Jamaican-born boot dealer who had spent the last thirteen years in Kimberley, South Africa. Booth by name, he had come to agitate in Britain and America against the pass laws, the liquor canteens, and the compounds that oppressed Africans at Kimberley and Johannesburg. The compounds for migrant workers were, Booth said, little more than "slave pens." But his bitterest words were reserved for Cecil Rhodes, "as the prime mover in all oppression," and Dr. "Jim" (Jameson), "whom he seemed to consider one of the negro's worst enemies."

Booth's words were picked up in the Cape Town newspapers and in the London journal *South Africa,* which headlined the story "More anti-Rhodes bunkum." It added that the *Christian World* had recently become an admirer of Olive Schreiner, a militant agnostic, because she gave weight to the (*Saturday Review's*) contention that Khama, Sebele, and Bathoen "are now over here trying to avoid being seized and sucked dry by the Rhodesian crew." [15]

There was perhaps more than a hint of Christian socialism in the late Victorian disquiet with capitalist ethics that historians now call "Tory romantic anticapitalism."

TEN

A Thing to Look at with the Teeth

◆━━◗ ◖━━◆

BY WEDNESDAY, OCTOBER 9, THE THREE CHIEFS AND their retinue were in the industrial North of England once again—at Stockport in Lancashire, just south of Manchester. Here they visited a large hat and cap manufacturer, and a large cotton-mill—where "Khama expressed delight with the machinery."

That evening they addressed another crowded LMS centenary meeting, at Heaton Mersey Congegational chapel, where Willoughby's brother-in-law, the Rev. A. H. Cullen, was the pastor. Also in attendance was Rev. Stanley Rogers, a Congregational worthy and local representative of the LMS who made it his business to make the visit of the Bechuana to the Northwest a success.

After a hymn, a prayer, and a choral anthem ("O Worship the Lord in the Beauty of Holiness"), the three chiefs were introduced to the congregation. Khama told them, "Although we did come from our country to deal with things pertaining to the State, yet we rejoice to see Christian men and Christian women in this land.—(Applause)." Sebele told the congregation: "With joy and astonishment we see what God had done for the people of England." Bathoen praised the work of the missionaries and added: "God can help both you and us together—black and white.— (Loud applause.)" [1]

An editorial in next morning's *Manchester Guardian* noted that Khama, Sebele, and Bathoen were "neglecting no opportunity of making friends" in their struggle against Mr. Rhodes and the Chartered Company. The *Guardian* recalled that this was not the first time native Africans had been seen on LMS platforms in this country. Sixty years earlier the "once well-known missionary" John Philip had taken a "Hottentot" (Khoe) and a

"Kaffir" (Xhosa) with him around Britain "to rouse public opinion" against the government of Cape Colony.

The *Manchester Guardian* was impressed by the fact that the chiefs preferred "to spend their time in addressing meetings than in seeing 'sights.'" But the latter is precisely what they had done the next day, when they visited a hatting works and a cotton mill in Stockport.[2]

FRIDAY, OCTOBER 11

The reception of the Bechuana chiefs in Liverpool, the great port city of the northwest that dominated sea traffic with Ireland and North America and West Africa, had many similarities with their experience in Birmingham two weeks before. There was undeniably an element of competition between the cities in the welcome given to the chiefs. One of the members of Parliament for Liverpool (Kirkdale) was Khama's old friend George Baden-Powell, who, though he was unavoidedly absent on urgent business as a commissioner of the Church of England, at the church's annual conference in Norwich, would have done all that he could to ensure a smooth pathway for the chiefs.

Amid a flurry of officials from rival railway companies checking trains from London and Birmingham at the main stations, the chiefs arrived quietly and unostentatiously at the Cheshire Lines Committee Station on the 11:15 Stockport train, during the morning of Friday, October 11. According to the *Liverpool Courier* the chiefs "left the precincts of the station almost unnoticed, being attired in quiet-toned English clothes."

The *Liverpool Post* had quite a different story when the chiefs emerged into the Liverpool streets:

> The appearance of the highly ebonised party attracted much attention in Water-street. Khama particularly coming in for a lion's share of the attention. He is tall, grizzled, well-formed, and intellectual looking.
>
> The Bechuanese dialect is rich and sonorous, and the ideas of the people are full of poetic imagery. The sound is not unlike a mixture of Italian, Spanish, and French, a word resembling "alors" [*njalo*, "now"?] occurring frequently in conversation, while the abundance of vowel sounds was very striking.

Their first appointment after depositing their bags in the Junior Reform Club was an inspection of the Liverpool overhead electric railway, where they were shown over the electricity-generating station by Mr. Cottrell, the manager. According to the *Courier:*

> Various experiments were made for their benefit, some of which occasioned among them the utmost wonder. So awe-stricken were they with

the manipulation of the electric forces ["electric fluid" as the *Post* would have it] by Mr. Cottrell that, when he made a flash of lightning through the building, Chief Khama, through the interpreter, designated him "the chief ["master" said the *Post*] of lightning" [—a pretty compliment in which all the other chiefs concurred].

Rev. Stanley Rogers, their general guide and host in Liverpool, then took the Bechuana back to the Junior Reform Club for a wash and brush-up before lunch. After introductions to members,

> Four of the suite remained at the club for lunch, their visit exciting much interest amongst the members present. After lunch they were taken to a smokeroom, where cigars and coffee were duly dispensed.
> Unfortunately, the enjoyment of the visitors appeared to be somewhat marred by the coldness of the weather, and although greatcoats were sent for and a snug circle was made around the blazing fire, the guests did not seem to be altogether free from a regrettable tendency to shiver.

Khama, Sebele, and Bathoen went to attend a grand civic luncheon at one o'clock in the town hall on Dale Street, where the heavily robed lord mayor (Mr. W. H. Watts) and members of the city council and distinguished guests were waiting to meet them. Those present included Thomas Lipton the tea merchant and grocery millionaire, the mayor of Bootle, and members of Liverpool merchant families like the Holts of West African fame.

> The three chiefs arrived after most of the other guests had taken their seats, and as they proceeded up the stairway to the banqueting-hall the Police Band, which was discoursing music in the vestibule, played a weird sort of tune, which was variously described as "the native war dance," and [as] the African National Anthem.

The tune in question cannot have been *Nkosi sikelel'i-Afrika* ("God Bless Africa"), the South African (Xhosa) hymn that was composed two years later. Possibly it was a tune of West African origin or, equally likely, a piece of mock-Ethiopian minstrelry composed by a white American. Or could it possibly have been an early echo of jazz from New Orleans?

The lord mayor began to speak when the guests had finished eating and the plates were cleared away. After reading apologies for nonattendance from the bishops of Liverpool and Chester and from George Baden-Powell, he delivered a paean of praise for Khama and then proposed a loyal toast to "The Queen."

The lord mayor then rose again to propose a toast to the health of the three guests, Khama, Sebele, and Bathoen:

> I suppose it is the first time in the history of this country that we have been honoured with the presence of three African kings at one time. That fact

emphasises the universal brotherhood of man as few things can. (Hear, hear.)

He then went on at length about the "high state of religious culture and civilisation" of the three chiefs, who "reign with more or less of absolute sway over a large territory in the south of the continent of Africa, in separate kingdoms adjoining each other." Their fear, he added, was being put under the rule of a Chartered Company that would not restrain the liquor traffic:

> Gentlemen, we seek commerce, but let that come by improving and elevating those with whom we trade, not by demoralising them. I am sure of your sympathy, and will now ask you to drink success to the mission of these noble chiefs. (Loud applause.)

The *Liverpool Courier* adds, "The toast was drunk with much cordiality." The irony of toasting temperance by ritual quaffs of alcohol on the part of nonteetotal guests was not remarked upon.

Khama then delivered a direct, political speech, returning to themes previously raised in Birmingham:

> When we came away from our land we heard that the company had been given our territories by the Government, and we found in that no cause for rejoicing for us black people. (Hear, hear.)

Khama went on to raise, wittingly or unwittingly, the bogey of Liverpool's past—as the chief port and profit center of the Atlantic African slave trade in the eighteenth century.

> We are not content to be dealt with as things that may be sold by their owners—(applause)—and so of course we came to the Government that we might tell . . . we prefer to judge our own people and to remain under the British Government.
>
> We felt pained, because our Government had been making progress, and we have been going forward in teaching, and we are accustomed to think of ourselves as people, and not as things. (Applause.)

Once again, Sebele put his audience at ease in his first few words:

> I rejoice to see Europeans, and especially to salute you Englishmen, and above all I rejoice to see those that have assembled in the love of the chief of this village to-day. (Laughter and applause.) . . .
>
> Nevertheless while you look at us three chieftains, to-day, you ought to know that we have a little sorrow right in the centre of our three hearts. Our sorrow is born of our objection to go from the hand of the Government into the hand of the Chartered Company. (hear, hear.)

He then went on to regret that some Liverpool newspapers were reproducing the story (from Flora Shaw's editorial in the *Times* that Monday) that the chiefs and the Chartered Company had agreed to come to terms.

I want you to know that this is a lie. (Applause.) We have never had a meeting with this company. We have not spoken about these things with them, and we say, as we said before, we want the Government and nobody besides. (Hear, hear.)

To this thing we ask your help, saying to you, "You, who are the people of this nation, can you not speak your thoughts and your words, so that your chieftains may not hand us over into the power of the company?"

As for us we have no power to restrain them, we are but weak in the hands of those who are mighty. But you have all power, for is the nation not yours?

This moving appeal to the rights and powers of the British people over their own government was greeted by heavy applause.

Bathoen, as usual, suffered from the disadvantage of speaking last:

All the words that are spoken by us three are words of this kind, they are one: and the words that have been spoken by my two neighbours are my words, just as if they had been spoken with my lips. (hear, hear.) And I say it is God who can help both you and us. (Applause.)

More toasts followed, to the London Missionary Society and to the lord mayor himself. The lord mayor rose once more to speak. He touched on the iniquitous past of "Liverpool, as a city":

He could not help thinking that now they had [had] such an eloquent appeal made to them, [that] every one of them would feel humiliated at the past, and thankful that they had an opportunity of helping to do right to Africa and those that had that day been before them. (Applause.)[3]

From the town hall the Bechuana visitors went down to the nearby Liverpool docks. Here they boarded the tender *Skirmisher* and puffed over the Mersey to the Sloyne, where the great transatlantic Cunard liner the *Campania* lay at anchor. There were a dozen guests besides the chiefs, in the charge of Sir William Forwood, a director of the Cunard Company. One of the guests, by the name of G. H. Hewitt, claimed to have been a friend of Lobengula and other African chiefs, including Sebele's late father Sechele.

As the *Skirmisher* crossed the wide river estuary, the chiefs looked back on the grand dockside buildings of the city of Liverpool and at the numerous small craft that dotted the water:

"Uriri! uriri!" or some musical expression like that [*ruri!* "truly!"; *o rile* "you have said"?], continually escaped from the king's lips. "It is a great water," he said; "greater than London, and the city is great and beautiful."

Questioned as to his impressions of the docks, cut into the side of the city and displaying hundreds of tall masts of oceangoing sailing vessels as big as clippers, as well as steamers, Khama replied:

Oh, it is mighty; there are forests of fallen trees such as no man has seen together.

As the *Skirmisher* drew up close to the *Campania* the chiefs stared, and one of them said, "we grow less, but the great water-kraal grows bigger before our eyes." And so it did.

Two trumpeters on board the *Campania* blared off a royal salute, and Khama gracefully acknowledged the compliment with a bow. The king, preceded by Sir William Forwood, nimbly ran up the gangway, where he was introduced to Captain Hewitson, with whom he cordially shook hands, as he had previously done with Mr. Morrison, who was in charge of the tender.

Their "majesties" were received by a turnout of all the crew on board, and then visited in royal procession the various apartments of interest: the music-room, the smokeroom, the library, &c. Afterwards a visit was made to the captain's deck, where the African royalties or semi-royalties were initiated into some of the mysteries of the great ocean palace.

Khama, when told that two trains could pass each other in the funnel, simply opened his mouth, and stared, the significance of which was great. He did not, however, quite believe the funnel could be so immense. Curiously enough, he was more interested in the masts. He was told a sailor could go up these.

"How?" said Khama; "it is impossible; he must have wings, then." Being told that the wings were ropes, the king was more puzzled still. At last he struck a bright idea, which seemed to him to knock the bottom out of the story about the man going aloft.

At this point in the story the correspondent of the *Liverpool Post* lapses into mock-minstrel talk that he could not possibly have heard from Khama, who was anyway being interpreted into English by Willoughby—"If man goes up there, man no gets down again."

He was told he would get down in the same way as he got up, but the "king" could not see it, and remained incredulous. The party afterwards proceeded to the dining saloon, where tea was served.

Sir William Forwood, through the interpreter, told the chiefs something about the provisions made for the journey across the Atlantic—including such items as 8,000 lbs. of mutton, 24,000 lbs. of beef, 16,000 to 20,000 eggs each way, &c.

Khama opened his mouth again and showed his ivories to the roots. He pondered a little, and then said, "you eat a hundred farms at once." Told that eighteen tons of potatoes were consumed on one journey, he opened his mouth again.

"Why does he open his mouth so?" said an inquisitive member of the party. "That is an African custom," said the interpreter, and Khama, speaking with musical intonation, supplied the key to the enigma by observing: "It is a thing to look at with the teeth," which also being interpreted means that his astonishment was inexpressible.

Just then the Rev. Stanley Rogers tripped up to the music-room over-head and played a piece on the organ, which had a fine effect. The chiefs were surprised at hearing the sound, which came, as one of them said, "out of the air."

After some more talk, the Rev. Stanley Rogers thanked the Cunard Company and Sir William Forwood for their courtesy. The party then returned [on the tender] to the [landing] stage [at Liverpool], and pro-ceeded to their destination on an omnibus carriage of the London and North-Western Railway Company.

Khama in particular was obviously in high spirits after all the sea air, despite the chilly weather. Khama enjoyed the cold: one of his praise names was *Mma-Mariga* ("Mother-Winter") because he liked to sit apart from the fire on cold nights.

Khama got upon the box beside the driver. Asked why he did this, one of the party replied: "Khama says, 'I'm [the] King, and the King goes first.'"

And so off he went on the dickey, sharing his royalty for the time being with the driver, who was abreast of him.

All through his wandering in Liverpool, Khama has always ridden on the dickey, and all attempts to get him inside the carriage have been un-availing, his answer always being the same—"I'm the King, and the King goes first."[4]

It is scarcely surprising that Sebele and Bathoen were beginning to show their resentment at all the attention given to and demanded by Khama.

That night there was a "vast meeting, organised by the Nonconformist Council of Liverpool," in Great George Street chapel on the south side of the city. Once again the lord mayor, Mr. Watts, presumably himself a Nonconformist in religion, presided over the meeting. He had now had time since luncheon to ponder further and crafted his words more care-fully, though once again speaking at length. After some words on the ne-cessity to spread "the humanising and civilising Gospel of Christ" across the world, and upon the worthy mission of the chiefs in opposition to the Chartered Company, Watts returned to his theme:

Already we owed a deep debt to Africa. There was a heavy balance against us. We had not always dealt fairly with her. Many a slave cargo had been carried in Liverpool ships, and many a fortune had been founded in that way.

In 1700 the first vessel sailed from this port to Africa—doubtless for legitimate trading, but in sixty years it had grown to ninety-six [vessels], and our merchants had found out that a human negro paid better than merchandise. It was on record that in 1766 Captain Simmons returned from Africa with 400 slaves. In 1767 advertisements appeared that several young men were to be offered for sale in this city.

Since then we had done something to purge ourselves from this inhuman traffic. The British flag, wherever it floated, proclaimed liberty and freedom to all alike, and Liverpool, whatever might have been her sins, had confessed them and made what atonement was in her power. Were we again to forge fresh chains for the poor African? . . .

The three chieftains present might well look with anxiety at what was going to happen. The dark continent was being opened up, and there was an unseemly scramble for territory. "Spheres of influence," forsooth, they called them now.

The three chiefs were here on a noble mission to plead with us to keep out the accursed thing [liquor]. There could be but one response to that appeal. The Christian people of this great country could give but one answer to it, and he felt sure from this great meeting and from others throughout the country their answer would be that their request must be conceded (loud applause).

Watts had thereby further compounded the confusion of the chiefs' political cause against Chartered Company rule with that against the liquor traffic. In doing so he reflected Liverpool realities. At Chamberlain's request, the Liverpool Chamber of Commerce had already been meeting to consider ways of curbing the native liquor traffic in (West) Africa,

While the lord mayor left to fulfill an engagement elsewhere, the three chiefs were welcomed by representatives of Baptists, Calvinistic Methodists, and the local Peace Society. The chiefs were presented with an album as a memento of their visit to Liverpool—an album consisting of photographs of Queen Victoria, Robert Moffat, David Livingstone, and the lord mayor.

The speeches of the three chiefs in thanks were "identical in bearing with those delivered at the luncheon earlier in the day." The reporter of the *Liverpool Courier*, however, was not impressed by the chiefs' speeches— or, rather, was impressed by the apparent confirmation of his or her own racial prejudices:

the one thought which they created in the minds of those who listened was that they are "groping! groping! groping!," crawling patiently and slowly from the blackness of barbarism into the sickly light of the outer pale of civilisation. Chiefs with majestic frames and kingly spirits, they have but minds—judged from our standard of civilisation—steeped in the obscurity which in England is only illumined after the evolution of centuries and the spilling of the blood of the martyrs.

When Khama, Sebele, and Bathoen had spoken, Willoughby once again gave his extended account of missionary life in Khama's country. After a collection was made of contributions for the LMS centenary, the meeting passed a resolution urging the colonial secretary to "accede to the wishes" of the three Bechuana chiefs for continued imperial rule.[5]

That night the chiefs stayed at the home of Rev. Stanley Rogers at

No. 51 Anfield Road, in a suburb next to Everton on the north side of the city center. There was some dissension among them about who was to keep the album of their Liverpool visit. As Rogers explained, the album contained not only the photographs of the two premier missionaries to Bechuanaland but also those of the queen and of the lord mayor, "for whom they have conceived a very warm admiration, and whose able and enthusiastic advocacy of their cause they very highly appreciate." Rogers continued:

> The first chief to enter [my house] had the album in his hand, and as soon as he got to the light looked at it, and when my wife began to speak to him he placed it on the sofa [as he stood up]. After that they took their seats, and he sat down beside it, leaving it there when he went into supper. On retiring to rest he took it upstairs with him.

The reporter from the *Liverpool Courier* constructed a rather different story from offhand comments by Willoughby the next morning:

> one of the chiefs annexed the present from the table and clung tightly to it during the whole of the night. He went to lie on a couch and placed the book under his head, and when bedtime arrived he concealed it under his coat and took it to his bedroom, to the disappointment of his companions.

The reporter seemed gratified to find that "the three manly and solemn visaged kings," who "did not in their personal habits reveal the slightest traces of savagery," had proved "they had not been properly brought under the influence of civilisation"—by resorting to such childlike behavior.

Rogers sprang to the defense of the Bechuana chiefs in subsequent letters to the *Courier:* "I feel sure each of them would appreciate a copy, but am equally sure no bitter feeling will arise between them on account of it." But the fact remains that there seems to have been some bad blood between the chiefs over the actions of one of them in trying to appropriate the album, and between Rogers and Willoughby over their failure to settle the issue. Willoughby asked Rogers to decide which chief should keep the album, but Rogers admitted, "I shrank from the ordeal."[6]

SATURDAY, OCTOBER 12

The next morning, before they left for the station, Rogers tried to jolly along his guests by playing on the piano. The tune "Old Calcutta" particularly pleased the chiefs:

> The set appearance of their dark faces relaxed into smiles, their eyes sparkled, and King Khama loudly clapped his hands—a manner of demonstrating his pleasure which he is proud of having learned during his stay in this country. It turned out they had been familiar with the tune many years ago.

But it was not a happy crew that arrived at Central Station shortly after ten o'clock to catch the 10:30 train for Manchester. As Rogers acknowledged,

> there seemed to be a look of consternation on their countenance when they found themselves at the station and about to depart. On asking the interpreter [Willoughby] its meaning, he told me they were sorry to leave, and had hoped they were going on the river again.

There were no crowds to see them off, and people scarcely noticed them on the platform. They entered their first-class compartment and sat (some of them) "stolidly smoking their cigars." The gloom was penetrated only by the arrival of Hewitt, the African traveler whom they had met on the *Campania*. He presented them with three small bouquets of flowers:

> What to do with these they did not at first seem to know, and held them gingerly in their big black hands. But when at length with a little delicate tact one of the company had placed the pretty flowers in their coat buttonholes they grunted short guttural exclamations of satisfaction.
>
> Next Mr. Hewitt presented Sebele with a little packet said to contain a cigar case, and given by Mr. Hewitt as a memento of a stay he had once made with the chief's father. He accepted it without the slightest facial expression—for immutability of countenance is a principle with them—and said, through an interpreter, "I thank you."

Sebele had been singled out for special treatment, instead of Khama. This may have served to release some of the tension between three headstrong middle-aged men. But it could not entirely dissipate the pressures of living so tightly together for so long.

The *Courier* reporter tackled Willoughby with the question, "What did the chiefs think of the agitation in the States for the disenfranchisement of the negroes?" Willoughby snapped back that the question was too long and complicated for the time they had in hand before the train left. Besides, he added not wholly truthfully, the chiefs probably didn't even know where America was. Then, no doubt by way of apology for his shortness, Willoughby outlined the next week's itinerary and made his incidental comments to the *Courier* on the dispute over the lord mayor's album and the pleasure that "Old Calcutta" had given the chiefs.

Once again, through Willoughby, the chiefs left behind a letter of thanks to all their hosts. Rogers added that they "were also mindful of the splendid discipline of the police force of this city, and the kindly protection given to them wherever they went." [7]

The Bechuana were going to the great city of Manchester, on this occasion, "simply to see the sights." They would return in a week's time to speak and attend meetings. It appears that they spent Saturday afternoon indulging their newfound passion for ship watching on the recently opened Manchester Ship Canal, which brought cargo ships of oceangoing size between Manchester and the river Mersey.

From Manchester they would go on that same day by train through the Pennine chain of rugged hills and moors that separates Lancashire from Yorkshire, beyond Huddersfield to the town of Dewsbury in the industrial area of West Yorkshire.[8]

SUNDAY, OCTOBER 13 – TUESDAY, OCTOBER 15

As always the Sabbath was spent in relative inactivity. The Bechuana stayed Saturday and Sunday nights at the home of Mr. J. Walker, a local magistrate at Dewsbury, and no doubt attended services at the local Congregational chapel.

On Monday and Tuesday the chiefs continued with their assault on Yorkshire—Monday in Bradford and Saltaire, Tuesday in Leeds. They made what had become set speeches to large attendances, while local bodies supported them with motions and petitions.[9]

A "large number" of people in Halifax, a West Yorkshire town that the chiefs had not intended to visit, had already petitioned the Right Hon. Joseph Chamberlain, MP, on "the subject of the proposed change in the administration of Bechuanaland." Their petition, published in the *Bradford Observer* of October 15, was recommended as a model to be followed by citizens elsewhere and is typical of the kind of petition now beginning to pour in from the provinces to the Colonial Office in London. It is thus worth reproducing in full:

> That a proposal has been made for a change in the mode of administration of the Bechuanaland Protectorate, in South Africa, by which, if the same is carried into effect, such territory would cease to be under the direct control of the Imperial Government as heretofore, and would be subject to the British South Africa Company.
>
> That such a step is contrary to the wishes of the native inhabitants of the said territory.
>
> That such inhabitants cannot justly be held bound by any promises which may have been made by former Governments for the handing over of the administration of their territory to the company, since such inhabitants never consented to such proceeding. Your memorialists further believe that such promises were made without full knowledge of the actual circumstances of the case.
>
> That the proposed step is unnecessary. Your memorialists have reason to believe that current statements as to the cost of the present system of administration of the territory are fallacious, since such statements do not distinguish between the proportion of the cost attributable to the Crown Colony of Bechuanaland and that attributable to the Protectorate. Moreover, the

greater part of such cost is incurred on account of the Bechuanaland Border Police, a semi-military force, which has become unnecessary.

That the said inhabitants are willing to pay a poll-tax, which, together with the revenue available from other sources, would be amply sufficient to meet the costs of administration on lines similar to those adopted in the case of Basutoland, where the revenue amply covers the cost of administration. That the principle of handing over the administration of a remote territory to a company whose object is necessarily the acquisition of gain is open to strong objection, and should not be adopted except on cases where no other plan is practicable, since the real welfare of the natives is likely to be subordinated to the interest of the company. No guarantee entered into by such a body could in the judgment of your memorialists be regarded as adequate or reliable, since it cannot be assumed that the motives of such a body or the spirit in which the affairs of the territory would be administered by it would always be beneficent.

That the inhabitants of the said territory deserve exceptionally favoured treatment, since they are increasingly industrious, law-abiding, and to a large extent Christian, and they and their chiefs have always been friendly and loyal to the British, while, as is well known, the Chief Khama in particular is a conspicuous example of enlightenment and of fidelity to the best interests of his tribe.

Your memorialists therefore earnestly desire that you will take the unanimous request of the inhabitants of the said territory into your favourable consideration, and that their wishes and interests may not be subordinated to those of the company; and that you will see fit to advise Her Most Gracious Majesty and Her Ministers accordingly.[10]

In Bradford on the Monday the chiefs first toured a textile mill and a school. They were interested to find wool from South Africa being used in textile manufacture. That night they addressed a public meeting in the Bradford Mechanics' Institute, convened in honor of the LMS centenary.

Sebele was principal speaker, beginning with an apologia for being "only a black man, who was not worthy to speak." He continued by making a trenchant criticism of "native policy" in the Transvaal (South African Republic), indicating that it demonstrated the uselessness for the protection of African rights of any piece of paper signed by white-settler rulers.

The *Bradford Observer* accepted the point about the irresponsibility of colonial power unfettered by direct imperial supervision by referring to the recent Stokes case in the Congo Free State.

An evening meeting held the next day in the Victoria Hall, Leeds, ostensibly to celebrate the LMS centenary, was attended by a large crowd. The *Yorkshire Post* estimated the crowd at the so-called *conversazione* at between twelve and fourteen hundred people. Again Sebele was principal speaker. The petition adopted followed the Halifax model.[11]

✣ ✣ ✣

At some time on October 14 or 15, Khama received an important telegram relayed from London. Dated October 14, from his son Sekgoma, whom he had left as regent at Palapye, the cable read:

KAR[E] TLA KWANO KAPELA GONE LE DIKGAN TSA GOUTA LE DIBENTLHE BA EWA PALA SENWAUPE LE LOTSANE

The Setswana was somewhat cryptic and, mindful no doubt of the fact that the telegraph was owned and operated by one of Cecil Rhodes's companies, there was no English translation attached. It appeared to read: "Attention. Come back quickly as there is news [troubles] of gold and stores. They refuse to move from Senwaupe and Lotsane." [12]

Khama interpreted this as the incursion from the north of white people digging gold and erecting stores, moving into the heart of his country without permission. The long-feared invasion of Bechuanaland by Rhodes's Chartered Company might have begun. The Chartered Company had some explaining to do.

✤ ✤ ✤

The weekly business journal *South Africa*, published in London and edited by E. P. Mathers, had up until about now been fairly indulgent toward "Khama and his confrères," under the incorrect assumption that Jameson and Rhodes had almost converted Khama before he left Cape Town. The editor had harbored the expectation that the chiefs would soon become "fully enlightened" and thus acquiesce in Rhodes's takeover of their countries. But in its issue of October 19, 1895, *South Africa* turned testy. Under the heading "Khama cantankerous," the journal bemoaned the

> great change that has taken place in Khama's attitude since he landed in England. At first he maintained a discreet silence; then he began to speak guardedly and diplomatically; now, seemingly under the exhilarating influence of the course of religious dissipation he had undergone, he has begun to speak unadvisedly with his lips, and to fling about reckless charges in a way that cannot fail to damage his cause.

While acknowledging that "the fineness and delicacy of the different shades of meaning must necessarily be lost in the process of translation," *South Africa* claimed that "thinking people" rather than "faddists and the mob" would now no longer take Khama's "striking speeches" seriously, but would suppose them to have been "made under the influence of teetotal ecstasy, or missionary meeting fervour." [13]

South Africa was undoubtedly a molder of informed white colonial opinion when its copies reached South Africa itself. Both Rhodes and Jameson appear to have regarded it as a major source of intelligence.

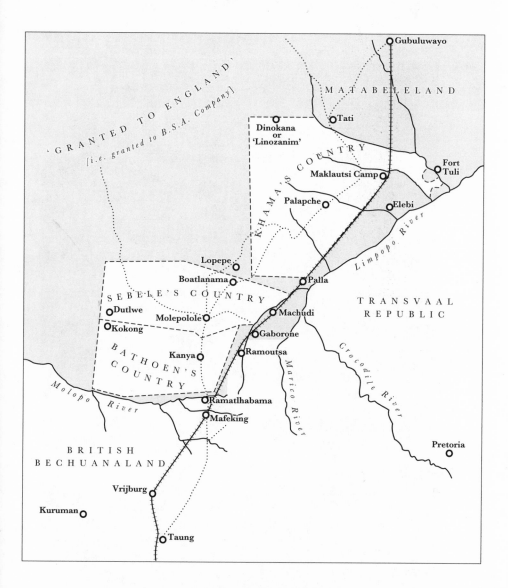

Map 3. "Mr. Rhodes's Maximum Offer," October 26, 1895. (Map by author from original in CWM/LMS Archives; courtesy of the School of Oriental and African Studies Library, University of London.)

Figure 18. Khama, Sebele and Bathoen seated in front of the conservatory of a country house with their attendants. Standing *(from left):* Kehutile Gohiwamang, Simeon Seisa (Khama's secretary and personal interpreter), David Sebonego, and Kwenaetsile (Bathoen's brother-in-law). (Reprinted from W. Douglas Mackenzie and Alfred Stead, *South Africa: Its History, Heroes and Wars.*)

Figure 19. Thursday, September 19: Somali Village at Crystal Palace.
The three Chiefs' reactions to seeing these people from a very different part
of Africa are not recorded. (Reprinted from *Illustrated London News*
106 [1895]: 677.)

Figure 20. The Chiefs at Enderby (1): arrival near the lych gate of the Anglican parish church in Leicester Lane. Alice Young's father Thomas Young and the Congregational minister Rev. G. H. Dickenson flank the Bechuana visitors on the cart. Alice's brother-in-law George Gamble and brother Thomas (in bowler hats) stand near Harry Biggs, who holds aloft a framed address of welcome. (Reproduced by permission of Mr. David North, Enderby.)

Figure 21. The Chiefs at Enderby (2): luncheon in the Congregational schoolhouse. Willoughby and Khama are at the far end of the table on the left. On the right Bathoen, Sebele, and Simeon Seisa sit next to Alice Young's mother and father (mid-table), Alice's brother Percy and sisters Jane, Ellen and Elizabeth, stand in line on the left. (Reproduced by permission of Mr. David North, Enderby.)

Figure 22. The Chiefs at Enderby (3): group photograph of the extended Young family and guests outside the Young home in Seine Lane. Rev. Dickenson on the left sits next to Sebele, Bathoen, Khama, Willoughby (with his own son), Kwenaetsile, and Alice's brother William (holding baby May). Alice's mother and father can be seen standing above Bathoen and Khama. (Reproduced by permission of Mr. David North, Enderby.)

Figure 23. The Chiefs at Enderby (4): Khama and Mrs. Young.
(Reproduced by permission of Mr. David North, Enderby.)

KHAMA.
"I think the king is but a man, as I am."
Henry V. iv. 1

Figure 24. KHAMA: "I think the king is but a man, as I am"
(*Henry V,* act iv, 1). A reponse to the "Khama Boom" in *Moonshine*
magazine, 6 October 1895.

Figure 25. The Idols of the Hour: Khama and the Lord Provost of Glasgow,
Sebele and Willoughby, at the Glasgow City Chambers, October 24, 1895.
(Reprinted from *Glasgow Times,* 25 Oct. 1895.)

Figure 26. Studio Portrait of Bathoen *(left)*, Sebele *(center)* and Khama
(right) seated, with Revs. W. C. Willoughby *(left)* and Edwin Lloyd *(right)* standing.
(Reproduced by permission of the Council for World Mission [formerly the
London Missionary Society]; photograph courtesy of the School of
Oriental and African Studies Library.)

From a Photograph by RUSSELL & SONS, *Baker Street, London, W.*

Khama

Figure 27. The portrait and signature of Khama that made Sebele and
Bathoen jealous, when it was colored and imprinted on a Staffordshire
porcelain plate. (Reprinted from Edwin Lloyd,
Three Great African Chiefs, frontispiece.)

JOHN BULL.—Sorry you can't join your friend, but trespassers will be prosecuted.

OOM PAUL.—Ugh! What business have *you* here?

JOHN BULL.—I'm the Man in Possession–that's all!

OOM PAUL.—The Man in Possession! Pray, whom for?

J.B.—FOR A UNITED SOUTH AFRICA.

Figure 28. Vaal Drifts Crisis (1): July 1895 cartoon from the Cape press of the reason why Kruger put sanctions on the British in Cape Colony. The Transvaal's road to the sea, and to possible naval alliance with the German Kaiser, is blocked by Britain's annexation of Tongaland and Zambaan's country (between British Zululand and Portuguese Delagoa Bay). The "man in possession" refers to a 1891 speech by Chamberlain which justified seizure of land for colonial development. (Reprinted from *Cape Times Weekly Edition*, 31 July 1895.)

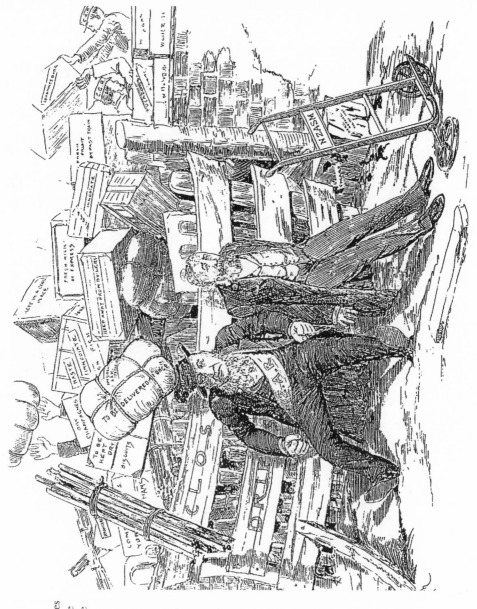

Figure 29. The Vaal Drifts Crisis (2): October 1895 cartoon from the Cape press of the consequences for the Transvaal of trying to close the Vaal river drifts (fords) to Cape waggon traffic. Kruger and Middelburg, head of NZASM, the Dutch company running the newly opened Transvaal railway to Delagoa Bay in Portuguese East Africa, attempt to hold back the flood of urgent goods for Johannesburg arriving from Cape Government Railways (CGR). (Reprinted from *Cape Times Weekly Edition*, 16 Oct. 1895.)

Figure 30. Wednesday November 13, 1895, at Chatham. Seated *(from left)*:
Kwenaetsile, Bathoen, Khama, Sebele, General Sir Charles Warren,
Warren's aide-de-camp; Standing: Gohiwamang, Simeon Seisa,
Willoughby. (Reproduced by permission of Duggan-Cronin Gallery,
McGregor Memorial Museum, Kimberley.)

After Khama and his fellow chiefs, Sebele and Bathoen, had been introduced to the Queen, they advanced and laid their presents at Her Majesty's feet. The Queen then in a graceful speech thanked them, and they each received through Mr. Chamberlain, the Secretary for the Colonies, a handsomely bound Bechuana Testament and a framed portrait of the Queen, as presents from her Majesty

THE BECHUANA CHIEFS AT WINDSOR CASTLE

DRAWN FROM LIFE BY SYDNEY P. HALL

Figure 31. Wednesday November 20, 1895: King Khama being presented through Joseph Chamberlain with a photographic portrait of Queen Victoria, as well as an Afghan shawl and a Setswana New Testament (inscribed by her with the words "The Secret of Khama's Greatness"). (Reprinted from *The Graphic* 52 [1895]: 664.)

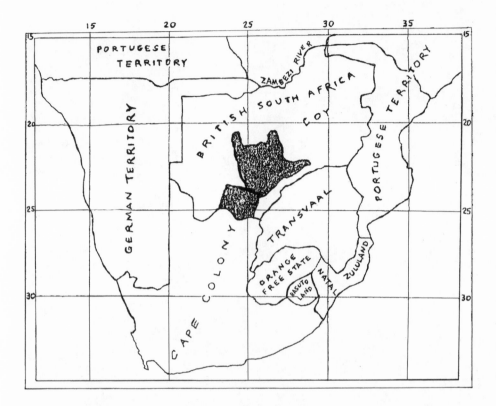

Figure 32. Responses to the Chamberlain Settlement (1): "The New Black Wedge: Will It Last?": December 1895 cartoon from the Cape press. It is an outline map of southern Africa with the reserves of Khama, Sebele and Bathoen as a black man's hand and cuff sporting a thumbs-up sign. (Other "black wedges" of territory in the Eastern Cape had been progressively eaten up by white settlers over the previous century.) (Reprinted from *Cape Times Weekly Edition*, 25 Dec. 1895.)

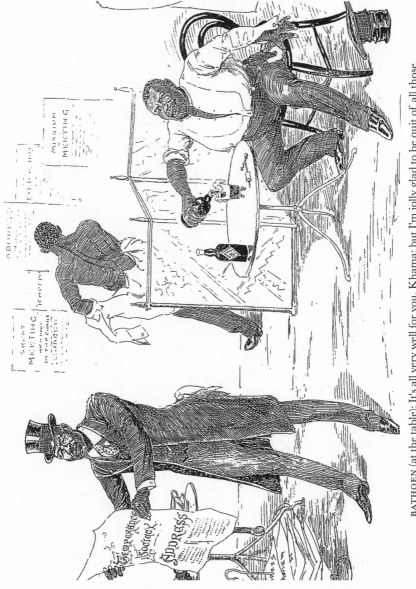

Figure 33. Responses to the Chamberlain Settlement (2): "It's all very well for you, Khama. . .": a South African newspaper cartoon after the Chiefs' arrival back at Cape Town. The cartoonist would have done better to portray Sebele rather than Bathoen drinking. (Reprinted from *Cape Times Weekly Edition*, 18 Dec. 1895.)

BATHOEN (at the table): It's all very well for you, Khama; but I'm jolly glad to be quit of all those Teetotal Meetings and blackcoats, and able to sit down to a decent glass of stout again. Eh, Sebele?

Figure 34. Advertiser's View of African Colonization (1): the Bechuana Chiefs in London: One of a series of advertisements for advertisements in March 1896. Khama is said to have been impressed by the "Handsome Pictures hung up in the Streets of London." (Reprinted from *Illustrated London News* 108 [1896]: 639.)

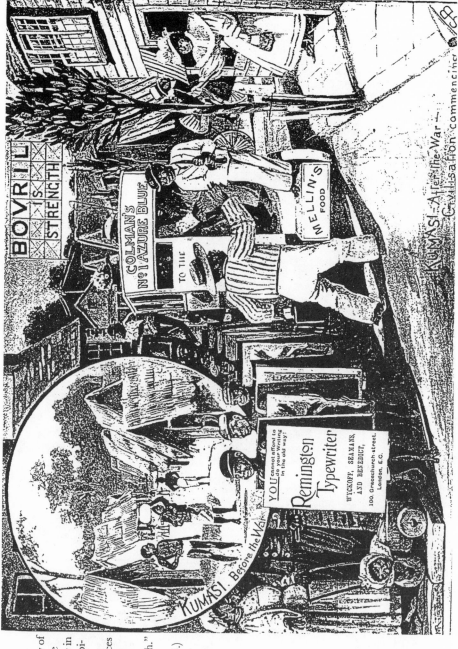

Figure 35. Advertiser's View of African Colonization (2): the Anglo-Asante (Ashanti) War in West Africa. The Asante capital of Kumasi: "After the War—Civilisation commences —Forecast of the probable results of the occupation of the country by the English." (Reprinted from *Illustrated London News* 108 [1896]: 413.)

Figure 36. Advertiser's View of African Colonization (3): The Jameson
Raid in South Africa. "THE TRANSVAAL: SOME MORE SECRETS REVEALED. New
and important reasons alleged as the cause of the appeal to Dr. Jameson by the
inghabitants of Johannesburg"–the call for international brand consumer
goods. (Reprinted from *Illustrated London News* 108 [1896]: 671.)

ELEVEN

In Every Town We Have Found Friends

◆►══◗ ◖══◄◆

ON WEDNESDAY, OCTOBER 16, THE CHIEFS AND THEIR followers were back in London. The Bechuana then split into two parties. Bathoen, with his brother-in-law Kwenaetsile and his attendant David Sebonego, took a train for Wales the next day, accompanied by the missionary Edwin Lloyd.

Lloyd had until now been largely engaged in writing *Three Great African Chiefs (Khâmé, Sebelé, and Bathoeng)*. The book was being rushed through the press, both as a celebration of the LMS centenary and as another propaganda weapon for the chiefs' mission, by the publishers—Messrs.T. Fisher Unwin of Paternoster Square in London, where the *Times* newspaper also had its offices.[1]

The decision to split Bathoen temporarily from Khama and Sebele may also indicate that it was he who had had the fit of jealousy over the lord mayor's album in Liverpool. Bathoen was undoubtedly under pressure from his half brother Kwenaetsile, who reckoned that he was as good as Bathoen, and no doubt pushed Bathoen to assert his equality with Khama and Sebele. Willoughby may have felt that a couple of days apart would have helped to mend fences between the three chiefs, who had been living too cramped up with one another.

Alternatively, the splitting of Bathoen from the other two at this stage was entirely fortuitous. Lloyd was after all Bathoen's missionary back home at Kanye in Bechuanaland, and he was simply taking Bathoen off to the land of his own fathers. Lloyd hailed from Llandovery in the mountains of mid-Wales. In the eyes of the missionaries, Bathoen should also be rewarded with adulation as much as Khama, as he was—unlike Sebele "the sinner"—a full and supportive member of a London Missionary Society church.

THURSDAY, OCTOBER 17 - FRIDAY, OCTOBER 18

On Thursday October 17, a beautiful fine day in the Southeast of England, Khama and Sebele and Willoughby traveled from London on the 11:50 train to Ipswich on the river Orwell near the Suffolk coast. Here, in the East Anglian countryside, was the heart of the agricultural lands recovered from marshes that had given England its "agricultural revolution" in the eighteenth century.

After lunch in Ipswich, the party repaired by train a dozen miles northeast to the Rendlesham stock-breeding establishment and dairy institute, near Wickham Market. Here Khama was much taken with the wooled sheep that he saw, contrasting them favorably with the hairy sheep back home. The *East Anglian Times* noted that Khama "evidently possesses a fund of dry humour" after he remarked that in his country, by contrast to England, hair had been put on the backs of the sheep and wool had been put on the heads of the people.

Khama and Sebele appear to have been greatly at ease viewing livestock on that fine autumn day. They were staggered by a cow named "Bushy Betty" that produced six thousand gallons of milk in one year. (The secretary of the dairy institute offered to send out machinery and trained instructors to Bechuanaland.) But they were horrified that calves were slaughtered so young for veal. Sebele was much taken with some horses, probably of the heavy draft or powerful cart-horse variety, on display.

After catching the 5:19 train back from Wickham Market, the two chiefs attended a very large LMS centenary meeting in Ipswich's Tacket Street chapel. Sebele was the main speaker, and a motion of deep sympathy and overwhelming support was passed.

The next morning the two chiefs visited an Ipswich canvas factory that supplied South Africa with sacks and hessian cloth. They were pleased to recognize the source of a product that was already familiar. Khama correctly identified some green canvas as being the same as that on Willoughby's wagon back in Bechuanaland. Once again, Sebele and Khama experienced some difficulty in negotiating a narrow staircase. Khama quickly retired from the tarring department, complaining of the obnoxious smell. The smell did not bother Sebele.

In the flag room Khama amused himself and Sebele, chuckling all the while, by taking a small flag or two and parodying the actions of a semaphore signaler of the Bechuanaland Border Police.

Next the local newspaper press, the *East Anglian Times*, was visited. The chiefs were impressed by the speed of its printing machinery. Then it was on to the foundry of the Orwell Works of Messrs. Ransome, where farm machinery was manufactured. According to the *Sketch,* Sebele and Khama were intensely interested in the huge steam-hammers and hydraulic presses that stamped and molded parts for steam-driven agricultural machinery and for iron or steel plows. They followed all the operations with "very intelligent attention."

Khama and Sebele then drove out to the fields where new machinery was tested. They were photographed by Mr. Frank Gray of the company with plows that were presented to them as gifts. Khama chose a light plow with which he personally plowed a furrow in the fields, "guiding the instrument with his own royal hands." Sebele was delighted with a double-furrow plow, which could readily be retracted and lifted up over an obstacle in the furrow. The bystanders were amused to see royalty so obviously adept in techniques of cultivation. Probably neither man had plowed before with horses rather than oxen.

Willoughby remarked that there were hundreds of American plows in Botswana now. On an earlier occasion Khama had told a journalist that plows came from Sweden as well as America.

Khama, Sebele, and Willoughby then caught the 4:22 P.M. train back to London.

The visit to Ipswich paid dividends. The *East Anglian Times* got up a "memorial . . . to the Colonial Secretary" to be signed by "the inhabitants of Ipswich"—in the belief that "In matters of state policy, public opinion carries great weight" in this and "all other large towns in the kingdom." [2]

✛ ✛ ✛

On the night of Thursday, October 17, Bathoen and Lloyd spoke at Abercarn—a small town in the Ebbw Vale, the greatest of the tightly packed valleys of South Wales and Monmouthshire, famous as much for its Nonconformist chapel culture as for its coal mining.

On the Friday night they spoke in the tabernacle at Newport, the coastal port and industrial town some miles downriver where the valleys converged, east of Cardiff. The chairman of the meeting on the Friday night was no less than the chairman of the Monmouthshire County Council, demonstrating once again how the Bechuana attracted the support of provincial political figures no less than religious ones.

There were soon petitions from Wales as well as from England arriving on the desks of the Colonial Office in London. [3]

SATURDAY, OCTOBER 19 – SUNDAY, OCTOBER 20

The chiefs kept their heads low in London over the weekend, as private negotiations began with the representatives of the Chartered Company who came round to Armfield's Hotel at nine o'clock on the Saturday morning (see chap. 12).

Meanwhile the good impressions left by the chiefs on their tours around industrial England continued to work their way into the press. As the *Keighley News* remarked from the North of England on October 19:

> The appearance of Khama and his brother chiefs from South Africa upon missionary platforms in Bradford and other large towns has brought home to great numbers of persons in a very lively way events which else might have made but little impression on them.[4]

These issues and events included the threatened French invasion of Madagascar and the threatened British invasion of the Ashanti (Asante) kingdom on the hinterland of the Gold Coast, and continuing disquiet over *l'affaire* Stokes in the Congo Free State. But the main issue in the colonial pages of the British press was the so-called Vaal drifts crisis.

On August 28, 1895, President Kruger of the Transvaal republic had announced that the Vaal "drifts" (fords) would be closed on October 1. This was part of a tariff war between competing railway systems in South Africa. With the lucrative market of the Witwatersrand just about to be served by two new lines to the ports of Durban in British Natal and Delagoa Bay in Portuguese East Africa (Mozambique), both with high capital costs to pay off by high freight tariffs, Kruger was trying to squeeze the well-established low-tariff lines from Cape Colony. Cape Railways had countered by establishing a back-door route, transshipping goods from the Kimberley line by ox wagon across the Vaal drifts into the Transvaal.

Kruger was to back down, reopening the Vaal drifts five weeks later—when the new railway link with Durban was ceremonially opened and soon after Chamberlain's threat of armed intervention. But the crisis fell directly into the arms of Rhodes and his allies, who were plotting and inciting rebellion among the *uitlanders* (foreign whites) of the Witwatersrand at Johannesburg. The Cape press and its London connections, through Reuter's and Flora Shaw of the *Times*, played up the Vaal drifts crisis for all it was worth.[5]

Jingoism in Cape Colony and London, and the related "Kaffir boom" in South African shares on the London stock market, had its equal and opposite response in Britain, especially in the "provinces." Newspapers such as the *Newcastle Leader*, the *Bradford Observer*, and the *Manchester Guardian* made a virtue of their independence from metropolitan opinion. All this no doubt encouraged the Bechuana chiefs to identify Cape-based Rhodes and the London-based Chartered Company, rather than simply Liquor, as the main enemy. Editorials in provincial newspapers began to go beyond the gentle sophistries with which the Bechuana cause was greeted at first.

The *Stalybridge Reporter* (from east of Manchester) of October 19 argued that Khama was being threatened by the dirty, muddy head of the wave of advancing civilization. The Chartered Company's aims must therefore be opposed. A Halifax reader's letter published in a Bradford newspaper the same day held similar views.

In Bradford the next day, Sunday the twentieth, a minister preached a fiery sermon against the Chartered Company, saying that like a cormorant a ring must be put round its neck to stop it swallowing Khama's country. He added:

> I thank God for this force of righteousness in the public Press, and wish it would arouse every pulpit and every church to a universal demand that justice must be done.[6]

MONDAY, OCTOBER 21

The last provincial tour of Khama, Sebele, and Bathoen was particularly carefully planned by Willoughby as their tour manager. Willoughby had received on the chiefs' behalf hundreds of invitations from towns and villages all over Britain. Willoughby chose the three major cities that had so far been neglected—Manchester in England, and Edinburgh and Glasgow in Scotland. In addition he chose Sheffield and Halifax in the industrial North of England, and Hanley near Stoke-on-Trent. He explained that all six places "were seats of distinct industries." But it is difficult not to see the choice of the latter three places as a reward for the strong support that they were already showing for the Bechuana chiefs.

The chiefs arrived in Manchester on Monday, October 21. They were greeted at a reception in the State Apartments of the town hall, an imposing building barely eighteen years old. In a speech of warm welcome the lord mayor jokingly tried to detain the chiefs in Manchester, guaranteeing that as long as they stayed in his city he would do everything to further their interests. Khama responded in spirit, telling his hosts, "In every town we have found friends, and we are glad indeed."

Sebele tuned into the mood of genial informality and gave the audience the benefit of his rather relaxed views of recent Bechuanaland history. He contrasted the mild impact of the Warren Expedition in 1885, which had declared the queen's protectorate, with the sting in the tail of the threat now posed by the Chartered Company.

> And while we were continuing to live in comfort in our own country, there came Sir Charles Warren in [our] midst. And Sir Charles Warren said to us, you had better enter the protection of the Great Queen. And we believed him and accepted his words, and we lived comfortably in this belief. . . . [But then] it was said to us you are to be given as a present to the company. . . .

We object to having our country cut up into little bits that they may be given away by the white man. A country full of boundaries, what is it worth?

People who attended the reception were pleased to find that the three chiefs were quite as impressive as their press notices made them out to be.

While in Manchester the chiefs managed to squeeze in a visit to the large industrial works of Whitworth's, where "they saw the casting of an immense ingot and many large guns in process of manufacture." Here, or later on the tour northward,

They could not, they said, understand it all, but the tour had given them subjects on which they will be able to talk for the rest of their lives.

That evening Sebele expanded on his theme of imperial abandonment of Bechuanaland at an LMS centenary meeting held not far from the Manchester Town Hall, in the Free Trade Hall. He told the packed audience that the Bechuana objected to being sold off to the highest bidder, and referred to the 1885 declaration of the protectorate as having been achieved through mutual agreement with the chiefs of Bechuanaland:

We are not oxen, we are people. . . . We desire that we may continue under the direct control [he also said "shadowing"] of the Queen, according to the agreement with Sir Charles Warren.

The meeting responded by adopting a unanimous memorial to be sent to the colonial secretary. This petition had been signed by no less than fourteen thousand people by the time it was forwarded to the Colonial Office on Thursday morning, and the local organizers claimed "that the number could have been largely increased had a longer time been allowed." The petition was duly acknowledged by the Colonial Office, assuring the petitioners that

you may rely on the just rights of the chiefs being respected; but that it should be borne in mind that certain pledges have been given by [Chamberlain's] predecessors which cannot be entirely be disregarded.[7]

The urgency of the chiefs' case was underlined by the news in the papers the day they arrived in Manchester that the British government had already started giving away small parts of the Bechuanaland Protectorate to the BSA Company. Rhodes's company had been given, with immediate effect, full administrative powers over the territories of Chiefs Montshiwa and Ikaneng in the southeast, ostensibly for the purpose of railway construction out of Mafeking northward toward Gaborone.

The *Manchester Guardian,* mouthpiece of the Liberal establishment, fully supported Khama and his brother chiefs—saying there was no need for the Crown to interfere in their "most interesting experiment in native self-government." The *Manchester Courier* on the other hand, while recognizing the importance of the visit of the three chiefs, saw the Rhodesian takeover as inevitable—and Khama, Sebele, and Bathoen should follow Montshiwa and Ikaneng in conceding gracefully. Better to be ruled by British Rhodesians than the Afrikaners of the Cape or the Transvaal.[8]

TUESDAY, OCTOBER 22 - WEDNESDAY, OCTOBER 23

The next morning the party took an express train from Manchester northward through the furthermost marches of England into the lowlands of Scotland, where the express obligingly stopped for them to alight a few miles short of Edinburgh at Esbank halt. That night they stayed in the village of Dalkeith at Glencairn, the house of Mr. and Mrs. R. Somerville. Dalkeith, on the outskirts of Edinburgh, was the home village of the LMS foreign secretary Wardlaw Thompson, who, however, remained in London.

Sebele and Khama already had a keen sense of how Scotland differed from England. They had known and been influenced by Scotsmen who had come to their countries to hunt and to preach. Besides the missionaries Livingstone and Mackenzie, closely associated with the upbringing of Sebele and Khama respectively, there had been famous hunters and traders like Roualeyn Gordon Cumming and David Hume with whom they had hunted and traded as youths. Cumming had hunted in his kilt, and kilts and plaids appear to have exercised a continuing fascination for Khama in particular.

Some Scots felt that they had a special claim on the Bechuana over and above that of the English. A few days before the three Bechuana chiefs arrived in Scotland a consortium of Scottish capitalists, styling themselves the Scottish African Corporation Limited (of No. 1 How Street, Edinburgh) wrote to the Colonial Office offering to take over responsibility for Khama's country from the British South Africa Company. This "purely" Scottish company would give Khama "the principal place" in the development of his country. The corporation's managing director, J. Hay Thorburn, attempted to assure Chamberlain, "As Scotch [*sic*] enterprise has long been associated with all that is best in the history of African civilization, this proposal might be found of practical value."

On the afternoon of Wednesday the twenty-third at three o'clock, Khama and his fellow chiefs arrived in the city of Edinburgh by horse carriage. They drove on the cobbles of the principal streets for an hour, over and under the great road bridges that spanned the valleys south and north of the old city, and along the Royal Mile that ran west to Edinburgh Castle and east to Holyrood Palace. They were suitably impressed by the beauty of the windy city's views to the sea over the New Town and to the massive hill in the southeast known as Arthur's Seat.

At four o'clock the chiefs were received by the lord provost and senior magistrates of the city for afternoon tea in the City Chambers, on the Royal Mile opposite the High Kirk of St. Giles. Their entry passage across Exchange Square was marked by a red carpet flanked by ceremonial sword bearers. A military band from Edinburgh Castle played outside in the square while the reception proceeded. The large company inside the City Chambers reportedly included advocates, baronets, and ministers of religion. There was a crush of well-wishers in the corridor as well as in the actual reception room, who would not leave until the chiefs had shaken their hands. "The chiefs, remarked the *Edinburgh Dispatch,* "conducted themselves with great dignity."

After tea, Khama was first to speak:

> I, Khama, especially rejoice to see this great town because it was from this country that one of my missionaries, Mr Mackenzie, came forth, and for his sake I am glad to see the town of this country.
>
> He was never tired of telling me what Scotland was like, and he has told me many times about this town of Edinburgh, and I am glad to have seen it with my own eyes, and I praise this town because I find friendship in it.
>
> I say as I stand here among you that it is just like being at home among my people. (Laughter and cheers).

Sebele reserved his usual comments on David Livingstone and expressed his pleasure instead at last to see the home of Robert Moffat. He concluded:

> I rejoice to see this town so great from which so much teaching has gone forth to other parts of the world.

The chiefs were then conducted by the lord provost though the museum in the City Chambers and signed the visitors' book while the castle band continued to play outside.

That night the chiefs and Willoughby addressed an LMS centenary meeting held in the Free Church Assembly Hall.[9]

THURSDAY, OCTOBER 24

At ten o'clock on the morning of Thursday, October 24, the chiefs left Edinburgh's Waverley station on the Glasgow express.

Glasgow prided itself on being a very different city from Edinburgh and was not about to bestow the same adulation on the chiefs unthinkingly. Unlike Edinburgh, where the smoke of "Auld Reekie" came from domestic hearths, the smoke of Glasgow contained the black soot of heavy industry, which coated the grandest of new buildings in a matter of months and penetrated clothes in a matter of hours with the tang of damp tar.

Glasgow's major export to Africa was the characteristic cast-iron guttering, drainpipes, and railings of Walter Macfarlane and Co., which were incorporated into the new buildings of places like Johannesburg. In 1890 Macfarlane boasted a two-thousand-page catalog of its designs and employed more than a thousand workers on a ten-acre (four-hectare) site.

The chiefs' train arrived in Glasgow at 11 : 15 at Queen Street Station, where they were received by municipal dignitaries—headed by Baillie Primrose, the senior magistrate, with Lord Overtoun and John Wilson, MP, at his side. Khama was dressed in a gray tweed suit with a red satin necktie in a sailor knot, a light overcoat, and a satin top hat. There was a large crowd at the station, more curious than enthusiastic, but people responded with a slight cheer when Khama tipped his hat to them.

The sun was shining through a faint haze as the Bechuana were whisked off in landau carriages on their first industrial excursion, raising slight cheers from bystanders on the way, toward the Parkhead Forge, on the south side of the city center. The *Glasgow Evening Times*, both skeptical and patronizing, takes up the story:

> The marvels of the Parkhead Forge—the boiling metal, the Goliath hammer, the mighty shears, and other things, seem to have deeply impressed them, as vast physical phenomena must do such people, rather than the subtle quality of ideas.

The *Evening Times* was disparaging about these "Bechuana Apostles to the British Gentiles," who had come as missionaries to teach the British government its duty.

They "witnessed the casting of a 50-ton steel ingot, the rolling of armour plates, and other massive work." The *Scotsman*, an Edinburgh newspaper, reported that Khama showed the keenest interest, getting so close he was almost showered in sparks. The party, no doubt exhausted by the heat and deafened by the Goliath hammer, repaired to the Cockburn Temperance Hotel for lunch.

That afternoon Khama, Sebele, and Bathoen were received at 3 : 30 by the lord provost of Glasgow and city magistrates, and a crowd of over a thousand people, in the City Chambers. The lord provost made a stirring speech, full of complex sentences:

> If the history of the Dark Continent different from the history of the past was ever to be written, it would be by men of the same standing and the same moral force and Christianity embraced by these three Chiefs of Africa. (Applause.)

Sebele spoke first on the political background to their visit, followed by Bathoen, and then by Khama, who said again how glad he was to be in Scotland. The audience was won over. A cartoonist portrays the lord provost and Khama as twin figures on the platform, and Sebele as "The Idol of the Hour" after his speech interpreted by Willoughby. Young women cluster round the chiefs to shake their hands.

That evening, back in their temperance hotel, Khama received a delegation from the Scottish Temperance League headed by its chairman, Rev. George Gladstone. Khama was tired out from the day's events and went to bed at 8 P.M. [10]

FRIDAY, OCTOBER 25

Excursions the next morning began with the University of Glasgow—the only British university honored with a visit by the Bechuana chiefs on their 1895 mission. Khama told the principal (equivalent to the vice-chancellor of an English university) how impressed he was by the institution. Glasgow was regarded as one of the premier British universities in research and teaching in a broad range of disciplines—engineering and medicine particularly in its case. Its main building, a striking Victorian-cum-Scottish baronial edifice six hundred feet long, had been designed by Gilbert Scott Senior (the architect of St. Pancras station hotel in London) and his second son, Oldrid.

The remainder of the morning was spent at the Clyde Bank Shipbuilding Yard, looking at the ships being constructed on the riverside. The greatest shipyards in the world, which built the world's greatest ships such as the Cunard liners, lay on the banks of the river Clyde. The ships on the stocks inspected by the chiefs were both naval vessels, the *Jupiter* and the *Terrible*.

The tour of Clydebank ended with a tour of the Singer Sewing-Machine Works, where the Bechuana were also given an informal lunch. Another informal lunch followed almost immediately at the industrial establishment owned by Lord Overtoun. The chiefs may also have visited the works of Messrs. J. and G. Thomson in the afternoon.

That night there was an LMS centenary meeting held in the St. Andrew's Hall, which was almost but not completely full. Willoughby spoke in place of Khama, who was again much tired. Willoughby's speech can hardly have endeared him to all the citizens of Glasgow. He said that he "found the natives [in Bechuanaland] more honest than the natives of Glasgow." Something of the old anti-Establishment *enragé* missionary also came out in Willoughby, when he scathingly referred to the exorbitant costs being spent by the British exchequer on the Bechuanaland Border Police, "to maintain a force which did not nothing but create friction among the people and find snug berths for somebody's younger sons."

The meeting passed a motion of support for the chiefs, proposed by John Colville, MP. The chiefs then returned to the Cockburn Hotel, where they were greatly interested to hear a dance going on elsewhere in the building. "The dancers gave Sebele a round of applause when he popped his head inquiringly between the curtains of the doorway." [11]

SATURDAY, OCTOBER 26 – SUNDAY, OCTOBER 27

Saturday morning began with fifteen degrees (Fahrenheit) of frost, but the chiefs left Glasgow somewhat reluctantly—because they had hoped while in Scotland to be called to an audience with Queen Victoria. She was still at her summer residence of Balmoral Castle, in the Grampian mountains west of Aberdeen. They were disappointed not to receive the call.

Knowing they were going to Scotland, the chiefs had written through Willoughby on September 24 to the Colonial Office to fix a visit to see the queen at Balmoral. Wardlaw Thompson of the LMS wrote again on October 8, saying that the chiefs wanted to see her before they left Britain. The reasons Thompson gave for urgent action are interesting for the light they throw on the three chiefs and their resources at this time. He explained that the cold weather that was approaching would worsen the continual colds of two of them, and they were also running short of money. They were not being entertained by Englishmen with quite the same generosity as they were accustomed to showing Englishmen at home.

Thompson added that if they left Britain without seeing the queen, the chiefs would be frustrated and dissatisfied.

Albert Spicer of the LMS also saw Meade of the Colonial Office about a Balmoral visit. But the Colonial Office answer on October 15 stated that Chamberlain did not advise such a visit to the queen's personal Balmoral residence, where she rests "from her great labours in reigning over this Empire." Chamberlain would only contact her on her return to Windsor in southern England, her main official residence, after her arrival at 9:30 A.M. on November 15. It may be questioned whether Chamberlain, as a lapsed republican who was not (unlike his American wife) entirely in Victoria's favor, would have dared to push for a Balmoral reception. [12]

On leaving Cockburn Hotel in Glasgow on Saturday the twenty-sixth, the Bechuana signed their names in the guest book: "Sebele, Molepolole"; "Khama, Phalapye"; "Bathoen, Kanye"; "Gohiwaman, British South Africa"; "David, Bechuanaland"; "Tsime, Bechuanaland"; "Seisa, Phalapye."A small crowd, including Fred Moir of the African Lakes Corporation (a Scottish venture on Lake Malawi), gathered to give them a slight cheer as they left St. Enoch railway station on a 10 A.M. train.

The weekend of October 26–27 was spent in the North of England at Langhill or Broomhill, Sheffield. The chiefs were to stay with Batty Langley, a Sheffield alderman and MP, who had been one of the leading lights at the Congregational Union convention in Brighton. The arrival of the chiefs on the Saturday was announced in the *Sheffield Independent,* which understood they would be coming from Balmoral. Their visit, said the newspaper, had created a wide interest in Sheffield not "based altogether on mere vulgar curiosity." [13]

MONDAY, OCTOBER 28 – WEDNESDAY, OCTOBER 30

The chiefs' last stops on their last provincial tour of Britain were three days spent in Sheffield, Halifax, and Hanley near Stoke-on-Trent. In each place they were given the support of LMS centenary meetings with memorials directed to Chamberlain.

After the Monday night meeting in Sheffield, Khama and an attendant (probably Seisa) were taken the next day by their host Batty Langley to ride with Lord Galway's hunt in North Nottinghamshire around the town of Worksop. Khama rode on one of Langley's horses, a fine Irish hunter named General.

> Khama is a fine horsemen. With a good seat and splendid nerve, he appeared quite at home, and derived great enjoyment from his experience. . . .
>
> A stout fox broke at Belby [Bilby] Flush. Khama manifested an intense pleasure as he saw Reynard [the fox] stealing sharply away, with the hounds in full cry after him. When Reynard crossed the [Chesterfield] canal and the railway, and got into Manton planting, the hunting became slow, and a number of ladies and gentlemen, including Khama, turned their horses' heads homewards.
>
> Those who remained followed the fox through Manton Wood, beyond which he was killed, and the brush [tail] has been sent to Khama at Halifax.
>
> Khama told Alderman Langley once or twice of the enjoyment he had derived out of the sport, and how well he liked English horses and the English country. He was introduced to several members of the Hunt, to whom, in his quiet dignified way, he made himself very agreeable.

So much did Khama appreciate the delights of foxhunting that he told Alderman Langley he would like to go again, but was afraid his public engagements would compel him to deny himself the pleasure.

Khama is reported to have "dined" in the town of Worksop, before catching the 4:26 P.M. train to Sheffield. At Sheffield's Victoria Station "he had to wait some time for the fast train for Halifax, and spent the time in the refreshment room, where, sitting near the fire, he was an object of curiosity to those who were there." In Halifax he rejoined the rest of the Bechuana.[14]

The next day, Wednesday, October 29, the chiefs made their last speeches and received their last accolade of support in the provinces at Hanley, the twin town of Stoke-on-Trent, in the Staffordshire pottery and brick manufacturing area north of Birmingham.[15]

✦ ✦ ✦

It was in Staffordshire that "the green-eyed monster" finally bubbled out between Bathoen and Sebele on the one hand and Khama on the other. The *Western Daily Mercury* reported, "Sebele and Bathoen . . . are rapidly developing an ill-concealed jealousy" over all the attention lavished on Khama.

Khama had been presented with North Staffordshire pottery in the form of a porcelain plate with his smiling photographic portrait burned onto it. Bathoen complained aloud: "Khama gets all the presents." Sebele added: "We get no presents. Khama gets everything." The three chiefs were of course meant to be equals in status.

The journal *South Africa* was gratified to learn from this piece of intelligence that, despite all the fuss made over them as superhumans, Khama, Sebele, and Bathoen were "but mortal after all."[16]

The eruption of jealousy at this time is confirmed by the reminiscence about twenty-seven years later of a young woman student, who remembered the chiefs' visit to Hackney (Congregational) College for young women in North London, on Friday, November 1, 1895. Khama, Sebele, and Bathoen, accompanied by Willoughby and Lloyd, went to the college for afternoon tea. Elsie West recalled: "There was great excitement and preparation for the momentous occasion. . . . You know it is not every day that one has a King to tea!" The guests were received by the principal, Dr. Cave, who took them into his study.

> One of the missionaries, Mr. Lloyd, I think, told us quietly to be sure not to make the slightest difference in the treatment of the chiefs. . . . Sebele and Bathoen would be extremely jealous if Khama was made more fuss of than they. Presently we found how true that was!

At the principal's invitation, Khama tried on the principal's doctoral gown and hood, and velvet mortar board, and sat in the principal's chair "hugely delighted," calling himself "Doctor Khama" and asking for a mirror. It was then discovered that Bathoen "had slipped away, and going into the drawing room [we] found him sulking there terribly, because he had not tried the gown on. . . . However, he was soon pacified, and smiled broadly when it was put on him." They then sat down at the tea table, at which, Elsie West recalled, all the ham sandwiches had been removed after one of the missionaries said the chiefs would not sit down if there was "pig" on the table. The students watched every move the chiefs made and were amused by "funny incidents" at the table, "mainly in the chiefs' use of the knife for jam, etc., and their huge delight at the sugar!"

After tea Khama, Sebele, and Bathoen were shown over the college by the students. "King Khama was immensely interested in everything, and asked innumerable questions (always through his interpreter of course)." He was amused by a student's cuckoo clock and talked about wanting to see the queen, and about his desire as a widower to get married again—to a bride who would wear a veil and orange blossom.

The evening ended with a chapel service, conducted by the principal, with Khama and the two missionaries addressing the students. They all sang "Abide with Me" together, though the chiefs sang in Setswana while the rest sang in English. And "we felt how close after all, are all the ties that bind us, and that white and black alike are one in Jesus Christ." [17]

TWELVE

Khama Will Play the Old Gooseberry

⋆⟫═◉ ◉═⟪⋆

KHAMA, SEBELE, AND BATHOEN RETURNED TO LONDON
at the end of October 1895, to negotiate with the Colonial Office. Chamberlain was just about to return from his Mediterranean holiday and
would be under public pressure to make a settlement with the chiefs as
soon as possible after he returned.

The Chartered Company had been determined to annex the whole
Bechuanaland Protectorate in one gulp. When W. T. Stead was preparing
his character sketch of Khama for the October 1 edition of *Review of Reviews,* he was approached by Rutherfoord Harris of the Chartered Company to help facilitate the transfer of the whole protectorate—and was
puzzled by Harris's sense of urgency.[1] But the success of Khama, Sebele,
and Bathoen, in gaining access to Chamberlain and the support of people
like Stead, forced Cecil Rhodes into "much cogitation" in early October
on how to revise the strategy of acquisition. He concluded that annexation
of the protectorate would have to proceed piecemeal.

The company's immediate need—for the purposes of the planned
Jameson Raid on the Transvaal republic—was to acquire a continuous
strip of land along the eastern border, from Fort Tuli and Rhodesia in the
north to the "Barolong farms" and Mafeking in the south. This would
enable the BSA Company as the legally constituted administrative authority of the strip to bring its forces from Bulawayo in Rhodesia to the
"jumping-off ground" for the raid. The pretext for the immediate acquisition of the border strip would be its necessity for the promotion and
protection of "railway works," pushing the track along a railway strip
north from Mafeking through Gaborone on line for Bulawayo.

North of Gaborone the so-called railway strip was a geographical and
engineering chimera. It was a ploy to get Khama to surrender his eastern
frontier with the Transvaal so that the Chartered Company could be le-

gally constituted as the "border authority" and could sell off well-watered settler farms along the Limpopo to finance the railway. The Gaborone-Bulawayo section of the railway had always been intended to go through the middle of Khama's country, with a station near Khama's capital at Palapye. There is no reason to suppose that any other route was ever seriously considered. But the revised plans put forward by the company in October 1895 sent the railway line lower down the Limpopo valley as far as Fort Macloutsie (Motloutse), instead of gradually climbing up to the higher plateau to the north. Company and Colonial Office insiders kept resolutely discreet about this chimera until the railway strip along the Limpopo had been negotiated with Khama.

Meanwhile, the first priority was for the company to acquire the railway strip for the Mafeking-Gaborone section.

Chiefs Montshiwa and Ikaneng at the southern end of the strip had the most suitable jumping-off ground for the raid and had their arms twisted into surrendering their territories by imperial and company officials on the spot. Chiefs Bathoen and Sebele were in London and had to be dealt with through the Colonial Office. Chiefs Linchwe and Khama, to the north of Gaborone, were less pressing cases, but might provide pretexts for assembling military forces in the south for the protection of "railway works" as they extended northward.

In the second week of September, Chamberlain authorized High Commissioner Robinson in Cape Town to proceed with the transfer to the Chartered Company of the Barolong farms area of Montshiwa and the Lete territory of Ikaneng (after Robinson had satisfied himself that Ikaneng was not a tributary chief under Bathoen). The British Treasury, which kept a watching brief on colonial expenditure, expressed its fears about the giving away of capital assets. But the Colonial Office assured the Treasury on September 19 that alienation of these two small enclaves would not lead to transfer of the whole territory "for the present." [2]

On September 23, Resident Commissioner Shippard and Frank Rhodes, one of the older brothers of Cecil Rhodes, left Cape Town for the north to persuade Montshiwa and Ikaneng to voluntarily concede these territories to the Chartered Company. The concessions were obtained by variants of the classic ruse of getting the chiefs to agree to one document but to sign another. As the historian Anthony Sillery points out, Frank Rhodes first bamboozled Ikaneng and then together with Shippard managed to trick the much older and shrewder Montshiwa. The company also bought from Israel Molema, one of Montshiwa's councillors, the site for a police camp at Pitsane (Phitsane Potlhoko) at the north end of the Barolong farms.

The two enclaves were formally annexed, and Leander Starr Jameson was designated their resident commissioner, on October 18—by Proclamation No. 10 of the Bechuanaland Protectorate. Arrangements were put in hand on October 20 to bring BSA Company forces south from Bulawayo to assemble and drill at Pitsane, where they began to arrive by November 30. It was such troop movements, even before the "jumping-off ground" had been formally acquired, that had panicked Khama's son Sekgoma, in Bechuanaland, into cabling his father in Britain on October 14.

Meanwhile, with the annexation of British Bechuanaland by Cape Colony due to take final effect on November 16, arrangements were also made for imperial police—the Bechuanaland Border Police—to assemble at their Mafeking headquarters to be "diluted" from that date. The officers and men of the police were to be given the option of staying on at Mafeking in the employ of the BSA Company Police.

After acquiring Montshiwa's and Ikaneng's territories, Robinson and Rhodes carried on with plans to take Linchwe's territory north of Gaborone. Linchwe was portrayed as having rebellious inclinations against British rule, necessitating the bringing of troops from Rhodesia. The process of handing over Linchwe's territory to Chartered Company administration was formally initiated by a further proclamation of the Bechuanaland Protectorate on December 11.[3]

While these moves were made in Africa, the Colonial Office had to deal with the three Bechuana chiefs who had come to Europe.

Because of the conspiracy, cover-up, and destruction of records after the failure of the Jameson Raid, there is controversy among historians about who in the Colonial Office was in conscious league with the Chartered Company in its plans for the jumping-off ground.

Sir Robert Meade at the Colonial Official was undoubtedly part of the conspiracy, but how far up and how far down did the conspiracy go? Sir Robert Herbert, a retired head of the office, was probably the person who arranged for the cover-up and destruction of documents. Circumstantial evidence points to both the current head, Sir Edward Fairfield, and his political boss, Joseph Chamberlain, having also been in the know. Chamberlain would only admit, privately, to having inherited the vaguest outline of the plans from his Liberal predecessors. He managed to maintain official ignorance by shutting up Rhodes's envoy, Dr. Rutherfoord Harris, whenever Harris looked as if he might be indiscreet in their formal interviews at the Colonial Office. Fairfield actually took the rap for the raid (or rather, for its failure) and died embittered, while Chamberlain got away free. Both men have had strong defendants among their later relatives—the novelist Rebecca West for Fairfield, and the historian Elizabeth Pakenham (Lady Longford) for Chamberlain.

How far down did the conspiracy go in the Colonial Office? Meade's underling F. Graham certainly seems to have still been in the dark when he scribbled a minute on an October 8 dispatch from Robinson to Chamberlain:

> I cannot see why the Chartered Co. are in such a hurry to establish their Administration and Police along the Railway line.

Perhaps he was subsequently enlightened by Flora Shaw, the *Times* colonial correspondence who—to Fairfield's annoyance—had the run of the Colonial Office corridors and had been put in the know by Rhodes himself a year before. It was another old Rhodes ploy—to compromise one's critics by giving them sufficient knowledge and interests in the grand plan to make them feel privileged, to keep quiet and tag along, a ploy that would succeed for only as long as Rhodes himself was held in awe as the Great Colossus.[4]

✤ ✤ ✤

On September 24 (as we have seen in chapter 6), the chiefs communicated their grievances, as expressed verbally in their interview of September 11 with Chamberlain, in a formal letter to Meade at the Colonial Office.

The formal reply from the Colonial Office to the chiefs' letter was returned on October 7. Meade advised the chiefs that Chamberlain wished them to consult with the British South Africa Company before his return to England from his Mediterranean holiday.[5]

The "official mind" in the Colonial Office was evidently somewhat divided on what to do next. Meade, as one of Rhodes's key accomplices, was pushing the claims of the Chartered Company, writing to another Colonial Office official on October 5 that the continuance of imperial rule over the Protectorate was impossible—and therefore the chiefs should be persuaded to submit to the company as soon as possible. But Selborne, Prime Minister Salisbury's son-in-law and parliamentary undersecretary for the colonies (i.e. assistant minister), who was evidently not part of the Rhodes-ian conspiracy, could not agree.[6]

On October 8 Rhodes's envoy in London, Dr. Rutherfoord Harris, wrote Willoughby a smoothly diplomatic letter from the Chartered Company's London offices, to open up negotiations with the chiefs. Harris first notified Khama and Willoughby that Rhodes had accommodated Khama's dissident brother Raditladi in Chartered territory at Mangwe, north of the Shashe River. He then told Willoughby that the company's accredited agents were Albert (Earl) Grey and Rochfort Maguire, and that they awaited the pleasure of an interview with the chiefs.

Albert Grey was a humanitarian who had sat on Mackenzie and

Chamberlain's South African Committee in the later 1880s but had been won over by Rhodes to sit on the Chartered Company's board. Maguire—a former fellow of All Souls' College at Oxford—was an Irish Nationalist MP who had recently married the daughter of the retiring Speaker of the House of Commons.

Harris's letter to Willoughby contained the implied threat that, since the transfer "of the balance of the Protectorate" to the Company's takeover was inevitable, the chiefs would do well to settle the issues of their land, laws, and liquor rights now before they lost that chance forever. There was also a strange final statement apparently aimed at Willoughby himself:

> There are reasons, which I would rather mention in conversation, why a postponement of the question can only be detrimental both to Khama and to ourselves.

The chiefs sent a prompt reply on October 9, from Heaton Mersey in Lancashire. They agreed to hearing Rhodes's envoys, but insisted that this should be kept secret from the press. Any leak to the newspapers would prejudice the chiefs against further talks. They were acutely aware of previous Rhodes-ian attempts to prejudice their negotiating position through false reports fed to the British public, especially in the *Times* newspaper. The time suggested for the meeting by Willoughby was Saturday, October 19, between 9 A.M. and 12:30. This was accepted by Harris in a telegram sent on October 10 and in a letter of the eleventh, which ended with an appeal to Willoughby's sense of patriotism:

> I am very much obliged to you for having used your influence in favour of this interview, as several friends have informed us that the Chiefs would not meet us. Had this been so I am sure that all who are interested in the English advancement of Africa would always have regretted it.[7]

On the same day Meade wrote to Bathoen and Sebele from the Colonial Office, asking them to cede eastern frontier lands for the railway strip. These concessions would be drastic, removing the two chiefs' best-watered territory. But Meade played this down as what he called, slipping into appropriate idiom, a "little word" to be kept separate from the big word they had to say with Khama.

Meade fretted with impatience at the delay in an answer from the two chiefs, while they were away from London. But he tried hard to play down this part of the negotiations. He wrote again on the eighteenth asking for an answer, again emphasizing how little a matter the railway strip was.

Sebele and Bathoen received Meade's letter on Wednesday, October 16, when they returned to London. It was read and discussed that evening. Their response, communicated by Willoughby to Meade on the eighteenth, the day before the chiefs were to meet the Chartered Company's delegates, was that it was no "small word":

> They evidently look on it as a very serious matter, and do not see why it should be separated from the larger question, since it is a question of the administration of a certain part of their country. They have asked me to say that they are considering it and will try to give you an answer in a few days.[8]

Bathoen was constrained by the fact that he had already granted a concession for railway construction in his country to another commercial company. This, of course, was considered as no inhibition by either the Colonial Office or the Chartered Company.

SATURDAY, OCTOBER 19

On October 19—five days after Khama's son and regent Sekgoma had urgently cabled his father about filibustering whites who had just appeared in his country—Rutherfoord Harris, Maguire, and Earl Grey visited the chiefs for the first time.

The Chartered Company put forward its modified proposals. They no longer wanted the whole of Bechuanaland Protectorate, only that part which lay outside the countries of the three chiefs. In return, the chiefs should assist the Chartered Company by granting it a railway strip along their eastern borders. Bathoen, Sebele, and Khama would grant to the company those parts of the Transvaal frontier not owned by Montshiwa, Ikaneng, and Linchwe.

Rutherfoord Harris outlined what he called "Mr. Rhodes' maximum offer." The "maximum offer" revived and exploited for Chartered Company purposes the "magnificent offer" by the chiefs ten years earlier—generous frontier lands, offered to and turned down by the imperial government, an offer long considered by all parties as having lapsed. Using the map of the chiefs' drastically reduced territorial reserves contained in the Blue Book of the 1885 negotiations, Harris outlined a settlement obviously already worked out with the Colonial Office. Inside their reserves, the chiefs would retain all jurisdiction that did not touch on whites and alien Africans and would be responsible to a resident commissioner representing the imperial government and not subject to the Chartered Company.

The Chartered Company promised to support Khama, Sebele, and Bathoen against all pretenders to their thrones, guaranteeing them tenure for life. Direct taxation, along the lines of the company's hut tax in Matabeleland and Mashonaland, would of course be necessary to cover the costs of administration. The chiefs could collect this (at their own expense) as long as the queen's officer supervised the collection. Mr. Rhodes would fence Khama's side of the railway against cattle and would pay for the surveying and beaconing of the land settlement himself.[9]

Willoughby visited the Colonial Office, at Fairfield's request, soon after the Saturday morning interview of the chiefs with the Chartered Company. Harris then bombarded Willoughby with letters.

On Monday, October 21 Harris wrote to Willoughby asking him to "obtain Bathoen's consent now" to conceding land for a ten-mile-wide railway strip—because Sebele had already consented.

On Tuesday, October 22, Harris wrote to assure Khama that Jameson would expel any infiltrators identified in Sekgoma Khama's telegram of October 14. He also promised a written record of Saturday's meeting between them, with a map. This promise was fulfilled on October 24 with a nine-page memorandum and a large colored map of the "maximum offer."

Harris's memorandum of the twenty-fourth made it clear that the Chartered Company would pay Sebele £225 a year in return for his part of the railway strip. Bathoen's concession of railway rights to the Kanya Exploration Company was deemed to be invalid (but the Chartered Company would accommodate his concession of ten thousand morgen—about twenty thousand acres—to Rev. James Good, Lloyd's father-in-law.[10]

The chiefs had been in the dark about Rhodes's exact territorial plans and had asked for a map to be drawn. The map, professionally drafted, now made it clear how small were the reserves promised to the three chiefs by contrast with the great bulk of "The remainder of the Protectorate to be transferred to the Company with a view to development and colonization."

The map showed that Khama would have to concede a wide belt of land along the Limpopo, from Palla Camp in the south to the Shashe River in the north. The railway was marked as running "in a fairly straight line" along the new border of Khama's country, set back a dozen miles or so from the Limpopo. It was to run from Palla, down the Limpopo valley but over the Tswapong Hills, to the Macloutsie (Motloutse) police fort, from whence it would cross a stretch of Khama's country directly north to Bulawayo. This contradicted all previous announcements of the railway route in Parliamentary Blue Books and in the press. But Khama may have welcomed the idea of the morally corrupting railroad bypassing his capital.

The accompanying letter laid out Rhodes's "maximum offer" to each chief. Each was defined by reference to the "Warren map" of 1885, with extremely restricted borders on the west. Khama would have been agitated that the Chartered Company was cutting him off on the north as well as the west and was denying him the whole of the Motloutse-Shashe "disputed territory." The railway would now dissect the "disputed territory," and Harris justified the company's taking a ten-mile-wide strip of its eastern frontier "to keep open the wagon traffic route and for our telegraph and postal offices at Tuli." Hence Khama would lose his entire Limpopo River frontage with the Transvaal. Furthermore, Harris threatened that Fort Macloutsie (rather than Fort Gaborones in the south) would become the protectorate headquarters of the company's police—the sure recipe, as previously at the Mafeking headquarters of the border police, for a white-settler town developing there.

Once again Harris ended with implied threats. The chiefs would not get such generous terms "from any of the self-governing communities" (i.e. white-settler states) in South Africa. They should compromise as soon as possible because Rhodes reserved the right to change his offer "should the local conditions in South Africa change from what they now are before our agreement is arrived at." So "it will be a mistake, from the point of view of the chiefs, if the day of settlement is postponed, and I am sure time will show the correctness of what I say should no agreement now be arrived at."[11]

✤ ✤ ✤

The chiefs were less than persuaded by "Mr. Rhodes' maximum offer." Their feelings were turned to positive hostility after the *Times* appeared, on the Monday morning after the Saturday meeting. It stated that the chiefs and the company had come to an agreement. This crude attempt to compromise the chiefs provoked immediate uproar in the press. Even publications previously friendly to the Rhodes-ian camp, such as the *St James' Gazette,* denounced the report as a deliberate fraud.

The press had been alerted to the tricks of Rhodes-ian propaganda by press articles appearing in the previous week. The *African Critic* of Wednesday, October 16, had carried a long article entitled "Khama and *The Times*," arguing that that newspaper had used its great influence most unfairly against Khama—carrying stories that Khama was going back on agreements with Jameson and Rhodes. The *Times,* according to the *African Critic,* was being fed with misinformation from the Cape. Saturday, October 19's *South Africa* agreed. Rhodes, said *South Africa,* must find the offenders and punish them. To do any less would create a strong public reaction in favor of Khama in Britain; and the Chartered Company would lose all it stood to gain.

Thus the emperor was seen to have no clothes when the *Times* carried its exclusive story on Monday, October 21. The voice of W. T. Stead urging moderation on Rhodes was joined by that of another great editor on

October 26, when Frank Harris, the libidinous editor of the *Saturday Review*, attacked Rhodes for trying to prejudice the case of the three Bechuana chiefs with false reports. Rhodes, more powerful than any European individual besides the czar of Russia, concluded Frank Harris, had the London *Times* like the softest of wax in his fingers.

The public image of the Chartered Company had never been lower. An article by Wardlaw Thompson that appeared in the monthly *Chronicle of the London Missionary Society* for October 1895 referred to the money madness of "That remarkable combination of dukes and stock-jobbers, the British South Africa Company, which was so largely the product of the genius and enterprise of Mr. Rhodes." [12]

All this press reaction and support helped to strengthen the resolve of the three Bechuana chiefs not to give in to the Chartered Company. On Tuesday, October 22, in Manchester, Sebele had been provoked into comment on "Mr. Rhodes' maximum offer": This was the occasion on which Sebele objected to "our country [being] cut up into little bits," adding the striking phrase, "A country full of boundaries, what is it worth?" [13]

SATURDAY, NOVEMBER 2

On the morning of Saturday, November 2, the chiefs and the Chartered Company's representatives met again and reached deadlock, waving Blue Books and maps in the argument. Having at last seen a map of the company's claims, leaving them with small "native reserves" isolated from major rivers, the chiefs were dead set against negotiations.

Rutherfoord Harris cabled his master in Cape Town after the meeting:

Native chiefs decline our proposal but we hope they will make counter proposal. J. Chamberlain will put pressure on them to settle. Fear we must increase Khama's boundary. . . . Country Press very much in favour of Khama.

Khama pressed his land claims far to the north of the meridian being offered by Rhodes. Harris had already remarked, "You know the way Khama will play the old gooseberry with the blessed British public." Now he was coming under such prickly tactics himself. He was obliged to send a second cable to Rhodes on November 2, adding: "Willoughby and Khama state you promised them land up to Panda Ma Tenka. . . . Telegraph authoritative denial." No such denial was returned by Rhodes, leaving Harris to go along with Chamberlain's recognition of Khama's country well to the north of the line drawn on the map of "Mr. Rhodes' maximum offer." [14]

In a letter to the Chartered Company drafted on Monday, November 4, reiterating the views they had put forward on the Saturday, the

chiefs pointed out how Rhodes had completely gone back on his Cape
Town promise that he did not want the chiefs' land.

> You speak to us as if you had taken our land in war and we had to beg it
> from you. The land is ours, not yours, and we cannot speak of giving the
> best parts to you. We occupy the waters [referring to the Ngotwane, Lim-
> popo, and other rivers] with our cattle and our gardens, and we cannot
> remove our people for the sake of letting you sell our country.

Also on Monday, November 4, the day of the Grosvenor House breakfast in their honor, the chiefs drafted a letter written by Willoughby to
Chamberlain. The first draft, presumably taken from the chiefs' dictation,
was a long plaint, asking: "Is the Great Queen not able to protect us from
the Chartered Company? Or does the Great Queen wish the Chartered
Company to steal our land?" The word "steal" was used frequently in the
first draft, in referring to the Chartered Company's land lust, but was
crossed out and replaced by "take" and "seek." A particular point was
made of the company's attempt to grab the "best part" of the chiefs'
lands—especially along the Ngotwane and Limpopo Rivers, and "even
the Makarikari Lakes" in Khama's country.

An offer by Khama to give Chamberlain (rather than the company) his
land north of the Nata River, that is, through Pandamatenga toward the
Zambezi, was first written in and then crossed out. The most important
statement in the letter appears to be an afterthought, as it was added in a
starred footnote: "We are willing also to give you land for the Railway."

There is good evidence (see below) that these offers were pressed on the
chiefs by Willoughby, to provide Chamberlain with leeway for negotiation. Willoughby's final draft of the letter was altogether more diplomatic
than the first one dictated by the chiefs—beginning with, "We do not wish
to talk again with the Company; we will talk with you," and ending with:

> If you will keep us under the protection of the Queen we will give you a
> part of our country and we are willing to speak with you about this matter.

Meanwhile the Rhodes-ian plot to obtain the "jumping-off ground"
thickened. Also on November 4, Rhodes's agent Flora Shaw of the *Times*
probably went to see her old friend Chamberlain to pass on Rhodes's
personal ideas about the railway strip. On the next day Meade of the
Colonial Office had another meeting with Rutherfoord Harris of the
Chartered Company. Any records of the meetings were subsequently
destroyed.[15]

✤ ✤ ✤

All evidence suggests that the deadlock in negotiations was indeed broken
and brokered by the missionary friends of the chiefs.

The London Missionary Society had been denied any official role or direct representation in the triangular talks between the Colonial Office, the Bechuana chiefs, and the Chartered Company. But its executives and directors, notably Wardlaw Thompson and the Spicer brothers, were active behind the scenes.

Wardlaw Thompson, the foreign secretary of the LMS, wrote a letter dated November 1 to Meade of the Colonial Office. Thompson said that he had been told by Willoughby that whereas the Bechuana chiefs were now in a mood to concede nothing to the Chartered Company, they would make over to the queen's government exactly those territorial concessions that the company wanted. So, Thompson suggested, why not persuade the chiefs to give them to the government in order that the imperial government might give them to the company—although "I appreciate that some questions of delicacy might arise in arranging this matter." Thompson added that the idea was entirely his own, and that he had not consulted the chiefs at all about it.

Fairfield then wrote from the Colonial Office to Chamberlain in Birmingham on November 4:

> Khama is utterly obdurate as regards the Company, and will grant them nothing whatever, but will (so the missionaries say) grant anything to you in reason. . . . give Khama a blue-pencil boundary on the map, which he will show you how to trace, and ask Khama & Co. to give up their country to you (it being perfectly understood that you are going to give it to the Company). This, according to the missionaries, the chiefs will agree to.

The next day, Rutherfoord Harris went round to the Colonial Office and reported back to Rhodes by telegram: "We have seen E. Fairfield, Hon. R. H. Meade, Colonel Goold-Adams, and we have agreed to what land we give native chiefs."

How far the three chiefs were collaborators in the charade of giving land to the Crown, in order that the Crown might give it to the company, is debatable. It seems that Sebele had already "sold out" to the Company by October 21, but Khama, in Rochfort Maguire's words, "would rather have twopence from Mr. Chamberlain than half a crown from the Company."

Bathoen and Khama continued to resist being collaborators in their own deception until the last moment—when, in Willoughby's words a year and a half later, they "knew . . . that the strip [being conceded to the Crown] was for [Chartered Company] railway purposes." The record of the "final" meeting with Chamberlain on November 6 shows that Bathoen and Khama were initially resistant but soon caved in, while Sebele seems to have developed a bad case of funk—claiming illness to stay away from the meeting altogether.

Wardlaw Thompson later said that he had had "a good deal of serious talk with the Chiefs before the settlement." He had told the chiefs that there was no hope of imperial rule in perpetuity, so they should push merely for a delay of transfer to the company for seven or ten years. (The idea of a delay until the year 1900 was also being put forward in the press.) But it was of course Willoughby who had the most crucial role in molding the chiefs' views as their main interpreter and adviser.[16]

Is it perhaps not curious how in the eyes of the company and the Colonial Office Willoughby moved from being the "*enragé* missionary" to being the most vital participant in the talks after the chiefs themselves? How much personal influence did he have on the final settlement? How far was he drawn away from simply representing the chiefs' views and persuaded that there were wider British imperial issues at stake that might override the chiefs' interests?

The suggestion that "Our Good Mr. Willoughby . . . might have himself fallen under the Rhodesian influence" was first made in the *African Critic* on September 21, which remarked how "the Cape Premier has devious ways of working his will with Downing Street." A week later the *African Critic* added: "I have had no reply from the rev. gentleman which would amount to a disclaimer."[17]

In the *Birmingham Post* of September 27, Willoughby was interviewed at length and expressed admiration for Cecil Rhodes:

> I went out to South Africa with a very strong prejudice in favour of Imperialism. My views today in that respect are unchanged. The "Little England" party, as it is called, has no charms for me, and I admire the Imperialism of Mr. Cecil Rhodes, immensely. He is our incarnation of Imperialism as applied to South African affairs. I have not always agreed with his methods, but there has never been a time when I have not agreed with his aims as far as I have understood them.
>
> I can understand the arguments of men who say that a company like the British South Africa Company, being more elastic in its methods than the Imperial Government can possibly be, is better adapted to govern a new territory—a hitherto unacquired territory—than the Imperial Government. Whether I quite agree with them I am not sure. Still, the argument is one that can be appreciated.
>
> I can understand the position taken up by men who say that the Chartered Company had gripped Matabeleland and Mashonaland, and if they had not gripped it, it would have gone from the British power to some other power; and painfully I have to confess that I think they are right.

But, he added, he could not understand why the Chartered Company should be given the Bechuanaland Protectorate as well. It might be good for the company's shares, "but I fail to see what service it can possibly render to the Imperial Government or to the native races living in those lands."

The company . . . has already a vast territory, more than it can possibly hope to utilise for the next ten years. To saddle it with more is to put upon its shoulders a burden that we have no proof of its ability to bear, especially when we consider that the natives which it is proposed to hand over are eminently disloyal to it. But these people are loyal, to the Imperial Government.

He was "very chary" about taking away the judicial rights of chiefs—"in Khama's town even the Europeans prefer that their disputes shall be adjudicated on by the Chief, in as much as they know they can obtain justice equal in quality and without all the expense and circumlocution that are the inevitable accompaniments of British law."

Willoughby concluded with "one further argument" on the expenses of colonial administration—"if the company are going to make it pay, why can't the Imperial Government?" (The protectorate administration's estimated revenue for 1894–95 was £17,340 matched against expenditure of £57,968, but of that expenditure no less than £39,000 was on an arguably unnecessary military police force, and a mere £1,027 was on the office of the assistant commissioner at Palapye.)

> The country could very easily be administered for £20,000 a year, with little or no risk of any serious disturbance, unless an attempt be made to take the land from the chiefs and give it out in farms.
>
> The £20,000 could be raised by means of licenses, fines, and poll-tax, the protectorate's share under the Customs Union, and the duties paid on goods imported into the territory. Why not try that plan for ten years to come?
>
> In the meantime we should see what the company did and if it turned out that it would be better to hand the land over to them, it would be done with sufficient and satisfactory guarantees.

Willoughby told the *Birmingham Post* that these were his own views and not those of the chiefs but might well be acceptable to them.[18]

It was the publication of this interview in the London *Daily Post* that convinced Dr. Rutherfoord Harris of the Chartered Company that he could after all deal with the missionary previously characterized as a hothead. But how much did Harris take Willoughby into his confidence? On October 8, Harris wrote to Willoughby about "reasons, *which I would rather mention in conversation* [emphasis added], why a postponement of the question can only be detrimental both to Khama and ourselves."[19] What reasons? Was Willoughby made complicit to at least enough of the Jameson Plan to compromise him? Rhodes had "squared" or silenced other opponents by making them privy to information that they could neither repeat nor forget. He had done this with the leaders of the Cape parliamentary opposition in May 1895 by showing them confidentially printed Colonial

Office correspondence that appeared to promise the Bechuanaland Protectorate to the Chartered Company.

Why did Harris thank Willoughby so profusely, on October 11, for arranging a meeting on October 19, with flattering phrases on Willoughby's help to "English advancement in Africa"? Why did Harris write to Willoughby on October 21—that since Sebele had now consented to the loss of a ten-mile-wide border strip, "I feel you will be able to obtain Bathoen's consent now"?[20] This implies that Harris had some prior understanding with and trust in Willoughby.

The suspicion lingers that Willoughby was compromised by being told "too much" about the Jameson Plan. After 1895 he was a changed man. Willoughby began to advocate the destruction of "tribalism" and the integration of the Bechuana into "modern," white-settler-dominated society. But there is no evidence that Willoughby was ever in the pocket of Rhodes and the Chartered Company.

THIRTEEN

Chamberlain's Settlement

ON THE MORNING OF MONDAY, NOVEMBER 4, KHAMA, Sebele, and Bathoen were due to be entertained to a public "breakfast" (in Victorian usage the first meal of the day but not necessarily early), at Grosvenor House, near Hyde Park Corner and Marble Arch in London, by the duke of Westminster.

The British South Africa Company was fully aware that the Grosvenor House breakfast was to be the climax of the campaign by the temperance supporters of the Bechuana chiefs to press their case on the colonial minister. Rutherfoord Harris had telegrammed Rhodes the day before to say that he would try to lobby all the people slated to speak at the breakfast—who were to include Westminster himself and the bishop of London, Sir George Baden-Powell, Lord Loch, and Frederick Lugard. This lobbying on Rhodes's behalf appears to have taken the form of a reminder

> that the Chartered Company subscribe to the Society for the Prevention of the Liquor Traffic with Natives, and that [its directors] the Duke of Fife and Mr. G. Cawston are both strong supporters of the Society.[1]

There may also have been, of course, subtle hints by Harris about the deeper interests for the whole future of the empire that might be upset by any delay in the transfer of the Bechuanaland Protectorate to the Chartered Company.

The seventy-year-old first duke of Westminster—like his lineal descendant a century later—was generally reckoned to be the richest man in Britain, because of his extraordinarily valuable landholdings in Mayfair and Belgravia near Buckingham Palace in the West End of London. He had other large landholdings in Cheshire and Flintshire. He was a former Whig and was now "a staunch Unionist" supporter of Joseph Chamberlain. He had held the honorific position of lord-lieutenant of the County of London since 1889 and was a prominent figure in humanitarian organizations. He presided over protest meetings against the ill treatment of Armenian Christians in the Ottoman Turkish Empire—the cause so close to Gladstone's heart. He was also president of the United Committee for the Protection of the Native Races from the Liquor Traffic, and it was in this capacity that he held the breakfast in honor of Khama and the other chiefs.

The breakfast was a great social occasion for the British temperance and humanitarian establishment, held at the duke's palatial West London residence, Grosvenor House. As well as by members of his United Committee, the breakfast was attended by people from the (Roman) Catholic Total Abstinence League of the Cross, the Church of England Temperance Society, the (Quakers') Friends Temperance Union, the National Temperance League, the (Women's) Band of Hope Union, the London Temperance Hospital, the Good Templars, and the United Kingdom Alliance (of temperance societies); the LMS, the Wesleyan Missionary Society, the ("broad" Anglican) Society for the Propagation of the Gospel, and the ("high" Anglican) Universities' Mission to Central Africa; the Royal Colonial Institute and the Aborigines' Protection Society. Other dignitaries present included Bishop Frederick Temple of London (former headmaster of Rugby School and future archbishop of Canterbury) and Canon Wilberforce of Westminster Abbey, the marchioness of Ormonde, and Ladies Frederick and Edward Cavendish (members of the rich and powerful family of the dukes of Devonshire).[2]

MONDAY, NOVEMBER 4

The guests gathered in the "splendidly decorated salon, with its choice art treasures displayed on every side."

> In the drawing room the first object that struck the eye was Sir J. Reynolds' splendid painting of Mrs. Siddons as "The Tragic Muse," whilst on the opposite wall was Gainsborough's famous "Blue Boy." All the names of the great masters were to be seen on the pictures that were hanging everywhere. Titian, Raphael, Rubens, each having several specimens of their works.
>
> But splendid though it all was, and glorious as the pictures are, they did not in the least seem to appeal to the Bechuana chiefs. For all the effect the splendours of Grosvenor House had upon them, the glories of Khama's home at Palapye would seem to outshine those of the grandest of our English palaces. At any rate, all three seemed stolid and unmoved.[3]

Another view of the chiefs' entry was more sympathetic:

> People very generally were inclined to feel a kind of pity for the black men, imagining that they would feel miserable and uncomfortable in the presence of the glitter, formality and dignity of such an occasion.

But tears started to many eyes and many hearts beat with warm admiration when, through the great reception hall of Grosvenor House, even though a certain silence fell over the large assemblage, Khama entered and moved forward with as much ease and composure and dignity in his manner as the noblest there to greet his host.[4]

Soon after the chiefs arrived, a move was made toward the dining room, where the breakfast meal was awaiting the guests. The room also had walls overlaid in silver and gold, and hung with famous paintings. Khama and Westminster sat on the high table on either side of Lady Loch. A musical interlude after the meal was provided by the Queen's Westminster Band.

The proceedings started with apologies from the archbishop of Canterbury and the prime minister for not being able to be present. Other regrets came from Lord Knutsford (former colonial secretary), Sir Wilfrid Lawson (head of the United Kingdom Alliance), and Sir Charles Warren.

The first speech was by the bishop of London, who proposed a motion of support for the maintenance of prohibition of liquor in the future administration of Khama's territory in Bechuanaland. He made no direct reference to the British South Africa Company, but referred to "the most dreadful curse" of liquor being imposed by British commerce "all over the world" on "native races," and paid tribute to the "high character" of Khama.

Sir George Baden-Powell seconded the motion, recalling his experience in 1885 under "that great Christian warrior" Sir Charles Warren, when

> they found a native chief ruling a native state in the wilds of tropical Africa in a way that would have done credit to the administration of any British Colony. (Applause.) They found him a thorough-going Christian man, a splendid instance of practical and muscular Christianity. . . .
>
> If this country, with its great Empire, were in any way to go contrary to the noble wishes of Khama it would be doing a crime that might sap the very foundations of justice on which the Empire rested. (Applause.) . . .
>
> The alternative to [Khama's] becoming a sort of feudatory State, after the Indian fashion, was that he should pass to the care of the great Chartered Company. He (Sir George) believed that the Chartered Company could only succeed with Khama on the distinct understanding that the liquor prohibition was perpetuated, and the Imperial Parliament would see to it that this prohibition would be an essential element in the conditions of the surrender of the territory.

The resolution was then carried on the vote of the meeting. Note that both the resolution, and the speeches so far, contained no element of opposition to the Chartered Company hand-over. Harris had evidently done his lobbying well.

The duke was next to speak, welcoming "a gathering that was unique."

It was England's duty as a Christian country to support "very noble and splendid" Khama's prohibition of strong liquor—though Khama "had not been so successful with native beer, which was looked on more or less as a temperance drink, much as porter was in Ireland. (Laughter.)"

Westminster then presented Khama in person with a "handsomely illuminated" framed address "mounted in gilt with a very handsome white stucco frame,"

> To Khama, Paramount Chief of the Bamangwato, Distinguished Chief.
> We, the President and Members of the Native Races and Liquor Traffic Committee, unite in offering you a hearty welcome to this country, and we desire to express our deep sympathy with you. . . . We have also much pleasure in welcoming your companions and fellow chiefs. . . .
> We join with you in the strong hope you then [in 1888] expressed "that not even a little door should be open to intoxicating drinks." We are confident that this enlightened policy will tend to the permanent establishment of legitimate trade, and to the highest moral and spiritual welfare of your people, for "righteousness exalteth a nation, but sin is a reproach to any people." [5]

The biblical quotation "righteousness exalteth a nation" was to be engraved on Khama's gravestone three decades later.

After the contribution of the Belgian member on the United Committee, Dr. Moeller, it was Lord Loch's turn to speak. It is not clear how and why Loch infuriated Rhodes and the Chartered Company by his speech, but it is clear that he did.

Loch began by disclaiming any intention of touching on the politics of Bechuanaland's future and went to great pains to defend the policies of the high commissioner for South Africa, the Cape Colony, and the Chartered Company on the supply of liquor to African natives.

The point at which Loch offended Rhodes must have been his account of the 1893 Anglo-Ndebele War. Loch referred to the "active part" of imperial troops, of whom Khama's men constituted the majority. He added that Khama had acted "with great gallantry" when he "fought in the only action with the Matabele in the open, and that he charged the Matabele at the head of his regiment, and successfully pressed them back. (Applause.)"

This was a denial of the myth so assiduously propagated by the Chartered Company over the previous eighteen months, that its first "Jameson raid" had been solely responsible for victory over the "Matabele," the very same myth of self-delusion that was even now driving the Chartered Company to destruction in attempting to repeat its version of history in the Transvaal.

The Rhodesian historian Hugh Marshall Hole claims that Loch's speech was "received coldly" at the Grosvenor House breakfast.[6]

Khama's succinct speech followed Loch's. He appealed for his audience's help against white people working to import strong drink into his country. The Chartered Company "will be causing strong drink to pass through my country to Buluwayo [sic], and I know that it will be stored in houses in my town before it can be forwarded to Matabeleland, and my people will see it from day to day, and it will be a very great temptation to my people. (Loud applause.)"

The penultimate speaker was Captain Frederick Lugard, a glamorous though slight figure with a large yoke-shaped moustache, fresh from the colonial pacification of parts of East Africa and West Africa and even now being recruited to go to northern Bechuanaland. Lugard "said it was surprising the liquor traffic should be supported by Government officials, because the outlay on drink destroyed the productive and consuming power of the people, and the drinking of foreign-made spirits prevented the importation of British-made goods"—as on their Lagos and Niger coastal colonies in West Africa.

The last speaker, before some closing remarks by the duke, was Wardlaw Thompson of the LMS. He singled out the issue of a liquor license at Kanye, Bathoen's capital, for a bar to serve only ten resident whites, as an example of the sort of colonial administrative policies they were fighting against.

(S. M. Molema, a Motswana physician and historian writing twenty-five years later in *Bantu Past and Present,* described white indignation when the news of the duke of Westminster's lavish entertaining of a black man reached South Africa. Molema compared this to the storm raised in the United States when President Theodore Roosevelt entertained to dinner in the White House the black educationist Booker T. Washington.)[7]

WEDNESDAY, NOVEMBER 6

The Grosvenor House breakfast must have increased the confidence of the chiefs in having the moral support of the British establishment. But it may also have given the Chartered Company the impression that the way had been cleared of the liquor obstacle in its takeover bid for the rest of the Bechuanaland Protectorate. Nor can the fulsome praise for Khama at the breakfast have helped relations between the three chiefs, exacerbating the jealousy felt by the other two.

The final interview with Chamberlain at the Colonial Office was fixed for 3 P.M. on Wednesday, November 6. With characteristic insensitivity, Fairfield, the head of the African department at the Colonial Office, had written to Willoughby asking him to persuade the chiefs not to open their mouths too wide and not to stick out for any and every old cattle post where some old cow may have wandered off in search of grass during a year of scarcity.[8]

When Chamberlain met the chiefs that afternoon he dictated a settlement, interpreted into Setswana by Edwin Lloyd, and previously cleared with Dr. Rutherfoord Harris of the Chartered Company. Sebele was ill, but Willoughby deputized for him. Other people present at the meeting in the Colonial Office were Wardlaw Thompson, Colonial Office officials, and representatives of the Chartered Company. The officials were Lord Ampthill, Meade, Fairfield, Graham, and Harry Wilson, Chamberlain's private secretary, who took the minutes. Colonel Goold-Adams sat in on the meeting, as a Setswana-speaking aide and local expert for Chamberlain. The company men were Rutherfoord Harris, Rochfort Maguire, Earl Grey, and the duke of Fife. Sixteen people in all were present.

Wilson's minutes of the meeting survive in a typescript preserved in the Botswana National Archives:

> CHAMBERLAIN: Glad to see them. Sorry Sebele is unwell. Let us go to business. I must decide this question at once as I have very little time. I will speak about the land of the Chiefs, and about the railway, and about the law which is to be observed in the territory of the Chiefs. . . .
>
> It is necessary that the railway should be made and I understand the Chiefs are ready to give me land for the purpose. I have consulted the people who know the country, and I see that it must go along Kruger's country.
>
> Now let us look at the map . . .

Chamberlain turned to speak with Bathoen. He asked him for a ten-mile-wide railway strip. Bathoen refused to grant it. Chamberlain then threatened to take it without Bathoen's consent. Bathoen agreed to six miles. But Rutherfoord Harris, sitting nearby, interjected that the Chartered Company needed a railway strip at least nine miles wide.

Chamberlain then took on Willoughby as the absent Sebele's authorized representative, turning back to Bathoen to say that the railway strip would be between six and nine miles wide. Adding significantly: "It is only for the railway we want the land."

Turning to Khama, Chamberlain was equally peremptory over the so-called railway strip, demanding a strip of land along the Limpopo of between ten and twelve miles wide. Overriding Khama's continuing expressions of dissent, discussion of the question of the railway strip was brought to a close:

> CHAMBERLAIN (to Willoughby): I will deal with Khama as I did with Bathoen. We will take the land that we want for the railway, and no more, and if we take any of his garden ground (we shall not take much) we will give him compensation elsewhere.

At this point, Khama himself began to compromise and was drawn along by Chamberlain to surrender both a border strip along the Limpopo and a line-of-rail across his country (from Fort Elebe to Fort Macloutsie) across the Motloutse to the Shashe:

> KHAMA: I say, that if Mr. Chamberlain will take the land himself, I will be content.
>
> CHAMBERLAIN: Then tell him that I will make the railway myself by the eyes of one whom I will send and I will take only as much as I require, and will give compensation if what I take is of value.
>
> KHAMA: I would like to know how [i.e. where] the railway will go.
>
> CHAMBERLAIN [through Willoughby]: It shall go through his territory [*sic*] but shall be fenced in, and we will take no land.
>
> KHAMA: I trust that you will do this work as for myself, and treat me fairly in this matter.
>
> CHAMBERLAIN: I will guard your interests.

Chamberlain then opened the question of the chiefs' western (Kalahari) borders, turning again first to Bathoen. Up to this point no mention had been made, except implicitly in Harris's intervention, of the fact that the border territories surrendered by the chiefs to the British Crown would then be donated by the Crown to the ownership and administration of the British South Africa Company. But now the question was posed by Bathoen about the Kalahari:

> BATHOEN: Who will be the ruler of this country?
>
> CHAMBERLAIN: The Company, under the Queen.

The interview had been largely a dictation of terms by the colonial secretary. The meeting continued to be one-sided but now became more conciliatory and relaxed, as Chamberlain outlined how imperial administration, liquor regulations, and police might be conducted within the chiefs' three territories. Bathoen and Khama were invited to listen to Chamberlain—and to respond, with Sebele, in writing. Chamberlain's words were to be laid out—in Harry Wilson's English and Lloyd's Setswana—in a letter the next day.

Finally, the colonial secretary ended with words that were to be quoted in modified form ("The Chiefs will rule their own people much as at present") for many years to come:

> CHAMBERLAIN: The Chiefs shall rule their people themselves as hitherto-fore, but in serious questions there shall be an appeal.[9]

The historian Elizabeth Longford paints a word picture of what she imagines to be the last scene of what she calls the "great indaba" in the Colonial Office. Khama, Sebele, and Bathoen leave first, "as befits distinguished strangers." Then Chamberlain shakes the hands of the assembled Chartered Company men—company president duke of Fife, Rhodes's envoy Harris, and Earl Grey last, who "lingers for a few friendly words while the room is emptying." Harris "engages in last minute chit-chat" with Harry Wilson, who is shepherding them out.

Somehow a verbal message was got across to the company men, a message that was summed up the next day by a telegram from Harris to Rhodes:

> Secretary of State says you must allow decent interval and delay fireworks for a fortnight.

What this meant is anyone's guess—but it was obviously a message about delaying explosive developments. Could Chamberlain have possibly supposed that Jameson's armed intervention into the Transvaal was all ready to go (on the imperial behalf)?

It was a momentous couple of days for Chamberlain as well as for the three Bechuana chiefs. Chamberlain went on that evening from the "great indaba" at the Colonial Office to a dinner in Northumberland Avenue, to celebrate the opening of the new Natal-Transvaal railway link. There he made his famous "Spread-eagle speech," his first major public pronouncement on imperial policy as colonial secretary. Though, as the journal *South Africa* remarked, "He was, perhaps, not very judicious to pledge himself to the marvellous riches of the mines of Mashonaland [Rhodesia] . . . which [still] remains to be proven."

Next day came news that Kruger was also celebrating the new railway link, on a celebratory trip to the port of Durban in Natal, by reopening ox wagon traffic across the Vaal drifts north of Kimberley—thus backing down in the face of Chamberlain's recent ultimatum threatening imperial armed intervention if Kruger did not do so. Was this what the "fireworks" were about, and did this now mean that they were postponed indefinitely? [10]

Thursday, November 7

The next day's letter from Edward Fairfield at the Colonial Office to the Rev. W. C. Willoughby laid out Chamberlain's settlement in great detail. Presumably it reflected further conversation between Chamberlain and Rutherfoord Harris, Edwin Lloyd, and others, after the chiefs and Willoughby had left the room.

The letter began by remarking that Khama and Bathoen had "agreed to abide by whatever Mr. Chamberlain might decide as to the future of their countries along the general lines indicated at the interview."

Chamberlain's settlement dealt first with the railway strip along the

Transvaal border that the chiefs were to give to the queen. It would be between six and ten miles wide in Bathoen's country.

> In the case of Khama's country, owing to physical circumstances, Mr. Chamberlain reserves a somewhat larger discretion as to the variation in width at different parts. But this discretion he will only use either for Khama's good or because of the difficulties in making the railway. . . . as far as possible garden grounds of natives shall not be interfered with. . . . the railway will be fenced on the side of the chiefs.

On the railway route through Khama's country, geographical confusion was worse confounded, as the line of rail was spelled out only to the Motloutse and not to the Shashe—thus suggesting that Chamberlain had not intended to hand over the Motloutse-Shashe "disputed territory" to Khama until the last moment:

> It will probably be necessary that from the Elebe Fort to the Makloutsi River, or at all events from the Pakwe River to the Makloutsi River, the railway shall pass through the middle of Khama's country.

Fairfield's letter then turned to the main matter of the Chamberlain settlement:

> Each of the three chiefs, Khama, Sebele, and Bathoen, shall have a country within which they shall live as hitherto under the protection of the Queen. The Queen will appoint an officer to reside with them. The chiefs will rule their own people much as at present. . . .
> The people under the chiefs shall pay a hut tax, or tax of a similar nature; but, as the chiefs wish it, they may collect it—at all events for the present—themselves, and pay it over to the Queen's officer; but this is not to be made a reason for paying too little.
> White men's strong drink shall not be brought for sale into the country now assigned to the chiefs, and those who attempt to deal in it or give it away to black men will be punished. . . .
> The Queen's officer will have one or two officers with him to help him, and he and they will have a few white mounted men to carry their messages and do their bidding. There will also be a force of black mounted police, who will be men not addicted to strong drink.

The Chamberlain settlement then outlined the turning points of the three chiefs' territorial-reserve boundaries. Bathoen's western boundary was defined as "a line drawn north and south so as to include the present most western cattle post of any member of his own tribe." Sebele's was defined as "the extension northward of the Bangwaketsi boundary already described."

Khama's loss of land in the east—including a strip along the Limpopo from a point six miles up the Motloutse River "in a direct line to the

Junction of the Shashi and Tuli rivers"—was compensated for by territory in the north running up the Shashe River to its source, then "running
as nearly north as possible" to the Maitengwe and Nata Rivers, which
flowed into the Makgadikgadi Pans. Thus Khama was awarded both the
Motloutse-Shashe "disputed territory" and the Bokalanga (Bokalaka) area
so assiduously claimed once by Lobengula and until now by the Chartered
Company. (Bokalanga was referred to as the "man's head" by Rhodesian
cartographers because of its shape on the map.)

Outside these reserves, the rest of the protectorate would be administered by the British South Africa Company, but the chiefs (and their
peoples?) would continue to enjoy hunting rights there, with an agreed
annual closed season.[11]

✤ ✤ ✤

The Bechuana chiefs' written answer to Fairfield's letter of November 7
was dispatched on the morning of Monday, November 11. Addressing the
colonial secretary as *Motlotlegi eo o Mogolo* ("Your Excellency"), they laid
out three minor differences with the settlement.

First, they wanted no AmaXhosa ("Amacosa") or AmaNdebele in the
new African police force. After the Colonial Office had inquired as to who
the "Amacosa" were, Chamberlain agreed.

Second, the chiefs objected that the right of appeal from their courts
to the queen's officer could be misused by malcontents to challenge and
undermine their authority. Chamberlain in reply assured the chiefs that
this right of appeal was only for criminal and not political cases.

Third, Khama wanted an official ban on white traders paying for livestock and other African produce with credit notes, rather than with hard
cash. This would ensure that people had the cash with which to pay the
new colonial tax. Chamberlain avoided the question by saying that this
should be left to negotiation between Khama and the high commissioner
in Cape Town—where it was to be turned down flat. As Lord Lugard
was to point out later, this apparently innocuous request by Khama had
had radical implications. Rhodes's explicit purpose for hut tax was to
oblige younger men to go and earn wages on white farms, towns, and
mines. Khama wanted the new tax to stimulate the local market economy in indigenous produce, and to retain labor in productive employment
at home.[12]

The publication of the Colonial Office letter of November 7, and the
acceptance by the Bechuana chiefs of Chamberlain's "final" settlement of
their affairs contained in their letter of November 11, led the journal *South
Africa* to remark in its November 16 edition:

Khama has accepted the proposals of Mr. Chamberlain. . . . in Khama's case his affirmation is considered necessary, and the statement published herewith becomes a treaty without further meetings.[13]

✠ ✠ ✠

The "final" settlement had been a hasty compromise imposed by Chamberlain, to get things moving for the Chartered Company. But if the company seemed satisfied at first, that satisfaction was not to last.

Rutherfoord Harris had won a strip of frontier farmland all the way along the eastern frontier of the Bechuanaland Protectorate, from the company's "jumping-off ground" at Pitsane in the south to Fort Tuli in Chartered territory in the north. Harris had also won the western and northern bulk of the rest of the protectorate, both thirstland and marshland, with long-term potential ranching, mineral, and irrigation value. But Harris had not had the time and opportunity to negotiate the £200,000 subsidy that the Chartered Company expected from the British government, in return for building the Bechuanaland Railway from Mafeking to Bulawayo.

The five principals of the Chartered Company in London, according to W. T. Stead, were happy with the details of the Chamberlain settlement, despite the "sacrifice" of the two hundred thousand pounds. As well as all the other territorial gains at the chiefs' expense, Rutherford Harris had reason to congratulate himself on having pushed Khama's border claim south from Pandamatenga to the Nata River. *South Africa*, indeed, thought Khama had been hard done by, in not having been awarded all the land he had claimed in 1885, stretching north from the Nata as far as the Zambezi. Cecil Rhodes thought otherwise. As he digested Khama's gains over his "maximum offer" on the map over the next few days, he grew steadily more furious and began to unleash a flurry of telegrams at Harris in the London offices of the Chartered Company.[14]

FOURTEEN

Rhodes Beaten by Three Canting Natives

-+>=⊃ ⊂=<+-

ON THE EVENING OF THE DAY THAT THE CHIEFS SENT OFF
their written response to Chamberlain's settlement, Monday, November 11, they were interviewed by a Reuter's press agency correspondent.
Their attitude toward Chamberlain's settlement of their affairs was generally warm but still cautious.

> We very much approve of Mr. Chamberlain's views concerning the
> drink question. We rejoice also to know that officers of the Imperial
> Government will live among us. Now, if we speak, our words will reach
> Mr. Chamberlain—we rejoice greatly at that. We think goodness only of
> Mr. Chamberlain. We have been glad to see him. He is verily a chief.[1]

Sebele dubbed Chamberlain "Moatlhodi"—meaning the Conciliator, the
man who rights wrongs. The newspapers were delighted to have a rival
praise-name to "Silomo," the name given to Ashmead-Bartlett, MP, by
Swazi royal delegates in England a year before.

"Three cheers for Khama and ginger-pop!" was the good-natured response in the *Pall Mall Gazette*. *Punch* portrayed Chamberlain as a Native
American chief sitting down to a drinking party with his African braves
in a circle, toasting each other with a glass of water. A poem elsewhere
in *Punch* concluded: "Each patriot who knows what's what must join the
Moatlhodi party." The London press was now almost as enthusiastic as
the provincial press had been. When King Carlos of Portugal visited
London on November 8, he received less press space than Khama, Sebele,
and Bathoen.[2]

✤ ✤ ✤

The three Bechuana chiefs were anxious to return home but had been put
under official pressure to prolong their stay in Britain—the incentive be-

ing that the queen would receive them soon after her return to Windsor from Scotland on November 15.

It was not generally appreciated that Khama, Sebele, and Bathoen were in Britain at their own expense, covering their own travel and subsistence. They rarely stayed in private homes and were expected to cover their London hotel bill.

Willoughby was later to record that Khama's total expenses from his home back to his home were £559 11s. 8d. (for which Khama had previously deposited £400 in cash and £226 in checks with Willoughby). Sebele's expenses were to total £371 16s. 9d. Bathoen's expenses are not precisely known, in the absence of Lloyd's accounts, but must have been between those of Sebele and Khama. The three chiefs had originally budgeted to leave Britain in early November. When they were obliged to stay on for another two or three weeks, they were put on the edge of some financial embarrassment. At this juncture Wardlaw Thompson stepped in to the rescue, by arranging to have their final bill at Armfield's Hotel paid for by the London Missionary Society.

The Colonial Office and other official bodies began to offer all sorts of daytime engagements to entertain the Bechuana chiefs during the final waiting period. Fairfield had asked Willoughby on October 28 to set aside November 5–19 for "Mr. Chamberlain etcetera and amusements combined"—though Fairfield could not fix any "amusement engagements" until he knew Chamberlain's appointments diary.

Officials at the Colonial Office had been rather cool toward the chiefs at first, no doubt suspicious and snooty about the lower-middle-class Nonconformist company they kept. But after a month Meade, the permanent undersecretary and head man among the civil servants at the Colonial Office, was calling the chiefs "by far the most favourable native products that I have seen from any part of Africa." Sebele and Bathoen did not have sufficient aristocratic demeanor in Meade's eyes to be classified as "gentlemen": he compared them with well-to-do middle-class traders. But Khama was given the ultimate accolade, as "a tall spare man with all the manners and address of a gentleman."

Fairfield, who was Meade's assistant under secretary, began inquiring from Willoughby which sights the chiefs wished to see in London. By November 2 Fairfield wanted to know if the chiefs liked ginger beer or lemonade, or just plain water, with their meals—and did they smoke?[3] (The answer to the latter was Khama no, Sebele probably yes, and Bathoen possibly no.)

Not all the chiefs' suggestions of places they wished to visit in London were equally acceptable to the Colonial Office. Fairfield wrote back to Willoughby objecting to one such suggestion:

As for your taking the Chiefs to see a prison, I hardly like the idea. Prisoners feel keenly the humiliation of being looked at by visitors, and it would be a new experience for the oldest to be looked at by Kaffirs [*sic*]. Besides, is it wise to give [the chiefs] the means of telling their country men that they have seen so many of the White Race in such degraded circumstances? [4]

"High society" had now, by early November, returned to London from holidays abroad. But after they saw Chamberlain at the Colonial Office, the chiefs had no major social engagements until the morning of Saturday, November 9, while they prepared their written response to Chamberlain. If they had social engagements in the evenings, they were probably minor ones restricted to the circle of people with which the chiefs were already in close contact—such as Albert Spicer, MP, the treasurer of the London Missionary Society.

Many years later Spicer recalled entertaining Khama "perfectly at ease in his dress clothes at a dinner party in Lancaster Gate." His brother Evan played a prank on Bathoen and Sebele and the attendants:

He got Khama—unbeknown to the others—to speak into the gramophone and make a record. Sir Evan then waited till one evening all of the Africans were sitting in his billiard-room, when he quietly turned the gramophone on.

The astounded Africans saw their chief quietly sitting in an armchair in one corner while from the other side of the room came his voice talking to them in their own tongue. The magic was altogether too much for them! [5]

SATURDAY, NOVEMBER 9

With the Chamberlain settlement virtually signed and sealed, the round of metropolitan entertainment began in the City of London, the one-square-mile financial district at the heart of Britain's "gentlemanly capitalism" and imperial economic dominance.

The chiefs visited the Bank of England in the City of London and had a place of honor as spectators of the Lord Mayor's Show, on Saturday, November 9. This show was the traditional triumphal procession through the streets of the City of the newly elected lord mayor of London. A new lord mayor was elected every year, and the procession displayed his connections with particular craft guilds in the City. The retiring lord mayor then held a farewell banquet on the Monday after the Saturday.

The chiefs were suitably impressed by a tour of the vaults of the Bank of England, which had almost doubled its holdings of gold bullion since the Baring Crisis of 1890—through its Rothschild-managed importation of the gold production of the Transvaal. After the tour, with its ritual handling of extremely heavy gold bars by the chiefs, they were entertained to luncheon by senior officials of the bank. They were then shown to their places on an upper floor of the bank building, the "Old Lady of Threadneedle Street," from which they watched the horse-drawn floats of the Lord Mayor's Show pass by in the crowded street below.

The accession of the lord mayor of the City of London was celebrated by a show featuring his chosen guilds of Leathersellers and Farriers (horse doctors and shoers), as well as reflecting current obsession with money-making from South African gold shares. The procession through the streets included a man on horseback dressed up as St. George (the semi-mythical Roman-Libyan patron saint of England and of the City of London) and horsemen dressed as King Arthur and the knights of the Round Table. There were horse-drawn cars or floats portraying former lord mayors such as Dick Whittington (with obligatory cat), and others representing British India and British South Africa.

The South African car was accompanied by soldiers dressed as a detachment of the Cape Mounted Rifles as of 1853. The float featured white hunters and gold miners, people dressed as African "natives," and Coloured people from the Cape of Good Hope advertised as being from the "Afrikaner negro population." There were also wild animals, undoubtedly stuffed:

> A detail of the car appealed directly to Khama, as he and his party detected on the moment. This was the presence amongst the animals of a particular kind of antelope which stands for his crest. The "duiker," as the beast is called, stood trustingly gazing towards the royal-looking lion which dominated the car.
>
> Here was a grouping—most likely wholly accidental—which suggested a pretty piece of symbolism. Read England for the lion, and Khama and his mission for the "duiker," and the symbolism is apparent.
>
> It was so explained to Khama [by Willoughby?]—who, indeed, hardly needed to have it explained—and the thing delighted him. "Duiker" and the lion will no doubt go down to history among Khama's people as typifying the result of his present appeal to England.
>
> The only pity is that the animals used for crests by Sebele and Bathoen [both used the crocodile] did not happen to be in evidence, since even kings of Africa may be jealous.[6]

MONDAY, NOVEMBER 11

After a Sunday no doubt devoted to religious services and contemplative inaction, in the area of central London, the chiefs mailed their response to Chamberlain on the Monday morning and set off to Kirby Gate, near

Melton Mowbray in Leicestershire. They had been invited there for the day by Albert (Lord) Grey of the Chartered Company, to join him on a fox hunt "meet."

Accompanied by Selborne, Chamberlain's assistant minister, the chiefs caught the 7:30 A.M. Northampton train from Euston Station in London. At Northampton they changed to a special train hired by Grey, which took in them on to Melton Mowbray by 10:30. From there they were driven in carriages to Kirby Gate.

Khama is said to have recalled the day thus:

> In England the people are sometimes very funny. Having heard from South African hunters that I had shot big-game and that I was a good horseman, they invited me to ride after hounds that were chasing a little fox!
>
> The horse picked out for me to ride was a fine animal, but with only a short tail. Although he seemed wild, I mounted him. Off we galloped after the hounds which kept their noses to the scent of the fox. My horse got very excited. He jumped the hedges without touching them, while I all the time stuck firmly in the saddle.
>
> At the finish a fox's brush was set aside for me and, after being mounted with silver and inscribed "From the Earl of Selborne to Khama," it was presented to me.[7]

Overall it appears that Khama was less than complimentary about English fox-hunting:

> He thinks hunting a poor sport—as practised in England! Why gentlemen should excite themselves and spend money as well over such things as foxes, he cannot understand. But then Khama is used to "big game."[8]

TUESDAY, NOVEMBER 12

On Tuesday, November 12, the chiefs were given what Fairfield called their first "treat" by the British army. At noon they visited the Knightsbridge barracks of the Life Guards, on the southern edge of Hyde Park, with a young official called Baillie Hamilton as their Colonial Office "minder." The chiefs were entertained by a show of mounted horsemen, trotting and wheeling across the parade ground, wearing the shining metal breastplates and metal helmets with swaying pony-tails that were characteristic of the royal household cavalry.

The chiefs were "much struck with the splendid physique of the men." They were particularly impressed by their uniforms and helmets.

After the cavalry show the chiefs went half a mile down Sloane Street to the residence of Lord Methuen, the colonel of the regiment, at No. 32 Cadogan Square. Methuen, an old hand in South African frontier warfare, gave them luncheon in his house and showed them round the splendid Guards' Chapel, where regimental "colors" (flags or banners commemorating various battles and used as ceremonial standards at the head of the cavalry) were hung in display around the walls.[9]

Possibly it was Methuen who arranged for the chiefs to acquire Life Guards officers' uniforms and armor for themselves. Khama may have already possessed such a uniform, though that of the Royal Horse Guards or "Blues." Six years earlier he had been pictured wearing its uniform and armor, when three officers of the Blues passed through his country to present a copy of the royal charter of the British South Africa Company to King Lobengula in Matabeleland.

Such military uniforms, with their heavy clanking breastplates and tin helmets, were worn by Sekgoma son of Khama, Sebele I, and Bathoen I, on special occasions at least from 1900. Some of their successors were seen in such uniforms as late as 1960, when Harold Macmillan, the British prime minster, landed in the Bechuanaland Protectorate en route to deliver his "Winds of Change" speech in Cape Town.[10]

WEDNESDAY, NOVEMBER 13

The next morning the three chiefs and three of their four attendants, with Willoughby, all in thick greatcoats, left their hotel in Finsbury. (David Sebonego was ill and stayed behind under care of a doctor.) They were met at Holborn Viaduct Station by G. V. Fiddes of the Colonial Office, their guide for the day. Together they boarded a 9:55 A.M. train of the London, Chatham and Dover Railway. The brick railway viaduct almost immediately crossed over Ludgate Circus—one of the most famous views of Victorian London, as seen from Fleet Street. A view recorded in numerous photographs, as well as by the artist Gustav Doré, is of an elevated train belching smoke along the viaduct with St. Paul's Cathedral in the background on the summit of Ludgate Hill.

After crossing the Thames, the train took the Bechuana over the soot-gray cobbled streets of southeast London and the green fields of north Kent to Chatham—one of the Medway towns, strategically located where the river of that name flows into the marshes of the Thames estuary. Chatham had long been the military base that protected the approaches to London from invasion from the Low Countries.

At Chatham station the party was met by army officers, who escorted them in carriages to the Brompton army garrison. Their first stop was the Royal School of Military Engineering, followed by a visit to the Royal Engineers' Institute and a demonstration of artillery firepower in the Royal Engineer Park.

The chiefs seemed to have been "astonished and amused" more by human than mechanical achievements, when they witnessed the gymnastic feats of a squad of garrison recruits being put through their paces by the gymnasium superintendent Lieutenant Logan. They were then taken to one of the parade grounds, where the 1st Royal Scots demonstrated their "evolutions" of bayonet and rifle-firing exercises, which "much interested" the chiefs.

Before they were handed over by the army to the navy, there was time for lunch with Major-General Sir Charles Warren of the Royal Engineers, at "Government House." It was extraordinary that the commander in chief of the Chatham (South-Eastern) Command of the British army should be a man so well known to the Bechuana—who knew him simply as "Ragalase," the man with the glasses. (His officers in the 1885 expedition had simply called him the "Boss.") Warren, as we have seen in chapter 2, was a great admirer of Khama, describing him as the finest man he had ever met.

After being photographed with Warren and a Royal Engineers aide-de-camp, the chiefs were taken down to Chatham's Royal Naval dockyard. Here they were "received by Admiral-Superintendent Andoe and Captain Lord Charles Beresford, and were conducted through the principal workshops of the establishments by Staff-Commander H. J. Dockerell." At this time Chatham was still a dockyard where great naval vessels were constructed, as well as a repair yard for the fleet.

> The chiefs seemed very much impressed with the colossal proportions of the giant battleship *Magnificent,* now completing; and were equally delighted with the sister vessel *Victorious,* only recently launched.
>
> The torpedo boat-destroyer *Lightning,* lying in a disabled position in dock after her recent collision, claimed a full share of their attention, and they asked many questions about the vessel's battered bows and bent propellor blades.

By late afternoon the chiefs had seen enough and asked enough questions to be satisfied, and returned to London.[11]

THURSDAY, NOVEMBER 14

On Thursday Khama and Willoughby went off together for a morning's visit to seed farms in the flat farmlands of Essex, between Chelmsford and Colchester. They traveled by express train to Kelvedon between Tiptree and Coggeshall, where Khama "expressed his pleasure at the modern appliances and improved methods of cultivation." This brief foray back into the East Anglian countryside, in the drained marsh country facing the Netherlands across a short stretch of North Sea, may be the reason for the otherwise inexplicable tradition that Khama visited Holland during his 1895 mission to Britain.

Why Bathoen and Sebele did not go to Kelvedon is not known. Maybe they were exhausted by a cold in the head or by the thought of more tripping in the company of Khama and Willoughby. Maybe they preferred to rest or to catch up on some shopping. But they were ready to go to Woolwich that afternoon.

This time they took a train from yet another railway station, such was the profusion of privately owned lines running out of London. They were met on the platform of Cannon Street Station, the south-facing terminus of the South-Eastern Railway on the north bank of the Thames, by Mr. Powell Williams, the financial secretary of the War Office and by his secretary. The party of twelve then proceeded in two special saloons attached to the 2:20 P.M. for Woolwich.

Less than half an hour later they were met on Woolwich Arsenal Station by Dr. Anderson, the director general of Royal Ordinance factories, who escorted them to the Arsenal factory on the banks of the Thames. Their tour around the extensive factory grounds was conducted along private tram lines in two saloon carriages, with a small steam locomotive "appropriately decorated."

> They first visited the Government Proof Butts, and witnessed the firing of several rounds from a heavy gun. The Chiefs subsequently saw the forging of an ingot of red-hot steel under the 40-ton steam hammer at the Radiel crane and south boring mill. At the examination branch of the Royal Gun Factory they witnessed the latest productions in breech-loading and quick-firing guns. The visitors also inspected the wheel factory and woodworking machinery, the Royal department carriage machine shop, and various portions of the Royal Laboratory.
>
> The chiefs manifested intense interest in what they saw.

Satisfied if not sated by this display of military-industrial pyrotechnics, the Bechuana returned to London on the 4:57 or 5:20 P.M. train.[12]

This was to be the last inspection of an industrial establishment in Great Britain by the Bechuana chiefs in 1895. They had scarcely had the extensive exposure experienced, say, by Peter the Great of Russia two hundred years earlier, when he stayed for more than a year working in the royal dockyards of Deptford a few miles upstream from Woolwich. But their exposure to modern industrial technology must have given them an understanding of the techniques of metallurgy and weapons manufacture that, if useless in practical home circumstances, was extraordinary among overseas potentates on the brink of the twentieth century. It was not inappropriate that a new Smith small-arms factory in Birmingham was subsequently named the Khama Works.[13]

Friday, November 15

Friday began with a visit to the Royal Mint, where coins were cast and promissory notes manufactured for the Bank of England. The appointment had been fixed with the deputy master and comptroller of the mint (the ex officio master being the chancellor of the exchequer) for 10:30 A.M., to allow for a two-hour visit—giving people there sufficient time so that they could as usual "brush off work at 1." [14]

This gave time for the chiefs to squeeze in another visit—to Westminster Abbey—before another fashionably late luncheon in midafternoon.

As pilgrims and politicians as well as industrial visitors to Great Britain, the chiefs had spoken in a large number of Nonconformist chapels around the nation but had rarely entered the buildings of the established church— except as casual tourists in London inspecting St. Paul's Cathedral and the David Livingstone memorial in the nave of Westminster Abbey. But the Grosvenor House breakfast on November 4, addressed by the bishop of London, marked the rise to acceptability of the Bechuana chiefs among the hierarchy of the Church of England (as well as in the temperance movement of the Roman Catholic Church).

Now, on the morning of November 15, the chiefs made a full and official visit to Westminster Abbey, where they were escorted around the sights of the building by its dean and listened to organ music. The abbey and its daughter church, St. Margaret's, stood opposite the Parliament buildings of the Palace of Westminster. It also faced across Parliament Square a building (demolished within a decade and replaced by Methodist Central Hall) called the London Aquarium. It was there that the impresario Giliarmi Farini ten years earlier had displayed families of "Bushmen" en route to the Coney Island entertainment center near New York— recruited in 1885 from Lehututu in the west of the Kalahari, at the same time as Warren's expedition in the east was proclaiming the British protectorate to Gaseitsiwe, Sechele, and Khama.

The tour of the abbey was followed by a luncheon hosted by Canon and Mrs. Samuel Wilberforce. Both Khama and Wilberforce made speeches expressing their pleasure in each other's company. Wilberforce had been one of the speakers at the Grosvenor House breakfast. The canon was a prominent supporter of the Native Races and Liquor Traffic Committee, as well as being a member of the famous antislavery family and the son of "Soapy Sam" Wilberforce, the outspoken opponent of Darwinian ideas of evolution.

Other guests at luncheon, who were introduced to the chiefs, included Lady Frederick Cavendish and other female members of the nobility— Lady Henry Somerset, Lady Battersea, the Hon. Maude Stanley, and the

Hon. Mrs Eliot Yorke. Boy choristers from the abbey sang in the background while the diners partook of the meal.[15]

The chiefs were asked what they thought of England now, after a long stay. They replied:

> We think astonishment only of England, and beyond that we know not what to say. The people surpass the locusts in multitude, and the things they possess are innumerable. They work with their hands and their feet, with metals, with fire, and even with lightning. In music [i.e. organ music] they use both hands and feet.
>
> Beyond the Lord Mayor's Show we were astonished at the money in the Bank. Such a thing we never thought of at home.[16]

SATURDAY, NOVEMBER 16 – SUNDAY, NOVEMBER 17

All indications are that Sebele and Bathoen were now as jealous of each other as of Khama, but they managed as yet to keep that jealousy within bounds. They were at least relieved from the burden of Khama and Willoughby's presence for the rest of the weekend, as the two men disappeared to the remote southwestern county of Cornwall.

Bathoen and Sebele, in the company of Lloyd and their attendants, spent a quiet weekend. Their only appointment was attendance at the morning service of Upton Congregational Church, at the junction of Upton Lane and Romford Road on the fringes of Essex in northeast London. The area was a new lower-middle-class suburb called Forest Gate, set on the edge of the Wanstead flats beyond the working-class districts of Stratford-at-Bow and West Ham.[17]

Meanwhile Willoughby and Khama had arrived on Saturday night at Redruth, only twenty-five miles short of Land's End at the extreme southwestern corner of Great Britain, not unnoticed by local folk at the railway station. A mildly ironic correspondent in the *Royal Cornwall Gazette* reported:

> After sundry disappointments Redruthians could on Saturday hardly believe their senses were not deceiving them, when it was announced that King Khama had travelled into Cornwall by the Cornishman [express train from London], and alighted at Redruth railway station. Statements by eye-witnesses convinced them.

Willoughby had been brought up locally and had gone to school in Redruth and no doubt felt it was his filial duty to visit his widower father before he left again for Africa. Old Mr. Willoughby lived in a cottage in the hamlet of Cara Brea, just west of Redruth on the road and rail to Cambourne.

Khama and Willoughby thus spent two nights in a Cornish cottage, the simplest dwelling that they had stayed in for months, an experience that no doubt appealed to Khama's sense of asceticism. One imagines that Khama and Willoughby took advantage of the opportunity for healthy walks in the closely set small hills and valleys of Cornwall, with views toward the sea, including perhaps the climb up to a nearby Iron Age hill fort.

The *Royal Cornwall Gazette* tells us that Khama and Willoughby came to the 6 P.M. Sunday evening service at Redruth's Wesleyan chapel, already packed with people from floor to balcony ceiling by quarter of an hour earlier. The local minister, Reverend Gibson, introduced Willoughby and Khama on the rostrum to the congregation, and Willoughby began to deliver a sermon. But it was Khama the people had really come to see, and there was much disappointment when Willoughby excused Khama from speaking—because he did not speak in public on Sundays, which must have surprised even the most strict Sabbatarians among them.

Willoughby preached, as usual, at length, about his experiences as a missionary in Khama's country. He told of building houses and roads, of extracting teeth, and of trying to master the local language. He implied, so said the local newspaper, that "Were it not for the work of the European missionaries, instead of coming over to the British Government in the way they have, these three gentlemen could have settled the matter at the point of an assagai." [18]

✤ ✤ ✤

Meanwhile the Chartered Company was trying to unpick the threads of the November 6 Chamberlain settlement. This is clear from surviving cables and correspondence, despite later attempts to hide or destroy Chartered Company communications between Cape Town and London dating from the last half of 1895.

Cecil Rhodes's response to the settlement of November 6, as expressed in a telegram to Rutherfoord Harris on November 8, seems to have begun innocently enough—sharing some of the geographical confusion over what territory had been gained or "lost" in the Bechuanaland Protectorate. But any such confusion was soon replaced by Rhodes's indignation at Harris's allowance of excessively large "native reserves" and the financial loss of a massive railway subsidy.

Harris had to defend himself, cabling petulantly to Rhodes on November 11 (the day his colleague the fourth Earl Grey was entertaining the chiefs hunting in Leicestershire), "Native chiefs and Willoughby acted like pigs." Rhodes cabled back on November 12: "It is humiliating to be utterly beaten by these niggers." On November 13 Harris went further in self-justification: "Native Chiefs with Lord Loch and Temperance carried

England with them." Ten days later, Rhodes was still smarting when he cabled Harris:

> I do object to being beaten by three canting natives especially on the score of temperance, when two of them, Sebele [and] Bathoen, are known to be utter drunkards.[19]

It would be difficult to redraw Khama's borders without raising political embarrassment, but the vagueness of definition of Bathoen and Sebele's western borders could be exploited. Above all Rhodes was determined to lay hands on the £200,000 subsidy. Grey was instructed to reapproach Chamberlain and did so on Sunday, November 17, in a personal letter addressed to Chamberlain's London residence. The letter is now lodged in the National Archives of Zimbabwe and has been unearthed by the historian Jeffrey Butler.

Grey's basic argument was simple: "Now that the area given to Khama has been so greatly enlarged, the position is altogether changed."

> I also know that you would be the last person in England who would consent to our being fined £200,000, because our desire to place ourselves in a position to help British Interests in the Transvaal in the event of anything taking place there, has made us [too] eager to obtain at once, without counting the cost, what we know must come to us eventually.

Jeffrey Butler argues that the letter shows "beyond doubt" that the major reason for the company's haste in negotiations was the need to have a territory and a military force stationed there ready for intervention in the Transvaal—and that Chamberlain was aware of this.[20]

Renegotiations were set in train at the Colonial Office. Goold-Adams, as the designated boundary commissioner, worked closely with the company on how to minimize the extent of the "native reserves" within the protectorate. The Chartered Company finally accepted the arrangements for transfer to it of the Bechuanaland Protectorate, in a letter to the Colonial Office of December 28, 1895. Though that eventuality was not to materialize, because of the developments of the next few days and weeks, the protectorate was burdened with paying off the £200,000 subsidy to the Bechuanaland Railway as a major slice of its budgeted expenditure until 1908–9.[21]

FIFTEEN

I Had No Idea She Was So Small

◦⊷⊸⊜⊷ ⊷⊜⊶⊷◦

IT WAS THE BECHUANA CHIEFS' LAST WEEK IN BRITAIN. AS Khama and Willoughby returned on the long train journey from Cornwall to London, they must have been experiencing great excitement about the high point of the odyssey to come on Wednesday—the audience with Her Majesty the Queen at Windsor Castle, preceded by dinner with Secretary of State Chamberlain on the previous night.

The figure of Queen Victoria had been exploited by British imperialists until, according to a white Rhodesian historian, "her name became invested with a sort of mysterious reverence, akin to . . . the feelings which the Bantu races entertain for their own departed chiefs."

The image of the Great (White) Queen or Great (White) Mother was so assiduously propagated that it sometimes preceded the colonialists. An aged Kalanga (Nyai) man, watching the troops of the Rhodesian Pioneer column pass in 1890, had shouted: "Oh, white men, white men! alas! You are going to be sacrificed on the spears of Lobengula's warriors; and the White Mother will weep for her lost children." Lobengula himself had had good reason to doubt whether there was a queen at all, if she sent out the likes of Rev. John Smith Moffat and Sir Sidney Shippard to trick him into accepting the Chartered Company.[1]

Such skepticism was widespread enough for the Bechuana chiefs to have made a point of it soon after their arrival: "If we return and say we have not seen her they will say—'I see, it is as we said, all lies.' We believe it would be of great use from a diplomatic point of view for us to have audience of Her Majesty."[2]

There were also more mundane matters of final shopping, and packing of all their newly acquired goods and presents, to be attended to by Willoughby and the chiefs during the final week. The chiefs' accounts record modest purchases of items such as lantern slides illustrating Britain, saddles, a watch, a compass, trunks, and perfume for the fur karosses they were giving to Chamberlain. Willoughby's accounts were recorded in a small fifty-page notebook. These had to be coordinated with Lloyd for Bathoen's account, and with the London Missionary Society, which would cover the bill at Armfield's.[3]

TUESDAY, NOVEMBER 19

The night before the trip to Windsor, the Chamberlains held a dinner in honor of the chiefs at their home at No. 40 Prince's Gardens, off Exhibition Road on the Knightsbridge frontier with South Kensington, opposite the towered Imperial Institute and not far from the most famous Victorian buildings of all—the Royal Albert Hall and the Victoria and Albert Museum. The attendants, who were not to go to Windsor, were invited to the reception party afterward, when ladies as well as gentlemen would be present and there would be "some fun" organized by Chamberlain's bright young American wife and her friends.

The all-male guest list for the dinner consisted of Khama's friends Loch and Baden-Powell from the Lords and Commons, Methuen from the army, Canon Wilberforce from the Church of England and Fox-Bourne of the Aborigines' Protection Society, Sir Albert Rollit representing British industry, Chamberlain's thirty-two-year-old son Austen (but not his other son, Neville), and Selborne, Fairfield, and Meade from the Colonial Office.

Each chief had already given "Moatlhodi" a perfumed kaross. He in turn gave them each a hunting saddle and bridle, with writing desks for each attendant. Chamberlain arranged for these presents to pass through the Cape Town customs and excise without duty being paid. On the night of November 19, he also gave each chief a gold signet ring with his crest *(seboko)* embossed on a bloodstone—*kwena* or crocodile for both Sebele and Bathoen, and *phuti* or duiker (a miniature antelope) for Khama. (These gold rings later entered Tswana mythology as pledges of eternal connection from the queen's government, but they were not presents from the queen herself.)

The "some fun" after dinner consisted of entertainment by a professional conjuror and magician, one Mr. Sidney Gandy with Miss Inglefield as his assistant. What tricks he played is not known, but his sleight of hand is said to have been truly mystifying, and the chiefs said that they would like to take him home to Africa.[4]

WEDNESDAY, NOVEMBER 20

At 1:20 P.M. the next day Chamberlain and the chiefs, accompanied by
Selborne, Willoughby, and Lloyd, left Paddington Station in London on
the Great Western Railway for their audience with Queen Victoria at
Windsor Castle. Fairfield had advised the chiefs to wear their "nice frock
coats," which "will do for the Queen." They were met shortly before two
o'clock at Windsor Station by Lord Ampthill, Chamberlain's private secretary, who had been checking all the arrangements. People crowded inside the station to watch their arrival and their departure for the castle
in two landau carriages from the royal mews, closed against the showery
weather.[5]

Once inside Windsor Castle the party proceeded straight to luncheon.
The queen was not present at the meal. She may have had other preoc-
cupations. Her twenty-six-year-old granddaughter Maud was announcing
her engagement to marry a prince of Denmark (subsequently King Haakon
VII of Norway, who ruled 1905–57). No doubt the queen was also concerned about the health of her former private secretary, Sir Henry Pon-
sonby, who was on his deathbed. (He was to die early the next morning.)
The chiefs are said to have been "duly and properly impressed with everything that they saw—from the guard of honour of Life Guards on duty at
the castle down to—or, 'up to,' according to taste—the gorgeous flunkies
who waited at the luncheon table of the Royal household."

At table the distinguished visitors from London sat down with ladies-
and lords-in-waiting and gentlemen equerries of the royal household at a
table of twenty-two people. The aging dowager Lady Southampton sat
between Chamberlain and Khama, who sat next to Willoughby and the
earl of Clarendon. Sebele sat opposite Khama with the Hon. Mrs. Mallet
and Selborne on his right, Edwin Lloyd and Bathoen on his left. Bathoen
was flanked by Miss Lambart on his left and sat opposite Clarendon and
near three military equerries. The master of the household, Colonel Lord
Edward Pelham Clinton, sat at the head of the table. According to *South
Africa* (probably using Selborne as its source),

> Luncheon was served immediately on the arrival of the party, and the
> three chiefs, being in excellent health and spirits, were exceedingly lively
> during the meal.
>
> Khama can be solemn and dignified on occasion; but, like many other
> great men, he isn't above unbending or cracking a joke or two when he
> finds himself in a regal atmosphere or congenial company.
>
> Laugh! Why, I have it on excellent authority that one of the hon. ladies
> with whom Khama lunched "thought she would ha' died" at his funny
> little ways—just for all the world like her humbler sisters in the coster
> ballad!

After lunch Chamberlain became the stage manager and rehearsed the drama of how the chiefs should be presented to Her Majesty. Selborne and Ampthill were to hover around with Chamberlain. Lloyd and Willoughby were to remain at the back of the room, pitching their voices forward as remotely controlled interpreters while Chamberlain and the chiefs went forward to the throne.

> As the Ghost with Hamlet, so Mr. Chamberlain with Khama, Bathoen, and Sebele—he found them "apt," though probably expecting them to prove "duller . . . than the fat worm that rots itself at ease on the Lethe wharf."[6]

After the rehearsal the company proceeded down the richly carpeted corridors of the castle to the Green Drawing Room, where the seventy-six-year-old queen sat on a throne awaiting their presence. Perhaps with memories of the figures in Madame Tussaud's waxworks as well as the statues in the street, Sebele soon afterward told a newspaper:

> The corridors of the magnificent palace where she lives [were] all lined with stalwart soldiers, as big as I am, in glittering uniforms. None ever moved. They all stood erect and motionless like the marble statues in the streets of London.
>
> While passing along their line I boldly tested one of these giants. I thrust my finger almost into his eye to make certain he was a living being, and not a statue placed there to add to the grandeur of the place. To my great surprise he never flinched, but merely rewarded me with a smile.[7]

When they reached the Green Drawing Room, according to *South Africa:*

> The chiefs advanced in Indian file—"all in a row," in fact—and bowed as they did so. My informant says that they acquitted themselves extremely well—for natives. The Queen, like the Strand Theatre *Niobe*, was "all smiles," and, in good sooth, no one can be more gracious than Queen Victoria.
>
> Mr. Chamberlain introduced the trio—good Mr. Willoughby and Mr. Lloyd [interpreting the words spoken] being, of course, in the background.

The queen had her youngest child, thirty-eight-year-old Princess Beatrice, and her invaluable (East) Indian factotum and confidant Abdul Karim at her side. She read a short speech of "kindly words to her dusky visitors," in a clear voice periodically interpreted into Setswana by the voice of Lloyd:

> I am glad to see the chiefs, and to know that they love my rule.
>
> I confirm the settlement of their case which my Minister has made. I approve of the provision excluding strong drink from their country. I feel strongly in this matter, and am glad to see that the chiefs have determined to keep so great a curse from the people.

The chiefs must obey my Minister and my High Commissioner. I thank them for the presents which they have made to me, and I wish for their prosperity and that of their people.

Lloyd interpreted the reply of each chief to the queen, sentence by sentence. The gist of their replies is reflected in a newspaper report:

> It was, in each instance, to the effect that they were grateful to be permitted to bask in the sunshine of the Royal countenance, and to express the hope that they and those they represented would continue to live under her august and direct rule.
> They were extremely thankful to Her Majesty and to her representatives for a final settlement of the business that had brought them to this country.

At this the queen bowed her head to each chief in gracious acknowledgement. The chiefs now presented in turn their gifts to her. Sebele's gift was "a very fine jackal skin kaross," while Bathoen and Khama presented "magnificent karosses made from leopard skins." Then,

> Her Majesty personally presented each one of the chiefs with a beautiful bound copy of the New Testament in Sechwana, the royal arms being shown on the covers. Her other gifts were autograph [large framed photographic] portraits of herself, Indian shawls for the wives of the chiefs, and magic-lantern slides, bearing a portrait of her Majesty, to be shown to the tribes. ["In Khama's case—he being a widower—the Royal shawl will descend to his eldest daughter."][8]

One newspaper referred to the gift of shawls from Her Majesty as "inevitable." The shawls in question were sent as annual tribute to Queen Victoria from Afghanistan, as a gesture of friendship from a still independent state that preferred not to be periodically invaded by the British army. The queen usually gave them as wedding presents to her innumerable European royal and German princely relatives. The three African rulers were indeed privileged to receive one each.

Even more privileged was Khama, when he opened his copy of the New Testament. There, inscribed in the royal handwriting on the frontispiece, were the words uttered by the queen to him as the book was placed in his hands: "The Secret of Khama's greatness." (This most valued possession survived until it was consumed in a fire at Serowe in 1950.)[9]

With the ceremony over, "they one and all backed out of the Royal presence as pleased as Punch."

> The visitors were then shown over the Castle, when they expressed their admiration in the most enthusiastic terms of the beauties and richness of the different apartments.

They said:

It is far beyond anything we have ever seen. We could not imagine such grandeur. We have seen incalculable wealth. The Bank of England has great wealth, but Windsor Castle, too, is riches made beautiful. In every room there was gold.

Sebele expanded on the causes for marvelment:

When I was in one of Her Majesty's splendid apartments, I was greatly astonished to see an ordinary, tiny housefly! It was a puzzle to me to know how it got there, for I could hardly believe that even death could enter such a palace.[10]

The chiefs, Chamberlain, and the rest then returned to the Great Western station to catch the 4:15 train to London. Just as they were about to enter the train, the queen herself was driven past the Thames Street entrance to the station and looked out of the carriage window. Evidently she was showing the same interest in them as they were in her.[11]

✢ ✢ ✢

After their arrival at Paddington Station, the press was anxious to record the chiefs' impressions of their visit to the mysterious "widow at Windsor."

The three chiefs expressed the highest satisfaction at having beheld one whom they had been inclined to regard as a myth, saying: "Now, when we return, we shall be able to tell our people that England has truly a Queen, for we have seen her face and spoken with her, and should any doubters speak we can show them her presents to us."

South Africa deduced that "they had, to some extent, suspected Her Majesty of being a sort of regal Mrs. Harris" (referring to the mythical friend of Mrs. Gamp in Dickens's *Martin Chuzzlewit*), but when they actually "beheld her in the flesh they were charmed at her sweet voice and affable condescension."[12]

Sebele, as usual, had the most quotable views, though not all newspapers agreed how to quote him:

Her Majesty is [a very] charming [old lady]. She has a kind [round, beautiful] face and a [very] sweet voice. But I had no idea that she was so short and stout.

I have long desired to see the Chief of so many millions, as my father did [desire] before me, but I have seen her now, and shall go back home contented.

At least one newspaper preferred to credit Sebele with calling Her Majesty "small," rather than "short and stout."[13]

The ironical and not a little racially prejudiced correspondent of *South*

Africa caught Khama back at his hotel. The correspondent approached and said: "And so, Khama, you have seen Her Majesty the Queen?"

The chief addressed, [responded] sprightly as one of his own native duikers, grinned and grinned with such fantastic glee that for a moment his face bore quite a marvellous resemblance to a gargoyle.

Then Seisa, the interpreter, who stood hard by, translated; and the chief, as he replied, immediately grew grave.

"Yes, I have seen the Queen," came the answer, delivered in all the soft unctuosity of the educated native.

"And was the Queen kind to you?"

A pleased, satisfied smile illumined the ebon countenance as Khama, through Seisa, replied: "Yes: the Queen was very good to me—and I was very good to the Queen."

At such a naive reply (says our man) I found it difficult to refrain from smiling; but was on the point of putting another question when Khama added, with a sententiousness that irresistibly recalled Jo in "Bleak House":

"Yes: she was very good to me!"

Whether it was the recollection of the Indian shawl, or the embossed copy of Holy Writ which Her Majesty had shed upon him, that affected Khama the most I cannot say; but certainly the chief spoke with a wonderfully convincing earnestness.

"And what did you think of Windsor Castle?"

"He thinks," quoth Seisa, glancing at the all-smiling face of his chief, "he thinks Windsor Castle is a wonderful place, full of gold and rich things; a place fit for such a Queen."

"Did you go all over the Castle and inspect the grounds?"

"Yes," said Seisa. "Khama says he saw many wonderful things, both inside and outside the Castle."

"Plenty of mooi veld?" I hazarded.

Khama laughed before the question was translated, as if he understood—as there is no doubt he did—and nodded his head vigorously.

"Yes; Khama says he saw much beautiful veld [pasture] and plenty of trees."

"And, Chief, are you satisfied with your mission to England?"

"Khama says he is quite satisfied" translated Seisa.

"And shall you ever return?"

"Khama says he may come back some day, but if he does not his son may come in his stead."

"You have received much kindness, Chief, since you came amongst us?"

"Khama says"—returned the native phonograph—"that everybody has been most kind to him."

"And you will be glad to get back?" I added.

"Yes; Khama thinks he will be glad to be in his own land again. The weather is cold [here] now."

All this time we had been standing in the hall of "Armfield's" Hotel, at South Place, Finsbury Pavement.[14]

Meanwhile in Africa, the *Cape Argus* received such intelligence with the observation that Khama was not after all humorless: "Certainly he is no innocent abroad":

> Much feasting has made Khama facetious. . . . Khama's meteoric career across the provincial seventh heavens has terminated at Windsor and Downing-street in a blaze of fireworks.[15]

Another Cape newspaper brought together the story of Khama's visit to Windsor in its list of latest cables with another on the engagement of Princess Maud of Wales, to produce a remarkable headline suggesting an unexpected connection between the widower of Palapye and the widow of Windsor: "Royal Betrothal—Khama and the Queen."[16]

THURSDAY, NOVEMBER 21

A great farewell "conversazione, followed by a public meeting" for the chiefs was arranged for the evening of November 21 by the London Missionary Society. It was to be held at the Queen's Hall in Langham Place, just north of Oxford Circus, a vicinity later famous as the headquarters of the home radio services of the BBC.

An immense crowd—"for the most part ladies of venerable aspect, and a fair sprinkling of gentlemen with a plentiful lack of hair and shining pericraniums"—assembled in the Queen's Hall at five o'clock. Let the journal *South Africa* once again take up the story:

> Tea was provided, and alarming quantities of that refreshing beverage were consumed by the good folk present. But by half-past five or so the tables were cleared, and people began to think about the business of the evening. Up to this time, Khama, Bathoen, and Sebele had not put in an appearance; but three chairs in front of the platform indicated where they would presently be in evidence.
>
> When the three chiefs first showed themselves the general curiosity was fired, and found vent in excited greetings. As the chiefs passed through the throng to the vacant chairs, the anxiety to behold their features or to touch the hem of their garments was such that the stewards had much ado to prevent an indecent mobbing. It suggested nothing so much as scene from "Martin Chuzzlewit," [at] what time that young hero was being introduced to some of the "most remarkable men" in America.
>
> As every visitor passed, he or she shook hands with each of the three chiefs, and "Good-bye"'d and "God bless"'d them most fervently. The three *stood* it—literally—for a long time, but finally re-seated themselves and "received" thereafter with all the dignity of an infirm European monarch.

It was my good fortune to be seated within two or three yards of the chiefs; and immediately in front of me were seated Seisa, the native interpreter, and three other gentlemen of ebon persuasion, whom, I understood, were the chiefs' attendants.

To reach the spot where the three chiefs were seated, the public had first to pass these gentry, and it was amusing, but not a little nauseating, to witness the fuss that everyone made of *them*. Each was shaken by the hand with something bordering on ecstatic fervour. Ladies of apparently high degree wasted their sweetness on these men.

Why? In the name of common-sense, why? What have *they* done that they should be petted and caressed in a manner that would strike many a colonist I wot of dumb with astonishment and indignation.

"What *dear* fellows!" exclaimed one lady, as she scrutinised them through her *pince-nez*. "Charming," agreed her companion. One elderly female I verily thought would have imprinted a chaste salute upon the fattest of the attendants [Bathoen's half brother]; and it is a solemn fact that a young lady caused some confusion in the line of progress by suddenly producing an autograph book—nor would she "move along please," until she had obtained the signatures of each of the attendants!

(This account carried in *South Africa* was widely disseminated in South Africa. The next issue also the carried the comments of the *Sketch* criticizing those who "beslobber" over "educated niggers." *South Africa* was the basis for the account of the Queen's Hall meeting that appears in *The Passing of the Black Kings* by Hugh Marshall Hole, published in 1932: "society women flocked up to shake them by the hand—some in their ecstatic fervour bestowing the same attention on their native servants who stood behind them.")

The account in *South Africa* continues with a lighter touch:

As the crowd continued to pour in and the task of shaking hands became a fatigue, the stewards admonished all and sundry in passing to "shake hands *gently* please, and pass along!"

The excitement rose considerably when, presently, a little girl daintily dressed in white, approached the chiefs and presented Khama—somewhat to his perplexity, methought—with a floral offering nearly as big as herself. The trophy was of red and white flowers, horse-shoe fashioned, and was "supported" by a miniature garden fork and rake.

Khama seized the little one's hand and kissed it with great gravity. At the same time there were presented to each of the chiefs a lily-of-the-valley "button-hole" and to Khama an illuminated and framed address—inscribed "to the chiefs, Khama, Sebele, and Bathoen."

It will be interesting to know which of them will retain possession of the address. Perhaps they'll toss for it. But that there's bound to be heart-burning over this presentation I feel certain—judging from the glum looks of Sebele and Bathoen when the gift was handed to Khama.

Shortly afterwards, the three chiefs vacated their chairs and disappeared from view, thus disappointing many who were anxious to be "received" by them and to grasp "King" Khama's "royal" hand. Then the organ was played—for which relief I sighed my many thanks.

By this time the vast and beautiful hall was thronged in all its parts. The sight was an impressive one, and if Khama did not think so he should have done. When he and his colleagues re-appeared, and mounted the platform, the enthusiasm knew no bounds. But neither of the three took the slightest apparent notice. They seated themselves and gazed straight in front of them with that sphinx-like gravity they know so well how to assume, [during] which time old gentlemen shouted excitedly and old ladies, in a delightful state of flutter, waved their handkerchiefs at them.

Maybe they wondered what it was all about—and perhaps asked themselves whether it was meet that British respectability should do such homage unto them.

The meeting was called to order by the chairman, Albert Spicer, MP, the treasurer of the LMS. He said that "no one would accuse him of exaggerated language when he described this as a unique incident in the history of foreign missionary enterprise."

> Their friends the chiefs had been in the country three months. They had travelled all over the land; they had met all sorts and conditions of men; and he was thankful to say that they had had an audience with Her Majesty. (Applause.)
>
> Wherever the chiefs had gone they had been recognised as Christian gentlemen. (Hear, hear.)

After Spicer had paid tribute to his political opponent Joseph Chamberlain, to the Colonial Office, and even to the British South Africa Company, Wardlaw Thompson, the foreign secretary of the LMS, took over. Thompson's main message was one of reassurance over events in Madagascar, an LMS mission field currently being conquered by French troops. The French were displaying "exemplary behaviour" and assuring complete liberty for mission work. He also paid tribute to Chamberlain.[17]

Next Willoughby spoke with what the historian Hugh Marshall Hole, following the account in *South Africa*, calls "wise and patriotic words." *South Africa* claimed somewhat misleadingly that previous speakers "vied with each other in praise of Khama, Khama, Khama . . . Khama *ad nauseam;* and one rejoiced to think that the English tongue was but imperfectly understood [*sic*] by that gentleman." What Willoughby did, *South Africa* pointed out, was to correct the impression that it was the drink question that brought the chiefs to England. It was only a side issue: "He explained that they had come over to appeal to Her Majesty's Government against their incorporation by the wicked Chartered Company. . . . Mr. Willoughby didn't say 'wicked,' but his tone, I thought, seemed to imply it."

There followed speeches by two advocates of temperance and one of aborigines' rights—including that rarity in late Victorian Britain, a woman speaker. Lady Henry Somerset, born Lady Isabella Caroline Somers Cocks, was a remarkable person. She was currently engaged in setting up a rural shelter for the recovery of "inebriate" urban women, at Duxhurst near Reigate in Surrey. Wealthy in her own right, she was editor of the *Woman's Signal* and president of the British Women's Temperance Association, which had somewhat fallen out with its American sister organization because it advocated only temperance and not absolute prohibition of alcohol. Now, at Queen's Hall, Lady Henry Somerset delivered "an apparently impromptu and moving address," which the tongue-in-cheek *South Africa* correspondent said "referred to the three chiefs as being amongst the most significant and pathetic figures of the century."

Sir Wilfrid Lawson, the religious radical MP, known for his humor as well as his "puritan energy" in Parliament, was more fully reported. His speech had a somewhat risqué beginning when he said that "he appeared before them as a native. (Laughter.) . . . He was a pure full-blooded white prohibitionist." But then he added that Khama was the same, and he harked back to antislavery abolitionist days by using the slogan "Is he not a man and a brother?"

The meeting was then addressed by Sebele, Bathoen, Khama, in that order.

Sebele began by confessing, "I fear I shall forget some of my speech through my great joy. (Cheers.)" Once more he spoke in praise of the missionaries:

> we have now seen all the goodness that used to be spoken of by our missionaries. We have been entering into your houses just as we have been used to enter into our mothers' homes. We give thanks for the decision which we have received from the Judge [*Moatlhodi*] Chamberlain. (Cheers and laughter) . . .
>
> I say to you—"remain nicely" [*salang sentle*]. (Cheers and laughter.) I also am going nicely. May you remain with the love of God and continue to send missionaries to us. (Cheers.)

Bathoen rehearsed the political grievances that brought them to the country and went on to stress the need for a high school nearer than Lovedale:

> If you, the leaders of the missionary work in this country, desire a piece of land in our countries, we shall rejoice to let you have it for a school. (Applause.) I mean in the countries of us, the three Bechuana chiefs. This help we beg of you now.
>
> . . . We have seen a great heart of love amongst you, and it looks as if you were giving us the whole of that heart of love, but we ask you to leave a little for your own people at home. (Cheers and laughter.) We also ask you, as you are helping to restrain strong drink in this country, to give us your help in restraining it in our countries. (Cheers.) And now we rejoice

that God has turned our faces homewards to our own countries. May you remain nicely. (Laughter.) May God preserve us together—even those who depart and those who remain. (Great applause.)

Khama spoke last:

Friends, I give you greetings today. Our time has now gone by, and I don't know whether we shall ever meet again. We have delayed very greatly in your country, because we have been lacking all the work which brought us to this country. And now we have spoken with the Government, and the Government has decided to agree to our request. We did not rejoice at the idea of having to live under the rule of the Company. We now rejoice because the British Government has separated us from that Company. (Cheers.)

He continued eloquently:

We were delayed by our waiting to see the Queen of England. We had written to say that we wished to see Her Majesty, and now we have seen her, and we are glad. (Cheers.) We went to see . . . [18]

It was probably at this point—according to a Wesleyan missionary interviewed by the historian S. M. Molema many years later—that there were gasps and murmurings in the crowd, when Lloyd, who was interpreting, said, "We went to see the old woman yesterday." Lloyd had blunderingly translated the familiar word for the queen *(Mma-Mosadinyana)* somewhat too literally. He had to hurriedly correct himself by saying, "We went to see the Queen yesterday," maybe adding the respectable gloss, "the little old lady of many years." [19]

Khama also talked of the need for schooling:

A word I wish to leave with you—a request I make of you. My word is this: I wish to speak with you about our desire to have a school for our youths and a school for our maidens in our country; and I ask you who have children who are here to-night: Do you parents not desire, when you have a son, a school in which your son can be taught, so that he can go forward in all that is good and right? (Cheers.)

We have some schools now, but they are not equal to the demand. We want a large school where our young people can all be taught; even those belonging to the nations at home. We have amongst us young men who desire to go forward in the teaching which you usually provide. They wish to learn to do all sorts of work, such as carpentering, blacksmith's work, and such-like works as those. It will be good if our boys can be like your boys, and learn, as your boys are learning, not only knowledge, but trades and employments, so that our nation may still go forward.

He went on to make some general observations:

We have seen many wonderful and useful things in this country. We have been struck, too, by seeing that there is no difference in this country be-

tween men and women—(laughter)—that the women learn as well as the
men; the women also are wise like unto the men. (Renewed laughter.)

We have difficulties in our way, and the ancient customs of our tribes
amongst us. We have not yet got rid of our old superstitions. We want you
to know that we have there our difficulties.

Khama asked for their prayers:

We ask you to pray to God in order that the worldly customs of our country may diminish more and more, and that the love of God may enter our
countries and destroy all that is evil.

Since I have been in this country I have seen many friends; and although I am now going back to my country I do not say that in the future
I may not come back again and visit you once more. (Loud applause.) I
say I shall be very glad if I ever come back again to England.

May God preserve you, is my word to you, and may He cause every
good custom and every good work to stand firmly in your country. (Pro-
longed applause.)

The last word on the evening is that of the correspondent of *South Africa:*

The inevitable collection was made during the proceedings, and several
hymns were sung. The proceedings closed with the singing of the National
Anthem ["God Save the Queen"], after which Khama, Bathoen, and
Sebele were for the last time affectionately mobbed.[20]

FRIDAY, NOVEMBER 22

On the Friday, the last full day in London, there were probably numerous
personal farewells from people coming to Armfield's Hotel.

One of the callers was a Mr. D. C. Morrison, "a well-known farmer
and politician in the Highlands [Lochiel], who is going out to South
Africa to try his fortunes there." He was sent round by Harry Wilson,
Chamberlain's private secretary, with a note to Willoughby thanking him
for "your wise and patriotic words last night at the Queen's Hall." Wilson
wanted him to talk to the chiefs about stock and sheep breeding. No doubt
Willoughby resented this imposition, but it was at Chamberlain's behest;
Wilson also referred Morrison to Maguire of the Chartered Company.[21]

In the afternoon there was an unrecorded meeting between Rutherfoord Harris of the company with Khama and Willoughby, set up by a
telegram to Willoughby the previous day: "Very important we should see
you and Khama tomorrow afternoon . . . at hotel." Harris had been under
telegraphic bombardment from Rhodes and no doubt wanted to make
another change in the company's position. Khama's attitude was that all
such changes were too much and too late, as the Chamberlain settlement
was irrevocable. But if Harris withdrew from Armfield's with a flea in his

Table 1.   Copy of Settlement of Accounts of Bathoen Made by W. C. Willoughby
Friday Afternoon, 22 Nov. 1895

CREDIT	£	s	D
To Bathoen's Private a/c* paid by me	35	15	9
To Bathoen's share of general a/c paid by me	38	14	7 1/2
To Bathoen's share of Hotel gratuities			
paid by me	1	0	0
Total	75	10	4 1/2

DEBIT			
To Khama's share of a/c paid by Lloyd		10	6
To Sebele's share of a/c paid by Lloyd	1	1	10
To Cash received from Lloyd at King's Cross	5	0	0
To cash received from Lloyd on "Arundel Castle"	35	0	0
Due to Mr. Thompson (unless already paid)	32	0	0
Total	75	10	4

BATHOEN'S PRIVATE A/C			
Doctor's fees	2	2	0
Medicine		6	9
Medicine		2	8
Collars	3	0	
Haberdashery		11	9
Civil Service a/c	15	12	1
Compass		9	9
Oil paper		1	0
Scent for Kaross		3	0
Medical attendance	1	1	0
Dress suit	7	15	6
Laundry	7	7	3
Total	35	15	9

*I add details of Bathoen's private a/c as I fancy that is the one that Mr. Lloyd found it so difficult to remember. The Hotel also is nowhere mentioned in these figures; because that bill was always (after the first week?) made out in Mr. Lloyd's name and handed to him direct. That is between him and the Hotel people: I have nothing to do with it. But we arranged to give gratuities in one sum and the agreed proportion is entered here.

ear, then Hercules Robinson (the high commissioner) was to return to the attack on Rhodes's behalf when Khama arrived in Cape Town.[22]

Also on the afternoon of the twenty-second Willoughby and Lloyd made a provisional financial settlement on Bathoen's accounts, totalling £75 10s. 4d. (table 1).

As for Sebele, Wardlaw Thompson had hoped to have "a good long talk" with "the sinner" before he left London. But "The Chiefs were always together, always being interviewed, or visited, or fussed about in some way, and it was impossible to get hold of them alone."[23]

SATURDAY, NOVEMBER 23

On Saturday, November 23, a very rainy day, the chiefs, their attendants, and Willoughby left Waterloo Station in London on the 10:45 train for

Southampton. (Willoughby's son was also probably in the party: he was too young to be left at the School for the Sons and Orphans of Missionaries, in Independents Road, next to Blackheath railway station in southeast London.)

They marched along the platform at Waterloo, a few moments before the train started, with all the airs of men of great importance. The great Cecil [Rhodes] himself could not have attracted more notice. . . . the royal chiefs seemed hugely to enjoy it.

At Southampton a deputation of ladies awaited Khama and Co. on the platform, and presented each chief with a huge bouquet of flowers, tied with flowing ribbons, and, if I mistake not, a buttonhole.

At all events when they entered the saloon of the tender they were each decorated with large chrysanthemum buttonholes that looked top-heavy, and silver-paper stalk upward, refused to keep their equilibrium.

The attendants, as regardlessly trim in their attire as their masters (who wore Bond Street up-to-date overcoats, shining bell toppers, and I verily think "spats"), with white cuffs and collars aggressively to the fore, were carrying a long mysterious roll of paper.[24]

Willoughby added that there had been the usual rush of passengers to get seats in the small tender that took them out to the ship anchored in the harbor. There were more than a few intoxicated emigrants for South Africa in the packed tender, anxious to board the ship and see the last of England.[25]

They boarded the *Arundel Castle*—"all that is spacious, comfortable and luxurious, and her deck cabins are quite too beautiful," leaving behind "a farewell letter of blessing for the English people," addressed to them via the editor of a new London periodical called the *Times of Africa:*

SIR,—As yours is a paper devoted to African matters, we have thought it right to use its columns to bid farewell to the English people. We thank them very cordially for the great kindness which they have, without exception, shown to all our party. They have made us feel as though we were, indeed, brothers of theirs. We have partaken of their hospitality, and seen the inside of their homes. We shall return to our own country with very grateful recollections indeed. And now we have, one and all, to say that we hope that God will bless this great country of England, and that we Bechuana and you Englishmen may be long linked together in bonds of mutual friendship, serving one Queen.

We wish to say also that it has been impossible to answer all the kind letters which have been sent to us, although our friend Mr. Willoughby has stayed up till two and three o'clock in the morning for weeks together in the attempt to do so.

And now farewell.

We are your friends.

KHAMA
BATHOEN
SEBELE [26]

The ubiquitous correspondent of *South Africa,* almost certainly its editor Mathers, who was permitted to have luncheon on board ship before it sailed, remarked of the moments before he returned to shore on the tender:

> Of the three chiefs, I liked Khama least, and Sebele best. Bathoen, though of characteristic appearance, is shorter and more common-place than his stately friend, Sebele. I did not like Khama—he looks deep, and there is far too much of the Hottentot about him to appeal to one's sympathy. But this did not prevent our shaking hands with the three chiefs, and smiling in return to their magnificent rows of white teeth.[27]

The ship sailed off into bad weather with 483 passengers. "It was one of those miserable 'drizzling' days," wrote Willoughby, "that make it easy for an Englishman to leave his native land."[28]

SIXTEEN

Dr. Jameson, You Have Got a Smooth Tongue

◦⊹⟶ ⟵⊹◦

THE *ARUNDEL CASTLE* SAILED SOUTHWESTWARD THROUGH the cold and damp of the Channel into the Atlantic. It was a poor boat in rough weather, without the sleek lines and speed of the *Tantallon*. The weather continued vile and sick-making as the ship crossed the Bay of Biscay. It was windy (moderate to strong) all the way to Grand Canary Island, with high seas and dull and showery weather. Thus far only Bathoen and Sebele proved to be "good sailors," able to come up from their cabins to take all meals: Khama, Willoughby, and all the attendants were seasick. The ship left Las Palmas, the port town on Grand Canary, on Friday, November 29, at 1 P.M. There was fine weather all the way from Las Palmas across the equator to the twentieth parallel south, where a strong head wind and high seas were encountered up to Cape Town.

Captain Winder and his officers were kind and courteous to the Bechuana, and Willoughby remarked that "our fellow passengers were certainly the best set I ever travelled with." (Among them were at least twenty-eight Jewish emigrants.)

The chiefs joined in deck games, low-key athletics, and games with rubber balls and quoits. "But more than this they enjoyed sitting still and listening to the Ship's Band as it discoursed sweet music on deck in the evenings." As they watched passing ships, signaling with colored flares at night, Willoughby remarked that the chiefs were quite evidently longing for home.

There was plenty of time for cogitation and reflection on the great odyssey while the chiefs and Willoughby sat and walked and slept on board the *Arundel Castle*. Willoughby smoked and sorted through his papers. No doubt the chiefs pored over their volumes of press clippings, read out to them and translated by their interpreters. The clippings and their memories may have served to open up old jealousies. Khama was suffering from "his old foe, dyspepsia," while

> The Bañwaketse were very troublesome on the way home. They grumbled at everything that was done for them and at everything that was not done. Bathoeñ was alright. There was some row between them, because they wished to get all they could of the things he [Bathoen] had bought while in England.[1]

✧ ✧ ✧

The *Arundel Castle* arrived at Cape Town on the morning of Sunday, December 15, at 10 A.M., after a passage of twenty-one days, nine hours, and forty minutes. But the passengers were not to disembark on the Sabbath but to stay on board until Monday morning. A party of temperance supporters, from the local branch of the Society of Good Templars, came on board on the Sunday afternoon, to present Khama with a congratulatory address. There were both white and black Templars, and their brass band played alongside the ship.[2]

Next morning the Bechuana disembarked while Willoughby stayed on board temporarily to deal with customs over the luggage. The chiefs were met on the dockside by George Hepburn, who summoned them to see the high commissioner, Sir Hercules Robinson. Sebele or Bathoen suggested waiting for Willoughby to join them, but Khama was impatient: "He had evidently tired of having to lean on another, and it is not surprising that he had." Thinking it was to be a purely social call, the chiefs went at once with young Hepburn.[3]

Hercules Robinson was brutally terse. He told Khama that Rhodes was withdrawing his promise to take Raditladi and his followers into Chartered territory—because the Chamberlain settlement had given Khama the land where Rhodes had proposed to settle Raditladi. He added that Chamberlain had wired saying that Khama must either take Raditladi back or give him the (Bokalanga) area stretching from Sua to Tlhabala. (Willoughby thought "Chamberlain had been misled" but concluded that Robinson had been hand in glove with Rhodes from the start.)

Robinson insisted on Khama's absolutely immediate reply to Chamberlain's cable. Khama saw red and refused to choose either alternative. But Robinson put such pressure on him, insisting on an immediate decision, that Khama grumpily agreed to take Raditladi back rather than lose part of his land.[4] His mood was not helped by his worsening dyspepsia or by Willoughby's attitude:

> Khama was in a very bad mood about this when I [Willoughby] returned to the hotel. He asked my advice, but I told him that it was too late to have advice; he had decided.

The next morning the chiefs attended "non-political" demonstrations at Cape Town churches, which were fully reported in the Cape press— "notwithstanding that the Cape press is dominated by millionaires and monopolists." They were then summoned for a second time by Sir Hercules Robinson. This time Willoughby went too. Robinson proved to be in affable mood. In answer to Willoughby's inquiries he showed him Chamberlain's telegram. It was a "breach of faith" on the government's part, and an act of provocation "eminently calculated to prejudice us in the eyes of the natives," said Willoughby. He told Robinson about Rhodes's previous promise to the chiefs in Cape Town—as a man of his word—to take Raditladi. Robinson's reply was that it was a pity that Willoughby had not been present to say that yesterday. It was all too late now.

> Khama was in very nasty mood for days after; and he seemed to think that I could do something to put the thing right if only I chose, but that I would not try.[5]

On arrival at Cape Town Willoughby had collected on behalf of the chiefs the £110 that had been left for safekeeping with David Mudie, the LMS agent. But now they felt impecunious enough to book second-class rather than first-class tickets on the train home.

On the night of Tuesday, December 17, 1895, the Bechuana party left from Cape Town's Adderley Street station in the homeward-bound train with a saloon carriage of their own. They were in the train from Tuesday night to Friday morning, the maximum speed being twelve miles (twenty kilometers) per hour on the last stretch. Khama found Willoughby sitting alone in one of the compartments and told him:

> Now that Raditladi and his party are coming back, I cannot speak to my people about giving more land for a school. We shall perish if we have no land.

Willoughby shrugged off the threat to the LMS college scheme: he must have been aware of alternative locations outside Khama's country.

On the evening before they reached their destination, Sebele and Willoughby were sitting on the open balcony of the wooden carriage, taking the air. Sebele said he would not drink again—not even *bojalwa*, sorghum beer. Willoughby scoffed and said Sebele would drink the next bottle of whisky given him by trader Harry Boyne at Molepolole.[6]

On arrival at Mafeking on Friday, December 20, they immediately heard that the BSA Company was massing a large military force in the town and at Pitsane (Phitsane Potlhogo) that was preparing for imminent action. The result must have been an atmosphere of fear and expectancy for the chiefs. Most people said that the force was going to invade the

Transvaal, but others said it was going to punish Chief Linchwe, the Chartered Company's new subject, "who was on the point of rebelling against the Company." Some even said that the force was there to smash Sebele and Bathoen and their peoples.

Leaving the train at Mafeking, the chiefs spent the rest of the day packing and preparing their wagons for the onward trek—while Willoughby had a lazy day. While still at Mafeking, Khama "received a message from two of Dr Jameson's friends, saying, that Dr Jameson wished to see him." Jameson and "Johnny" Willoughby were assembling and drilling their troops thirty miles (fifty kilometers) north of Mafeking at Pitsane, Jameson's makeshift administrative headquarters as resident commissioner of the Chartered Company's enclaves in the Bechuanaland Protectorate.[7]

The wagon train left for the north on Saturday, December 21. On the way north Khama and his wagons camped the first night halfway to Pitsane at Ramatlabama—a dry stream where British Bechuanaland ended and the Bechuanaland Protectorate began. Here they heard that Dr. Jameson was stopped for the night on his way south to Mafeking at a campsite nearby. (He was going to coordinate final arrangements with the other half of his Transvaal invasion force, at Mafeking, under Major Grey and the Hon. "Bobbie" White.)

Accounts of the meeting of the two men vary, but it is evident that Jameson was extremely angry with Khama about his actions and pronouncements in Britain, and a long bandy ensued. Khama made the mistake of going to meet Jameson without Seisa as interpreter, taking only his secretary Ratshosa, who was not fluent enough in English. (Reverend Willoughby's wagon was a few hours behind Khama's wagons.) One account of the incident was written down in later years by Simon Ratshosa, the son of the man who was with Khama, and no doubt reflects Ratshosa family tradition:

> The Chief on horseback, accompanied by Ratshosa, rode to the Doctor's camp to meet him. On [Khama] alighting from his horse, Doctor Jameson without losing time enquired from the Chief his meaning of sailing to England without the Chartered Company's directors' knowledge [i.e. approval?].
>
> " . . . I must tell you point blank you had no reason to visit England" said Doctor Jameson.[8]

Jameson followed the line of argument propagated from London by the journal *South Africa*. As Willoughby explained from hearsay, "Khama was accused by the Doctor of having made a dead set on the Company whilst in England on the Liquor Question."

What made matters worse was the Setswana interpreter supplied by Jameson, who inadequately translated Khama's words for fear of infuriating his master further. The cowering interpreter suggested to Khama that he blame Willoughby's translations for any offense to the Chartered Company. Khama adamantly refused to do so, but the interpreter still twisted his words to seem apologetic. The result was even worse confusion between Jameson and Khama.[9]

> KHAMA: Dr. Jameson, you have got a smooth tongue; I have known you for many years. If as you say I should have relied on your guardianship and peaceful intentions, can you tell me why are these things in front of you? (meaning big guns). What is their object[?] . . . are these guns you have not the sign of destruction and death? Please don't think you can cheat me and take me for a child, my old friend. Your ambition is but one[,] to kill.
> JAMESON: Oh, no, no, Khama, you must not say that. I am proceeding to Mafeking on some important business to perform, and am only going down with these guns to have them repaired.
> KHAMA: No, doctor, don't take me for a blind [man], I can see this is an expedition. Go forward with your expedition, which will bring you nothing but shame and disgrace. When I went over to England, I was afraid of these big guns. [But now I am not.][10]

Jameson might once again blame an interpreter for his misunderstanding with Khama. But it was also true that any quarrel with Khama was a good "cover" for Jameson's military preparations, which might then be said to be aimed as much against Khama as against Linchwe. How much Khama knew of this one does not know, but the threat of invasion would have helped to concentrate his mind on the way home.

The Kuruman newspaper of the London Missionary Society, *Mahoko a Becwana,* states that the three chiefs were met at Kgorwe, the Ngwaketse-Rolong border point north of Ramatlabama on the road to Kanye, by a large crowd of mounted horsemen come to greet them. It was noteworthy that the horsemen were drawn not only from the BaNgwaketse of Bathoen and the BaKwena of Sebele but also from other neighboring "tribes" expressing their approval of the mission of the three chiefs—from the BaLete of Ikaneng and the BaKgatla of Linchwe, and also from the Manyana group of BaKgatla and the BaTlokwa of Gaborone. Was such a force also an allied Tswana counter-commando in the making against the Jameson threat?

The arrival of the chiefs at Kanye, Bathoen's capital, on Tuesday, December 24, Christmas Eve, was a scene of even greater rejoicing as women and children joined in. One or more men even did what was described as a war dance. But Sebele and Khama declined to stay over at Kanye on Christmas Day, which was no great festival of feasting among puritan Congregationalists, and instead departed for Molepolole that morning. They arrived at Molepolole on the twenty-eighth, and Khama departed on his long trek north on Wednesday, January 1.[11] (The length of stays in Kanye and Molepolole was another indicator of the stress between Bathoen and his attendants on the one hand and Khama and Sebele and the other.)

Khama's wagons were slow-moving, while Willoughby's wagon was faster, and the missionary took advantage of this to stay on a bit longer at Mafeking and Molepolole and then catch up with Khama. Khama was not, however, good company: "All along the road from Cape Town he was very dyspeptic and rather difficult to get along with"—not actually quarreling, but doing "too much of the incarnate thorn-bush kind of thing." Khama confirmed this by his own account, related thirteen years later:

> When we left the train, & travelled in our wagons, we kept apart from each other. At Khunon Mrs. (Willoughby) called me to eat with them, & said the meal was ready, but I refused, I never ate with them once of that journey.[12]

As he approached his capital town, reported by *Mahoko a Becwana*, Khama was met on the Tawane River by an advance party led by his son and regent Sekgoma Khama, on the night of Monday, January 6. The greeters approached Khama's wagons, singing:

> God, Our Father, which art in Heaven, we praise Thee that we behold the lamp of the Bamañwato still shining. The winds of the sea, Jesus, Lord, Thou didst rebuke to stop them. We praise thus that the name of our Father in Heaven may be honoured, and that His Government may be seen here at Phalapye and in all lands always.

Such was the emotionalism of the occasion that one Disang a Makgasane cried out, "I am near to being a Christian today." Khama's wagons traveled on through the night.

> People from the gardens, women, came running, chanting with singing mixed with weeping. They said, "Is it he, or do we dream as those who sleep?" Men danced before him, rushed in among the horses, seized him by the hands and kissed him.[13]

At the Lokakulwe stream the next morning the party halted for a formal greeting by the white traders of Palapye come out to meet their *Kgosi*. Unfortunately, Charlie Clarke, who presented the embossed address to Khama, "had been imbibing beyond his usual extent," and Khama's *bête blanc* "Tom Fry was almost mad with drink." Khama's reply to the address was somewhat haughty: "he went rather out of his way to say that he would not have people in the stad [town] who did not do the right thing, and those who meddled with liquor would have to go."

Here at Lokakulwe, Khama mounted a splendid horse brought to him from Palapye. "And when we entered the town," wrote Willoughby, "there was a great noise; they fired guns; women chanted; they rejoiced." Local trader Loosely took commemorative photographs (not known to survive) of the welcome in the Palapye *kgotla*.

On the next morning, Wednesday, January 8, there was a great prayer meeting in the *kgotla*, at which Psalm 116 ("I am well pleased that the Lord hath heard the voice of my prayer . . . ") was sung in gratitude. Khama told of his journey and the receptions by the churches of Britain, Mr. Chamberlain, and the queen. The *Mahoko* report claims that Khama stated that Queen Victoria "rejoiced to see these three Chiefs, since it was then for the first time that she saw black people from Africa." [14]

Khama was still unwell and took to his bed. The dyspepsia that had developed on the boat had increased at Cape Town and grown even worse on the road home. When Khama and Willoughby settled financial accounts, the chief gave his missionary a "few" extra pounds to cover any extra expenses on the trip. "I suppose," complained Willoughby, "I must take that as evidence of appreciation." He was feeling quite sorry for himself when he replied to thanks sent him by Wardlaw Thompson:

> They are the only words of serious appreciation that I met with from anyone who was neither a blood relation nor a Brightonian. The chiefs showed no signs of appreciation, throughout; but many Bamañwato have thanked me for what I did, and I am inclined to think that the chief has expressed satisfaction to them. I do not know.

Khama supplied a rather different account of Willoughby's "few" extra pounds thirteen years later, as part of a long verbal complaint made about Willoughby to Edwin Lloyd:

> I took £600-0-0 to England. Seisa (his Secretary) stole some of the money. I told Olloby [Willoughby] to buy something for Mrs. (Willoughby) in England, either clothes or anything else he liked, & he bought her a saddle, as my gift to her. When we returned to Phalapye, Olloby gave me £60-0-0, which was the amount remaining over from the £600, and I returned £50 to Olloby, as my gift. [15]

When Khama emerged to resume his public duties after two weeks, he was no longer liverish and resumed a more friendly attitude toward Willoughby. He gave a lecture to his people on his travels one night in the Palapye *kgotla*, illustrated by Willoughby's lantern slide projector on a screen of white sheeting. "But there were so many thousands present that many could neither see nor hear what was going on." The illustrated lecture had to be repeated three times that week, in the large enclosed church building, once for each of the three divisions or "wards" of the town.

I wish I had space to give you some of Khama's remarks. The most interesting was his description of the intelligent sheep-dog that he saw in Sussex. The people were immensely pleased that the Queen had sent her [lantern slide] portrait for them to see, and these slides elicited much applause.

But the high-water mark of enthusiasm was reached when the photo of Mr. Chamberlain was shown. He is better known here now than [any] English politician has ever been.[16]

✣ ✣ ✣

How far had Khama, Sebele, and Bathoen been changed by the experience of their odyssey?

As for Khama, the opinions of white people differed. Some said yes, some said no. That he was testy on his return, having been forced to take back Raditladi, can be understood. But Raditladi and his followers refused to return and were given a home in Southern Rhodesia in return for helping the Chartered Company to suppress the Ndebele rising of that year. And the failure of the Jameson Raid resulted in the disgrace of Rhodes's Chartered Company, with the whole of the Bechuanaland Protectorate reverting to imperial overrule. Khama's mood undoubtedly improved. In March 1896 Willoughby wrote:

> But as far as I can see there is no change in him, except that he has seen a little more of the world, and knows more of what England is like. "There are no Englishmen here," he said the other day; "if you want to know what an Englishmen is, go to England and see him."

Willoughby added: "remarks like that made in public will hardly do him much good," that is, with Southern African English settlers.[17] The *Bulawayo Chronicle* reported at some time in March or late February:

> As was sometimes feared . . . Khama's temper and manner do not seem to have been improved by his lionising in England. . . . There are very few men able to keep their heads much through a London season when they have been the centre of attention, and it would have been more than wonderful if Khama had returned as sensible and as plain a man as when he went away.[18]

The French Protestant missionary François Coillard, on the other hand, was more positive and enthusiastic when he met Khama around the same time:

> There was the noble chief Khama, whose friendship (now of twenty years standing) has always been so precious to me, and whom I found totally unchanged and unspoilt by his visit to England. How delighted he was to tell me about all the wonders he had seen and the kindness he had received.[19]

As for Sebele, after three months without a drop of alcohol, he resumed drinking almost at once after his return to Molepolole—"though I cannot imagine him so far forgetting himself as to get drunk whilst Khama was here." (Harry Boyne's liquor license had been renewed on the ground that his store at Gaborone now fell in BSA Company territory surrendered by Sebele to the queen.)

When Sebele met Miss Partridge, the new LMS schoolteacher for Molepolole, he also made the distinction between English people from England and those from southern Africa: "Out here men call themselves Christians but we cannot see their spoor [i.e. tracks]. In England we can see their spoor very plainly." [20]

It was a distinction between the colonial and the imperial that, while sometimes unfair to individual "settlers," was now reinforced among the people of the Bechuanaland Protectorate. It was to serve them well by emphasizing direct connections with Great Britain that overrode the claims of South Africa and Southern Rhodesia to take their country.

As for Bathoen, some of his impressions of Britain were gleaned from him in 1900, during the South African War, when he appeared "on a splendid white horse," wearing his Life Guards officer's uniform, to greet British forces cut off by the siege of Mafeking. He was preceded by a mounted headman bearing his sword. One of the British soldiers told him that he had seen him before in Sheffield, and he replied that "he liked Sheffield better than London, because in Sheffield he could go where he liked, but in London he had to follow the stream of people." Bathoen also added a jab at local white settlers: "the Queen's stables, he said, were cleaner than any white man's house in Africa."

Bathoen's quarrel with Kwenaetsile, which developed during the voyages of 1895, was to plague him for the rest of his life. [21]

Perhaps the most affected by 1895 was the fourth and youngest member of the team that went to England, Rev. William Charles Willoughby. The experience appears to have hardened and matured him. This was how he appeared to an outside observer (Frederick Lugard's brother) in mid-1896:

> Willoughby ran Khama's trip to England, and I could see he was *engrossed* in all the politics of the land. He seemed a shrewd little man . . . very hard-working, and he evidently considered that he was Khama's political, as well as spiritual guide! He knew all about boundary awards, and political workings below the surface, etc., etc! He is a nice, obliging little man, very anxious to help . . . but is *very* self-important, evidently fancies himself extremely! and wants to teach you how to do it! [22]

✢ ✢ ✢

On Monday, December 30, 1895, the *Cape Argus* carried an important editorial, intended to cover up the fact that Rhodes (on intelligence from Johannesburg and ultimately at the behest of Chamberlain) had called off the "Jameson Plan" indefinitely:

> Amongst the absurdest of the rumours relating to the Transvaal crisis is that which alleges that for some time the Chartered Company's forces have been quietly massing on the Transvaal frontier, ostensibly because of possible trouble with Khama [*sic*], really for use at Johannesburg. No better refutation of such statements could be formed than a bare statement of the facts.

The editorial ran through the bare facts of the dissolution of the Bechuanaland Border Police at Mafeking, with the option of joining the British South Africa Company Police. Then it explained why detachments of the BSA Company Police had come south from Rhodesia to Pitsane:

> It may be added that the company will in future station the major part of their police in the Protectorate portion of their territory, for the simple economical reason that there is no horse-sickness as there is at Buluwayo [*sic*], and a man can be kept at half the expense. In case of need these men could be transported to Matabeleland in a few days.[23]

Too late. Next day's *Argus* carried the news of Jameson's "unexpected" foray into the South African Republic, condemned by the Chartered Company and the high commissioner alike.[24]

Jameson's men had survived some heavy Christmas drinking at Pitsane, a flat area of hot open grassland marked by two very small conical hills, noted for its skylarks soaring high in the sky. Jameson's column from Pitsane, and Grey's column from Mafeking, then crossed the border into the Transvaal on the night of Sunday, December 29. "It's all bosh about fighting Linchwe," an officer told his former Bechuanaland Border Police troopers at Mafeking as they prepared to move.

The two columns, numbering together an inadequate five hundred men, effected a junction the next morning at 5 A.M., for breakfast, in the wooded vale of Malmani, or Mosega, where Mzilikazi had had a capital town six decades before. This alerted the Boers in nearby Zeerust, whose telegraph to Rustenburg and Pretoria Jameson's scouts had forgot to sever.

From Malmani it was a short climb onto the highveld ridge of the western end of the Witwatersrand, and easy riding through grass country along an established road toward Johannesburg. Galvanized iron sheds full of food and fodder had been set up along the road. The first dash was to get through a valley around lead mines, where they could have been ambushed by the Boer forces shadowing them. Tired troopers slept rather than ate and rode the same tired horses for two days, rather than risk riding the broken-down carriage horses provided halfway as remounts.

Finally, deadened by fatigue, confused by false guiding around Krugersdorp west of Johannesburg, and failing to receive the promised reinforcements of armed *uitlanders*, the Jameson raiders were ambushed and brought to the point of surrender on Thursday, January 2, 1896, near what is now the western edge of Soweto.[25]

With an irony that would have escaped white people at the time, but that is quite piquant from the perspective of a hundred years later, the Anglican vicar of St. Mary's Church (later cathedral) in central Johannesburg preached a muscular sermon against Boer oppression on the evening of Sunday, December 30, 1895—at the very moment when Jameson's expedition was setting off to save his *uitlander* parishioners. The vicar "said it was preposterous to imagine that the majority could be worked [*sic*] for an indefinite period by a minority." [26]

✛ ✛ ✛

Readers may be curious as to the eventual fates of Khama, Sebele, and Bathoen, and indeed Willoughby. It would take more than another book to furnish a satisfactory answer to these questions. Khama is already the subject of an extensive biographical literature, though Sebele is the subject of less and Bathoen of virtually none at all.[27]

Bathoen ruled his people for another fifteen years after returning from Britain, until his death in 1910. He remained moderate and temperate and mild mannered, despite the fractiousness of relatives. During 1908–9 Bathoen worked closely with Sebele (and less closely with Khama) to oppose another threatened takeover of the Bechuanaland Protectorate, this time by the impending Union of South Africa—and was noted for the cogency of his arguments. (His "dialectic" was described as very good by the Colonial Office.) Perhaps the most remarkable thing about him was his wife, the one-eyed Gagoangwe, daughter of Sechele, a woman of "high character and religious convictions" whose wisdom in governance after Bathoen's death preserved the chieftainship for her grandson, Bathoen II— whose rule ended only in 1969, when he resigned to join party politics as an opposition leader.[28]

Sebele lived a few months longer than Bathoen. Known for his geniality and good humor as a host, he lacked the drive and acquisitiveness of Bathoen and Khama—with both of whom he appears to have remained on equally good terms. He also proved less adept than them at dealing with factions and fractiousness and left behind a seriously weakened chieftainship. Struck down by pleurisy in July 1910, he spoke of "the dark river" ahead and spent much of his time reading Scripture, dwelling on Psalm 51: "Behold, I was shapen in wickedness; and in sin hath my mother conceived me. But . . . Thou shalt purge me with hyssop, and I shall be clean; thou shalt wash me, and I shall be whiter than snow." He retired to his cattle post, where he "received a great shock to his system" after being misdirected to use a strong lotion in his eyes, returning home to Molepolole and dying there on January 23, 1911.[29]

Khama lived the longest of the three Bechuana chiefs who had gone to Britain. After settling back home in 1896 he resumed his customary initiative and reforming spirit, though concentrating his energies on administrative and economic rather than cultural or religious reforms. He grew steadily more estranged from Willoughby and the London Missionary Society, who refused his offer of buildings at (Old) Palapye for a new college and chose instead Tiger Kloof, south of Vryburg in Cape Colony. Willoughby became the principal of Tiger Kloof Institution and led a faction of the LMS that called for the integration of Africans into mainstream colonial society.

On June 6, 1909, Khama called on Edwin Lloyd and delivered a long indictment of a recent speech by Willoughby on "The relation of the Bechuana tribes to the future of South Africa":

> he is always speaking about the land, for I know that he wants to see our land divided into farms, & given to the white people. . . . I have long known Olloby [Willoughby] & I went to England with him. There I was helped by Monare Thompson & Mr. Albert Spicer. I do not reckon that Olloby helped me at all. When in England, he kept me away from people to whom I wished to speak. After our business had been settled, I observed that a great change came over Olloby, & I could not work with him any longer. This was most marked on board ship on our return voyage. Then Olloby went one way, & I went the other way, & we never again agreed.[30]

Khama was reconciled with his missionaries in 1915, after Willoughby left Tiger Kloof. But disillusion with colonial administrators set in, because they sabotaged (at the behest of a big-business combine in South Africa) his successful attempt at a state trading corporation. From 1916 onward, after a serious horse-riding accident, Khama concentrated on leaving a united nation for his son Sekgoma II (and grandson Seretse Khama), by patching up the differences caused by his previous reforms. Around 1920 he told visitors: "I am still looking to England with both eyes and listening with both ears," though "I receive nothing of the good laws of England but oppression from the Officials." He died aged almost ninety, on February 21, 1923, having caught pneumonia after a long, wet horse ride.

Willoughby went on to become an author and academic, an expert on "race relations" and traditional African religion, and professor of missions in the heartland of American Congregationalism at Hartford Seminary College, Connecticut. He was there when Khama died and had the last word on him in a long but somewhat dismissive obituary titled "Khama: A Bantu Reformer," which appeared in the *International Review of Missions* in January 1924.[31]

CONCLUSION

Half a Loaf?

WHAT, AFTER ALL, DID THE BECHUANA CHIEFS ACHIEVE by their odyssey in late Victorian Britain? On January 6, 1896, before the consequences of the Jameson Raid had become clear, John Mackenzie in South Africa wrote a letter to Wardlaw Thompson in London, suggesting that the chiefs had achieved little. Mackenzie pointed out the great value of the Chartered Company's free acquisition of the western and northern parts of Bechuanaland, as well as the eastern border strip. The way was now cleared for the Chartered Company to build a Walfisch Bay–Kalahari-Beira Railway. Mackenzie could not believe that the retention of an imperial protectorate over the countries of Khama, Sebele, and Bathoen was anything more than a temporary expedient, to be withdrawn when it suited the other parties.

Wardlaw Thompson replied:

> I quite agree with your feeling. . . . But this is emphatically a case in which half a loaf is better than no bread, and if you had been in England when the Chiefs came, and had been able to realize how tremendously strong was the influence on the side of the Chartered Company . . . you would, I think, have felt with us that the present settlement represented a very great victory indeed.[1]

Mackenzie had his own agenda. For him the full loaf would have been the annexation of the Bechuanaland Protectorate as a Crown Colony under direct imperial control, with a government in which the chiefs and their peoples would be represented and progressively integrated.

✤ ✤ ✤

The Chamberlain Settlement of November 1895 secured the countries of Khama, Sebele, and Bathoen as Bechuana islands in a Rhodesian sea. Or, as the *Cape Times Weekly Edition* of December 25, 1895, portrayed them— "The New Black Wedge: Will It Last?" Cape colonists would have been familiar with black wedges of territory in the Eastern Cape that had not outlasted white land hunger. The article carried a cartoon map portraying Bathoen and Sebele's countries as the silhouette of a coat cuff, from which the wrist of Khama's country protruded with a black fist giving a thumbs-up sign toward the north.

But the failure of the Jameson Raid resulted in the reversal of most Chartered Company gains in the Bechuanaland Protectorate—besides those parts of the railway strip conceded to the queen by Bathoen, Sebele, and Khama. What the company had already annexed it was forced to give back; what it was about to annex it was not allowed to have. Proclamation No. 1 of 1896 of the Bechuanaland Protectorate reversed Proclamation No. 10 of 1895, taking back the Lete territory of Ikaneng and the Barolong farms under Bechuanaland Protectorate administration. Nothing more was heard of the company taking over the Kgatla territory of Linchwe as directed by High Commissioner Robinson on December 11, 1895.[2] But how permanent was even the post-Jameson Raid settlement intended to be?

The Chamberlain settlement of 1895 became the Magna Carta of the chiefs of the Bechuanaland Protectorate—much like the 1900 Buganda Agreement in Uganda. Thus in the 1930s when Khama's son Tshekedi and Bathoen I's grandson Bathoen II sued the high commissioner, in an attempt to stop the promulgation of the Native Administration Proclamations, they claimed that the new laws were "a breach of the treaty made between the late Queen Victoria's Ministers and our fathers."

This viewpoint was taken up when the Bechuanaland Protectorate became independent as the Republic of Botswana in the 1960s. Khama, Sebele, and Bathoen were portrayed as the nation's founders, who preserved its autonomy from white Rhodesia and white South Africa.[3]

Some revisionist historians of Botswana, notably Jeff Ramsay and Barry Morton, have quibbled. Chamberlain's hasty settlement had given away to the company more than it had kept for the chiefs. The protectorate's autonomy had been preserved by the failure of the Jameson Raid, not by the 1895 Chamberlain Settlement. The irrelevance of the settlement is shown by the 1936 Watermeyer Judgement in reply to Chiefs Tshekedi Khama and Bathoen II—citing the Westminster Parliament's Foreign Jurisdiction Act of 1890, which asserted that British power in any dependent territory was "not limited by Treaty or Agreement."[4]

It has also been suggested, by the eminent social anthropologist Isaac Schapera, that the events of 1895–96 greatly enhanced the personal powers of traditional rulers in the Bechuanaland Protectorate. Each of the three chiefs had been given "a hearty mandate to go to Britain" by an assembly of their male elders. But on their return in 1896 they neglected to convene such an assembly to get their people's explicit consent to the terms of the treaty made in England. This precedent enabled the chiefs to ride roughshod over traditional constitutional constraints in the future[5]—

at least until the 1930s, when the British colonial authorities began the assault on chiefly prerogatives taken up by the independent republican authorities in the 1970s.

Probably the best way to put the 1895 odyssey in historical context is to ask what would have happened if Khama, Sebele, and Bathoen had *not* gone to Britain. Look at Chiefs Montshiwa, Ikaneng, and Linchwe, who either did not go overseas or had their envoys turned back. They lost their lands willy-nilly. This suggests that—if Khama, Sebele, and Bathoen had not been in Britain at the time—the whole Bechuanaland Protectorate would have been taken over by the Chartered Company in October–November 1895.

What the three Bechuana chiefs did in Britain was to recruit on their side the Nonconformist conscience that constituted Joseph Chamberlain's own electoral power base. This strengthened Chamberlain's better instincts. He felt obliged to make partial concessions to the chiefs and was held back from throwing his lot completely into the Rhodes-ian camp.

The success of the mission of the three Bechuana chiefs to Britain also helped to cause the failure of the Jameson Raid. Preparations for the raid were made immensely more complicated by the lobbying of the chiefs in London—delaying and reducing the transfers of land and police forces to the BSA Company that were essential preconditions for a successful military expedition.

After the failure of the ill-prepared Jameson Raid in 1896, Chamberlain and the Colonial Office had to extricate themselves from complicity in the Chartered Company's plans for the raid, that is, from the previous year's exercise of granting most of the Bechuanaland Protectorate to the BSA Company for "railway works." This they did by generalizing the Chamberlain settlement—retaining imperial protection for three reserves—from part of the protectorate to the whole country. It was a symbolic, almost costless, gesture of punishment: taking away from the Chartered Company that which was not yet possessed. It was a sop to the anti-Rhodes forces conjured up by Khama, Sebele, and Bathoen's mission that avoided the really effective punishment of taking away the company's royal charter—which was being demanded by some politicians.

Without the success of the mission of the three chiefs to Britain in 1895 there would have been no precedent of retaining imperial protection to follow in 1896, nor any identifiable political lobby of supporters for the Bechuanaland Protectorate in Britain to appease. If the whole of Bechuanaland had been swallowed whole without effective protest in 1895, it would have become just as natural a part of "Rhodesia," as Mashonaland and Matabeleland were already, or as Barotseland and "Northern Rhodesia" were to become.

As it was, Khama was still obliged to hand over yet more territory to the British government in 1896, for it to donate to the BSA Company, when the Bechuanaland Railway under construction reverted to the route direct from Gaborone to Palapye and thence to Tati (Francistown) and Bulawayo. Surveyors set out to survey the "old" route on the same day as Jameson's raiders surrendered in the Transvaal. The "new" border route along the Limpopo agreed on with Chamberlain could now be seen as a complete fraud, concocted for purposes of preparing the way for the Jameson Raid. But Khama refused to reclaim the border strip, so as not to modify or undermine the cherished Chamberlain settlement in any way. Under protest, he conceded an extra hundred-yard strip through his country for the Bechuanaland Railway in 1896 but resolutely refused to sign title deeds for stations in his country on the Magalapye River or at Palapye Road.[6]

The symbolic punishment of the Chartered Company by the British government in 1896 was not necessarily, however, intended to be permanent. Bechuanaland was placed under an administrator closely linked to the Chartered Company, and its white police were integrated with the BSA Company's police. There was still talk of the protectorate becoming part of Rhodesia by the year 1900, but this deadline was lost in the South African War and its aftermath. Thereafter it was often argued that the compact with the British government of Khama, Sebele, and Bathoen was a personal one and would end with their deaths.[7]

If that was so, the very longevity of the three chiefs must count as an important factor in the survival of the Bechuanaland Protectorate's territorial autonomy. Bathoen did not die until 1910, Sebele not until 1911, and Khama not until 1923. By that time the BSA Company was losing its charter to rule Rhodesia, and the Southern Rhodesian claim to take over the Bechuanaland Protectorate was more than counterbalanced by the claim of the new Union of South Africa.

✥ ✥ ✥

The 1895 odyssey developed its own mythology in the history of Botswana. It also seems to have affected the deeper historical mythology of the Tswana people, helping to "rewrite" the traditional history of earliest times.

Edwin Lloyd's *Three Great African Chiefs (Khâmé, Sebelé, and Bathoeng)* (T. Fisher Unwin, 1895) told the following tale about the BaKwena of Sebele, the BaNgwato of Khama, and the BaNgwaketse of Bathoen:

> Long, long ago, these three tribes lived together as one tribe. . . . The Chief who ruled over them had three wives; the head wife was called Mma-

Kwena, or mother of Crocodile; the second wife was named Mma-Ngwato or [Mma-]Ngwatwe; while the third wife, having a son named Ngwaketse, was spoken of as Mma-Ngwaketse, or mother of Ngwaketse.[8]

In works published over the century since 1895 this has become simplified and defeminized, referring to a founding father called Malope who had three sons—Kwena, Ngwato, and Ngwaketse.[9]

But other historical traditions tell different tales. Thus the traditions of the ancestral BaKwena published in a *Short History of the Native Tribes of the Transvaal* (1905), compiled from sources unconnected with the Bechuanaland Protectorate, refer to Malope's son Mmutla as having had two wives, called Mma-Kwena and Mma-Ngwato. On the other hand Ngwaketse is given as the name of Kwena's grandson who quarreled with his brother Motswasele. There are also other traditions that refer to Ngwaketse as an older sister who challenged Motswasele.[10]

Lloyd was Bathoen's missionary, and he acknowledged Bathoen as his major source. Did Bathoen tell Lloyd that Ngwaketse had been the brother of Kwena and Ngwato—to upgrade his own ancestry and to anticipate and validate the essential equality of the three chiefs in 1895? If this was so, what is all the more remarkable is that Sebele and Khama, and their peoples, accepted this version subsequently.

✠ ✠ ✠

What, if any, was the significance of the odyssey for British history, besides being an illustrative exercise for the "new journalism"? Was it just forgotten along with the long hot summer? R. C. K. Ensor's volume of *The Oxford History of England* (1936) covering the years 1870–1914 acknowledged the mission to London led by Khama in 1895 as an event in the political history of England.[11] But the tour of the three chiefs around Britain has otherwise been ignored in narratives of British history covering 1895.

Coverage in works of imperial-colonial history has often been dismissive. Thus Ian Colvin's *Life of Jameson* (1922) referred to Khama and the other two Bechuana chiefs being "used by their friends . . . the philanthropists." Frederick A. Madden in *The Cambridge History of the British Empire*, volume 3 (1967) incorrectly asserted that Khama's visit to London was a rare "impressive triumph" for the Aborigines' Protection Society— when in fact the visit was not even referred to in the society's journal at that time! Lord Hailey (1953) had much better grounding when he observed: "The success of a visit by Khama to London did much to consolidate the tradition . . . that 'native interests' are the special responsibility of the Imperial Factor."[12]

Reaction against the success of Khama's visit also helped to reinforce a prosettler tradition in British political life profoundly sympathetic to white (and especially Rhodesian) colonialism. This alternative tradition was exemplified at the time of the visit by the writings of the editor of the London-based journal *South Africa*, Edward P. Mathers. Further examples toward the end of Khama's visit were mocking and entirely fictitious anecdotes of Khama's sporting prowess that were carried in "The Smoking Room" of Rider Haggard's *African Review*. One tale was about when Khama went pheasant shooting and peppered Willoughby's buttocks with shot; and another was about when he played golf—missing his first four shots and then driving the fifth for seventeen yards, and completing the eighteen holes in 257 swings.

Pro-native and prosettler traditions clashed, literally, in a bar-room brawl inside Rider Haggard's Anglo-African Club in London, just before the Bechuana chiefs left England. Prosettlers, led by the French traveler Lionel Décle, clashed with pro-natives led by H. A. Bryden, who in the pages of the *Saturday Review* had accused "Mr. Rhodes and the monopolists" of trying to seize and suck the three chiefs dry.[13]

How soon were the chiefs forgotten in Britain? On the one hand there is Wardlaw Thompson's despair in January 1896, as the scandal of the Jameson Raid was beginning to unfold:

> Unfortunately the interest created by the Chiefs' visit has been entirely swallowed up and dissipated by the exciting news which have taken place since then.[14]

On the other hand there is the fact that when pestilence and famine struck the Bechuanaland Protectorate a few months later, Wardlaw Thompson managed to organize a London "Bechuanaland Protectorate [famine] relief" committee headed by the duke of Westminster, with thirty-five prestigious members including Sir George Baden-Powell as honorary treasurer and Wardlaw Thompson as honorary secretary. Chamberlain was one of the members: he contributed twenty guineas to its funds. The lord mayor of London issued the following circular for an inaugural meeting to be held in the Mansion House at 2:30 on the afternoon of Monday, June 29, 1896:

> The visit of Khama and his fellow chiefs to this country last autumn is not forgotten. Their manly and modest bearing, their contention on behalf of the moral as well as the political interests of their tribes, their bright works in the causes of Christianity and temperance, and their successful appeal to remain under the direct government of the Queen awakened a very widespread interest in them and their country, which is the scene of the present distress and famine.[15]

There is other evidence to suggest that the odyssey of the three chiefs left traces deep in British society, in the broad class and provincial coalition that sympathized with and supported the Bechuana cause. With the passing of Queen Victoria and her replacement by Edward VII, an exponent of the new "immorality," the Nonconformist conscience and the temperance movement came to be regarded as relics of a bygone age. But the figure of Khama undoubtedly retained moral prestige in influential corners of British society. In 1913 the British colonial minister noted that for so long as Khama was alive "the bare suggestion of handing him over to the Union [of South Africa] would bring the whole missionary world and others upon me at once." [16]

Seven years after Khama's death, another Khama came to London on a mission against commercial exploitation—Tshekedi Khama. Once again the London Missionary Society provided channels into influential circles, now Labour as well as Liberal. Then, twenty years later in London, Khama's grandson Seretse Khama married an English woman, quarreled with his uncle Tshekedi and upset British–South African relations, setting off a political crisis that almost felled the Labour government and rocked the subsequent Conservative government. Seretse Khama also began to draw on a broad alliance of supporters in British society—a few of whom could still remember the events of 1895. The name of Khama once again filled the British newspapers. [17]

✠ ✠ ✠

The odyssey of Khama, Sebele, and Bathoen in 1895 remained fresh in the memory of many people in Britain and became a founding myth of the Botswana nation that kept its autonomy from white-settler rule and achieved independence in 1966. The odyssey also had an unexpected consequence in the Soviet Union many years later.

After the first Russian revolution of 1905, when Russia was undergoing its first experiment with Western-style democracy, the Houses of Parliament in London gave a collection of published British parliamentary papers to the Duma in Petrograd. This collection, consisting of hundreds of bound volumes, was locked away during the Soviet period and remained largely unread. After the Second World War, however, it was discovered by a young Soviet scholar of Western studies called Apollon Davidson. His eyes lighted on a Blue Book of 1896 (C. 7962), entitled "Correspondence relative to the Visit to this Country of the Chiefs Khama, Sebele, and Bathoen." It was this Blue Book that began Apollon Davidson's lifelong fascination with the character of Cecil Rhodes, and that set him on the road to become the leading Africanist historian in the Soviet Union. [18]

APPENDIX
BALLADS OF THE 1895 TOUR

KHAMA, KHAMA, KHAMA!
Lionised and Poetised

Headline from *Cape Times Weekly Edition*, October 2, 1895

According to *Cape Argus,* January 12, 1895, the following ballad was "softly warbled" by an anonymous member of the crowd awaiting the arrival of Khama at Cape Town fire station, "with apologies to the author of 'Princess Ida.'" Alfred Tennyson's poem *The Princess* of 1847 was the basis for the 1884 operetta *Princess Ida* by W. S. Gilbert and Arthur Sullivan.

> Searching through the panorama
> For a sign of royal Khama,
> Who has come to see its wonders
> Of Cape Town and its blunders,
> Legion is their name.
>
> Some misfortune evidently,
> Has detained him consequently.
> Searching through the panorama
> For a sign of royal Khama,
> Chief of loyal fame.
>
> He was seen at Garlick's lately,
> With his stick and helmet stately,
> Gazing at the lift sedately,
> As up and down it went.
>
> On the Witter sprinkler's showers,
> And its fire-resisting powers,
> Or the artificial flowers,
> Gloves, handkerchiefs, and scent.
>
> Some say they've cracked a bottle,
> Just to liquidate his throttle,

Now he's far from daub and wattle,
In Cape Town of to-day.

And he feels he cannot leave 'em,
Thought of parting which will grieve him,
For the manner they receive him
Is princely, royal, and gay.

(Khama was then seen looming in the distance.)

See through the panorama
Looms the form of Royal Khama,
Who has come to see the wonders
Of this city, and its blunders.
Legion is their name.

No misfortune, evidently,
Has befallen him consequently,
Looming through the panorama
Comes the form of Royal Khama,
To see the firemen's game.

This poem was found scribbled on the back of a House of Commons seat reservation card, according to the weekly journal *South Africa*, August 24, 1895.

Bechuanaland

The Brewers have this House returned
To follow their command,
Yet Drink's to be tabooed, we've learned,
In Bechuanaland.
The Bechuana men are black,
So Prohibition's right;
For here it is a dreadful thing
For Englishmen are white,
But we shall get it here ere long,
Proceeding on this track
For Tories vote that black is white,
And also white is black.

"King Khama and the English Government" appeared in the *Manchester Guardian*, September 16, 1895 (also *Christian Million*, September 26, 1895).

King Khama and the English Government
KHAMA: Great chieftain of the white man's race,
I fall before thee on my face,
And from yourself and Queen I crave
My countrymen to guide and save;

So long as Christians drink supply,
　　By drink they fall, by drink they die.
Great chieftain, may it be thy will
　　To save them from this cruel ill,
And thus to remedy the griefs
　　Of Khama and his brother chiefs.

CHAMBERLAIN:　Oh, Khama, of the Afric race,
　　I joy to meet thee face to face;
Though Bamangwato's far away
　　From Birmingham, where I hold sway,
Yet are our hopes the same.
"Social reform" is all our aim,
　　Jesse and Williams, too, combine
In following the self-same line,
　　And in six months, I tell you, King,
We the millennium mean to bring.

KHAMA:　These words have made my bosom burn,
　　You've sworn, no doubt, strong drink to spurn,
And Khama learns, with great delight,
　　How you will bless both black and white.
The chieftain of the Midland fields
　　From ill, the weak and helpless shields,
And blessings on the head of Joe.
　　Shall flow from far Bamangwato.

CHAMBERLAIN:　Yes, yes, great King, the Emperor Joe,
　　To save the black is never slow,
And soon 't shall be our greatest boast
　　We've banished drink from all your coast.

KHAMA:　'Tis well, your words are good, great chief,
　　My tribe will hail this great relief,
And statues to the Emperor Joe
　　Shall rise in far Bamangwato.

CHAMBERLAIN:　I joy my praise should there be sung;
　　But here my greatest friend is Bung.
In fact, if you more knowledge crave
　　I'm really nothing but his slave.
He's guardian of my high career,
　　He put me in, he keeps me here,
He tells me what to do or say,
　　He gives the word and I obey.
He says, "Let loose the flood of drink,
　　Till all beneath the torrent sink,"
And we like wax within his hands
　　Must simply do what he commands.

But in this case, as now you see,
     He says the black man may be free,
So you and I and Bung agree,
     And Bamangwato may be free.
But now, oh King, I'm forced to go,
     A brewer's agent waits below,
He's come to start a scheme I think,
     For selling here more stocks of drink,
And I must help him, for you know,
     We are not in Bamangwato!

"The Ballad of Bechuana," or "The answer Mr. Punch would like Mr. Chamberlain to be able to make to Khama" appeared in *Punch*, September 21, 1895:

Air— "Oriana"

We sympathise with your great woe,
     Bechuana.
There's little rest for Chiefs below,
     Bechuana.
In sultry climes, in climes of snow,
The drink will come, the land will go.
     Bechuana.
The ways of trade were ever so,
     Bechuana!

The Chartered Company seems growing,
     Bechuana.
The liquor interest is crowing,
     Bechuana.
Bung is blowing, drink is flowing,
Rhodes like one o' clock is going,
     Bechuana.
Where they will stop there is no knowing,
     Bechuana.

In black kingdoms, as in white,
     Bechuana,
Men are given to getting "tight,"
     Bechuana,
KHAMA, it is a grievous sight.
And you, you seem to have done right,
     Bechuana,
Since you your troth to us did plight,
     Bechuana!

Sober, industrious, fond of peace,
     Bechuana,
You've kept your tribe. May it increase,
     Bechuana.

If you would have the traffic cease,
Why should your heart not have that ease,
　　Bechuana?
Sobriety is the best police,
　　Bechuana!

It is a vile, corroding curse,
　　Bechuana.
We do not wish, quite the reverse,
　　Bechuana,
That, just to fill a huckster-purse,
Your tribe should go from bad to worse,
　　Bechuana.
'Twere a foul shame! That true and terse,
　　Bechuana!

Let Gain go hang, let Bung be blowed,
　　Bechuana.
Rather than drunkenness corrode,
　　Bechuana.
The realm whereby Molopo flowed.
To Khama Britons much have owed,
　　Bechuana;
The boon you crave should be bestowed,
　　Bechuana!

This strange, racist doggerel, entitled "Savages. To Khama, Sebele and Bathoen," by
Victor Plarr, was published in the *Speaker*, 28 September 1895. Additional lines by "L."
(not reproduced here) were published in the same journal a week later.

As stags that o'er some moonlit pasture range,
　　Obscurely they emerge upon our ken,
Those lithe fierce forms, pathetical and strange,
　　Those changeless savage men!

Sometimes it is the prairies' twilight brood
　　That, for a moment, doth affront our noon:
The stark ghost-dancers rave for white men's blood,
　　Their bare feet drum in tune.

Sometimes, with unimagined faith possest,
　　The dark religious Mahdists rush in swarms
Upon an impious and intruding West,
　　Impregnable in arms.

Anon, the meek Kanáka steals in view,
　　And respite for a little space implores,
While drink, disease, and long debauch undo
　　His palm-embattled shores.

Again, with praying lips and patient eyes,
    Some Aethiop tribe uplifts a sombre face,
And pleads articulate before it dies
    For the great White Man's grace.

Commerce, the sluggish-footed Maenad, creeps
    Through their borders, laying stealthy hands
Upon the harvest of all virgin deeps,
    The fruit of all lone lands!

She leaves a bleaching line of savage bones
    Her royal road to mark and to define:
Cairns of their murdered kings are her milestones,
    Kings of some perishing line.

Vainly these strove and cried, nor ever found
    A breathing-space, a time to love and toil,
A strip of hunting-ground or burial-ground
    No trader dared despoil!

Types of the ancestral races whence have sprung
    The polished Aryans of the happier West,
Types of the babe who hung when Time was young
    Upon Earth's lonely breast,

Shall these belated elemental men
    Still inarticulately strive and cry,
And find no rest until the day dawn when
    Mortality shall die?

"Farewell to Sebele, Bathoen and King Khama" appeared in the *Globe* (London), November 20, 1895 and was quoted in *South Africa,* November 23, 1895.

Farewell to Sebele, Bathoen and King Khama!
    Farewell to the chiefs of the temperance clan!
They haste from our winter—no longer pyjama
    Seems sweeter than greatcoat with warm Astrakhan.

Farewell to King Khama, Sebele, Bathoen!
    Let's speed them at parting—no time should be lost—
For should they stay longer (teetotal path tho' in)
    They might take a nip just to keep out the frost.

Farewell to Bathoen, King Khama, Sebele!
    Let's cheer the three Africans three times and three!
We'll toast them in strong stirrup cups of tea freely;
    King Coffee's no more, but we've found a King Tea.

A poem addressed to Joseph Chamberlain by "Ariel" in the *Daily Chronicle* (London), n.d. was quoted in *South Africa*, November 20, 1895:

> Say, in what measure shall I hymn thy fame?
>> Choose in what lyric, dithyramb, or ode I
> Shall rouse the echoes with thy novel name,
>> O Moatlhodi!

> Silomo serves for Ashmead-Bartlett's need,
>> Buffalo Bill for mighty Colonel Cody
> Thy title is more sumptuous indeed,
>> Great Moatlhodi!

> What Ancient Briton, fiercely large and fine,
>> With brawny limbs, magnificently woady,
> Could sport so wonderful a name as thine,
>> O Moatlhodi?

> Let choirs of singers, chanting through the scale
>> From high soprano C to thrilling low D,
> Take up the musical and mystic tale
>> Of Moatlhodi!

> "The man that rights things," so the Afric chief
>> Has Birmingham's Right Honorable Joe di-stinguished
> by title, rather bright than brief,
>> Of Moatlhodi.

"Moatlhodi!" appeared in *Punch*, November 30, 1895.

Moatlhodi!

> O Midland "*Joe*," "*Silomo*"
>> Must envious feel of your new title;
> Which for a lot of party "rot"—In "calling names"—should
> prove requital.
> *Khama* & Co., O Chieftain *Joe!*
>> Ingenious seem in nomenclature.
> Which Temperance cranks move to warm thanks
>> And angry-faddists to good nature.
> Sir *Wilfrid* thinks you're down on drinks,
>> And *Lawson* laudeth anybody.
> Who givest tongue against tyrant Bung,
>> So gives three cheers for *Moatlhodi*.
> The angry Rad, who thought it sad
>> That Joe should turn a Tory-toady
> Thinks if you bar strong drink and war,
>> You are in sooth a *Moatlhodi*.

The might and sleight to "put things right"
   Is what we want, *Joe,* in our leaders.
If that's your game, in fact as name,
   From your side you'll find few seceders.
Then *Khama's* praise in sounding lays
   We'll echo with exuberance hearty;
Each patriot who know's what what
   Must join the Moatlhodi Party!

An encore from *Times of Africa* was reprinted in the *Times* and in *Punch,* November 28, 1895.

Encore "Moatlhodi!": a Ballad of South Africa

There were three black Bechuana men,
King *Khama, Sebele,* and *Batho-en*—Though far they'd
travelled, they fairly were gravelled
On seeing the Chief, *Jocham Berlen*

There had never appeared within their ken
Such a putter to rights as *Cham Berlen,*
"A fig for *Barnatos* and *Bamangwatos!*"
Said *Khama, Sebele, Bathoen.*

They journeyed to England and back agen,
This one to his kraal and that to his den,
And the third to his scanty remains of a shanty—They'd
seen, though, the Chief, *Jocham Berlen!*

They said "Let's make him a citizèn
of Umtiwayo, this *Cham Berlen*—A new blood-brother
to each and the other,"
Said *Khama, Sebele and Bathoen.*

What name for our country's new denizen?
Asked *Khama, Sebele* and *Bathoen;*
It was promptly bestowed, he was titled "*Moatlhod!*";
For He-Who-Rights-Things is *Cham Berlen.*

"*Moatlhodi*" they christened him there and then
No more to be known as *Cham Berlen;*
Their own novus homo to rank with *Silomo*
Have *Khama, Sebele,* and *Bathoen.*

Rider Haggard must look to the fame of his pen,
When *Khama, Sebele,* and *Bathoen*
Go stealing his thunder, and making us wonder
At names that they coin for *Joe Chamberlain.*

The English epilogue of Westminster School's Latin Play, Christmas 1895 was quoted in *South Africa*, December 21, 1895. The characters included SYRUS, mesmerist, modern magician, financier, etc.; SOSRATA, an American widow for sale; CANTHARA, a New Woman; SANNIO, a wine merchant; and DEMEA, a stern parent.

CANTHARA: Old England makes too little of our cause,
But Africa will give us freer laws.

SANNIO: I'll join with you; for niggers, wine make ready,
And soon grow rich, retailing spirits heady.

DEMEA: Are, them, the great chiefs naught to you, wine farmer,
Big Bathoen, huge Sebele, pious Khama?
Will you out there do what you didn't oughter?
Khama lets naught be sold but draughts of water.

NOTES

ABBREVIATIONS

BNA—S	Mafeking Secretariat series files, Botswana National Archives, Gaborone.
BNA—HC	Cape Town High Commissioner's office papers, Botswana National Archives, Gaborone.
BPP—C	British Parliamentary Papers (Command Papers or "Blue Books"), followed by command number of paper.
CO 417	Colonial Office correspondence with High Commissioner Cape Town, Public Record Office, London.
CO 879	Colonial Office confidential print Africa South ("White Books"), Public Record Office, London.
CWM/LMS Archives	Council for World Mission, London Missionary Society Archives, School of Oriental and African Studies Library, University of London.
LMS In	LMS in-Letters Africa South, CWM/LMS Archives.
LMS Mack	LMS John Mackenzie correspondence, 1890–99, Africa Personal Box 2, CWM/LMS Archives.
LMS Out	LMS out-Letters Africa South, CWM/LMS Archives.
LMS Will	LMS Willoughby "Papers Concerning Visit of Chiefs Khama, Sebele, and Bathoen," Africa Odds Box 29, CWM/LMS Archives.
WCW	Papers of Prof. William Charles Willoughby, Selly Oak (Theological) Colleges Library, Selly Oak, Birmingham, England.

INTRODUCTION

1. *Bristol Mercury*, 21 Sept. 1995; *Westminster Gazette*, 23 Sept. 1895.

2. Boswell's father quoted in Hesketh Pearson, *The Lives of the Wits* (London: Heinemann, 1962), 64. For Willoughby as *enragé* see Fairfield minute of 15 Aug. 1895 in CO 417/145. On missionaries among the Tswana see John L. Comaroff and Jean Comaroff, *Of Revelation and Revolution: Christianity, Colonialism, and Consciousness in South Africa* (Chicago: University of Chicago Press, 1991), vol. 1, chap. 6, "Conversion and Conversation," and chap. 7, "Secular Power, Sacred Authority."

3. *Morning Advertiser* and *Westminster Gazette*—both 23 Sept. 1895.

4. John Barrow, *A Voyage to Cochin China in the Years 1792 and 1793 . . . To which is attached an account of a journey, made in the years 1801 and 1802, to the residence of the chief of the Booshuana Nation* (London: T. Cadell and W. Davies, 1806). See also *Edinburgh Review*, July 1804, 443–579 on the "superior civilization in the *interior* of this unhappy continent" revealed by the chapter on the 1801–2 Trüter and Somerville expedition to the "Booshuana" in Barrow's *An Account of Travels in the Interior of South Africa*, vol. 2 (1804). For Baron Münchausen see Stephen Gray, *South African Literature* (Johannesburg: Ravan Press, 1979).

5. *African Critic*, 23 Sept. 1895.

6. *Westminster Gazette*, 23 Sept. 1895.

7. *Daily Chronicle*, 9 Sept. 1895.

8. *Times*, 28 Sept. 1895.

9. *British Weekly*, 21 Nov. 1895, 71.

10. *British Weekly*, 28 Sept. 1895.

CHAPTER ONE

1. Peter J. Cain and Anthony G. Hopkins, *British Imperialism: Innovation and Expansion, 1688–1914* (London: Longman, 1993), 2:105–446; Eric Hobsbawm, *The Making of Modern English Society*, vol. 2: *1750 to the Present: Industry and Empire* (Harmondsworth, Middlesex: Penguin, 1968). See also Keith Burgess, "Did the Late Victorian Economy Fail?" in *Later Victorian Britain, 1867–1900*, ed. T. R. Gourvish and Alan O'Day (Basingstoke, Hampshire: Macmillan Education, 1988), 251–70.

2. Colin Clark, *The Conditions of Economic Progress*, 2d ed. (London: Macmillan, 1957).

3. See Elizabeth Longford, *Jameson's Raid: The Prelude to the Boer War*, 2d ed. (London: Granada/Panther, 1982), quoting Churchill on title page and 25.

4. *Review of Reviews* 12 (1895): 425 and 9 (1894): 39; *South Africa* 26 (1894): 191 and 27 (1895): 267; *Illustrated London News* 108 (1896): 260.

5. *Review of Reviews* 9 (1894): 341, 345, 395, and 399.

6. *Cape Argus Home Edition*, 1 Feb. 1896, 4.

7. *Review of Reviews* 12 (1895): 226–27.

8. *Review of Reviews* 9 (1894): 399; Jacqueline Laks Gorman, "Historical Anniversaries," in *World Almanac and Book of Facts, 1995* (Morwah, N.J.: Funk and Wagnalls; New York: St. Martin's Press, 1994), 105; *Illustrated London News* 106 (1895): 127.

9. *Review of Reviews* 9 (1894): 399.

10. Cain and Hopkins, *British Imperialism*, 141–60.

11. See Ian R. Phimister, "Rhodes, Rhodesia, and the Rand," *Journal of Southern African Studies* 1, no. 1 (1974): 74–90 re John Hays Hammond report of October 1894 that there was no "Second Rand" in Rhodesia.

12. On *Kaffir* as an insulting word see *South Africa* 28 (1895): 161.

13. *Review of Reviews* 12 (1895): 318; *South Africa* 26 (1895): 391 and 415.

14. *South Africa* 28 (1895): 704; *Cape Times*, 17 Jan. 1895.

15. *South Africa* 26 (1895): 344, 27 (1895): 404–6, 28 (1895): 719.

16. *South Africa* 26 (1895): 174, 400; 27 (1895): 20, 80, 136, 304; 28 (1895): 410.

17. *Harper's Monday Magazine,* quoted in *Review of Reviews* 12 (1895): 319.

18. *Illustrated London News,* 106 (1895): 747.

19. *Review of Reviews* 12 (1895): 364; *Illustrated London News* 106 (1895): 299.

20. *Cape Argus Home Edition*, 16 Nov. 1995, 12; Ben Weinrab and Christopher Hibbert, eds., *The London Encyclopaedia* (London: Macmillan, 1987), 306; Stanley Jackson, *The Great Barnato* (London: Heinemann, 1970), 100.

21. *Illustrated London News* 106 (1895): 99; *Cape Argus Home Edition*, 2 Nov. 1895, 3; *Cape Times Weekly Edition / Home Budget* 5 (28 Sept. 1895): 1, and 6 (6 Oct. 1895): 6.

22. *Cape Times Weekly Edition / Home Budget* 3 (14 Sept. 1895): 21; *Illustrated London News* 107 (1895): 355, 357, 573, 595; *Review of Reviews* 12 (1895): 182, 367–74.

23. The cover picture of John M. Mackenzie, ed., *Popular Imperialism and the Military, 1850–1950* (Manchester: Manchester University Press; New York: St. Martin's Press, 1992), is a tableau from *Cheer, Boys, Cheer*.

24. *Illustrated London News* 106 (1895): 667 and 107 (1895): 571; *South Africa* 28 (1895): 36, 329, 339, 498.

25. *World Almanac 1995*, 105; *South Africa* 28 (1895): 325; *Review of Reviews* 12 (1895): 430; *Illustrated London News* 107 (1895): 549; *Cape Argus,* 28 Oct. 1895.

26. *Review of Reviews* 12 (1895): 319 and 9 (1894): 221.

27. *Cape Argus Home Edition*, 29 June 1895, 15; *Illustrated London News* 106 (1895): 19; *South Africa* 25 (1895): 700.

28. *Illustrated London News* 106 (1895): 703; *South Africa* 26 (1895): 150.

29. John A. Hobson, *The Psychology of Jingoism* (London: Grant Richards, 1901), esp. 3–11, 138.

30. *Cape Argus Home Edition*, 19 Oct. 1895, 2 (Clark's Embrocation); *Illustrated London News* 107 (1895): 28 and 108 (1896): 4, supplement.

31. Richard Ellmann, *Oscar Wilde* (London: Hamish Hamilton, 1987); *Cape Argus Home Edition*, 28 Sept. 1895, 13; *Cape Times Weekly Edition / Home Budget* 3 (14 Sept. 1895): 11.

32. *Cape Times Weekly Edition*, 25 Sept. 1895, 18; *Illustrated London News* 106 (1895): 102, 638, and 670; *Review of Reviews* 12 (1895): 145, 201, 231, and 235; *Cape Times Weekly Edition / Home Budget* 3 (14 Sept. 1895): 17.

33. R. C. K. Ensor, *England, 1870–1914*, vol. 15 of *Oxford History of England* (Oxford: Clarendon Press, 1936), 214; *Review of Reviews* 12 (1895): 393–94.

34. *Illustrated London News* 106 (1895): 318, 406, and 471; *Cape Argus Home Edition*, 26 Oct. 1895, 5; Elizabeth Longford, *Victoria R. I.* (London: Weidenfeld and Nicolson, 1964), 513; Kevin Shillington personal communication.

35. J. L. Garvin, *The Life of Chamberlain* (London: Macmillan, 1934), 1 : 490–93.

36. Peter T. Marsh, *Joseph Chamberlain: Entrepreneur in Politics* (New Haven, Conn.: Yale University Press, 1994), 185, 202, 226, 250, and 304–5; Longford, *Victoria R. I.,* 491.

37. Marsh, *Joseph Chamberlain,* 288–92, 312, and 319.

38. Longford, *Victoria R. I.,* 523.

39. Apollon Davidson, *Cecil Rhodes and His Time* (Moscow: Progress Publishers, 1988); Robert I. Rotberg, with Miles F. Shore, *The Founder: Cecil Rhodes and the Pursuit of Power* (New York: Oxford University Press, 1989).

40. *South Africa* 25 (1895): 32, 562, 684; Ellmann, *Oscar Wilde*, 405.

41. *South Africa* 25 (1895): 129, 132–34; Longford, *Victoria R. I.*, 65.

42. See Elizabeth Main, *Man of Mafeking: The Bechuanaland Years of Sir Hamilton Goold-Adams, 1884–1901* (Gaborone: Botswana Society, 1996), 238.

43. *South Africa* 27 (1895): 63, 79.

44. *Times*, 12 Aug. 1895, 10; Yvonne Kapp, *Eleanor Marx*, 2 vols. (New York: Academy Press, 1971); Anthony Sillery, *Founding a Protectorate: A History of Bechuanaland, 1885–1895* (The Hague: Mouton, 1965), 47–48; Marsh, *Joseph Chamberlain*, 227 and 312; *Cape Argus Home Edition*, 18 May 1895, 4; *Illustrated London News* 106 (1895): 319.

45. *South Africa* 25 (1895): 335, 349–50, 353–54, 371, 387, 444, and 641–44; 26 (1895): 370, 416–17, and 453; 27 (1895): 257, 273, 278, 295, 368, and 441–42.

46. *Review of Reviews* 12 (1895): 347; *Spectator*, 5 Oct. 1895.

47. *South Africa* 25 (1895): 191, 589–90; 26 (1895): 543.

48. *Morning Advertiser*, 7 Sept. 1895.

49. *Illustrated London News* 106 (1895): 253, 286, and 316; *South Africa* 26 (1895): 174, 630; 27 (1895): 66, 81, and 136.

CHAPTER TWO

1. John Augustus Ioan Agar-Hamilton, *The Native Policy of the Voortrekkers: An Essay in the History of the Interior of South Africa, 1836–1858* (Cape Town: Maskew Miller, 1928).

2. Sechele was described as "Livingstone's first (and only) convert to Christianity" in Isaac Schapera, "The Anthropologist's Approach to Ethnohistory," in *Historians in Tropical Africa: Proceedings of Leverhulme Inter-Collegiate History Conference—Salisbury, 1960*, ed. Terence Osborn Ranger (Salisbury, Southern Rhodesia: University College of Rhodesia and Nyasaland, 1962). See Schapera's Chatto and Windus (London, 1959–63) editions of Livingstone's southern African papers as listed in Tim Jeal, *Livingstone* (New York: Putnam, 1973), and I. Schapera, *David Livingstone: South African Papers, 1849–1853* (Cape Town: Van Riebeeck Society, 1974). See also Mackenzie on the "Christian soldier" in *Popular Imperialism*.

3. Daphne Trevor, "Public Opinion and the Acquisition of Bechuanaland and Rhodesia (1868–1896)," Ph.D. diss., London School of Economics and Political Science, 1936, 801.

4. Trevor, "Public Opinion," 630.

5. Trevor, "Public Opinion," 688 citing BPP—C 5918 (vol. 51 of 1890): dispatches nos. 15 and 28.

6. CO 879: Correspondence African (South), no. 439 (1892), 45ff.

7. Trevor, "Public Opinion, 883–84; *Manchester Guardian*, 15 Sept. 1893; *Times*, 5 Aug. 1893.

8. BPP—C 7383 (vol. 67 of 1894): dispatch no. 3.

9. CO 879: Correspondence African (South), no. 484 (1895), 76; Sillery, *Founding a Protectorate*, 215.

10. Neil Parsons, "Prelude to Difaqane in the Interior of Southern Africa, c. 1600–c. 1822," in *The Mfecane Aftermath*, ed. C. Hamilton (Johannesburg: Witwatersrand University Press, 1995), 347n. Derivation from Goa, the home of many Portuguese traders, has also been suggested by N. J. van Warmelo, "European and Other Influences in Sotho," *Bantu Studies* 3 (1927): 405–21, rpt. in *Foundations in Southern African Linguistics*, comp. Robert K. Herbert, African Studies Reprint series, no. 1 (Johannesburg: Witwatersrand University Press, 1993), 243.

11. James Walton, "Early Bafokeng Settlement in South Africa," *African Studies* 15 (1956): 38; P. W. Laidler, "The Archaeology of Certain Prehistoric Settlements in the Heilbron Area," *Transactions of the Royal Society of South Africa* 23, pt. 1 (1935): 54.

12. *St James's Gazette*, 7 Sept. 1895.

13. Frederick Jeffress Ramsay, "The Rise and Fall of the Bakwena Dynasty of South-Central Botswana, 1820–1940," Ph.D. diss., Boston University, 1991, 53–54.

14. Ramsay, "Rise and Fall," 64–89; Neil Parsons, "The Economic History of Khama's Country in Southern Africa," *African Social Research* 18 (1974): 643–73.

15. CWM/LMS Archives LMS Reports Africa South, Box 2 (1881–97): Howard Williams, "Molepolole 1890."

16. See note 2 above and Jackson Mutero Chirenje, *A History of Northern Botswana, 1850–1910* (Cranbury, N.J.: Associated University Presses, 1977).

17. Ramsay, "Rise and Fall," 90–168.

18. Ramsay, "Rise and Fall," 168–74.

19. LMS In: W. Ashton (Barkly West) to LMS, 5 Dec. 1895.

20. Edwin Lloyd, *Three Great African Chiefs (Khâmé, Sebelé and Bathoeng)* (London: T. Fisher Unwin, 1895).

21. Sillery, *Founding a Protectorate*, 192 and 195.

22. Sillery, *Founding a Protectorate*, 195.

23. *St James's Gazette*, 7 Sept. 1895.

24. Lloyd, *Three Great African Chiefs*, 150–54.

25. LMS In: John Brown (Taung) to LMS, 1 Jan. and 29 Feb. 1896.

26. James Theodore Bent, "Among the chiefs of Bechuanaland," *Fortnightly Review*, n.s. 31 (May 1892): 642–54; E. T. Gilliat, *Heroes of Modern Africa: True Stories of the Intrepid Bravery and Stirring Adventures of the Pioneers, Explorers, and Founders* (London: Seeley, 1911), 328–29.

27. Lloyd, *Three Great African Chiefs*, 174–75; Howard Williams, "The Passing of Bathoen Gaseitsiwe," *Chronicle of the London Missionary Society*, n.s. 18 (1910): 153–54.

28. *St James's Gazette*, 7 Sept. 1895.

29. John Mackenzie, *Ten Years North of the Orange River: a Story of Everyday Life and Work among the South African Tribes from 1859 to 1869* (Edinburgh: Edmonton and Douglas, 1871); Jackson Mutero Chirenje, *Chief Kgama and His Times: The Story of a Southern African Ruler* (London: Rex Collings, 1978); Parsons, "Economic History"; Neil Parsons, *The Word of Khama* (Lusaka: Historical Association of Zambia, 1972).

30. Anthony Sillery, *The Bechuanaland Protectorate* (Cape Town: Oxford University Press, 1952), 56 and 250; Watkin W. Williams, *The Life of General Sir Charles Warren* (Oxford: Basil Blackwell, 1941)—quoting Warren to E. A. Maund, E. A. Maund Papers, William Cullen Library, University of Witwatersrand, Johannesburg, copies in Royal Commonwealth Society Library, University of Cambridge.

31. Sillery, *Founding a Protectorate*, 40–44; LMS In: J. D. Hepburn (Palapye) to LMS, 24 Oct. 1890.

32. Trevor, "Public Opinion," 584 (Rider Haggard's *King Solomon's Mines* was first published in November 1885).

33. *Bradford Observer*, 17 Sept. 1895; James Theodore Bent, *The Ruined Cities of Mashonaland* (London: Longman, Green, 1892), 27.

34. William Harvey Brown, *On the South African Frontier: the Adventures and Observations of an American in Mashonaland and Matabeleland* (London: Sampson, Low, Marston, 1899), 90–92.

35. Sillery, *Founding a Protectorate*, 62 and 72, citing CO 417/85, CO 417/89, and CO 417/90.

36. Brown, *South African Frontier*, 62 and 90–92; W. T. Stead, "Character sketch: Khama, Chief of the Bamangwato," *Review of Reviews* 12 (1895): 312–15. See BPP—C 7290 (vol. 61 of 1893–94), 11, 42–43, and 86.

37. *Pall Mall Gazette*, 21 Oct. 1895; Trevor, "Public Opinion," 905, citing *Manchester Guardian*, 25 Sept. 1893; Elizabeth Pakenham [Longford], *Jameson's Raid* (London: Weidenfeld and Nicholson, 1960), 36 (no source cited); Hugh Marshall Hole, *The Passing of the Black Kings* (London: Philip Allan, 1932), 147 (citing BPP—C 1748 [vol. 60 of 1877]: Khama to Victoria) and 271–73.

38. Neil Parsons, "Khama III, the Bamangwato, and the British, with Special Reference to 1895–1923," Ph.D. diss., University of Edinburgh, 1973; Robert Unwin Moffat, *John Smith Moffat, C.M.G.: A Memoir by His Son* (London: John Murray, 1921)—citing J. S. Moffat letter, n.d.; Sillery, *Founding a Protectorate*, 211 and 214–45. For Fairfield's background see Brian L. Blakely, *The Colonial Office, 1868–1892* (Durham, N.C.: Duke University Press, 1972).

39. Quoted in Parsons, "Khama III."

CHAPTER THREE

1. Estelle Stead, *My Father* (London: Heinemann, 1913) 245; Sillery, *Founding a Protectorate*, 216 (Ripon to Rhodes, Nov. 1894).

2. Rotberg, *The Founder;* Lancelot Dudley Stafford Glass, *The Matabele War* (London: Longman, 1968); LMS Out: Thompson to Roger Price, 5 Jan. 1895. For Loch's attitude, see CO 879: dispatch no. 439 (Oct. 1892), 21.

3. *Cape Times*, 7, 10, 11 (interview with Khama), 14, 15 Jan. 1895; *Cape Argus*, 2, 5, 7, 10, and 12 (poem) Jan. 1895; LMS In: Willoughby to LMS, 18 Mar. 1895.

4. Vivian Bickford-Smith, *Ethnic Pride and Racial Prejudice in Victorian Cape Town: Group Identity and Social Practice, 1875–1902* (Cambridge: Cambridge University Press, 1995); *South Africa* 25 (1895): 513.

5. *Cape Times*, 14, 15, and 17 Jan. 1895; *Cape Argus*, 12 and 14 Jan. 1895; *South Africa* 25 (1895): 373, quoting *Western Morning News*.

6. LMS Out: Thompson to Mudie, 2 Feb. 1895; LMS In: Willoughby to LMS, 18 Mar. 1895.

7. CO 417/138: Loch to Ripon, 27 Feb. 1895, and CO 879: no. 484 (1895), 174; Sillery, *Founding a Protectorate*, 76; Sillery, *The Bechuanaland Protectorate*, 67 (misquoted in Jack Halpern, *South Africa's Hostages: Basutoland, Bechuanaland, and Swaziland* [Harmondsworth, Middlesex: Penguin, 1965], 90). For Robinson's previous career and dismissal see Kenneth O. Hall, *Imperial Proconsul: Sir Hercules Robinson and South Africa, 1881–1889* (Kingston, Ontario: Limestone Press, 1980).

8. LMS In: Beard to LMS, 21 Aug. 1895; *Times*, 1 July 1895; LMS Mack: Thompson to Mackenzie, 8 June 1895; Williams, *Life of Charles Warren*, 115.

9. Parsons, "Khama III"; Thomas Tlou, "Documents on Botswana History: How Rhodes Tried to Seize Ngamiland," *Botswana Notes and Records* 7 (1975): 61–65; Louis W. Truschel, "Accommodation under Imperial Rule: The Tswana of the Bechuanaland Protectorate, 1895–1910," Ph.D. diss., Northwestern University, 1971; CO 417/142 (correspondence re Ngamiland and Ghanzi).

10. *Times*, 3 May 1895, BPP—C 7932 (vol. 59 of 1896); Trevor, "Public Opinion," 954ff.; *South Africa* 26 (1895): 42.

11. *South Africa* 26 (1895): 562.

12. Marsh, *Joseph Chamberlain; Times*, 9 July 1895, 15; BPP—C 7932 (vol. 59 of 1896): Chamberlain to Robinson, 16 July 1895.

13. *Times*, 28 Sept. 1895 (Birmingham speech); Alfred Bertram, *The Kingdom of the Barotsi* (London: Fisher Unwin, 1899), 49; WCW, file 795, "The Bamañwato"; and BPP—C 7962 (vol. 59 of 1896) ("killed and eaten" petition); BNA—HC 182/2 (assaults on Bangwato north of BSA Company "customs line").

14. *Times*, 28 June, 12 July, and 1 Aug. 1895; LMS In: Beard to Thompson, 21 July 1895.

15. *Cape Times Weekly Edition*, 21 Aug. 1895, 2; LMS Mack: Thompson to Mackenzie, 20 July 1895; LMS Out: Thompson to Tiro, Morwe, etc., 27 July 1895.

16. CO 417/142: minute for Fairfield, 26 Aug. 1895 (dispatch no. 14966/95); *Daily Chronicle*, 9 Sept. 1895.

17. CO 417/142: enclosure in BSA Co. to Imperial Secretary, 9 Aug. 1895.

18. LMS Mack: Thompson to Mackenzie, 8 June and 20 July 1895.

19. *Times*, 12 July 1895; *The History of "The Times,"* vol. 3: *The Twentieth Century Test, 1884–1912* (London: "The Times" Office, 1947), 167–69; LMS In: Beard to LMS, 21 Aug. 1895; *Times*, 13 July 1895, 16; *Times*, 19 July 1895, 15.

20. LMS Will: H. Williams (Molepolole) to Willoughby (Palapye), telegram 29 July 1895; BPP—C 7962 (vol. 59 of 1896): petitions of Khama, Sebele, Bathoen, Lentswe (Linchwe); CO 417/141: dispatches nos. 396 and 397; CO 417/142: dispatches nos. 417 and 430; Sillery, *Founding a Protectorate*, 217; BPP—C 7962 (vol. 59 of 1896): dispatch no. 10.

21. CO 417/142: high commissioner to Colonial Office, 7 Aug. 1896; Lloyd, *Three Great African Chiefs*, 135; LMS Will: Willoughby (Palla Camp?) to Mrs. Willoughby (Palapye), n.d.

22. LMS Will: T. B. Shaw (Palapye) to Willoughby, 4 Aug. 1895.

23. CO 417/142: high commissioner to Colonial Office, 7 Aug. 1895 encl. telegrams Friday, 3 Aug. 5:30 P.M.; Saturday, 11:00 A.M.; Sunday morning; Sunday, 4:00 P.M.; Monday, 2:37 P.M. See also C. 7962 (vol. 59 of 1896).

24. Longford, *Jameson's Raid*, 12.

25. *Times*, 12 Aug. 1895, 5.

26. CO 417/142: dispatch no. 14126/95; Robert V. Rhodes James, *Rosebery: A Biography of Archibald Philip, 5th Earl of Rosebery*, 2d ed. (London: Reader's Union, 1964), 495.

27. CO 417/142: dispatch no. 14966/95, enclosure 15; Isaac Schapera to author, personal communication, 4 April 1967.

28. *Chronicle of the London Missionary Society*, Sept. 1895, 248; LMS In: H. Williams to Thompson, 30 Aug. and 20 Sept. 1895.

29. *News from Afar*, Oct. 1895, 147. See also LMS Out: Thompson to H. Williams, 22 Dec. 1895.

30. William Charles Willoughby, *Native Life on the Transvaal Border* (London: Simpkin, Marshall, Hamilton, Kent and Co., 1900), 180.

31. LMS Will: Robert Appelbe (Wesleyan parsonage, Mafeking) to Willoughby, 15 Aug. 1895; Gerrans (Mafeking) to Willoughby, 16 Aug. 1895; *Times*, 13 Aug. 1895, 5; BPP—C 7932 (vol. 59 of 1896): high commissioner to Colonial Office, 27 Aug. 1895.

32. LMS Will: stationmaster Vryburg to stationmaster Mafeking, 16 Aug. 1895.

33. LMS Will: Willoughby (at Cape Town hotel) to Appelbe (Mafeking), two draft telegrams, n.d., Appelbe (Mafeking) to Willoughby (Government House, Cape Town), telegrams 20 and 21 Aug. 1895; CO 417/142: dispatch no. 16334/95.

34. LMS In: Mudie to Thompson, 20 Aug. and 11 Dec. 1895; BPP—C. 7692 (vol. 59 of 1896): Robinson to Chamberlain, 21 Aug. 1895; LMS In: Beard to Thomp-

son, 21 Aug. 1895, Mudie to Thompson, 19 [20?] Aug. 1895; LMS Will: Khama draft letter (in Willoughby's handwriting) to Sekgoma Khama, n.d.

35. *African Critic* (London), 21 Sept. 1895.

36. LMS In: Beard to LMS, 21 Aug. 1895; CO 417/145: minute by Fairfield, 15 Aug. 1895; Pakenham, *Jameson's Raid*, 36; Sillery, *Founding a Protectorate*, 218.

37. *Times*, 19 and 21 Aug. 1895, 8.

38. *Cape Times*, 21 Aug. 1895; *Manchester Guardian*, 16 Aug. 1895; *Cape Times Weekly Edition*, 28 Aug. 1895, 6-8; Richard Rive and Russell Martin, eds., *Olive Schreiner Letters, 1871-99* (Cape Town: David Philip, 1987), 255-56.

CHAPTER FOUR

1. H. W. Lucy, *The Log of the Tantallon Castle* (London: Sampson, Low, Marston, 1896).

2. Leetile Disang Raditladi, "The Destiny of Seretse Khama, Royal Head of the Bamangwato People," photocopy typescript, c. 1955, Michael Crowder Papers, Institute of Commonwealth Studies, University of London; Capt. R. C. Robinson in *Outward Bound*, April 1923, 484-86; *Westminster Gazette*, 23 Sept. 1895.

3. LMS Will: Mosely to Khama, telegram, 2 Sept. 1895; Singleton (Brighton) to Willoughby, telegram, 2 Sept. 1895; *Times*, 7 Sept. 1895, 7; *Western Morning News*, 7 Sept. 1895; *Daily Chronicle*, 7 Sept. 1895.

4. WCW, file 54, "Expenses of Khama, Sebele, and Bathoen during the trip to England, 1895" booklet; *Western Morning News*, 7 Sept. 1895.

5. *Times*, 6 Sept 1895 (parliamentary report).

6. *Review of Reviews* 12 (1895): 298; *Times*, 4 Sept 1895, 12; *Bristol Mercury*, 10 Sept. 1895; LMS Out: Thompson to Mackenzie, 5 Oct. 1895; Åke Holmberg, *African Tribes and European Agencies: Colonialism and Humanitarianism in British South and East Africa* (Göteborg, Sweden: Akademiförlaget, 1965), 143-44.

7. *St James's Gazette*, 7 Sept. 1895.

8. Weinrab and Hibbert, *The London Encyclopaedia*, 74; LMS Will: Willoughby (South Place Hotel) to H. J. Wilson (Colonial Office), 10 Sept. 1895; *Manchester Courier*, 17 Sept. 1895; LMS Will: Willoughby to Chamberlain, draft letter, 6 Sept. 1895.

9. WCW, file 54, "Expenses" booklet.

10. *Daily News*, 9 Sept. 1895, also reported in *Yorkshire Herald*, 10 Sept. 1895; *Leicester Post*, 10 Sept. 1895; *News from Afar*, Dec. 1895, 185.

11. *Daily Chronicle*, 9 Sept. 1895; *Leicester Post*, 10 Sept. 1895; *Nottingham Express*, 11 Sept. 1895.

12. Weinrab and Hibbert, *The London Encyclopaedia;* Felix Barker and Peter Jackson, *London: 2000 Years* (London: Papermac, 1983).

13. Madame Tussaud's Wax-Works, 1894-95, catalog of exhibits (courtesy of Madame Tussaud's archives); Barker and Jackson, *London*, 286-87.

14. *Christian World*, 12 Sept. 1895.

15. *Chronicle of the London Missionary Society*, Oct. 1895.

16. *Chronicle of the London Missionary Society*, Oct. 1895, appendix 3; LMS Mack: Thompson to Mackenzie, 5 Oct. 1895; LMS Out: Thompson to Mrs. Hepburn, 9 Nov. 1895; James Davidson Hepburn, *Twenty Years in Khama's Country*, ed. C. H. Lyall (London: Hodder and Stoughton, 1895).

17. *Daily Graphic*, 7 Sept. 1895; *Bradford Observer*, 17 Sept. 1895; *Spectator*, 21 Sept. 1895.

18. *Review of Reviews* 12 (1895): 302-17; *Times*, 12 Sept. 1895; *Globe*, 11 Sept. 1895;

LMS In: Mackenzie to Thompson, 6 Jan. 1896; Albert Spicer in *Outward Bound*, April 1923, 486; LMS Will: Wilson to Willoughby, 10 Sept. 1895; Willoughby to Wilson, 10 Sept. 1895.

19. *East Anglian Daily Times, Daily Telegraph, Methodist Recorder, Morning Advertiser*—all 12 Sept. 1895; *England the Union*, 14 Sept. 1895.

20. *Outward Bound*, April 1923, 484–86 ("salted": inoculated by dousing in fluid from diseased cow's lungs); LMS Will: H. A. Bryden to Khama, 2 Sept. 1895; Sir George Baden-Powell to Khama, 7, 8, 9, and n.d. Sept. 1895.

CHAPTER FIVE

1. *St James's Gazette, Daily Telegraph, African Review, Modern Society, Nottingham Guardian, Western Morning News*—all 7 Sept. 1895.

2. *St James's Gazette, Lincolnshire Echo, Morning Post, Daily News*—all 9 Sept. 1895.

3. *Dundee Advertiser, Bristol Times, Newcastle Leader, Pall Mall Gazette*—all 10 Sept. 1895.

4. *Aberdeen Free Press, Times* (first leader)—both 11 Sept. 1895; *Daily Chronicle*, 9 Sept. 1895; *Realm*, 12 Sept. 1895.

5. *Times, Morning Post, Manchester Guardian, Realm, Globe*—all 12 Sept. 1895; *Yorkshire Post*, 13 Sept. 1895; *Punch*, 21 Sept. 1895, 139.

6. *Christian, Christian Commonwealth, Christian Globe, Woman's Signal*—all 12 Sept. 1895; *Rock*, 13 Sept. 1895.

7. *England and the Union, African Critic*—both 14 Sept. 1895; *Cape Argus Home Edition*, 14 Sept. 1895; *Illustrated London News* 107 (21 Sept. 1895). For German press see *African Critic*, 14 Sept. 1895, *Cape Times Weekly Edition*, 18 Sept. 1895, and *Liverpool Mercury*, 23 Sept. 1895. See also Jean van der Poel, *The Jameson Raid* (London: Oxford University Press, 1951), 52ff.

8. *Cape Times Weekly Edition / Home Budget, 14 Sept. 1895; South Africa* 27, no. 350 (14 Sept. 1895): 610–11. For Mathers see R. S. Roberts's introduction to *Zambesia, England's El Dorado in Africa*, comp. E. P. Mathers (London: King, Sell and Railton; Cape Town: Juta, 1891), rpt. Rhodesiana Reprint Library, Silver Series, vol. 18 (Bulawayo: Books of Rhodesia, 1977).

9. *South Africa* 27, no. 350 (14 Sept. 1895); *African Review*, 21 Sept. 1895; *Globe*, 13 Sept. 1895 (dated 12 Sept. in Bathoen's clippings); *Times*, 13 Sept. 1895, 8.

10. *Birmingham Post* and *Birmingham Gazette*, 21 Sept. 1895; *England and the Union*, 14 Sept. 1895; *African Review*, 21 Sept. 1895; George Baden-Powell, *Protection and Bad Times, with Special Reference to the Political Economy of English Colonization* (London: Trübner and Co., 1879); LMS Will: Sir G. Baden-Powell (Grand Hotel, Eastbourne) to Khama, telegrams, 7 and 9 Sept. 1895; Sir G. Baden-Powell to His Highness the Chief Khama, 8 Sept. 1895; Sir G. Baden-Powell to Willoughby, 8 Sept. 1895; Khama to Sir G. Baden-Powell, telegram, n.d.

11. *Times*, 13 Sept. 1895 (according to *African Critic*, 14 Sept. 1895, dinner was on Tuesday); Williams, *Life of Charles Warren* (referring to *Times* letter of 11 Nov. 1885); "Flora" (Mrs. Fenwick Miller) "Our interview with King Khama," *Echo*, 18 Sept. 1895; *Times*, 19 and 20 Aug. 1895; Robert S. S. Baden-Powell in *Outward Bound*, April 1923, 486.

12. *South Africa* 27, no. 350 (14 Sept. 1895); *Christian World*, 12 Sept. 1895 (Bathoen's famous comment).

13. *Cape Times Weekly Edition / Home Budget 5 (28 Sept. 1895): 2; William Charles Willoughby, Race Problems in the New Africa* (Oxford: Clarendon Press, 1923).

14. *Echo*, 18 Sept. 1895.

15. *South Africa* 27, no. 350 (14 Sept. 1895); *Illustrated London News* 107 (21 Sept. 1895): 366 ("Three Kings of Africa: The mission of Khama," by L.M.).

CHAPTER SIX

1. *Globe* and *Sussex Daily News*—both 16 Sept. 1895; *African Critic*, 21 Sept. 1895; *South Africa* 27, no. 351 (21 Sept. 1895); *Brighton Herald*, dated 21 Sept. 1895 (23 Sept. 1895); *Westminster Gazette*, 23 Sept. 1895; *Eastbourne Gazette*, 9 Oct. 1895; *Brighton Gazette*, 10 Oct. 1895.

2. *African Critic* and *England and the Union*—both 14 Sept. 1895; "Flora" in *Echo*, 18 Sept. 1895, picked up in *Christian World*, 21 Sept. 1895.

3. *Bristol Mercury*, 10 and 14 Sept. 1895; *Western (Daily) Press*, 18 and 20 Sept. 1895; *Times*, 19 Sept. 1895; *Bristol Times*, 20 Sept. 1895; *African Review* and *Bristol Mercury*—both 21 Sept. 1895; *Westminster Gazette* and *Western Mercury*—both 23 Sept. 1895; *African Critic*, 23 and 28 Sept. 1895; *Chronicle of the London Missionary Society*, Nov. 1895, 316.

4. *Daily Chronicle* and *Times*—both 19 Sept. 1895; *Reading Mercury*, 20 Sept. 1895; *African Review*, 21 Sept. 1895; *Westminster Gazette* and London *Evening News*—both 23 Sept. 1895.

5. *Illustrated London News* 106 (1 June 1895): 635 and 677; *South Africa* 26, no. 330 (27 April 1895): 191, no. 334 (25 May 1895): 389, no. 337 (15 June 1895): 543.

6. *Times*, 21 Sept. 1895; *Nottingham Guardian*, 22 Sept. 1895; *African Critic, Court Journal*, and *Devon (Daily) Gazette*—all 28 Sept. 1895; *South Africa* 27, no. 352 (28 Sept. 1895).

7. *Daily Chronicle*, 9 Sept. 1895; "Flora" in *Echo*, 18 Sept. 1895; *Leeds Mercury*, 19 Sept. 1895; *African Critic*, 21 Sept. 1895; *South Africa* 27, no. 351 (21 Sept. 1895); "Africa on England: how we impress the Bechuana chiefs," *Westminster Gazette*, 23 Sept. 1895—reprinted in *Westminster Budget*, 27 Sept. 1895—reported in London *Evening News*, 23 Sept. 1895; *Sheffield Independent*, 24 Sept. 1895; *Licensing World*, 27 Sept. 1895.

8. *Bradford Observer*, 19 Sept. 1895; *Belfast Witness*, 20 Sept. 1895; *Levant Herald, Naval and Military Review*, and *West Australian Review*—all 21 Sept. 1895; *Liverpool Mercury*, 21 Sept. 1895; "Our Good Mr. Willoughby," *African Critic*, 21 Sept. 1895; [J.M.], "Three Kings of Africa," *Illustrated London News* 107 (21 Sept. 1895): 366; "'Bung' in Africa," *Punch*, 21 Sept. 1895; London *Evening News, Lichfield Mercury*, and *Dundee Courier*—all 23 Sept. 1895; *New York Tribune*, 29 Sept. 1895.

9. *Daily News*, 21 Sept. 1895; *Daily Chronicle, Daily News*, and *Daily Telegraph*—all 23 Sept. 1895; *British Weekly*, 26 Sept. 1895, 356; *Times*, 26 Sept. 1895, 8; *Land and Water* and *St James's Gazette*—both 28 Sept. 1895; *Chronicle of the London Missionary Society*, Nov. 1895, 282; *News from Afar*, Dec. 1895, 178; For Chautauqua see, for example, Ivor H. Evans, comp., *Brewer's Dictionary of Phrase and Fable* (London: Cassell, 1981), 224.

10. *Daily Chronicle, Daily Graphic, Daily News, Daily Telegraph, Manchester Guardian, Morning Leader, Pall Mall Gazette, Sun*—all 24 Sept. 1895.

CHAPTER SEVEN

1. *St James's Gazette*, 28 Sept. 1895.

2. LMS Will: chiefs to Sir Robert Meade, draft, 24 Sept. 1895; fair copy in CO 417/158, printed in CO 879, no. 498 (1896); BPP—C 7962 (vol. 59 of 1896), "Cor-

respondence relative to the visit to this country of the chiefs Khama, Sebele and Bathoen."

3. *Bradford Observer* and *Leicester Daily Post*—both 24 Sept. 1895; *Times*, 25 Sept. 1895; *Birmingham Argus*, 26 Sept. 1895; *Northampton Mercury* and *Wellingborough Post*— both 27 Sept. 1895; *African Review*, 28 Sept. 1895; *South Africa* 27, no. 352 (28 Sept. 1895).

4. *Times*, 25 Sept. 1895.

5. *Leicester Daily Post*, 20, 24, 25, and 26 Sept. 1895; *South Africa* 27, no. 352 (28 Sept. 1895).

6. *Leicester Daily Post*, 26 Sept. 1895; personal communication to author from surviving eyewitness, 1972. See figures 20–23, courtesy of Mr. David North of Enderby, grandnephew of Alice Young.

7. *Leicester Daily Post*, 26 Sept. 1895; *Times*, 25 Sept. 1895; LMS Will: H. Beckwith (hon. sec. Leicester Temperance Society) to Willoughby, 25 Sept. 1895 with enclosure.

8. Editorial in *Leicester Daily Post*, 26 Sept. 1895.

Chapter Eight

1. *Birmingham Mail*, 20, 23, 26, and 27 Sept. 1895; *Birmingham Argus*, 26 Sept. 1895; *Birmingham Gazette* and *Birmingham Post*, 21, 27, and 28 Sept. 1895. On "municipal socialism," see Chamberlain and Birmingham in G. D. H. Cole and Raymond Postgate, *The Common People, 1746–1946* (London: Methuen, 1948), 408.

2. *Birmingham Argus*, 27 and 28 Sept. 1895; *Birmingham Gazette*, 25 and 27 Sept. 1895; *Birmingham Mail*, 26 and 27 Sept. 1895; *St James's Gazette*, 28 Sept. 1895; *Times*, 27, 28, and 30 Sept. 1895; *African Review*, 28 Sept. 1895; *British Weekly*, 3 Oct. 1895, 373 and 378; LMS Will: Joseph Hood (chairman Birmingham Sunday School Union scholars festival, Town Hall) to His Majesty King Khama, 26 Sept. 1895.

3. *Birmingham Argus, Pall Mall Gazette, Westminster Gazette*—all 28 Sept. 1895.

4. Willoughby interview in *Daily Post* and *Birmingham Post*—both 27 Sept. 1895; *African Critic*, 28 Sept. 1895.

5. *African Review, Birmingham Gazette, Birmingham Post, Globe*, 28 Sept. 1895; *South Africa* 28, no. 353 (5 Oct. 1895); *British Weekly*, 10 Oct. 1895.

6. *Birmingham Mail*, 27 Sept. 1895.

7. *Birmingham Post*, 27 and 28 Sept. 1895; *Birmingham Gazette* and *Daily Telegraph*— all 28 Sept. 1895; *Illustrated London News*, 1896 re Bournville.

8. Marsh, *Joseph Chamberlain*, 139–41.

9. *Birmingham Gazette* and *Birmingham Post*—both 28 Sept. 1895.

10. *Birmingham Gazette* and *Birmingham Post*—both 30 Sept. 1895; *African Review*, 5 Oct. 1895; *South Africa* 28, no. 353 (5 Oct. 1895). Compare chap. 3, n. 4 for Cape Town fire brigade.

11. *Licensing World*, 27 Sept. 1895; *Illustrated London News* 107 (28 Sept. 1895): 390; *African Critic, Belfast Telegraph, Penny Illustrated Paper,* and *St James's Gazette*—all 28 Sept. 1895; *South Africa* 27, no. 352 (28 Sept. 1895); *Birmingham Gazette*, 30 Sept. 1895.

12. *Globe*, 24 Sept. 1895; *Cape Argus Home Edition*, 28 (24?) Sept. 1895.

Chapter Nine

1. *South Africa* vol. 27, no. 351 (21 Sept. 1895), 657; *African Review*, 5 Oct. 1895.

2. *Brighton Herald*, 6 Oct. 1895.

3. *Sussex Daily News*, 1 Oct. 1895.

4. *Daily Chronicle* and *Daily News*—both 1 Oct. 1895; *Pall Mall Gazette,* 2 Oct. 1895; *Vanity Fair,* 3 Oct. 1895.

5. *Sussex Daily News,* 3 Oct. 1895; *Brighton Herald,* 6 Oct. 1895.

6. *Daily Chronicle* and *Pall Mall Gazette*—both 2 Oct. 1895; *Christian World,* 3 Oct. 1895; *South Africa* 28, no. 353 (5 Oct. 1895); *Brighton Herald,* 6 Oct. 1895.

7. *Sussex Daily News,* 3 Oct. 1895.

8. *Brighton Gazette,* 10 Oct. 1895.

9. For Kiralfy see John M. Mackenzie, *Propaganda and Empire: The Manipulation of British Public Opinion, 1880–1960* (Manchester: Manchester University Press, 1984), 102–15 and 152; Peter Greenhalgh, *Ephemeral Vistas: The "Expositions Universelles," Great Exhibitions, and World's Fairs, 1851–1939* (Manchester: Manchester University Press, 1988), 40–44ff.

10. WCW, file 54, "Expenses" booklet.

11. *British Medical Journal,* 12 Oct. 1895; *Liverpool Courier; News from Afar,* Dec. 1895, 185; *Illustrated London News* 107 (16 Nov. 1895): 578; Willoughby, *Race Problems,* 189; *Westminster Gazette,* 23 Sept. 1895; *Manchester Guardian,* 17 Sept. 1895 (Khama's thrift); *Primitive Methodist* (quoting *Liverpool Echo*), 3 Oct. 1895.

12. WCW, file 54, "Expenses" booklet re press clippings fees, medical prescriptions (George Spiller, 3 Wigmore Street, prescription for Bathoen's reading spectacles; 8 Oct. 1895).

13. *Sussex Daily News,* 2 Oct. 1895; London *Sunday Times,* 6 Oct. 1895; *Court Journal,* 12 Oct. 1895. .

14. Stead, "Character Sketch"; *Penny Illustrated Paper,* 28 Sept. 1895; London *Sunday Times,* 6 Oct. 1895; *Dundee Advertiser,* 5 Oct. 1895. On Stead and Rhodes see Stead, *My Father.*

15. *Cape Argus Home Edition,* 19 Oct. 1895, 13; *South Africa* 28, no. 355 (19 Oct. 1895): 123 and 145–46; *Penny Illustrated Paper,* 28 Sept. 1895; *London Sunday Times,* 6 Oct. 1895.

CHAPTER TEN

1. *Manchester Guardian,* 10 Oct. 1895; *Cape Argus Home Edition,* 12 Oct. 1895, 5.

2. *Liverpool Courier, Liverpool Post, Macclesfield Chronicle, Manchester Guardian*—all 11 Oct. 1895.

3. *Liverpool Courier* and *Liverpool Post*—both 12 Oct. 1895.

4. *Liverpool Post,* 12 Oct. 1895; Isaac Schapera, ed., *Praise-Poems of Tswana Chiefs* (Oxford: Clarendon Press, 1965), 200–213.

5. *Times,* 27 Sept. 1895, 5; *Liverpool Post* and *Liverpool Mercury*—both 12 Oct. 1895.

6. *Liverpool Courier,* 14 and 15 Oct. 1895.

7. *Liverpool Courier,* 14 and 15 (letter) Oct. 1895. (Sebele would have known David Livingstone's eldest child, Robert, as a child. Robert died at the age of nineteen fighting for the North in the U. S. Civil War after the Battle of Gettysburg: W. G. Blaiker, *The Life of David Livingstone* (London, John Murray, 1910), 65 and 285; G. L. Guy, "Robert Moffat Livingstone," *Africana Notes and News* 18, no. 6 (June 1969): 228–37.

8. See Willoughby note on itineraries in WCW, file 54, "Expenses" booklet.

9. *Leeds Mercury,* 16 Oct. 1895.

10. *Bradford Observer,* 15 Oct. 1895.

11. *Bradford Observer,* 15 Oct. 1895; *Leeds Mercury* and *Yorkshire Post*—both 16 Oct. 1895.

12. LMS Will: Telegram Sekgoma (Palapye) to Kgosi Khama (at LMS, London), 14 Oct. 1895; *Cape Argus Home Edition*, 19 Oct. 1895.

13. *South Africa* 28, no. 354 (12 Oct. 1895): 69, and no. 355 (19 Oct. 1895): 145–46.

CHAPTER ELEVEN

1. Lloyd, *Three Great African Chiefs*. See also "Chats with missionaries: Rev. Edwin Lloyd," *News from Afar*, Oct. 1895, 147. Another work going through the press that managed to mention Khama's visit to England in a note in chapter 8 on Khama was Bishop G. W. H. Knight-Bruce's *Memories of Mashonaland* (London: Edward Arnold, 1895; rpt. Bulawayo: Books of Rhodesia, 1970), 182n.

2. *Christian World*, 12 Sept. 1895; *East Anglian Times*, 18, 19 Oct. 1895; LMS Will: J. A. Smith (sec. and man. dir. Eastern Counties Dairy Institute, Ltd., Gippeswyk Park, Ipswich) to Willoughby, 18 Oct. 1895 with enclosure; *East Anglian Times*, 18 and 19 Oct. 1895; *South Africa* 28, no. 358 (9 Nov. 1895): 317, quoting the *Sketch*.

3. *Cardiff News*, 19 Oct. 1895.

4. *Keighley News*, 19 Oct. 1895; *Bradford Observer*, 19 Oct. 1895.

5. For strong provincial reports for the chiefs see editorials and features in *Bradford Observer*, 19 Sept. and 20, 23 Oct. 1895; *Keighley News*, 19 Oct. 1895; *Stalybridge Reporter*, 19 Oct. 1895; *Manchester Guardian*, 22 Oct. 1895; *Western Morning News*, 9 Oct. 1899. See also London *Sunday Times*, 6 Oct. 1895; *Penny Illustrated Paper*, 28 Sept. 1895; *Court Journal*, 12 Oct. 1895; *South Africa* 28, no. 355 (19 Oct. 1895).

6. *Birmingham Argus*, 28 Sept. 1895.

7. *Manchester Guardian*, 22 Oct. 1895.

8. *Manchester Guardian* and *Manchester Courier*—both 12 Oct. 1895.

9. *Scotsman*, 23 Oct. 1895, 5, and 24 Oct. 1895, 5; *Edinburgh Dispatch*, 24 Oct. 1895.

10. *Glasgow Evening Times*, *Glasgow Evening News*—both 24 and 25 Oct. 1895; *Scotsman*, 25, 26 and 28 Oct. 1895.

11. *Glasgow Evening News*, 24 and 25 Oct. 1895; *British Weekly*, 31 October 1895, 27; *Glasgow Herald*, 23 and 25 October 1895; *Scotsman*, 25 Oct. 1895.

12. *Scotsman*, 28 Oct. 1895.

13. *Sheffield Independent*, 16 and 26 Oct. 1895.

14. *Cape Argus Home Edition*, 2 Nov. 1895, 11.

15. *South Africa* 28, no. 357 (2 Nov. 1895): 255.

16. *South Africa* 28, no. 359 (16 Nov. 1895): 351, quoting *Western Daily Mercury*.

17. Elsie Alfreda West (Finchley), "An Afternoon with Khama," n.d. (1922?), typescript, LMS Africa Odds Box 1, LMS Papers.

CHAPTER TWELVE

1. W. T. Stead, *The Scandal of the South Africa Committee: A Plain Narrative for Plain Men* (London: Review of Reviews Office, 1899), 19; BPP—C 7154 (vol. 61 of 1893–94), BPP—C 7154 (vol. 57 of 1894): 277.

2. Sillery, *Founding a Protectorate*, 221–26; Paul R. Maylam, *Rhodes, the Tswana, and the British: Colonialism, Collaboration, and Conflict in the Bechuanaland Protectorate, 1885–1899* (Westport, Conn.: Greenwood Press, 1980), 161–86.

3. CO 417/143: Chamberlain to Robinson, 12 Sept. 1895; CO 417/142: dispatch no. 14965/95. Cf. Sillery, *Founding a Protectorate*, 221.

4. Pakenham, *Jameson's Raid;* van der Poel, *The Jameson Raid*, 98; CO 417/142: dispatch no. 15277/95; *Times*, 26 Sept. 1895 (cable datelined Cape Town, 23 Sept.); BPP—C 7962 (vol. 59 of 1896): dispatches nos. 25, 41; Sillery, *Founding a Protectorate*, 221.

5. BPP—C 7962 (vol. 59 of 1896): 13, 14, 17; *Review of Reviews* 12 (1895): 303ff.; LMS Will: Chiefs Khama, Sebele, and Bathoen to Sir Robert Meade, draft, 24 Sept. 1895.

6. Sillery, *Founding a Protectorate*, 221.

7. LMS Will: Chiefs Khama, Sebele, and Bathoen to Sir Robert Meade, draft, 24 Sept. 1895; Willoughby (Heaton Mersey) to Rutherfoord Harris (BSA Co.), 9 Oct. 1895; Rutherfoord Harris to Willoughby (Armfield's Hotel), 11 Oct. 1895; Hole, *Passing of Black Kings*, 217.

8. CO 879: no. 498 (1895), 105; Sillery, *The Bechuanaland Protectorate*, 69; Pakenham, *Jameson's Raid*, 38ff.; CO 417/142: dispatch no. 17644/95; LMS Will: Meade to chiefs, 11 Oct. 1895; Meade to Willoughby, 18 Oct. 1895; Fairfield to Willoughby, 24 Oct. 1895; Stead, *Scandal*, 29 and 51–53 (cablegrams 2, 6, and 81 of parliamentary select committee inquiring into Jameson Raid, 1896).

9. "Mr. Rhodes' maximum offer" in LMS Will: Harris to Willoughby, 26 Oct. 1895 and CO 879: no. 498 (1895), 119–20. See Maylam, *Rhodes*, 168 (citing National Archives of Rhodesia: British South Africa Company London Office Papers LO 3/1/ 31, 176). Map (twenty inches by twenty inches) in LMS Will: Harris to Willoughby, 26 Oct. 1895.

10. LMS Will: Willoughby to Rutherfoord Harris, 9 Oct. 1895; Rutherfoord Harris to Willoughby (Stockport), telegram, 10 Oct. 1895; Rutherfoord Harris to Willoughby, 11 and 26 Oct. 1895.

11. Willoughby, *Native Life*, 9–11; LMS Will: Rutherfoord Harris to Willoughby, 26 Oct. 1895.

12. *Times*, 11, 17, and 21 (letters) Sept. 1895; *African Critic*, 16 Oct. 1895; *Times*, 21 Oct. 1895; *Saturday Review*, 26 Oct. 1895; *Chronicle of the London Missionary Society*, Oct. 1895; *Review of Reviews* 12 (1895): 303ff.; Stead, *Scandal*, 15 and 19; *St James's Gazette*, 21 Oct. 1895; *Times*, 21 Oct. 1895; *South Africa* 28, no. 355 (19 Oct. 1895); *Manchester Courier*, 23 Oct. 1895.

13. See chap. 11, nn. 7 and 8.

14. LMS Will: chiefs to Colonial Office, 4 Nov. 1895; no source given for "gooseberry" quote in Longford, *Jameson's Raid*, 44, or Pakenham, *Jameson's Raid*, 38.

15. LMS Will: Khama, etc. to Rutherfoord Harris, draft 26 Oct. 1895; LMS Memorials No. 6: Thompson to Meade, 1 Nov. 1895, LMS Papers; Stead, *Scandal*, 29, 51–53.

16. LMS Mack: Thompson to Mackenzie, 5 Oct. and 1 Nov. 1895; LMS Memorials no. 6: Thompson to Meade, 1 Nov. 1895.

17. *African Critic*, 21 and 28 Sept. 1895; *South Africa* 28, no. 355 (19 Oct. 1895).

18. *Birmingham Post*, 27 Sept. 1895; on 1894–95 annual estimate see CO 417/142: enclosure in dispatch 5 Aug. 1895.

19. LMS Will: Harris to Willoughby, 8 Oct. 1895; *African Critic*, 28 Sept. 1895; *South Africa* 28, no. 355 (19 Oct. 1895); LMS In: Mudie to Thompson, 20 Aug. 1895; LMS Will: Willoughby (Heaton Mersey) to Harris, 9 Oct. 1895; Harris to Willoughby (Armfield's Hotel), 11 Oct. 1895; *Birmingham Post*, 27 Sept. 1895.

20. LMS Will: Harris to Willoughby, 11 and 21 Oct. 1895; Maylam, *Rhodes*, 179 and 186n (quoting LMS Africa Personal 6: Willoughby to Singleton, 9 June 1897), 167 and 182n; LMS Will: Harris to Willoughby, 21 Oct. 1895.

CHAPTER THIRTEEN

1. Stead, *Scandal,* cablegram 2 (Harris to Rhodes, 2 Nov. 1899).

2. Westminster was, according to another famous black man who dined with him, "said to be, I believe, the richest man in England, if not in the world"—Booker T. Washington, *Up from Slavery* (New York: Bantam Books, 1959), 201; A. E. Blackburn, *Khama, King of the Bamangwato* (London: Native Races and Liquor Traffic United Committee, [c. 1926]; *Times,* 7 Aug. 1895, 7 (Chester protest meeting over Armenians): *Illustrated London News* 107 (9 Nov. 1895): 574; *South Africa* 28, no. 358 (9 Nov. 1895): 334.

3. *South Africa* 28, no. 358 (9 Nov. 1895): 334.

4. W. Douglas Mackenzie and Alfred Stead, *South Africa: Its History, Heroes, and Wars* (Chicago: Monarch; London: Marshall, 1900), 301.

5. *South Africa* 28, no. 358 (9 Nov. 1895): 334–35.

6. Hole, *Passing of Black Kings,* 279.

7. Mackenzie and Stead, *South Africa,* 301; Silas Modiri Molema, *The Bantu Past and Present* (Edinburgh: Green and Son, 1920), 269–70.

8. LMS Will: Fairfield to Willoughby, confidential, 6 Nov. 1895; Fairfield to chiefs, 7 Nov. 1895 (dispatch no. 19638/95).

9. Sillery, *The Bechuanaland Protectorate,* 71–75 (Fairfield to chiefs, 7 Nov. 1895); LMS Mack: Thompson to Mackenzie, 9 Nov. 1895.

10. *South Africa* 28, no. 358 (9 Nov. 1895): 288–99; Marsh, *Joseph Chamberlain,* 366 and 378–79.

11. LMS Will: Fairfield to chiefs, 7 Nov. 1895; *Cape Argus Home Edition,* 16 Nov. 1895, 16; *South Africa* 28, no. 359 (16 Nov. 1895): 390.

12. LMS Will: Khama, etc. to Chamberlain, draft, 11 Nov. 1895; BPP—C 7962 (vol. 59 of 1896): 20; LMS Will: chiefs to "Motlotlegi eo o Mogolo" Chamberlain, Setswana letter translated by Lloyd from Willoughby's English copy, 11 Nov. 1895; Lord (Frederick) Lugard, *The Dual Mandate in British Tropical Africa* (Edinburgh: Blackwood, 1922), 251.

13. *South Africa* 28, no. 359 (16 Nov. 1895).

14. Stead, *Scandal,* 29; *South Africa* 28, no. 360 (23 Nov. 1895): 429.

CHAPTER FOURTEEN

1. Stead, *Scandal,* cablegrams 14 and 28.

2. *Punch,* 23 and 30 Nov. 1895; *Times,* 9 Nov. 1895 (arrival of king of Portugal).

3. LMS Will: Fairfield to Willoughby, 14 Oct. 1895; Fairfield to Willoughby, 2 Nov. 1895; Sillery, *Founding a Protectorate,* quoting Meade to Bigge, 5 Sept. 1895 (CO 417/162).

4. Fairfield to Willoughby, 1 Nov. 1895.

5. *Times,* 16 Nov. 1895; Sir Evan Spicer in *Outward Bound,* April 1923, 486.

6. *Cape Times Weekly Edition,* 13 Nov. 1895, 9; and *Home Budget* 9 (23 Oct. 1895): 2.

7. Julian Mockford, *Khama, King of the Bamangwato* (London: Jonathan Cape, 1931); LMS Will: Herbert Canning to Fairfield, 11 Nov. 1895.

8. LMS Will: Herbert Canning (BSA Co.) to Fairfield, 7 Nov. 1895; Fairfield to Willoughby, 11 Nov. 1895; *Illustrated London News* 107 (9 Nov. 1895): 575.

9. *South Africa* 28, no. 359 (16 Nov. 1895): 377; LMS Will: Fairfield to Willoughby, 2 and 9 Nov. 1895; Ampthill to Willoughby, 9 Nov. 1895.

10. *South Africa,* 10 Feb. 1900, 394; *Daily Chronicle,* 22 July 1925 (clipping in LMS

Press Cuttings vol. for 1920–30, with comment from Miss Sharp that Sekgoma Khama's uniform was brand new when acquired c. 1900). Tshekedi Khama said Khama wore his uniform on return from England, and speculated on his having been made an honorary colonel of the Royal Horse Guards (BNA—S 435/5: Resident Magistrate Nettelton, Serowe, to government secretary, Mafeking, 13 June 1935).

11. LMS Will: Fairfield to Willoughby, 2, 7, 9, 11, and 12 Nov. 1895; Fiddes (Colonial Office) to Willoughby, 11 Nov. 1895; Read (Colonial Office) to Willoughby, 11 Nov. 1895; *South Africa* 28, no 359 (16 Nov. 1895): 377.

12. *South Africa* 28, no. 359 (16 Nov. 1895): 377; LMS Will: Fairfield to Willoughby, 7 and 9 Nov. 1895; Read to Willoughby, 11 Nov. 1895.

13. Simon Ratshosa, "My Book on Bechuanaland Protectorate: Native Customs, etc.," original manuscript and typescript (c. 1930), Botswana National Archives, MSS 3 and S. 598/1.

14. LMS Will: Fairfield to Willoughby, 12 Nov. 1895.

15. See Shane Peacock, "Farini the Great," *Bandwagon* 34, no. 5 (1990): 13–20.

16. *South Africa* 28, no. 359 (16 Nov. 1895): 390.

17. *South Africa* 28, no. 360 (23 Nov. 1895): 426.

18. *Royal Cornwall Gazette*, quoted in *Cape Argus*, 21 Dec. 1895, 2; *South Africa* 28, no. 360 (23 Nov. 1895): 426.

19. Stead, *Scandal*, cablegrams 14, 18, and 26.

20. Jeffrey Butler, *The Liberal Party and the Jameson Raid* (Oxford: Clarendon Press, 1968), 56 and 295–96.

21. BSA Co. to CO, 28 Dec. 1895—i.e. just as the Jameson Raid was setting off; H. C. L. Hermans, "Towards Budgetary Independence: A Review of Botswana's Financial History, 1900 to 1973," *Botswana Notes and Records* 6 (1974): 89–115.

CHAPTER FIFTEEN

1. Brown, *South African Frontier*, 59; Trevor, "Public Opinion," 675–76; Hole, *Passing of Black Kings*, 14; Schapera, *Praise-Poems*, 165.

2. *Daily News*, 9 Sept. 1895.

3. WCW, file 54, "Expenses" booklet.

4. LMS Will: Lord Ampthill to Willoughby, 7, 15, and 19 Nov. 1895; Fairfield to Willoughby, 9 Nov. 1895; Graham to Willoughby, 22 Nov. 1895; *Cape Argus Home Edition*, 23 Nov. 1895, 11, and 14 Dec. 1895, 5; *South Africa* 28, no. 360 (23 Nov. 1895): 409.

5. BPP—C 7962 (vol. 59 of 1896): 26 and 34: Fairfield to chiefs, 18 Nov. 1895 (dispatch no. 20046/95); LMS Will: seating plan for Windsor Castle luncheon, 20 Nov. 1895.

6. *South Africa* 28, no. 360 (23 Nov. 1895): 438.

7. Mockford, *Khama*, 170.

8. *South Africa* 28, no. 360 (23 Nov. 1895): 438.

9. Mockford, *Khama*, 170.

10. LMS Will: Fairfield to Willoughby, 9, 12 Nov. 1895; Sir A. Bigge to Wilson (Colonial Office), 14 Nov. 1895; seating plan for Windsor Castle luncheon, 20 Nov. 1895; *Times*, 21 Nov. 1895, 6–7, and 22 Nov. 1895.

11. *Cape Argus Home Edition*, 23 Nov. 1895, 4.

12. *South Africa* 28, no. 360 (23 Nov. 1895): 438.

13. *Cape Argus Home Edition*, 23 Nov. 1895, 4; *South Africa* 28, no. 361 (30 Nov. 1895): 492.

14. *South Africa* 28, no. 360 (23 Nov. 1895): 438.

15. *Cape Argus,* 22 Nov. 1895, 4.

16. *South Africa* 28, no. 363 (14 Dec. 1895): 588.

17. *South Africa* 28, no. 360 (23 Nov. 1895): 438–40, and no. 361 (30 Nov. 1895): 492.

18. Hole, *Passing of Black Kings,* 281; *South Africa* 28, no. 360 (23 Nov. 1895): 438.

19. Silas Modiri Molema, *Montshiwa, Barolong Chief and Patriot* (Cape Town: Struik, 1966).

20. *South Africa* 28, no. 360 (23 Nov. 1895): 440.

21. LMS Will: Wilson to Willoughby, 22 Nov. 1895.

22. LMS Will: Harris to Willoughby, telegram, 21 Nov. 1895.

23. LMS Out: Thompson to H. Williams, 25 Jan. 1896.

24. *South Africa* 28, no. 360 (23 Nov. 1895): 462.

25. LMS In: circular letter of 7 Mar. 1896, encl. in Willoughby to LMS, 30 Mar. 1896.

26. *Times of Africa,* quoted in *Cape Argus Home Edition,* 30 Nov. 1895, 13.

27. *South Africa* 28, no. 360 (23 Nov. 1895): 462.

28. LMS In: Willoughby to LMS, 17 Dec. 1895; *Illustrated London News* 107 (23 Nov. 1895): 663.

Chapter Sixteen

1. LMS In: Willoughby to LMS, 27 Nov. and 13 Dec. 1895, circular letter of 7 Mar. encl. in 30 Mar. 1896; *Cape Argus,* 13 and 16 Dec. 1895, 2.

2. *Cape Argus,* 12 Dec. 1895, 6.

3. *Cape Argus,* 14 Dec. 1895, 5, and 16 Dec. 1895, 2; LMS In: Willoughby to LMS, 30 Mar. 1896.

4. LMS In: Willoughby to LMS, 30 Mar. 1896.

5. LMS In: Willoughby to LMS, 12 Feb. and 30 Mar. 1896. See also note 30 below.

6. LMS In: Willoughby to LMS, 30 Mar. 1896.

7. Ratshosa, "My Book"; LMS In: Willoughby to LMS, 30 Mar. 1896 and encl. circular letter of 7 Mar. 1896.

8. Ratshosa, "My Book"; LMS In: Willoughby to LMS, 30 Mar. 1896 and encl. circular letter of 7 Mar. 1896.

9. *Cape Argus,* 26 Dec. 1895, 5; *South Africa* 28, no. 364 (21 Dec. 1895): 665, and 29, no. 370 (25 Jan. 1896): 263.

10. Ratshosa, "My Book," quoted in Mockford, *Khama,* 182–83; LMS In: Willoughby to Thompson, 17 Dec. 1895, Mudie to Thompson, 11 and 18 Dec. 1895; Sillery, *The Bechuanaland Protectorate,* 78; LMS Will: Graham (Colonial Office) to Willoughby, 22 Nov. 1895.

11. LMS In: Willoughby to LMS, encl. circular letter of 7 Mar. in 30 Mar. 1896.

12. LMS In: Willoughby to LMS, 22 Feb. and encl. circular letter of 7 Mar. in 30 Mar. 1896, Lloyd (Shoshong) to LMS, 20 Aug. 1909.

13. *Mahoko,* quoted in LMS In: Willoughby to LMS, encl. circular letter of 7 Mar. in 30 Mar. 1896.

14. LMS In: Willoughby to LMS, 12 Feb. 1896.

15. LMS In: Willoughby to LMS, 30 Mar. 1896, Lloyd (Shoshong) to LMS, 20 Aug. 1909.

16. LMS In: Willoughby to LMS, encl. circular letter of 7 Mar. in 30 Mar. 1896.

17. LMS In: Willoughby to LMS, 30 Mar. 1896.

18. *Bulawayo Chronicle*, quoted in *South Africa* 30, no. 380 (4 April 1896): 40.

19. M. G. Edwards, "The Jubilee of a King" (1910), 47, LMS Africa Odds Box 8, CWM/LMS Archives, quoting Coillard. Coillard's presence in Palapye, when ill, is confirmed by LMS In: Willoughby to LMS, 16 Mar. 1896.

20. LMS In: Mary Partridge (Molepolole) to LMS, 13 Jan. 1896, H. Williams to LMS, 7 Jan. and 27 Mar. 1896.

21. Sillery, *The Bechuanaland Protectorate*, 141–42; *South Africa*, 10 Feb. 1900, 394.

22. "Major E. J. Lugard's Journal on the Expedition to Ngamiland, 1896–99," 77, Rhodes House Library (Bodleian), Oxford University, referring to dinner with the Willoughbys at Palapye, 21 June 1896. I owe this reference to Dr. Barry Morton.

23. *Cape Argus*, 30 Dec. 1985, 4; LMS In: Willoughby to Thompson, 17 Dec. 1895, Mudie to Thompson, 11 and 18 Dec. 1895; Mockford, *Khama*, 182–83; Sillery, *The Bechuanaland Protectorate*, 78; LMS Will: Graham (Colonial Office) to Willoughby, 22 Nov. 1895.

24. *Cape Argus*, 31 Dec. 1895.

25. Longford, *Jameson's Raid; South Africa* 29, no. 375 (29 Feb. 1896): 535–44 and 646.

26. *Cape Argus*, 31 Dec. 1895, 5.

27. Neil Parsons, "The Image of Khama the Great, 1868 to 1970," *Botswana Notes and Records* 3 (1971): 41–58; Chirenje, *Chief Kgama;* Ramsay, "Rise and Fall."

28. LMS In: Willoughby (Tiger Kloof) to LMS, 2 July 1910; Howard Williams, "Passing of Bathoeng Gaseitsiwe"; Neil Parsons, Willie Henderson, and Thomas Tlou, *Seretse Khama, 1921–1980* (Gaborone: Botswana Society; Braamfontein, Johannesburg: Macmillan Boleswa, 1995), see index under "Bathoen II."

29. LMS In: R. Haydon Lewis (Molepolole) to LMS, 27 July 1910; Mary Partridge (Gaborone) to LMS, 3 Feb. 1915.

30. LMS In: Lloyd (Shoshong) to LMS, 20 Aug. 1909. Compare with "a few pounds" in LMS In: Willoughby to LMS, 12 Feb. 1896.

31. Parsons, "Khama III"; Neil Parsons, "Khama and Co. and the Jousse Trouble, 1910–1916," *Journal of African History* 16 (1975): 383–408; William Charles Willoughby, "Khama, a Bantu Reformer," *International Review of Missions* 13 (1924): 74–83.

CONCLUSION

1. LMS Mack: Thompson to Mackenzie, 14 Mar. 1896.

2. *Cape Times Weekly Edition*, 25 Dec. 1895, 11; Sillery, *Founding a Protectorate*, 231–34; BNA—HC 182/5.

3. BNA—S 466/3; a booklet published to celebrate independence in 1966 entitled *Botswana, 1966* (Gaborone: Botswana [Government] Information Services, 1966), 30.

4. Lord Hailey, *Native Administration in British African Territories*, part 5: *The High Commission Territories: Basutoland, the Bechuanaland Protectorate, and Swaziland* (London: HMSO for Commonwealth Relations Office, 1953), 217–18; Michael Crowder, *The Flogging of Phinehas McIntosh: A Tale of Colonial Folly and Injustice, Bechuanaland, 1933* (New Haven: Yale University Press, 1988), 192–95.

5. Personal verbal communication from Prof. Schapera, 1967.

6. BNA—S 29/8.

7. Ronald Hyam, *The Failure of South African Expansion, 1908–1948* (London: Macmillan, 1972), 86–88.

8. Lloyd, *Three Great African Chiefs*, 10–12.

9. Thomas Tlou and Alec Campbell, *History of Botswana*, 2d ed. (Gaborone: Macmillan Botswana, 1997).

10. Transvaal Native Affairs Department, *Short History of the Native Tribes of the Transvaal*, ed. Knothe (Pretoria: Government Printing and Stationery Office, 1905; rpt. Pretoria: State Library reprint no. 24, 1964), 17.

11. Ensor, *England, 1870–1914*, 228.

12. Ian Colvin, *The Life of Jameson* (London: Edward Arnold, 1922), 1:31; A. Frederick Madden, "Changing Attitudes and Widening Responsibilities, 1895–1914," in *Cambridge History of the British Empire*, ed. E. A. Benians, J. Butler, and C. E. Carrington, 2d ed., vol. 3: *The British Empire-Commonwealth, 1870–1919* (Cambridge: Cambridge University Press, 1967), 354; Hailey, *Native Administration*, 29; see also W. M. Macmillan, *The Road to Self-Rule, a Study in Colonial Evolution* (London: Faber, 1959), 169.

13. *African Review* 6 (July–Dec. 1895): 867 and 1067.

14. LMS Out: Thompson to H. Williams (Molepolole), 25 Jan. 1896.

15. LMS Out: Thompson to Willoughby (Palapye), 30 June 1896; *South Africa* 30, no. 391 (20 June 1896): 671.

16. Hyam, *Failure*, 88.

17. Mary Benson, *Tshekedi Khama* (London: Faber, 1960); Parsons, Henderson, and Tlou, *Seretse Khama, 1921–1980*.

18. Prof. Apollon Davidson, director of Centre for Russian Studies, University of Cape Town, personal verbal communication, Mar. 1995.

BIBLIOGRAPHY

PRIMARY SOURCES

ARCHIVES

Catalog of Exhibits, 1894–95: Contents List. Madame Tussaud's Wax-Works, London.
Chief Bathoen's press cuttings, September–October 1895. National Museum and Art Gallery Library, Gaborone.
"Chief Kgari's [Chief Sebele's] Press Cuttings," September–November 1895, microfilm, Mss. Afr. s. 1611, Rhodes House Library, Oxford University. The original is property of the Bakwena tribal administration, Molepolole. Microfilm photographed by William Cullen Library, University of Witwatersrand, deposited in Rhodes House Library by Anthony Sillery c. 1958.
Colonial Office Series 417 Africa South correspondence in bound volumes: re Bechuanaland, vols. 10, 85, 89, 90, 138, 141, 142, 143, 144, 158, 162 (1886–96). Colonial Office African (South) ("White Books" of selected corr. from CO 417 etc., published for office use: also available unbound in Foreign and Commonwealth Office Library, etc.) re Bechuanaland nos. 439, 484, 498 (1892–96). Public Record Office, Kew Gardens, London.
Council for World Mission / London Missionary Society Archives, School of Oriental and African Studies Library, University of London. LMS In-Letters: South[ern] Africa in-letters to LMS foreign secretary, boxes 51–52 (1895–96). LMS Out-Letters: South[ern] Africa out-letters from LMS foreign secretary. LMS Memorials: Memorials from London board to government. LMS Mack: Africa Personal Box 2, letters of John Mackenzie to LMS (1890–99). LMS Will: file "Papers Concerning Visit of Chiefs Khama, Sebele, and Bathoen of Bechuanaland Protectorate to England, 1895, includes letters from Joseph Chamberlain," Africa Odds Box 29 (originally marked "Chiefs in England: Correspondence, 1895" in box of W. C. Willoughby papers at CWM / LMS Archives, Carteret Street, London).
E. A. Maund Papers, William Cullen Library, University of Witwatersrand, Johannesburg. Copies in Royal Commonwealth Society Library, University of Cambridge.
Khama III Papers. Khama III Memorial Museum Archives, Serowe.
Michael Crowder Papers (relating to Tshekedi Khama). Institute of Commonwealth Studies, University of London.

Papers of Lord Lugard. Mss. Brit. Emp. s. 81–84, Rhodes House Library, Oxford University.
Papers of Prof. William Charles Willoughby, Selly Oak Colleges Library, Birmingham, England.

MANUSCRIPTS AND TYPESCRIPTS

Edwards, M. G. "The Jubilee of a King" (1910), LMS Africa Odds Box 8, CWM/ LMS Archives.
Khama (Shoshong), letter to François Coillard (Zambezi), 17 July 1889, Royal Commonwealth Society Library, University of Cambridge. Reproduced in Donald Simpson, comp., "Khama and the People of the Great Queen," *Royal Commonwealth Society Library Notes*, no. 136, April 1968.
Raditladi, Leetile Disang. "The Destiny of Seretse Khama, Royal Head of the Bamangwato People." Photocopy typescript, c. 1955, in Michael Crowder Papers, Institute of Commonwealth Studies, University of London.
Ratshosa, Simon. "My Book on Bechuanaland Protectorate: Native Customs, etc." Original manuscript and typescript (c. 1930), Botswana National Archives—MSS 3 and S. 598/1.
Secretary of State. "Interview with 3 Bechuana Chiefs (Khama, Bathoen and Sebele) 6 Nov. 1895." Typescript, enclosed in high commissioner to resident commissioner, 27 July 1936, BNA—S. 466/3, Botswana National Archives, Gaborone.
West, Elsie Alfreda. "An Afternoon with Khama" (n.d.). LMS Africa Odds Box 8, CWM/ LMS Archives.

BRITISH PARLIAMENTARY PAPERS

"Blue Books." Command number (C.) followed by volume and year: C. 1748 (vol. 60 of 1877); C. 4224 and C. 4227 (vol. 55 of 1884–85); C. 4588: (vol. 57 of 1885); C. 5237 (vol. 59 of 1887); C. 5918 (vol. 51 of 1890); C. 7154 (vol. 61 of 1893); C. 7290 (vol. 61 of 1893–94); C. 7383 and no. 277 (vol. 57 of 1894); C. 7932: 1896 (vol. 59 of 1896); C. 778 (vol. 71 of 1896); C. 7962: Corr. re. Visit of Chiefs Khama, Sebele, and Bathoen (vol. 59 of 1896).
Colonial Annual Reports. British Bechuanaland (including Bechuanaland Protectorate) 1894–95. London: HMSO, 1896.
Hansard Parliamentary Debates. 4th series. Vols. 36 (12 Aug.–15 Sept. 1895) and 37 (11 Feb.–2 Mar. 1896).

PERIODICALS

Unless otherwise indicated, the place of publication is London.

African Review, vols. 3–10, 1894–97.
Anti-Slavery Reporter, series 4, vols. 13–16, 1893–95.
British Weekly, vols. 18–19, 1895.
Cape Argus (Cape Town, 1st and 2d eds.), January–December 1895.
Cape Argus Home Edition (weekly), January–December 1895.
Cape Times (Cape Town), January–December 1895.
Cape Times Weekly Edition, January–December 1895 (with *Home Budget*, September–October 1895).
Chronicle of the London Missionary Society, 1895–96.
Contemporary Review, January 1893–December 1896.
Graphic, January–December 1895.

Illustrated London News, January 1895–June 1896.
News from Afar, 1895–96.
Punch, or the London Charivaria, May–December 1895.
Review of Reviews, vols. 9–13, January 1894–December 1896.
South Africa, Conducted by Edward P. Mathers, vols. 25–30, January 1895–June 1896.
Spectator, May–December 1895.
Times, May–December 1895.
Truth, January–April 1893.

Chief Sebele's and Chief Bathoen's press cuttings include clippings from the following 135 titles:

London and national daily press: *Daily Chronicle; Daily News; Daily Telegraph; Evening News; Daily Graphic; Morning Advertiser; Morning Leader; Morning Post; Pall Mall Gazette; St James's Gazette; Star; Times; Westminster Gazette.*

London and national weekly/monthly press: *Black and White; British Medical Journal; Civil Service Gazette; Court Circular; Court Journal; England and the Union; Echo; Free Man; Fun; Globe; Illustrated Dramatic News; Illustrated London News; Inquirer; Land and Water; Licensing World; (Modern) Society; Moonshine; Naval and Military Review; New Budget; Pelican; Penny Illustrated Paper; Punch, or the London Charivaria; Realm; Record; Review of Reviews; St James's Budget; Saturday Review; Speaker; Standard; Sun; Sunday Times; Vanity Fair; Westminster Budget.*

London international periodical press: *African Critic; African Review; Colonies and India; Levant Herald; South Africa; Times of Africa; West Australian Review.*

Christian and temperance press: *British Weekly; Christian; Christian Advocate; Christian Commonwealth; Christian Globe; Christian Million; Christian World; Land and Water; Methodist Recorder; Primitive Methodist; Record; Rock; Tablet; Woman's Signal.*

South of England: *Bath Herald; Brighton Gazette; Brighton Herald; Bristol Mercury; Bristol Times; Devon Daily Gazette; Eastbourne Gazette; Reading Mercury; Shrewsbury Chronicle; Sussex Daily News; Sussex Gazette; Western Mail; Western Daily Mercury; Western Daily Press; Western Morning News.*

Midlands and East Anglia: *Birmingham Argus; Birmingham Gazette; Birmingham Mail; Birmingham Post; East Anglian (Daily) Times; Eastern Daily News; Keighley News; Leicester Daily Post; Lichfield Mercury; Lincolnshire Echo; Northampton Mercury; Northampton Guardian; Nottingham Express; Oundle Guardian; Wellingborough Post; Wolverhampton News.*

North of England: *Blackburn Standard; Blackburn Telegraph; Bradford Observer; Bradford Telegraph; Huddersfield Examiner; Leeds Mercury; Leicester Post; Liverpool Courier; Liverpool Echo; Liverpool Mercury; Liverpool Post; Macclesfield Chronicle; Manchester Courier; Manchester Guardian; Middlesborough Gazette; Newcastle Leader; Scarborough Post; Sheffield Independent; Sheffield Telegraph; Stalybridge Reporter; Stockport Advertiser; Yorkshire Evening Post; Yorkshire Herald; Yorkshire Post.*

Scotland, Ireland, Wales: *Aberdeen Free Press; Belfast Witness; Dundee Advertiser; Dundee Courier; Edinburgh Dispatch; Glasgow Evening News; Glasgow Evening Times; Glasgow Herald; Irish Times; Scotsman; Belfast Telegraph; Cardiff News.*

North America: *New York Times; New York Tribune.*

BOOKS AND ARTICLES

Baden-Powell, George. *Protection and Bad Times, with Special Reference to the Political Economy of English Colonization.* London: Trübner and Co., 1879.

Baden-Powell, Robert S. S. "Khama, for Boys." *London Missionary Society News from Afar,* April 1923. Reprinted from "The Passing of Khama—Glimpses of the Last Great African Chief," *Outward Bound* 3, no. 31 (1923): 484–86.

Barrow, John. *A Voyage to Cochin China, in the years 1792 and 1793: containing a general view of the valuable productions and the political importance of the flourishing kingdom; and also of such European settlements as were visited on the voyage: with sketches of the manners, character, and condition of their several inhabitants. To which is attached an account of a journey, made in the years 1801 and 1802, to the residence of the chief of the Booshuana Nation, being the remotest point in the interior of southern Africa to which Europeans have hitherto penetrated. The facts and descriptions taken from a manuscript journal with a chart of the route.* London: T. Cadell and W. Davies. 1806.

Bent, James Theodore. "Among the chiefs of Bechuanaland." *Fortnightly Review*, n.s. 31 (May 1892): 642–54.

———. *The Ruined Cities of Mashonaland.* London: Longman, Green, 1892.

Bertrand, Alfred. *The Kingdom of the Barotsi, Upper Zambezia. A Voyage of Exploration . . .* Trans. A. B. Miall. London: T. Fisher Unwin, 1899.

Brown, William Harvey. *On the South African Frontier: the Adventures and Observations of an American in Mashonaland and Matabeleland.* London: Sampson, Low, Marston, 1899.

Bryden, H. A. "A friend of Livingstone." *Chamber's Journal* (Edinburgh), 7 (July 1894): 420–21.

"Chief Khama at Mafeking." Interview. *Bechuanaland News* (Vryburg), 5 January 1895.

Colquhoun, Archibald R. *Matabeleland: the War, and Our Portion in South Africa.* London: Leadenhall Press, 1894.

Dachs, Anthony, comp. *Papers of John Mackenzie.* Johannesburg: Witwatersrand University Press, 1975.

Decle, Lionel. *Three Years in Savage Africa.* Intro. H. M. Stanley. London: Methuen, 1898.

de Waal, D. C. *With Rhodes in Mashonaland.* Cape Town: H. C. Juta, 1896.

Fritsch, Gustav. *Drei Jahre in Süd-Afrika.* Breslau: Ferdinand Hirt, 1868.

Hepburn, Elizabeth. *Jottings, by Khama's Friend Mrs J.D.H.* Cape Town, 1928.

Hepburn, James Davidson. *Twenty Years in Khama's Country.* Ed. C. H. Lyall. London: Hodder and Stoughton, 1895.

Hobson, John A. *The Psychology of Jingoism.* London: Grant Richards, 1901.

Hyatt, Stanley Portal. *Diary of a Soldier of Fortune.* London: T. Werner Laurie, 1910.

Imperialist [J. Rochfort Maguire]. *The Pioneers of Empire: being, a Vindication of the Principle and a Short Sketch of the History of Chartered Companies, with Special Reference to the British South Africa Company.* London: Methuen, 1896.

Johnston, James. *Reality versus Romance in South Central Africa.* London: Hodder and Stoughton, 1893.

"Khama." *Times* (London), 21 October 1893.

"Khama—a model African king, by one who has known him." *Pall Mall Gazette,* 21 Oct, 1893. Reprinted in *Anti-Slavery Reporter,* series 4, vol. 13, no. 5 (Sept.–Oct. 1893): 280–83.

Knight-Bruce, G. W. H. *Memories of Mashonaland.* London: Edward Arnold, 1895; rpt. Bulwayo: Books of Rhodesia, 1970.

Knight-Bruce, Laura [Mrs. W.]. *The Story of an African Chief: being, the Life of Khama.* London: Kegan Paul, 1893. Reprinted from *Murray's Magazine* 5 (1889): 452–65.

Livingstone, David. *Missionary Travels in South Africa.* London: John Murray, 1857.

Lloyd, Edwin. *Three Great African Chiefs: Khâmé, Sebelé and Bathoeng.* London: T. Fisher Unwin, 1895.

Long, Una, ed. *The Journals of Elisabeth Lees Price.* London: Arnold, 1956.

Lucy, Sir Henry. *Diary of the Unionist Parliament, 1895–1900.* London, 1901.

Lucy, H. W. *The Log of the Tantallon Castle.* London: Sampson, Low, Marston, 1896.

Mackenzie, John. *Austral Africa, Losing It or Ruling It: Being Incidents and Experiences in Bechuanaland, Cape Colony, and England.* 2 vols. London: Sampson, Low, Marston, Searle and Rivington, 1887.

———. "The Chartered Company in South Africa: a review and criticism," *Contemporary Review* 71 (March 1897): 305.

———. "Native Races and their polity." In *British Africa,* 2:168–94. 2d ed. London: Kegan Paul for South Place Institute, 1902.

———. *Ten Years North of the Orange River: a Story of Everyday Life and Work among the South African Tribes from 1859 to 1869.* Edinburgh: Edmonton and Douglas, 1871.

Mallet, Victor, ed. *Life with Queen Victoria: Marie Mallet's Letters from Court, 1887–1901.* London: John Murray, 1968.

Mathers, E. P. *Zambesia, England's El Dorado in Africa.* Intro. R. S. Roberts. London: King, Sell and Railton; Cape Town: Juta, 1891. Rpt. Rhodesiana Reprint Library, Silver Series vol. 18. Bulawayo: Books of Rhodesia, 1977.

Moffat, Robert Unwin. *John Smith Moffat, C.M.G., Missionary: A Memoir by His Son.* London: John Murray, 1921.

"The Passing of Khama—the Last Great African Chief." *Outward Bound* (London), 3, no. 31 (April 1923): 484–86.

Romilly, Hugh Hastings. *Letters from the Western Pacific and Mashonaland, 1878–1891.* Ed. S. H. Romilly. London: Nutt, 1893.

Schapera, Isaac, comp. *Ditirafalo. tsa Merafe ya Batswana ba Lefatshe la Tshireletso* (Traditional Histories of the Native Tribes of the Bechuanaland Protectorate). Alice, Cape: Lovedale Press, 1940.

———, ed. *David Livingstone: South African Papers, 1849–1853.* Cape Town: Van Riebeeck Society, 1974.

———, ed. *Praise-Poems of Tswana Chiefs.* Oxford: Clarendon Press, 1965.

Scott-Keltie, J. *The Partition of Africa.* 2d ed. London: Edward Stanford, 1895.

Shippard, Sidney. "The administration of justice in South Africa." *Proceedings of the Royal Colonial Institute* 28 (1896–97): 82.

———. "Bechuanaland." In *British Africa,* 2:46–88. 2d ed. London: Kegan Paul for South Place Institute, 1902.

Stead, Estelle W. *My Father: Personal and Spiritual Reminiscences.* London: William Heinemann, 1913.

Stead, W. T. "Character sketch: Khama, Chief of the Bamangwato." *Review of Reviews* (London) 12 (1895): 302–17.

———. *Joseph Chamberlain: Conspirator or Statesman?* London: Review of Reviews Office, 1900.

———. *The Scandal of the South African Committee: A Plain Narrative for Plain Men.* London: Review of Reviews Office, 1899.

Transvaal Native Affairs Department. *Short History of the Native Tribes of the Transvaal.* Ed. Knothe. Pretoria: Government Printing and Stationery Office, 1905. Rpt. Pretoria: State Library reprint no. 24, 1964.

Vindex [J. Verschoyle], comp. *Cecil Rhodes, His Political Life and Speeches, 1881–1900.* London: Bell, 1900.

Washington, Booker T. *Up from Slavery.* New York: Bantam Books, 1959.

Williams, Howard. "Death of two African Chiefs." *Chronicle of the London Missionary Society,* n.s. 2 (1893): 38–40.

———. "The Passing of Bathoen Gaseitsiwe." *Chronicle of the London Missionary Society,* n.s. 18 (1910): 153–54.

Williams, Ralph Champneys. *The British Lion in Bechuanaland: the Story of the Expedition under the Command of Major-General Sir Charles Warren, K.M.G., F.R.S.* London: Rivington, 1885.

Willoughby, William Charles. "Khama, a Bantu reformer." *International Review of Missions* 13 (1924): 74–83.

———. *Native Life on the Transvaal Border.* London: Simpkin, Marshall, Hamilton, Kent and Co., 1900.

———. *Race Problems in the New Africa: A Study of the Relation of Bantu and Britons in Those Parts of Africa Which Are under British Control.* Oxford: Clarendon Press, 1923.

Wills, W. A., and L. T. Collingridge. *The Downfall of Lobengula: the Cause, History and Effect of the Matabeli War.* London: African Review, 1894.

Wookey, Alfred J., comp. *Dinwao leha e e Dipolél—kaga Dic—tsa Secwana.* Tiger Kloof Institution, Vryburg: London Missionary Society Bookroom, 1913.

Secondary Sources

Agar-Hamilton, John Augustus Ioan. *The Native Policy of the Voortrekkers: An Essay in the History of the Interior of South Africa, 1836–1858.* Cape Town: Maskew Miller, 1928.

———. *The Road to the North: South Africa, 1852–86.* London: Longman, 1937.

Ahluwalia, D. Pal. Review of *Ethnography and the Historical Imagination,* ed. John L. Comaroff and Jean Comaroff. *Journal of Modern African Studies* 33, no. 34 (1995): 699–700.

Atmore, Anthony, and Shula Marks. "The Imperial Factor in South Africa in the Nineteenth Century." *Journal of Imperial and Commonwealth History* 3, no. 1 (1974): 103–39.

Barker, Felix, and Peter Jackson. *London: 2000 Years of a City and Its People.* London: Papermac, 1983.

Baylen, J. O. "W. T. Stead's *History of the Mystery* and the Jameson Raid." *Journal of British Studies* 4, no. 1 (1964): 104–32.

Beckson, Karl. *London in the 1890s: A Cultural History.* New York: W. W. Norton, 1992.

Benson, Mary. *Tshekedi Khama.* London: Faber and Faber, 1960.

Bickford-Smith, Vivian. *Ethnic Pride and Racial Prejudice in Victorian Cape Town: Group Identity and Social Practice, 1875–1902.* Cambridge: Cambridge University Press, 1995.

Blackburn, A. E. *Khama, King of the Bamangwato.* London: Native Races and Liquor Traffic United Committee, c. 1926.

Blaiker, W. G. *The Life of David Livingstone.* London: John Murray, 1910.

Blake, Robert. "The Jameson Raid and the Missing Telegrams." In *History and Imagination: Essays for H. R. Trevor-Roper,* ed. Howell A. Lloyd-Jones, Valerie Pearl, and Blair Worden, 326–29. London: Duckworth, 1981.

Blakely, Brian L. *The Colonial Office, 1868–1892.* Durham, N.C.: Duke University Press, 1972.

Bolt, Christine. *Victorian Attitudes to Race.* London: Routledge and Kegan Paul, 1971.

Brake, Laurel, Led Jones, and Lionel Madden. *Investigating Victorian Journalism.* Basingstoke, Hampshire: Macmillan, 1990.

Briggs, Asa. *Kew Bridge to Crystal Palace: Impact and Images of the Industrial Revolution.* London: Thames and Hudson for Ironbridge Gorge Museum Trust, 1979.

———. *Victorian Cities.* 1968; rpt. London: Penguin, 1990.

Brown, Lucy M. *Victorian News and Newspapers.* Oxford: Clarendon Press, 1985.

Buchanan, R. A. *Industrial Archaeology in Britain.* Harmondsworth, Middlesex: Penguin, 1972.

Burgess, Keith. "Did the Late Victorian Economy Fail?" In *Later Victorian Britain, 1867–1900,* ed. T. R. Gourvish and Alan O'Day, 251–70. Basingstoke, Hampshire: Macmillan Education, 1988.

Butler, Jeffery. *The Liberal Party and the Jameson Raid.* Oxford: Clarendon Press, 1968.

Cain, Peter J., and Anthony G. Hopkins. *British Imperialism: Innovation and Expansion, 1688–1914.* London: Longman, 1993.

Chirenje, Jackson Mutero. *Chief Kgama and His Times: The Story of a Southern African Ruler.* London: Rex Collings, 1978.

———. *A History of Northern Botswana, 1850–1910.* Cranbury, N.J.: Associated University Presses, 1977.

Chirgwin, A. M. "Khama, the Black Prince of Africa: A Negro Cromwell." *Outward Bound* (London), 3, no. 25 (1922): 55–59.

Clark, Colin. *The Conditions of Economic Progress.* 2d ed. London: Macmillan, 1957.

Cole, G. D. H., and Raymond Postgate. *The Common People, 1746–1946.* London: Methuen, 1948.

Colvin, Ian. *The Life of Jameson.* 2 vols. London: Edward Arnold, 1922.

Comaroff, Jean. *Body of Power, Spirit of Resistance: The Culture and History of a South African People.* Chicago: University of Chicago Press, 1985.

Comaroff, John L., and Jean Comaroff. *Of Revelation and Revolution: Christianity, Colonialism, and Consciousness in South Africa.* Vol. 1. Chicago: University of Chicago Press, 1991.

———. "Through the Looking-Glass: Colonial Encounters of the First Kind." *Journal of Historical Sociology* 1 (1988): 6–31.

———, eds. *Ethnography and the Historical Imagination.* Boulder, Colo.: Westview Press, 1992.

Cranfield, G. A. *The Press and Society: From Caxton to Northcliffe.* London: Longman, 1978.

Creswicke, Louis. *The Life of the Right Honourable Joseph Chamberlain.* 3 vols. Cape Town: D. E. McConnell and Co., n.d.

Crowder, Michael. *The Flogging of Phinehas McIntosh: A Tale of Colonial Folly and Injustice, Bechuanaland, 1933.* New Haven, Conn.: Yale University Press, 1988.

Curtin, Philip D. *The Image of Africa: British Ideas and Action, 1780–1850.* Madison: University of Wisconsin Press, 1964.

Dachs, Anthony J. "Missionary Imperialism in Bechuanaland, 1813–96." Ph.D. diss., Cambridge University, 1968.

———. "Rhodes's Grasp for Bechuanaland, 1889–1896." *Rhodesian History* 2 (1971): 1–9.

Davenport, T. Rodney H. *South Africa: A Modern History.* 4th ed. London: Macmillan, 1991.

Davidson, Apollon. *Cecil Rhodes and His Time.* Trans. Christopher English. Moscow: Progress Publishers, 1988.

Davies, Horton. *Great South African Christians.* London: Oxford University Press, 1951.

Deacon's Newspaper Handbook and Advertiser's Guide: Lists of all the Most Important London, Provincial, Colonial and Foreign Newspaper, etc. London: Samuel Deacon, 12th issue for 1895.

Dixon, Roger, and Stefan Muthesius. *Victorian Architecture.* London: Thames and Hudson, 1978.

Drus, Ethel. "Chamberlain and the Boers." *Journal of African History* 4 (1963): 144–45.

———. "The Question of Imperial Complicity in the Jameson Raid." *English Historical Review* 68 (1953): 582–93.

Ellmann, Richard. *Oscar Wilde.* London: Hamish Hamilton, 1987.

Ensor, R. C. K. *England, 1870–1914.* Vol. 15 of *Oxford History of England.* Oxford: Clarendon Press, 1936.

Fisher, Trevor. *Scandal: The Sexual Politics of Late Victorian Britain.* Stroud, Gloucestershire: Alan Sutton Books, 1995.

Fraser, Derek. "Joseph Chamberlain and the Municipal Ideal." In *Victorian Values: Personalities and Perspectives in Nineteenth Century Society,* ed. Gordon Marsden, 135–46. London: Longman, 1990.

Fraser, Peter. *Joseph Chamberlain: Empire and Radicalism, 1868–1914.* London: Cassell, 1966.

Galbraith, John S. "The British South Africa Company and the Jameson Raid." *Journal of British Studies* 10, no. 1 (1970): 145–61.

———. *Crown and Charter: The Early Years of the British South Africa Company.* Berkeley and Los Angeles: University of California Press, 1974.

Garson, Noel G. "The Swaziland Question and the Road to the Sea, 1887–1895." In *Archives Year Book for South African History,* 2:271–422. Parow: Cape Times, 1957.

Garvin, J. L. *The Life of Joseph Chamberlain.* 3 vols. London: Macmillan, 1934.

Gilliat, Edward. *Heroes of Modern Africa: True Stories of the Intrepid Bravery and Stirring Adventures of the Pioneers, Explorers, and Founders.* London: Seeley, Service and Co., 1911.

Glass, Lancelot Dudley Stafford. *The Matabele War.* London: Longman, 1968.

Gollock, Georgina A. *Lives of Eminent Africans.* London: Longmans Green, 1928.

Gorman, Jacqueline Laks. "Historical Anniversaries." In *World Almanac and Book of Facts, 1995,* 105. Morwah, N.J.: Funk and Wagnalls; New York: St. Martin's Press, 1994.

Gray, Stephen. *South African Literature.* Johannesburg: Ravan Press, 1979.

Greenhalgh, Paul. *Ephemeral Vistas: The "Expositions Universelles," Great Exhibitions, and World's Fairs, 1851–1939.* Manchester: Manchester University Press, 1988.

Guy, G. L. "Robert Moffat Livingstone." *Africana Notes and News* 18, no. 6 (June 1969): 228–37.

Hailey, Lord. *Native Administration in the British African Territories.* Part 5: *The High Commission Territories: Basutoland, the Bechuanaland Protectorate, and Swaziland.* London: HMSO for Commonwealth Relations Office, 1953.

Hall, Kenneth O. *Imperial Proconsul: Sir Hercules Robinson and South Africa, 1881–1889.* Kingston, Ontario: Limestone Press, 1980.

Halpern, Jack. *South Africa's Hostages: Basutoland, Bechuanaland, and Swaziland.* Harmondsworth, Middlesex: Penguin, 1965.

Harris, John Charles. *Khama the Great African Chief.* 2d ed. London: Livingstone Press, 1923.

Hermans, H. C. L. "Towards Budgetary Independence: A Review of Botswana's Financial History, 1900 to 1973." *Botswana Notes and Records* 6 (1974): 89–115.

The History of "The Times." Vol. 3: *The Twentieth Century Test, 1884–1912.* London: "The Times" Office, 1947.

Hobsbawm, Eric J. *The Making of Modern English Society.* Vol. 2: *1750 to the Present: Industry and Empire.* Harmondsworth, Middlesex: Penguin, 1968.

Hole, Hugh Marshall. *The Making of Rhodesia.* London: Philip Allan, 1926.

———. *The Passing of the Black Kings.* London: Philip Allan, 1932.

Hollis, M. G. "Joseph Chamberlain and the Jameson Raid: A Bibliographical Survey." *Journal of British Studies* 3, no. 2 (1964): 152–66.

Holmberg, Åke. *African Tribes and European Agencies: Colonialism and Humanitarianism in British South and East Africa, 1870–1895.* Göteborg, Sweden: Akademiförlage, 1966.

Hyam, Ronald. *The Failure of South African Expansion, 1908–1948.* London: Macmillan, 1972.

Jackson, Stanley. *The Great Barnato.* London: Heinemann, 1970.

James, Robert V. Rhodes. *Rosebery: A Biography of Archibald Philip, 5th Earl of Rosebery.* 2d ed. London: Reader's Union, 1964.

Jeal, Tim. *Baden-Powell.* London: Hutchinson, 1989.

———. *Livingstone.* London: Heinemann; New York: Putnam, 1973.

Jones, Gareth Steadman. "Working-Class Culture and Working-Class Politics in London, 1870–1900: Notes on the Remaking of a Working Class." In *Popular Culture: Past and Present,* comp. Bernard Waites, Tony Bennett, and Graham Martin, 92–121. London: Croom Helm for Open University Press, 1982.

Jones, R. Tudor. *Congregationalism in England, 1662–1962.* London: Independent Press, 1962.

Judd, Denis. *Radical Joe: A Life of Joseph Chamberlain.* London: Hamish Hamilton, 1977.

Kapp, Yvonne. *Eleanor Marx.* 2 vols. New York: Academy Press, 1971.

Kubicek, R. V. *The Administration of Imperialism: Joseph Chamberlain at the Colonial Office.* Durham, N.C.: Duke University Press, 1969.

Longford, Elizabeth. *Jameson's Raid: The Prelude to the Boer War.* 2d ed. London: Granada/Panther, 1982.

———. *Victoria R. I.* London: Weidenfeld and Nicolson, 1964.

Lovett, Richard. *The History of the London Missionary Society, 1795–1895.* London: Frowde, 1899.

Lugard, Lord [Frederick]. *The Dual Mandate in British Tropical Africa.* Edinburgh: Blackwood, 1922.

Macintosh, Christine W. *Coillard of the Zambezi.* London: T. Fisher Unwin, 1907.

Mackenzie, John M. *Propaganda and Empire: The Manipulation of British Public Opinion, 1880–1960.* Manchester: Manchester University Press, 1984.

———, ed. *Imperialism and Popular Culture.* Manchester: Manchester University Press, 1986.

———, ed. *Popular Imperialism and the Military, 1850–1950.* Manchester: Manchester University Press; New York: St. Martin's Press, 1992.

Mackenzie, W. Douglas, and Alfred Stead. *South Africa, Its History, Heroes, and Wars.* Chicago: Monarch; London: Marshall, 1900.

Macmillan, W. M. *The Road to Self-Rule, a Study in Colonial Evolution.* London: Faber, 1959.

Madden, A. Frederick. "Changing Attitudes and Widening Responsibilities, 1895–1914." In *Cambridge History of the British Empire,* ed. E. A. Benians, J. Butler, and C. E. Carrington. 2d ed. Vol. 3: *The British Empire-Commonwealth, 1870–1919,* 339–405. Cambridge: Cambridge University Press, 1967.

Main, Elizabeth. *Man of Mafeking: The Bechuanaland Years of Sir Hamilton Goold-Adams, 1884–1901.* Gaborone: Botswana Society, 1996.

Marks, Shula, and Stanley Trapido. "Lord Milner and the South African State." *History Workshop* 8 (1979): 50–80.

———. "Lord Milner and the South African State Reconsidered." In *Imperialism, the State, and the Third World,* ed. Michael Twaddle, 80–95. London: Institute of Commonwealth Studies, 1992.

Marsh, Cyril, ed. *South African Portrait Gallery.* London: Frederick Warne, 1897.

Marsh, Peter T. *Joseph Chamberlain: Entrepreneur in Politics.* New Haven, Conn.: Yale University Press, 1994.

Maylam, Paul R. "The Making of the Kimberley-Bulawayo Railway: A Study in the Operations of the British South Africa Company." *Rhodesian History* 8 (1977): 13–33.

―――. *Rhodes, the Tswana, and the British: Colonialism, Collaboration, and Conflict in the Bechuanaland Protectorate, 1885–1899.* Westport, Conn.: Greenwood Press, 1980.

Mendelsohn, Richard. "The Cape and the Drifts Crisis of 1895." M.A. diss., University of Cape Town, 1971.

Mitchell, Lewis. *The Life of the Rt. Hon. Cecil John Rhodes, 1853–1902.* 2 vols. London: Edward Arnold, 1901.

Mockford, Julian. *Khama, King of the Bamangwato.* London: Jonathan Cape, 1931.

Moffat, Robert Unwin. *John Smith Moffat, C.M.G., Missionary: A Memoir.* London: John Murray, 1921.

Molema, Silas Modiri. *The Bantu Past and Present.* Edinburgh: Green and Son, 1920.

―――. *Montshiwa, Barolong Chief and Patriot.* Cape Town: Struik, 1966.

The Newspaper Press Directory and Advertisers' Guide . . . London: C. Mitchell and Co., 1895. Jubilee issue.

Newman, Kenneth. *Birds of Botswana.* Johannesburg: Southern Book Publishers for Botswana Bird Club, 1989.

Ngcongco, Leonard Diniso. "Aspects of the History of the Ngwaketse to 1910." Ph.D. diss., Dalhousie University, 1975.

Pakenham [Longford], Elizabeth. *Jameson's Raid.* London: Weidenfeld and Nicholson, 1960.

Pakenham, Thomas Frank Dermot. *The Boer War.* London: Weidenfeld and Nicholson, 1979.

―――. *The Scramble for Africa, 1876–1912.* London: Weidenfeld and Nicholson; Johannesburg: Jonathan Ball, 1991.

Parsons, Neil. "Colonel Rey and the Colonial Rulers of Bechuanaland: Mercenary and Missionary Traditions in Administration, 1884–1955." In *People and Empires in African History: Essays in Memory of Michael Crowder,* ed. J. F. Ade Ajayi and J. D. Y. Peel, 197–215. London: Longman, 1992.

―――. "The Economic History of Khama's Country in Botswana, 1844–1930." In *The Roots of Rural Poverty in Central and Southern Africa,* ed. Robin Palmer and Neil Parsons, 113–43. London: Heinemann Educational Books; Berkeley and Los Angeles: University of California Press, 1977.

―――. "The Economic History of Khama's Country in Southern Africa." *African Social Research* 18 (1974): 643–73.

―――. "The Image of Khama the Great, 1868 to 1970." *Botswana Notes and Records* 3 (1971): 41–58.

―――. "The Impact of Seretse Khama on British Public Opinion." In *Africans in Britain,* ed. David Killingray, 195–219. London: Frank Cass, 1994.

―――. "Khama and Co. and the Jousse Trouble, 1910–1916." *Journal of African History* 16 (1975): 383–408.

―――. "Khama III, the Bamangwato, and the British, with Special Reference to 1895–1923." Ph.D. diss., University of Edinburgh, 1973.

―――. *A New History of Southern Africa.* 2d ed. Basingstoke, Hampshire: Macmillan, 1993.

―――. "Three Botswana Chiefs in Britain, 1895." Diploma in African Studies thesis, University of Edinburgh, 1967.

―――. *The Word of Khama.* Lusaka: Historical Association of Zambia, 1972.

Parsons, Neil, Willie Henderson, and Thomas Tlou. *Seretse Khama, 1921–1980.* Gaborone: Botswana Society; Braamfontein, Johannesburg: Macmillan Boleswa, 1995.

Peacock, Shane. "Farini the Great." *Bandwagon* 34, no. 5 (1990): 13–20.

Pearson, Hesketh. *The Lives of the Wits.* London: Heinemann, 1962.

Pelling, Henry. *A Social Geography of British Elections, 1885–1910.* London: Macmillan, 1967.

Peters, Margaret T. "The British Government and the Bechuanaland Protectorate, 1885–1895." M.A. diss., University of Cape Town, 1947.

Phimister, Ian R. "Rhodes, Rhodesia, and the Rand." *Journal of Southern African Studies* 1, no. 1 (1974): 74–90.

———. "Unscrambling the Scramble for Southern Africa: The Jameson Raid and the South African War Revisited." *South African Historical Journal* 28 (May 1993): 203–20.

Pieterse, Jan Nederveen. *White on Black: Images of Africa and Blacks in Western Popular Culture.* Trans. Pieterse. New Haven, Conn.: Yale University Press, 1992.

Porter, Andrew N. "In Memoriam Joseph Chamberlain: A Review of Periodical Literature." *Journal of Imperial and Commonwealth History* 3, no. 2 (1975): 292–97.

———. "Joseph Chamberlain: A Radical Reappraisal." *Journal of Imperial and Commonwealth History* 6, no. 3 (1978): 330–36.

———. *The Origins of the South African War: Joseph Chamberlain and the Diplomacy of Imperialism, 1895–1899.* Manchester: Manchester University Press, 1980.

Porter, Bernard J. *Critics of Empire: British Radical Attitudes to Colonialism in Africa, 1895–1914.* London: Macmillan, 1968.

Ramsay, Frederick Jeffress, Jr. "The Rise and Fall of the Bakwena Dynasty of South-Central Botswana, 1820–1940." Ph.D. diss., Boston University, 1991.

Rive, Richard, and Russell Martin, eds. *Olive Schreiner Letters, 1871–99.* Cape Town: David Philip, 1987.

Roberts, Ray S. "Rhodes, Rhodesia, and the Jameson Raid." *Zambezia* 1, no. 2 (1970): 77–80.

Rotberg, Robert I., with Miles F. Shore. *The Founder: Cecil Rhodes and the Pursuit of Power.* New York: Oxford University Press, 1989.

Saul, Samuel Berryck. *The Myth of the Great Depression, 1873–1896.* London: Macmillan, 1969.

Schapera, Isaac. "The Anthropologist's Approach to Ethnohistory." In *Historians in Tropical Africa: Proceedings of Leverhulme Inter-Collegiate History Conference—Salisbury, 1960,* ed. Terence Osborn Ranger, 11–15. Salisbury, Southern Rhodesia: University College of Rhodesia and Nyasaland, 1962.

———. *The Ethnic Composition of Tswana Tribes.* London: London School of Economics and Political Science, 1952.

———. *A Handbook of Tswana Law and Custom.* London: Oxford University Press, 1938.

———, comp. *David Livingstone: South African Papers (1849–1853).* Cape Town: Van Riebeeck Society, 1974.

Schapera, Isaac, with John L. Comaroff. *The Tswana.* Rev. ed. London: Kegan Paul, 1991.

Schreuder, Deryck M. *The Scramble for Southern Africa, 1877–1895.* Cambridge: Cambridge University Press, 1980.

Sedimo, O. L. "Bechuanaland Border Police, 1885–1895." B.A. University of Botswana, 1986.

Sillery, Anthony. *The Bechuanaland Protectorate.* Cape Town: Oxford University Press, 1952.

————. *Founding a Protectorate: A History of Bechuanaland, 1885–96.* The Hague: Mouton, 1965.

————. *Sechele, the Story of an African Chief.* Oxford: George Ronald, 1954.

Skota, T. D. Mweli. *The African Yearly Register, Being, an Illustrated National Biographical Directory (Who's Who) of Black Folks in South Africa.* Johannesburg: Esson for author, 1932.

Smith, Iain R. *The Origins of the South African War, 1899–1902.* Origins of Modern Wars series. London: Longman, 1996.

Sokolsky, W. "The Establishment of the British Protectorate in Bechuanaland." M.A. thesis, Columbia University, 1951.

Southon, A. E. *Khama the Conqueror.* London: Atlantis Press, 1930.

Taylor, Alan John Percivale. *The Struggle for Mastery in Europe, 1848–1919.* Oxford: Clarendon Press, 1954.

Thompson, H. C. *The Kuruman Mission.* Kimberley, South Africa: Diamond Fields Advertiser, 1953.

Thorold, Algar Labouchère. *The Life of Henry Labouchère.* London: Constable and Co., 1913.

Tlou, Thomas. "Documents on Botswana History: How Rhodes Tried to Seize Ngamiland." *Botswana Notes and Records* 7 (1975): 61–65.

————. "Melao yaga Kgama: Transformations in the Nineteenth Century Ngwato State." M.A. thesis, University of Wisconsin at Madison, 1969.

Tlou, Thomas, and Alec Campbell. *History of Botswana.* 2d ed. Gaborone: Macmillan Botswana, 1997.

Trevor, Daphne. "Public Opinion and the Acquisition of Bechuanaland and Rhodesia (1868–1896)." Ph.D. diss., London School of Economics and Political Science, 1936.

Truschel, Louis W. "Accommodation under Imperial Rule: The Tswana of the Bechuanaland Protectorate, 1895–1910." Ph.D. diss., Northwestern University, 1971.

————. "Political Survival in Colonial Botswana: The Preservation of Khama's State and the Growth of the Ngwato Monarchy." *Transafrican Journal of History* 4, nos. 1–2 (1974): 71–93.

van der Poel, Jean. *The Jameson Raid.* London: Oxford University Press, 1951.

Weinreb, Ben, and Christopher Hibbert, eds. *The London Encyclopaedia.* London: Macmillan, 1987.

Wells, James. *Stewart of Lovedale.* 3d ed. London: Hodder and Stoughton, 1909.

Williams, Basil. *Cecil Rhodes.* London: Constable, 1938.

Williams, Watkin W. *The Life of General Sir Charles Warren.* Oxford: Basil Blackwell, 1941.

Willing's British and Irish Press Guide, and Advertiser's Directory and Handbook 1895 (Twenty-Second Year). London: James Willing, 1895.

Woodhouse, C. M. "The Missing Telegrams and the Jameson Raid." *History Today* 12 (1962): 395–404, 506–14.

Young, Robert M. "Herbert Spencer and 'Inevitable' Progress." In *Victorian Values: Personalities and Perspectives in Nineteenth Century Society,* ed. Gordon Marsden, 147–57. London: Longman, 1990.

INDEX